Poets in the Public Sphere

Poets in the Public Sphere

THE EMANCIPATORY PROJECT
OF AMERICAN WOMEN'S POETRY,
1800–1900

Paula Bernat Bennett

PRINCETON UNIVERSITY PRESS

Princeton and Oxford

LIBRARY OF CONGRESS CATALOGING-IN-PUBLICATION DATA

Bennett, Paula.
    Poets in the public sphere : the emancipatory project of American women's poetry,
1800–1900 / Paula Bernat Bennett.
      p. cm.
    Includes bibliographical references (p.) and index.
    ISBN 0-691-02645-9 (cloth : alk. paper) — ISBN 0-691-02644-0 (pbk. : alk. paper)
    1. American poetry—Women authors—History and criticism. 2. Feminism and
literature—United States—History—19th century. 3. Piatt, Sarah M. B. (Sarah Morgan
Bryan), 1836–1919—Criticism and interpretation. 4. Women and literature—United
States—History—19th century. 5. American poetry—19th century—History and
criticism. 6. Feminist poetry—History and criticism. 7. Social problems in literature.
8. Sentimentalism in literature. 9. Sex role in literature. 10. Irony in literature. 11. Sex
in literature. I. Title.

PS310.F45 B46 2003
811'.3099287—dc21   2002069278

British Library Cataloging-in-Publication Data is available

This book has been composed in Minion

Printed on acid-free paper. ∞

www.pupress.princeton.edu

Printed in the United States of America

   9 8 7 6 5 4 3 2 1

TO THE STAFF

OF THE AMERICAN ANTIQUARIAN SOCIETY

AND

TO MY FATHER, PAUL BERNAT,

WHO TAUGHT ME WORDS,

Budapest, Hungary, 1904–
Brookline, Massachusetts, 1989

Contents

Illustrations

*Courtesy, American Antiquarian Society

Preface

This book, a historical-critical study of nineteenth-century U.S. women's poetry, originated in a critique made by an external reader of *Emily Dickinson: Woman Poet*. Why, she wanted to know, was I so dismissive of other nineteenth-century women poets, why so determined to depict Dickinson as an isolated talent with no connection to her peers? The query came too late to affect *Woman Poet*, which had already gone to press in England, but seconded by questions my own research had begun to raise, it nagged me long after the Dickinson book was published in the United States.

At the time I wrote *Woman Poet*, the groundbreaking research of Emily Stipes Watts (1978), Cheryl Walker (1982), and Joanne Dobson (1989) had already alerted Dickinson scholars to the existence of a significant body of poetry by other nineteenth-century U.S. women. However, since my book was on Dickinson, and Dickinson viewed herself as "the only Kangaroo among the Beauty," who was I to challenge her self-perception? Despite what I now know, I still think that this approach has some merit when applied to Dickinson herself. Not because it accurately reflects her situation—it does not—but because, accurate or not, this is how she construed it. Given the unique qualities of her verbal gifts, understandably so.

Where I erred, rather, was in dismissing other women poets, poets whom I either denigrated or, knowing nothing of them, omitted entirely from consideration. Despite friendly warnings from Joanne Dobson, I had never really questioned my assumption that nineteenth-century U.S. women's poetry, ex Dickinson, was a static field. A mere half-day's browsing in Rufus Griswold's *Female Poets of America* (1848) or Edmund Clarence Stedman's *An American Anthology* (1900) explains why. The poem that I and others thought "typical" of nineteenth-century U.S. women's poetry—genteelly narcissistic, domestically oriented, and largely apolitical in its concerns—can be found in abundance in both anthologies, albeit, as Stedman's demonstrates, men no less than women wrote such poems.

Ubiquitous as this poem was, however, I now know that it was only one piece in a complex story, a story whose complications I sketch out here. Far from presenting a seamless voice and perspective—that, as it were, of "The Angel in the House"—nineteenth-century U.S. women's poetry was a dynamic field in which the "angel" and the gender ideology for which she stood were contested ground at best. Originating in complaint, literature published by eighteenth-century women in their local newspapers, the poetry this book explores stands radically opposed to the narcissistic self-

engagement of the dominant genteel tradition, although rhetorically affili-
ated with it. Succinctly, in this alternative poetry, the sentimental conventions of nineteenth-century genteel verse are twisted to serve the political
ends of the complaint genre, usually, albeit not always, through ironization.
Taken thus, as a literature of quasi-political dissent, this poetry provides substantial evidence for nineteenth-century women's collective agency as civil
subjects in the liberal state, their lack of franchise notwithstanding.

However Victorian these writers' metrics and diction seemed to the generations of women writers who followed them, the poets discussed in this
book were the first to give "New Women" voice. Precisely because they were
feeling their way individually as well as collectively onto uninhabited ground,
they were, I believe, peculiarly open to their own differences, to their need
not to be fully absorbed by the genteel lyric's homogenizing voice or by the
bourgeois gender values that voice encoded. It is these women's struggle—
complex, contradictory, characterized, to use Mary Poovey's term, by the
"uneven developments" that distinguish the ideological commitments of individuals and groups during periods of rapid cultural change—that this
book maps. In doing so, it will not only give back to U.S. women's poetry
part of a history it has too long lacked but also, hopefully, bring into question any presentation of nineteenth-century women poets that takes "lack"
itself, as I once did, to be constitutive either of their writing or of the women
themselves.

Acknowledgments

As with any writing project that takes a decade or more to complete, this book comes with a trail of debts. To those who have read my drafts, helped me find sources, given me poems, loaned me books, checked my transcriptions, listened patiently or impatiently to my ideas, borne with my tempers and frustrations, and cheered me on, what can I say? Thanks? Even though I know that I risk unintentionally leaving someone or other out, here is my list in alphabetical order, with only two reserved for special mention, their assistance being on a heroic scale: David Anthony, Michael Batinski, Mary Bogumil, Edward Brunner, Lawrence Buell, Mary and Ken Carpenter, Kenneth Collins, Lee and Lu Cupp, Elizabeth Dillon, Joanne Dobson, Heather Dubrow, Ben Foster, Lucy Frank, Janet Gray, April Gentry, Todd Gernes, Paula Geyh, Eric Haralson, Susan Harris, Melissa Homestead, Linda Hughes, Mary de Jong, Paul Lauter, David Leverenz, Deborah Malmud, Mary Murrell, Cary Nelson, Margaret Piatt, Vivian Pollak, Kenneth Price, Marjorie Pryse, Patricia Reinstein, Elizabeth Renker, Eliza Richards, Katherine Rodier, Vernon Rosario II, Shirley Samuels, Ivy Schweitzer, Georgina Taylor, Julie Winch, Jean Fagan Yellin, Rosemarie Zagarri, my women's faculty support group at Southern Illinois University, the members of the Northeast Nineteenth-Century American Women Writers Study Group (all of you). Separately, I want to thank Karen Kilcup and John Evelev, not just for their willingness to read my entire manuscript in draft, but for the care and thoughtfulness of their critical commentary. There are some debts that can never be repaid, and the debts I owe you both are certainly in that category. Finally, to my daughters, Marta Hope and Erin Elizabeth, thanks for being you.

This book was written with the aid of a number of different internal and external grants: two grants from the Office of Research and Development, Southern Illinois University, Carbondale, a Bunting Fellowship, 1996–97; and a National Endowment for the Humanities–American Antiquarian Society Fellowship, 1996–97. The latter grant, in particular, was crucial to the development of this project, and I can never sufficiently express my gratitude to the society's dedicated and enthusiastic staff.

Abbreviations

AAA   *An American Anthology, 1787–1900*, ed. Edmund Clarence
        Stedman (Boston: Houghton Mifflin Co., 1900)

AWP   *American Women Poets of the Nineteenth Century: An Anthology*,
        ed. Cheryl Walker (New Brunswick: Rutgers University Press,
        1992)

F   *The Poems of Emily Dickinson*, ed. R. W. Franklin (Cambridge:
        Belknap Press of Harvard University Press, 1998)

FPA   *The Female Poets of America*, ed. Rufus W. Griswold (Philadelphia:
        Carey and Hart, 1849)

L   *The Letters of Emily Dickinson*, ed. Thomas H. Johnson and
        Theodora Ward (Cambridge: Belknap Press of Harvard University
        Press, 1958)

NAWP   *Nineteenth-Century American Women Poets: An Anthology*, ed.
        Paula Bernat Bennett (Oxford: Blackwell Publishers, 1998)

PB   *Palace-Burner: The Selected Poetry of Sarah Piatt*, ed. Paula Bernat
        Bennett (Urbana: University of Illinois Press, 2001)

PPA   *The Poets and Poetry of America*, ed. Rufus W. Griswold
        (Philadelphia: Carey and Hart, 1842)

Poets in the Public Sphere

Poetry in the Public Sphere

For poetry is itself one form of social activity, and no
proper understanding of the nature of poetry can be made
if the poem is abstracted from the experience of the poem
either at its point of origin or at any subsequent period.
—JEROME McGANN, *The Beauty of Inflections*, 1985[1]

On June 5, 1850, the *Louisville Weekly Journal* published "To My Child" by
an author who signed him- or herself "S." No editorial explanation accompanied the poem, only a notice indicating that it was written for the *Journal*;
that is, it was an original submission, not a reprint. In the poem, a female
speaker bids good-bye to her child. She does not explain why they are parting, but a number of possibilities occur. The child is illegitimate, and the
mother's relatives (?) are forcing her to give it up. The mother is a divorcée,
who under the law of coverture has no rights to her child, or a widow,
unable to support it. She could be a prostitute or criminal from whom the
child is taken for its own good or a slave whose child has been sold away.
More remotely, she could even be a Native American whose child is leaving
for some far-off boarding school, where its ties to her and to tribal culture
will be systematically destroyed.

Whatever narrative one invents—and historically speaking, any of these
scenarios could apply—one thing is clear: the poem's speaker has had her
deepest maternal feelings violated. Enraged by the forced separation, she
lashes out not just against the "the Father's Law" but against the "'father to
the fatherless,'" God. From her opening apostrophe to her concluding peroration, the speaker of "To My Child" resists her breaking, refusing to display the grief she feels lest her tears gratify those who injure her. Her willingness to "kiss the chastening rod" a thing of the past, she teases out for herself
what remains of her relationship to the Almighty instead:

Farewell! I will not part from thee in sadness and in tears,
Nor darken this, our parting hour, with vain and fruitless fears;
Though long and weary years may pass, ere we shall meet again,
I will not lose the present hour in tears as weak as vain.

Sweet baby! come and lean thy head upon my aching heart,
And let me look into thine eyes, one moment, ere we part,

And smile as thou art wont to smile in thy young childish glee,
That so thy joy may reach the heart that bleeds to part from thee.

No grief shall mark my death-cold brow, no sorrow dim my eye,
In bidding thee a last adieu when other eyes are by;
But *here*, with none but God and thee to witness, let me tell
How bleeds the heart, that seems so cold, in bidding *thee* farewell!

We are alone, my sweetest child, no friend is left us now,
Save Him who blesses every tear that falls upon thy brow;
And He *will* bless thee evermore, for He has sworn to be
"A father to the fatherless"—then will He care for *thee*!

I leave thee with a breaking heart, a dry and aching eye,
For none may know the thoughts that swell within my soul so high;
I press thee in a last embrace—and *can* it be the last?
Can all the love I felt for thee be but as shadows past?

I have bent o'er thy little form, when cradled on my breasts,
Thy dark eye softly folded in its sweet, unbroken rest,
And my wild heart has gone above in gratitude to God,
And I *have* bowed in spirit there, and kissed His chastening rod!

My child! if in this breaking heart one feeling lingers still,
Which anguish hath not changed to gall, nor wrong hath made an ill,
It *is* the deep, redeeming love that fills my heart for thee,
And forms the last link, yet unrent, between my God and me!

(NAWP 419–20)

For a poem so thoroughly Victorian in form, metrics, and style, "To My Child" raises a surprising number of un-"Victorian" questions. Most obviously, given the aura of sexual guilt hanging over the speaker, the poem seems an odd choice for a family newspaper, let alone one found so far from a major cosmopolitan center. Then there is the date, 1850. This places "To My Child"'s composition squarely in the middle of what Douglas Branch dubs the "Sentimental Years," 1836 to 1860, when, we are told, domestic ideology was in full flower and the "empire of the mother" uncontested terrain. Yet, for all that the speaker of this poem is a mother, she is hardly sentimentalized. With her "wild heart" and stubborn will, she is no Ellen Montgomery, eagerly embracing her own humiliation, or Uncle Tom, forgiving those who kill him. If anything, the literary figure she resembles most is Hawthorne's erring-and-proud-of-it Hester Prynne. And if this mother, as she repeatedly says, sheds no tears—those certain signifiers of the sentimental persona—then how can we? Why, that is, does this poem invoke so many sentimental conventions—the erring mother, the innocent babe, the hoped-for redemption—only to disappoint them in the end? Why refuse the consolation of sentimental closure? Put another way, why the "yet" before the "unrent"?

Then there is the mother herself. Neither Southern Belle nor True Woman, neither Bluestocking nor Coquette, certainly no Angel in the House, who is she? Prostitute, criminal, divorcée, pauperized widow, illegitimate mother, slave—any of these subject positions might fit, but which is hers? And how should we view her? Is she a sinner or one sinned against? Is her child a sign of her guilt or, as she herself insists, her only hope for salvation, a salvation others jeopardize? Why, moreover, does she repeatedly insist in this most public of private spaces—the anonymous newspaper poem—that she will never let anyone know her pain? Is this a poem in which, as T. S. Eliot puts it, the poet talks "to himself, or to nobody"?[2] Or is it a complaint, one whose very inwardness is transformed by the mere fact of publication into a vehicle for public work? In revealing the "injustice perpetrated against the speaker, or something the speaker represents," does this poem implicitly demand redress?[3] Indeed, if it is not the mother's complaint that matters here but its *publication*, what do we make of this fact? Whoever the author was, what did she (or he) hope to accomplish by placing such an ironic yet seemingly intimate and pain-filled work before the public eye?

I have chosen "To My Child" to open this study of American women poets in the public sphere, from 1800 to 1900, not because I have answers to these questions but because I do not. Indeed, I think many unanswerable, beginning with the author's sex. What makes this poem central for me is not what it says about one poet's concerns or even about one legally unentitled mother's plight, important though these matters are, but that it was published at all. As much by its provenance in a regional newspaper as by its resistance to closure, "To My Child" challenges key scholarly assumptions about nineteenth-century U.S. women and the poetry they wrote. Most especially, in publicizing one woman's (possible) transgressive behavior and (certain) tortured grief, "To My Child" suggests that the production of lyric poetry by nineteenth-century U.S. women may have more *political* significance than feminist literary and political historians have granted it to date.

"To My Child"'s publicity comprises this study's departure point and one of its principal concerns. Despite differences in theoretical framework, most mainstream twentieth-century Anglo-American literary scholars have, at least until recently, followed Eliot in situating lyric poetry within a late-Victorian/ early modernist aesthetic of high culture. The unstable product of a forced marriage between Matthew Arnold's liberal humanism and elite pre-Raphaelite aestheticism, this concept of poetry—the poet speaking "to himself, or to nobody"—sought to preserve poetic autonomy and authenticity against the devaluating impact that mass-market technologies were presumably having on popular taste. Like the Victorians, modernists insisted that art should transcend immediate and material concerns. Identified thus, as quasi-private or overheard speech largely devoted to meditative concerns—Wallace Stevens's "Sunday Morning," for example—lyric poetry's other function as a "social activity" was restricted, at least in theory, to the poem's engagements with other texts in the same free-standing literary tradition.

For such a model, one predicated on lyric poetry's transcendent status as aesthetic artifact, the figure of apostrophe—the direct address of an absent presence—has been taken, as Barbara Johnson takes it in "Apostrophe, Animation, and Abortion," as paradigmatic of lyric poetry's self-enclosed, intra-subjective nature as a whole. In an intricate argument to which I cannot do justice here, Johnson identifies lyric poetry as a literature of "demand," articulating "the primal relation to the mother as a relation to the Other,"[4] as in Shelley's "Ode to the West Wind," for example, or Dickinson's many poems to her "Master," a figure whose actual biographical reality remains moot. Intrusive in its peremptoriness, the speaker's voice commands what otherwise does not exist into being, animating it, as the voice in "S"'s poem animates her lost child. Viewed thus, lyric poetry is an internal drama of desire linguistically acted out. As such, it maintains tenuous ties at best to anything outside the author's head except those precursor texts to which it is generically related—whether Petrarch's sonnets or, as in the case of "To My Child," other women's complaint poems.

In valorizing a poem like "To My Child" as *public* speech, I am not denying lyric poetry's status as aesthetic artifact any more than I am denying apostrophe's importance to lyric production as a whole. Like "To My Child," many, possibly most, of the poems cited in this book address themselves to a someone or something not there, using the rhetorical conventions, whether satirical or sentimental, of their day. But even when structured apostrophically, poems, I would suggest, engage other, less theoretically abstract, audiences as well: a specific interpretive community, a magazine's readership, a biographically identifiable individual, other authors to whom the particular poet responds, a coterie of the author's friends, and so on. And it is the specific ways in which poems relate to these other, more concrete and historically specific audiences that concerns me here.

In this book, I bracket the text-based intrapsychic approach which using the apostrophic model enables in order to call attention to a body of poetry, largely complaint poems, whose social, cultural, and political affiliations give them historical value outside the aesthetic. Decontextualized or, as Jerome McGann puts it, "abstracted" from the specific social and material conditions which produced it, including the historically specific audiences to which individual poems are addressed, lyric poetry has, or seems to have, little to say to those concerned with the "cultural work" that literature does.[5] Scholarly interest in poetry has consequently steeply declined in the past few decades as literary theorists have shifted from viewing culture as text to viewing it, in Danky and Wiegand's terms, as "agency and practice."[6] Resituating nineteenth-century American women's newspaper and periodical poetry within the tradition of social dialogue and debate from which it sprang and to which it belongs, will clarify this poetry's function as a form of *public* speech addressed to concrete, empirically identifiable others. Doing so, it will establish the vital role that women's poetry, taken collectively, played within the intersubjective framework of the public sphere.

Drawing examples principally from national, regional, and special-interest newspapers and periodicals published between 1800 and 1900, I examine nineteenth-century American women's poetry in terms of what the German social philosopher, Jürgen Habermas, calls "everyday communicative practise."[7] That is, I treat this poetry as an instance of speech whose expressive and mimetic power is organized explicitly or implicitly for argumentative ends—in order to achieve a practical discursive goal: persuasion. In this poetic form of speech, the author produces aesthetic pleasure, typically, as in "To My Child," through manipulation of affect. However, this pleasure is not an end in itself any more than is the poem's expressive function, the sheer personal voicing of complaint or injustice. Rather, as in "To My Child," both pleasure and expressivity are put in service to swaying the judgments of others on matters of concern to all—in this poem, a mother's violated rights.

Obviously, not all nineteenth-century women's poetry fits this description. Much of the genteel poetry collected by nineteenth-century anthologists like Griswold and Stedman encouraged aestheticization along with (the illusion of) personal expressivity; and the conventions governing such poems have been richly explored by scholars like Mary Loeffelholz, Elizabeth Petrino, Adela Pinch, Yopie Prins, Eliza Richards, and Cheryl Walker.[8] But, at the same time, a substantial amount of nineteenth-century poetry by both sexes is directed implicitly or explicitly toward social and political concerns, the concerns of the Habermasian public sphere: building solidarity in particular racial and ethnic communities, questioning prevailing ideologies or laws, criticizing national policy—for example, the removal of indigenous Indian populations—and so on. In these poems, the boundaries between the aesthetic and the political and between the sentimental and the ironic are breached as genteel poetry's rhetorical conventions are twisted to meet complaint poetry's reformist ends.

In the poetry I discuss, white women and women of color, coming from every caste and class, region and religion, address the major social and political issues of their day and those of special interest to themselves, their own entry into modernity not least among them. As a result, we can use their poems to track not only women's opinions on a broad range of social and political questions but also fundamental shifts in their own self-definition as the century progressed. In the brief space of these poems—poems which, when added together, represent thousands of differently sited individual women—nineteenth-century women spoke out on who they thought they were and what they wanted for themselves and for their society. These are the issues that I explore here, treating their poetry as a specific form of communicative utterance directed toward real-world, or what Habermas calls "life-world," effects, by reaching "into our cognitive interpretations and normative expectations" in order to make us rethink and modify what we believe and do.[9] Although this book is about poetry, therefore, finally, it is even more about the women who wrote it and the political and cultural work their poetry did.

The best way for me to establish the cultural importance of the poetic praxis this book discusses is to describe, however briefly, the eighteenth-century publishing practices out of which it evolved. Newspapers had hardly started to appear in the colonies (circa the mid-1720s) when literate middle- and upper-class women began using them as venues for self-representation and public suasion on issues pertinent to themselves. Since early colonial newspapers were mainly devoted to disseminating commercial and political news, it seems likely that publishers viewed these female-authored complaints as harmless filler or else as cost-free ways to create community appeal. But whatever the case, by the mid-1730s, the spaces where women's writing appeared—typically, letter and poetry columns—had become the designated public sites for the discussion of gender issues.[10] In these sites, male and female writers, often directly rebutting each other, established an ongoing practice of gender debate that in various guises would persist right through the next century and was crucial, this book will argue, to the success of the women's rights movement in the United States.

To take a striking example, between 1724 and 1731, the *American Weekly Mercury* published the following: a letter from "Lovia," complaining of being forced into marriage with a man for whom she felt no desire; two poems by women, one describing the kind of man the author wanted to marry, the other, possibly by Elizabeth Magawley, critiquing this description; letters by "Martha Careful" and "Caelia Shortface" protesting a male writer's impugning of women; two letters of complaint against "Florio," one signed "Matilda," the other anonymous and advocating an end to the double standard; a letter by "Florio," defending his sex against women's complaints; an anonymous male's letter describing "our MODERN BELLES"; a long satirical poem, by a male author, entitled "The Journal of a Modern Lady" ("But let me now a while survey / Our Madam o'er her Ev'ning-Tea; / Surrounded with her Noisy Crew, / Of Prudes, Coquets, and Harridans"); a long editorial by the *Mercury's* editor, Andrew Bradford (a.k.a. "Mr. Busy-Body"), giving men matrimonial advice and railing against women, especially smart ones;[11] and finally, terminating this increasingly vitriolic, if witty, set of exchanges, "Generosa's" (Elizabeth Magawley's) heated debate in poetry and prose with men whom she dubs "The Wits and Poets of Philadelphia" over the relative merits of the sexes. "[A]s in your Sex," Magawley writes, "there are the several Classes of Men of Sense, Rakes, Fops, Coxcombs and downright Fools, so I hope, without straining your complaisance, you will allow there are some Women of Sense comparatively, as well as Coquets, Romps, Prudes and Idiots."[12]

Magawley, whom Sharon Harris describes as a "razor-sharp satirist," was apparently responding to Bradford's over-the-top editorial;[13] but one can find equally feisty sentiments expressed by women, whether in letters or verse, in other newspapers of the time also. "But what, in the Name of Dullness, most venerable Sirs, could move ye to endeavour to impose on us, so severe a Task as that of *Silence*: Or (which is little better) speaking no more than is necessary? Nothing less, I fear, ye unconscionable Creatures, than a barbarous Avarice of ingrossing all the Talk to your selves," challenged Penelope Aspen in the 1731 *South Carolina Gazette*, speaking, one suspects, for a significant portion of her sex.[14]

Admittedly, the publication of women's texts such as these was dependent on editorial goodwill and not the writers' right to write. After publishing Magawley and Aspen, for instance, both the *Mercury* and the *Gazette* cease publishing women's writing for a time, whether by accident or design. But then the debate resumes, or is conjured up elsewhere. In 1733, the *South Carolina Gazette*, for instance, published a poem by an upper-class twelve-year-old "young Lady," who, according to the editor, wrote it for her brother. Finding him "busied in making his School-Exercise," writing a poem. "[I]f that be all," says she, "I'll write it for you"; and the young lady does, with, what's more, no small bite: "Oh, spotless Paper, fair and white! / On thee by force constrained to write; / Is it not hard I should destroy / Thy Purity, to please a Boy!"[15] Reprints of British verse in the *American Weekly Mercury* during 1735 suggest, moreover, that editors might even publish poetic signs of the gender times from abroad. After describing the highly successful preaching of the "noted & celebrated" Mrs. Drummond, a British Quaker, one article ends with a poem "By a young Lady" praising Mrs. Drummond:

Too long indeed our sex has been deny'd,
And ridicul'd by man's malignant pride;
Who fearful of a just return forebore,
And made it criminal to teach us more.
That woman had no soul was their pretence,
And woman's spelling, past [*sic*] for woman sense;
'Till you most generous heroine stood forth,
And shew'd your sex's aptitude and worth.
Were there no more, yet you bright maid alone
Might for a world of vanity atone.
Redeem the coming age, and set us free
From the false brand of incapacity.[16]

A few months earlier, this same newspaper reprinted one of Mrs. Drummond's sermons in its entirety.

Published more than half a century before Mary Wollstonecraft's *Vindication of the Rights of Women* (1792), these exchanges make clear that both American and British women were keenly aware that their lack of education seriously disadvantaged them. They use rhetorical suasion in poems and letters in order to encourage men to treat them better; and, like the young South Carolinian, they frequently point to their facility at verse as prima facie evidence of their wasted potential. Outraged by an attack on women in the *Philadelphia Chronicle*, a self-described "Circle of Ladies" declared themselves fed up with being blamed for faults for which they were not responsible. "You, Sir, with better *sense*, will justly *fix* / Our faults on *education*, not our *sex*; / Will shew the source which makes the female mind / So oft appear but puerile and blind; / How many would surmount stern custom's laws, / And prove the want of *genius* not the cause; / But that the odium of a *bookish fair*, / Or *female pedant*, or '*they quit their sphere*,' / Damps all their views, and they must drag the chain, / And sigh for sweet instruction's page in vain."[17] When men trash them, which happens quite regularly, they trash back, their arguments, as befits authors in the "Age of Reason," as honed as those of any lawyer.

Although none of this literature suggests that these women were working out any kind of systematic feminist understanding of their oppression—that had to wait for the likes of Judith Sargent Murray and Mary Wollstonecraft—their complaints, like a low grade fever, do not go away. On the contrary, by the end of the eighteenth century, American women's published writing—much of it devoted to critiques of colonial and early republican gender politics—had swelled from a trickle to a stream. In this stream were the works in verse and prose of such notable authors as Phillis Wheatley, Ann Eliza Bleecker, Susanna Rowson, Sarah Wentworth Morton, Mercy Otis Warren, Hannah Adams, and Judith Sargent Murray, not to mention a plethora of other, less well-known names. As is now well recognized, by the first half of the next century, the stream had become a flood, which some male authors, Hawthorne among them, claimed was drowning their own voices out.

In citing the precedent established by this lively male-female newspaper debate, I am not claiming that the late-eighteenth-century public sphere that Habermas describes was other than a profoundly masculinist and class-bound institution. As Nancy Fraser, among others, has forcefully argued and Habermas since conceded, the eighteenth-century public sphere was a male-dominated form of social organization structured on exclusions of race, gender, ethnicity, religion, and class.[18] Indeed, to judge by John Adams's 1776 response to the plea of his wife, Abigail, to "Remember the Ladies," one of the public sphere's primary functions was to insure that men like Adams kept control. If women were not to be trusted out from under the "Masters'" collective thumb, neither were "Indians, Negroes, Hanoverians, Hessians, Russians, Irish Roman Catholics, Scotch Renegadoes, Tories, Landjobbers, Trimmers, Bigots [presumably religious ones], and Canadians."[19] If nothing else, the comprehensiveness of this list suggests just how tight a circle men like Adams were ready to draw around those they deemed capable—or incapable—of governing themselves.

Yet if this be true, it is also true, as Habermas passionately argues, that one of the major differences between his concept of the public sphere and conventional Marxist formulations of class-based power is that Habermas's thinking takes into account the bourgeois public sphere's own internal mechanisms for self-transformation. Agitation by labor and by feminists, Habermas writes, "transformed . . . the structures of the public sphere itself. . . . From the very beginning, the universalistic discourses of the bourgeois public sphere were based on self-referential premises; they did not remain unaffected by a criticism from within because they differ from Foucaultian discourses by virtue of their potential for self-transformation."[20] To Habermas, the promise of the bourgeois public sphere lay precisely here. Using the power of public suasion, women and other subjugated minorities—for example, those on Adams's little list—could take advantage of the public sphere's transformative mechanisms to alter radically their own situations.

Depending on what dates one adopts, how one defines inclusion, and, finally, how one defines the public sphere, this process took, where women were concerned, at least two hundred years. Not precisely a record to cheer for. Nevertheless, the point holds: because in the liberal state the principle of open access was foundational to the public sphere, the sphere did change, becoming more responsive to the needs and demands of the alien elements, as Adams viewed them, within it. This, as even Fraser allows, is its strength:

> [The] idea of the public sphere also functions here and now as a norm of democratic interaction we use to criticize the limitations of actually existing public spheres. The point here is that even the revisionist story and the Gramscian theory [of hegemony] that cause us to doubt the value of the public sphere are themselves only possible because of it. It is the idea of the public sphere that provides the conceptual condition of possibility for the revisionist critique of its imperfect realization.[21]

On however ad hoc a basis, the eighteenth- and nineteenth-century bourgeois women who published their complaints in newspapers and periodicals were using "the idea of the public sphere" as Fraser describes it. If, as we shall see, these women were no less ready to exclude others, those they would have excluded were nonetheless able to use "the idea of the public sphere" in precisely the same way. One need only look as far as Phillis Wheatley's newspaper publications, especially her brilliant and widely circulated open letter to the Mohegan minister, Samson Occom, in 1774, to realize just how powerful such interventions could be.[22]

In order to show how nineteenth-century women generally used their poetry to achieve similar political ends, I will approach my subject from two different directions at once, one historical, the other, literary. Historically, I address how the self-transforming mechanisms of the Habermasian public sphere did indeed work in one specific instance: to wit, the revolution in women's social and juridical status between 1800 and 1900. It is my thesis that, with limited means at their disposal to gain access to the public sphere, women used their writing, in particular, their poetry, to demand, model, imagine, produce, and defend reforms that ultimately led to their acquisition of civil free agency and hence, as they defined it, to their modernity. Literarily, this book will link women's demand for free agency to their exploitation of the complaint genre. In discussing women's complaints, I focus on their ironization of sentimentality because sentimental rhetoric was widely used not just by poets but (in some ways more crucially) by male and female prescriptive authorities to encode the gender notions that these women contested. These were the notions that denied women *civil* free agency prima facie by defining them only in relation to their *social* location within the home, as, for example, in the nineteenth century's use of "public" as an honorific for men and a term of degradation for women.[23]

At the same time, however, this book will also argue that women's social advances in the public sphere came at a cost to women's poetry itself. In particular, as the barriers to female civil agency came down, women poets were not only free to compete with men as equals in the professional arena but, as a result, to separate their verse from their lives, rendering the very kind of female complaint poetry that I discuss here not just out of date but without status as "art." As the coda will observe, some mainstream and, especially, minority women poets continued to write protest poetry after 1910, as indeed did some men. At least until the 1960s, however, self-styled "serious" women poets overwhelmingly positioned themselves alongside their male peers in an Anglo-American poetic tradition that stressed individual achievement over collective concern: the poet talking "to himself, or to nobody." Read from this perspective, this book is not about progress—as if progress were possible in art—but, rather, about a complicated set of exchanges, about loss as well as gain.

Because I believe so deeply that no one story can be told of nineteenth-century century women or their poetry, I have tried to balance the chronological arrangement of this book, dictated by its historical narrative of U.S. women's struggle for civil free agency, with chapters whose internal discontinuities mirror the sometimes stunning differences characterizing these poets' lives and works. This book is consequently neither a unified historical overview of nineteenth-century U.S. women's poetry nor a study of particular writers. Connections among writers exist but never apart from equally significant disjunctions. No single writer or unified set of writers is treated as "representative" of the whole. Where some writers like Sarah Piatt and the Canadian Mohawk writer, E. Pauline Johnson, are given greater scope, it is because the variety of their writing allows them to appear in different chapters on different grounds. If I have erred, it will be in paying, perhaps, too great attention to differences. But in a field that has been so reductively treated over such a length of time, imbalance may be necessary, at least as long as global allusions to "nightingales," "sweet singers," and "poetesses" persist.

However, my emphasis on difference also brings problems of its own. For one thing, although this book is committed to a historical approach, the absence of an effective copyright system for poetry in the nineteenth century makes dating, attribution, and the establishment of correct texts difficult at best. Typically, literary scholars have been able to avoid this problem by speaking of nineteenth-century women's poetry, always ex Dickinson, as if it were an undifferentiated mass. As it is precisely this view that I am contesting here, however, such an alternative is not open to me. On the contrary, one of the chief reasons I have focused on newspaper and periodical poetry, is because the circumstances of its publication allow us to achieve much greater accuracy in dating in particular. Since any poem could appear in multiple venues, in different versions, with different attributions (or none at all), over a period of decades (not just years), errors, however, are inescapable.[24] Quite simply, I have done the best I could.

On a more mundane level, my emphasis on differences has also made the obligatory chapter summaries difficult. Suffice it to say, that part 1 deals primarily with antebellum sentimental poetry by mainstream and minority women writers. In chapter 1, I set the stage for late-nineteenth-century women's entry into gender modernity by examining the vexed relationship that earlier women had with domestic ideology and with the sentimental rhetoric that encoded it, rhetoric that, like domestic ideology itself, was disabling and empowering at once. In tracing this latter paradox, I postulate two very different, and in some ways antithetical, strains within sentimentality itself.[25] The first, which I call "literary sentimentality," originated on the Continent in the imaginative writings of Goethe, Rousseau, and other late-eighteenth-century proto-romantics. All but entirely mediated by literary texts, this form of sentimentality became the culturally sanctioned discourse of refined bourgeois sensibility in the United States, as abroad. In its close alliance to domestic ideology, it also gave rise to the vague, idealizing romanticism that we now identify as characteristic of the sentimental or genteel lyric.

In chapter 2, I examine the century's second principal form of sentimentality, namely, "high sentimentality." Like literary sentimentality, high senti-

mentality also originated in the eighteenth century but as an ethical/epis-
temological discourse of social reform. Where antebellum women poets were
never entirely comfortable with literary sentimentality, largely because of its
romanticization of hearth and home, their adoption of high sentimentality
was, on the whole, as passionate and powerful as, today, it is problematic.
My goal in these chapters is to untangle these two strains of sentimentality,
which scholarly literature has largely conflated, and to suggest some of the
ways in which both strains, together with the domestic ideology that supported them, were used, critiqued, and not infrequently ironized by women
well before Seneca Falls.

Part 1's final two chapters focus on the extensive roles both forms of
sentimentality played in the writing of women from four of the United States'
principal minorities: African American, Irish American, Jewish American,
and Native American. Unlike their mainstream peers, minority women poets
tended to employ the strategies of literary and high-sentimental lyric poetry
unironically through most of the century. In these two chapters, I speculate
on why and explore how writers from each minority group inflected these
strategies for their own purposes. I then look in depth at the problematics of
minority representation as they appear in the work of four highly prominent
minority women poets: Frances Harper, Fanny Parnell, Emma Lazarus, and
E. Pauline Johnson. Of these writers, I argue that it was not "representativeness" but their peculiar positioning between minority cultures and the dominant society that enabled them to become such effective spokespersons for
peoples in many respects fundamentally unlike themselves.

In part 2 (chapters 5 through 8), I examine how mainstream women's
interrogation (repudiation?) of domestic ideology after 1850 led to their
ironization of sentimentality both as a lyric mode and as a discourse of
sociopolitical reform. Women no less than men continued to write genteel
lyrics well into the fin de siècle. However, after 1850, many women also
began to parody both gentility and literary sentimentality. As the social
change brought on by feminist agitation made possible a new generation of
professional woman writers, a deepening split developed between those
women still concerned with politics—most notably, minority women poets,
but also Sarah Piatt—and those whose desire for mainstream recognition led
them in more purely formal directions. As these chapters unfold, my attention will become noticeably more text-oriented, in keeping with changes in
the ways women wrote. Determined to separate themselves from both the
gender values and the perceived rhetorical excesses of their sentimentally
inclined predecessors, mainstream and minority fin-de-siècle poets made
control of affect, or what I call "affective irony," the signature of their modernity. That is, they made *anti*sentimentality a defining feature of themselves
as "New Women" and as artists of the "New."

However ironically, the success of these poets was thus predicated on the

demise of the very kind of writer who gave them birth. Some women continued to write in the social-protest tradition in the twentieth century, but the
modernist woman poet is best understood as one produced not by the political agitation that made her emergence possible but by the split between high
and popular culture that occurred in the final decade of the nineteenth century itself. In dismissing earlier nineteenth-century women poets *tout court*
as irremediably inferior artists, whose popularity rested in their (feminizing)
emotionality, fin-de-siècle women poets demonized their own roots, cutting
early modernist women off from them also. However, where male modernists could repudiate their Victorian precursors without impugning their own
authority as artists, serious twentieth-century women poets could not. Persuaded that to be a woman as they believed women were, or traditionally
had been, was necessarily to be a bad poet, female modernists languished in
a literary limbo for (if one believes Adrienne Rich) half a century or more,
never really granted equality with male writers yet fearing to appeal to a
(gendered) constituency of their own.

At its baldest, this is my argument. The complexities of its persuasion I
leave to the chapters themselves.

✦ **PART ONE** ✦

1

Literary Sentimentality and the Genteel Lyric

I wish to persuade women to endeavor to acquire strength, both of mind and body, and to convince them that the soft phrases, susceptibility of heart, delicacy of sentiment, and refinement of taste, are almost synonymous with epithets of weakness, and that those beings who are the only the objects of pity . . . will soon become objects of contempt.
  —MARY WOLLSTONECRAFT,
    A Vindication of the Rights of Woman, 1792[1]

The poems of Miss [Anne C.] Lynch are marked by depth of feeling and grace of expression. They are the natural and generally unpremeditated effusions of a nature extremely sensitive, but made strong by experience and knowledge, and elevated into a divine repose by the ever active sense of beauty.
  —RUFUS W. GRISWOLD,
    The Female Poets of America, 1848[2]

[D]elicacy of feeling, purity of sentiment, and grace of expression . . . without either remarkable strength or remarkable imagination, have made Mr. Stedman a deserved favorite among a large host of readers.
  —REVIEW OF Recent Poems, Harper's, 1878[3]

Between 1848 and 1849, three anthologies of nineteenth-century U.S. women's poetry were published: Caroline May's *The American Female Poets*, Thomas Buchanan Read's *The Female Poets of America*, and Rufus W. Griswold's anthology of the same name. May, a poet herself, put out the least pretentious volume (seventy-eight poets, something over 300 poems). An artist as well as poet, Read produced the most elegant, gracing his smaller selection (seventy-two poets, about 170 poems) with nine idealizing portraits of his illustrious authors, from Lydia Huntley Sigourney to Sara Jane Clarke (Lippincott). With its double columns and ten-point type, Griswold's anthology was the most commodious and, relatively speaking, the most diverse—the anthology, as it were, of record, with ninety-four poets, over 600 poems, and extensive biographical introductions. All three anthologies came out in nineteenth-century equivalents of the "coffee-table book," their tooled leather bindings and gilded edges bespeaking their status as ideal gifts for poetically inclined young ladies.

Like their British counterparts published in the same year, Frederic Rowton's *The Female Poets of Great Britain, Chronologically Arranged with Copious Selections and Critical Remarks* (1848) and George Bethune's *The British Female Poets* (1849), the U.S. anthologies were part of a continuum of publications, including gift books and annuals, targeting the middle-class's distaff side. These were women like *Middlemarch's* Rosamund eager "to display the very best taste."[4] However, mediating the latest literary fashions for ("silly"?) young women was only one of the functions these publications served. As Margaret Reynolds remarks in her introduction to *Victorian Women Poets* (1995), even high-culture women authors like George Eliot benefited from the role such publications played in establishing women writers' professional credentials.[5] Equally important, these venues helped build an audience ready to put down good money for what women writers, Eliot included, wrote.

Understood thus, the U.S. anthologies, like their British siblings, were fabulously successful. Impressed, it seems, by the sheer volume U.S. women were producing, Griswold forecasted an exciting future for their poetry, one that would make it a significant source of national pride. An enterprising man of letters, as well as the avuncular patron of many of the women he published, Griswold was eager that he and other members of the U.S. male literary establishment be properly credited for the remarkable efflorescence of female verse:

> The most striking quality of that civilization which is evolving itself in America, is the deference felt for women. As a point in social manners, it is so pervading and so peculiar, as to amount to a national characteristic. . . . The increased degree in which women among us are taking a leading part in literature, is one of the circumstances of this augmented distinction. . . . The proportion of female writers at this moment in America, far exceeds that which the present or any other age in England exhibits. (*FPA* 8)

Griswold's assertions were, as it happens, somewhat premature. According to Davis and Joyce's bibliographical survey, *Poetry by Women to 1900*, 1,609 U.S. women published volumes of poetry in the nineteenth century, as compared to 1,687 British women, with U.S. women outproducing their transatlantic rivals only after 1850. But since only 18 U.S. women published volumes *before* 1800, as opposed to 210 in Britain, the American anthologist still had good reason to crow.[6]

Along with evidence for the healthy production rate of U.S. women's poetry, Davis and Joyce's research provides subtler hints of the field's strength as well. For example, the bibliographers note that, contrary to popular opinion, these poets were not all from New England, or white, or from the Protestant middle class. They came "from all strata of society," "a true cross section of American . . . life."[7] Equally telling, "[t]hey did not hide behind male pseudonyms, they were not always obscure in their own lifetimes, and they did compete in the literary marketplace."[8] In sum, not only were there a great many nineteenth-century U.S. women poets but they were a diverse and visible lot who, far from being abashed at publicity, enthusiastically promoted both their own and—as May's anthology testifies—each other's work.[9]

But given this plenitude and diversity—so amply confirmed by my research into women's newspaper and periodical publication—what does one make of the close-to-mind-numbing sameness of the poetry in the anthologies themselves? Griswold, to be sure, points with pride to Phillis Wheatley, the noted eighteenth-century "slave poet"; Lucy Larcom, a former Lowell mill girl; and Maria James, a Welsh émigrée in service to the Reverend Bishop Potter. But his inclusion of these "others" does not create space in his anthology for racial or class difference any more than the presence of a sprinkling of women poets introduced gender diversity into his earlier anthology, *The Poets and Poetry of America* (1842). On the contrary, Griswold, like May and Read, features only one kind of poem, whoever the writer: that which met the age's idealizing genteel standard. "The sense of beauty . . . is the means through which the human character is purified and elevated. The creation of beauty, the manifestation of the real by the ideal, 'in words that move in metrical array,' is poetry" (*PPA* vi). Since, as Griswold sanctimoniously intones in *Female Poets*, "the muse is no respecter of conditions," in a democracy even a slave girl, if she loved beauty enough, could show signs of "genuine poetical inspiration" no less than the bourgeois woman next door (*FPA* 9 and 31). For this particular aesthetic—so oddly democratizing in its way—gender, class origins, and race played second fiddle to the elevated aspirations of the *nouvelle bourgeoisie*.

Edmund Clarence Stedman, Griswold's fin-de-siècle successor as anthologist of record, frames his gleanings in terms of an identical aesthetic of high-minded sameness, one in which "the tuneful sisterhood" now mingles imperceptibly with its brotherhood in song (*AAA* xxviii). Of the poets publishing between 1835 and 1875, Stedman writes in the introduction to *An American Anthology*: "With the exception of Poe, the *dii majores* . . . were interpreters of nature, sentiment, patriotism, [and] religion. . . . With the added exceptions of Whitman and Lanier, and of Lowell in his dialect satire, the leaders' methods and motives have had much in common." Nor, Stedman claims, did minor poets vary the tune. Rather, they followed "the spirit of the leaders . . . [in] the same measures and diction" (*AAA* xix). Even after 1875, when, according to Stedman's narrative, fiction usurped poetry's place as the genre of choice for serious writers, the choir sang on as before, filling the "twilight interval" with their "minor voices and their tentative modes and tones" (*AAA* xxviii). Early or late, major or minor, female or male, U.S. poets all sounded pretty much alike to Stedman, their poems "a rhythmical expression of emotion and ideality" (*AAA* xxix).[10] With this vague and aestheticized definition of poetry in hand, Stedman, like his midcentury precursor, packs his anthology with, basically, one poem, the "genteel lyric" or, since, practically speaking, they amount to the same thing, the lyric of "literary sentimentality."

One does not have to read far in the existing scholarship on nineteenth-century poetry to realize how profoundly influential the commitment of nineteenth-century anthologists to the genteel lyric—the "rhythmical expression of emotion and ideality"—has been. Operating under what, with a nod to Foucault, I would call "the homogeneity hypothesis," Cheryl Walker describes nineteenth-century women's poetry in terms fully compliant with those principles of selection that Griswold and Stedman used. "For the most part, these women saw their task as providing memorable expression for the prevailing sentiments of liberal Christianity, domestic piety, American nature romanticism, and nationalist fervor." "Modernist aesthetic principles," she observes, "privileging linguistic disruption, extreme perceptions, epistemological doubt, and trenchant political critique—were alien to the minds of most of them" (*AWP* xxvi–xxvii). According to Walker, the qualities distinguishing women's poetry are, rather, expansiveness, consistency of tone, comprehensive treatment of subject, and a general willingness to "operat[e] within the fixed boundaries of a shared discourse, rather than ai[m] at surprise." The "typical nineteenth-century work," she concludes, "is nothing like what twentieth-century critics, strongly influenced by Modernist aesthetics, construe as a 'good poem'" (*AWP* xxviii).

Generally speaking, Walker's description of nineteenth-century U.S. women's poetry as stylistically and thematically seamless—a "shared discourse" unmarked by "idiosyncratic" extremes—fits most of the selections of women's poetry in Griswold and Stedman. Despite Walker's inclusion of three black women, and one genuine eccentric (Adah Isaacs Menken),[11] the description also fits most of the selections in her own anthology, *American Women Poets of the Nineteenth Century* (1994). Like Stedman, she assumes that the genteel lyric that rose to dominance after 1825 maintained its hegemony through the century as a whole. Walker differs only in treating this lyric's genteel/sentimental properties as part of an explicitly female poetic tradition, a tradition she defined in her critical study *Nightingale's Burden* (1982) as the veiled expression of secret sorrow.

Although scholars coming after Walker—including Walker herself in subsequent writings—have greatly complicated her initial presentation, the assumption that nineteenth-century U.S. women's genteel poetry was a gender-
specific literary field has gone largely unchallenged, and understandably so,
given the vast quantity of genteel poetry women produced.[12] However, male
poets, if anything, produced even more, as any fair reading of Griswold's
Poets and Poetry or Stedman's *American Anthology* makes clear. Indeed, this
is precisely why Melville savages reviewers in *Pierre* (1852). "[E]uphonious
construction of sentences . . . judicious smoothness and genteelness of . . .
sentiments and fancies, and something they called 'Perfect Taste'"—which
Melville identifies with avoiding anything "coarse or new"[13]—were what reviewers admired, and on the whole these poets gave the reviewers what they
wanted.

But was the genteel lyric, even with its admittedly powerful cultural identification with the feminine, all that nineteenth-century women wrote? In this
chapter, I want to complicate our view of women's actual relationship to the
genteel lyric in two distinct but interrelated ways. First, I want to clarify the
lyric's own relationship to the feminine by resituating it in terms of its origins in late-eighteenth-century male-authored literature of sensibility, a literature that in its domestic values was sentimental to the core. Then, I will
look specifically at early-nineteenth-century women's ambivalent responses
to this sentimentality, especially as allied to domestic ideology and the
genteel.

In response to Ann Douglas's fierce attack on nineteenth-century U.S.
women's writing in *The Feminization of American Culture* (1977), feminist
defenders of women's literature have sought to redeem it by casting its affect-
laden rhetoric as a uniquely (and powerfully) female discourse. Nineteenth-
century women writers used sentimentality, they argue, to rewrite the masculinist values of Romanticism in terms of a woman-centered "domestic"
ethos or vision, one stressing community over individual aspiration. Like the
argument for homogeneity, this argument also has considerable evidence to
support it. A poem such as Sigourney's "The Alpine Flowers," for example,
in which the speaker apostrophizes the "Meek dwellers mid yon terror-
stricken cliffs," unambiguously treats its titular subject as a type for female
power, "bloom[ing] unblanch'd, amid the waste / Of desolation." In such
lines, Sigourney's apparently sentimental poem can be fairly construed as a
bold rewriting of the masculinist impetus behind the nineteenth-century Romantic sublime. Here, "pencil'd beauty," not "breathless awe," brings the
poem's (male) quester to God:

Man, who panting toils
O'er slippery steeps, or trembling treads the verge
Of yawning gulfs. . . .

. . . looks shuddering up,
And marks ye in your placid loveliness
Fearless, yet frail, and clasping his chill hands
Blesses your pencil'd beauty.—Mid the pomp
Of mountain summits rushing to the sky,
And chaining the rapt soul in breathless awe,
He bows to bind you drooping to his breast,
Inhales your spirit from the frost-wing'd gale,
And freer dreams of Heaven.

(NAWP 4–5)

First published in 1827, however, Sigourney's poem comes late in the evolution of the gender values it espouses. Associated initially with refined poetic sensibility, the qualities which constituted the nineteenth-century female sentimental—"depth of feeling," "grace of expression," "purity of sentiment," etcetera—were first associated with the valorization of home and family by *male* Continental writers publishing in the second half of the eighteenth century, in particular, Goethe and Rousseau. Far from offering a gender-specific female alternative to male Romanticism, therefore, this kind of genteel sentimental—what I call "literary sentimentality" because of its origins in belles lettres—is more properly understood as a discursive/ideological option proffered up by Romanticism itself in its own early stages. As such, it began and remained throughout its long career, a rhetoric of interiority first and foremost for the domesticated genteel male. It was that feminized form of Romanticism that even in its idealization of hearth and home was narcissistically tailored to suit male, not female, needs, even as Sigourney's flower is there to bring "Man"—not itself—to God.

Not surprisingly, then, even between 1830 and 1850, at the height of literary sentimentality's discursive dominance in the United States, some women writers contested its rarefied rhetoric and the "ideality" for which it stood. With cause. Middle-class women did indeed write a great deal of genteel verse, inscribing in it, as Sigourney does in "Alpine Flowers," their faith in domesticity's power. However, insofar as the power of domesticity came only through women's willing confinement to heart and hearth, domesticity's impact played out very differently in the lives of each sex. Baldly put, for men, female domesticity meant getting served; for women, serving. For men, it meant the enhancement of their private lives; for women, it meant restriction to them. Bourgeois women were bound, therefore, to respond both to domesticity and to literary sentimentality differently, given how differently they were positioned vis-à-vis the benefits derived.

It is this difference and, with it, women's resistance to the genteel lyric's discursive dominance, that will concern me both in this chapter and throughout this book. Behind the genteel aesthetic and inseparable from it lay a domestic ideology that made many so-called "feminine" psychic qualities fundamental to the refinement of male bourgeois subjectivity, not the least, a domesticized and sentimentalized focusing on the interior life itself. But whether the refining and redemptive qualities literary sentimentality and domestic ideology ascribed to women were in fact qualities that defined—or should define—women was an entirely different question. To what extent, if at all, women should identify with these qualities was, perhaps, for the poets I discuss, the single most important question driving them to write. As we shall see in later chapters, this was also the principal issue at stake in the emergence of female modernity (the "New Woman") in the fin de siècle.

The Literature of Sensibility and the Male Sentimental

> An angel! Nonsense! Everybody says that of the girl he
> loves.
> —GOETHE, *The Sorrows of Young Werther*, 1774[14]

The genealogical roots of the genteel lyric can be traced back to bourgeois/sentimental texts published on the Continent in the first half of the eighteenth century, that host of middle-class novels and plays that Erich Auerbach identifies with the *comédie larmoyante*.[15] Evolving between 1730 and 1770, this body of literature occupied itself with the trials and tribulations of the petite bourgeoisie. Eventually, it produced some of the best-known and most formative works of Anglo-European Romanticism's early stages, among them, Rousseau's *Julie; ou, La Nouvelle Héloïse* (1761) and *Émile* (1762), Laurence Sterne's *A Sentimental Journey* (1768), and Bernardin de St. Pierre's *Paul et Virginie* (1788). No work, however, says more about the close ties between nineteenth-century domestic ideology and the rise of the eighteenth-century literature of proto-Romantic sensibility than does Goethe's *Die Leiden des jungen Werthers* (1774). In this semiautobiographical epistolary novel, the constellation of qualities now identified with the genteel—rarefied emotionality, the idealization of the bourgeois woman in a domestic setting, etcetera—comes fatally together with Romanticism's nascent aesthetic of emotional excess to produce a bourgeois tragedy whose sentimentality is, to use one of Ann Douglas's more graphic terms, rancid to its core.[16]

"*Werther*," David Wellbery declares, "is the first European novel in which subjectivity *per se* acquires aesthetic concretization."[17] Wellbery would have better said male subjectivity, but the point is well-taken. Focused entirely on Werther himself, Goethe's tear-saturated novel treats the interior life of its eponymous hero as a subject of absorbing literary interest even while transforming the bourgeois/genteel home into a site for tragic/romantic excess. Indeed, few texts before or since have devoted themselves with such loving scrupulosity to the emotional life of a single, otherwise utterly undistinguished young man. With nothing but his sensitivity and self-absorption to recommend him, Werther became the beau idéal for generations of suicidally inclined romantic young.

Werther's relevance to this study lies in what is, in fact, the novel's best-known scene. In his letter of June 16, Werther relates to his friend, Wilhelm, his first encounter with Charlotte, the young middle-class woman with whom he falls in love despite knowing that she is engaged elsewhere. What gives this scene its importance is the way in which it situates romance in a domestic mise en scène. Werther falls in love with Charlotte while watching her perform a quintessentially domestic chore: giving "her" children (she and her younger siblings are motherless) their supper.[18] Like those key literary moments so richly explored by Auerbach in *Mimesis*, Goethe's handling of this scene points to a basic shift in the paradigms representing "reality" in Western literature. The young woman who moves Werther's passion as she carries out her domestic labor is in all basic respects indistinguishable from her later incarnation, the Victorian "Angel in the House." If Werther has nothing but romantic excess and self-destructive emotionality to recommend him, the gentle Charlotte has nothing but domestic self-denial and patient, loving service to offer in return. Much like Yopie Prins's Sappho in *The Victorian Sappho*, Charlotte is a trope with nothing behind it, a "place-holder," in her case, for mother-love and home:[19]

> a lovely girl of medium height, dressed in a simple white frock with pink ribbons. She was holding a loaf of dark bread in her hand, and was cutting slices for the little ones all round, in proportion to their age and appetite. She performed her task with such affection and each child awaited his turn with outstretched hands and artlessly shouted his thanks. . . . "Forgive me for causing you the trouble of coming for me and for keeping the ladies waiting but dressing and making arrangements for the house while I'm out made me forget my children's supper. They don't like to take it from anyone but me." I paid her some indifferent compliment, but my whole soul was absorbed by her air, her voice, her manner.[20]

Nurturant, virginal—the white dress and pink ribbons—caring, dutiful, intelligent, selfless, loving, and beautiful, withal, Charlotte sounds too good to be true. And is. In the novel's narcissistic economy, she is the unadulterated product of male fantasy, and she has but one function: to serve as the (oedipalized) object of male desire. As such, she provides the occasion for Werther, as male bourgeois subject/artist, to discover/explore the heights and depths of his own desires, his interiority, his quivering sensibility. What Charlotte lacks—using this term specifically for its Lacanian reverberations—is an interiority of her own. One-dimensional as any surface, hers is the half-life women live in the male imaginary. Indeed, this is what being an "Angel" is all about: to be without having a being. To be lack.

If to be "feminized" means becoming overly emotional and thoroughly narcissistic, then loving Charlotte feminizes Werther, and to this extent, the novel can be read as a feminization of otherwise masculine art, since Werther represents himself as a poet. (In their last meeting before Werther's suicide, he reads his weepy translation of Ossian's songs to Charlotte, dissolving them both in tears.)[21] But Werther's feminization is no woman's doing. Indeed, if a woman writer wants to find herself in this novel, she, like Judith Fetterly's unresisting reader, must either "immasculate" herself, that is, read from a male point of view, or accept Charlotte's total lack of an autonomous subjectivity, that is, her Angelhood, as her own.[22] "[P]oets, painters, and composers," Wollstonecraft scathingly comments in *Vindication of the Rights of Women* (1792), "pour sensibility into their compositions . . . moulding them with passion, giv[ing] to the inert body a soul; but, in woman's imagination, love alone concentrates these ethereal beams."[23] In Lacanian terms, women could only "do" (love) what men could write about (loving).

In this Wertherian paradigm, woman is a vacancy, a hole waiting to be filled. What life she has comes from another's desire, another's words—desire and words that erase even as they animate, just as Goethe erases "Charlotte," the historical woman, in Charlotte, Werther's Angel. Nor does the would-be woman writer escape this dilemma by identifying with Werther instead, since such an identification is no less equivalent to self-erasure. Despite the literature of sensibility's valorization of the feminine—or, rather, what it constructed as the feminine—this literature was precisely the unalterably masculinist discourse Wollstonecraft said it was. And as Prins has forcefully demonstrated, nineteenth-century British and American women poets who adopted its conventions erased themselves in the process, making death their recursively repeating end.

But do women's reproductions of this discourse constitute a female literary tradition and aesthetic, as Prins also seems to suggest? Yes and no. Like Walker with the myth of Philomela, Prins traces the putatively female authorial dilemma she describes back to an equally putative female ur-text, namely, the myth of Sappho and Phaon, a myth whose fame, like that of Philomela, rested on its Ovidian version. However, even if one ignores the major role that a male author like Ovid played in shaping and preserving the Sapphic fable, a passing acquaintance with the work of Charlotte Smith (1749–1805), said by some to be Britain's first romantic woman poet, should deeply trouble Prins's account. Written on the cusp between the eighteenth and nineteenth centuries, Smith's poetry, like Goethe's novella, balances between an outgoing literature of sensibility and an incoming romanticism in its presentation of authorial subjectivity. Her series of five sonnets, spoken by Werther, are typical of her work and especially enlightening as a result.

Published in Smith's highly influential *Elegiac Sonnets and Other Poems* (1784), these Wertherian rip-offs are saturated with the same kind of self-emptying self-pity that Prins identifies with the Sapphic "poetess" and that Walker identifies with the "Nightingale tradition." The invocation "To Solitude" will be sufficient to demonstrate what I mean. In this poem, "Werther" apostrophizes the "sequester'd vale" where he, like that "sweet songstress," the nightingale, has taken refuge. If the Sapphic poem is a poem of evacuated self, then this is a Sapphic poem, but its speaker is, as well he should be, a woman author masquerading as a man who masquerades at being like a woman (i.e., a suffering nightingale):

> O Solitude! to thy sequester'd vale;
>   I come to hide my sorrow and my tears,
> And to thy echoes tell the mournful tale
>   Which scarce I trust to pitying Friendship's ears!
> Amidst thy wild-woods, and untrodden glades,
>   No sounds but those of melancholy move;
> And the low winds that die among the shades,
>   Seem like soft Pity's sighs for hopeless love!
> And sure some story of despair and pain,
>   In yon deep copse thy murm'ring doves relate;
> And, hark, methinks in that long plaintive strain,
>   Thine own sweet songstress weeps my wayward fate!
> Ah, Nymph! That fate assist me to endure,
> And bear awhile—what Death alone can cure![24]

Given *Werther's* enormous cachet as a model for "male" poetic subjectivity, it is not surprising that women poets coming after Smith would turn—as, for example, Mary Robinson does in *Sappho and Phaon* (1796)— to Ovid's apocryphal story of Sappho's doomed love for Phaon in their desire for a "female" equivalent to Werther himself.[25] But the discourse that Robinson uses in her *Sappho*, like that Smith uses in "To Solitude" or Sigourney in "Alpine Flowers," remains a male invention, traceable back to eighteenth-century male authors of sensibility, not to the Greek woman poet herself.[26] As Adela Pinch argues, lyric poetry's apparent expression of personal emotion is, and has always been, a matter of convention, nowhere more so, I might add, than in love poetry.[27] Early-Romantic Wertherian melancholy was the very height of fashion when Smith and Robinson were writing. In cutting the Sapphic cloth to fit a Wertherian-Romantic model, women poets were doing no more than what poets typically do. But as a gender-specific poetic, the result is ambiguous at best. For not only was the Victorian poetess whom Walker and Prins describe—like the story of her origins, a male invention, but the "poetess" herself was a man.

It is, then, in terms of the masculinist valorization of middle-class domestic life and values, on the one hand, and early Romanticism's privileging of male sensibility, on the other, that the evolution of soft Victorian romanticism, that is, the sentimental genteel, must be understood. This discursive modality was not identified specifically as male because it did not have to be; maleness was the default position. What matters here is that neither the genteel's vision of domestic life nor its vision of gender difference were of women's making. They represent, all but exclusively, the thinking of male authorities like Rousseau and Griswold and those countless others—ministers, doctors, authors of conduct books—who made their livings by giving nineteenth-century men, women, and children advice. To say otherwise— that is, to claim literary sentimentality as a gender-specific female discourse—requires that one abstract the history of its discursive production from both its history as a romanticized discourse of male subjectivity, not to mention its history as a bourgeois discourse of family, nation, and class.[28]

Finally, it should be noted that where nineteenth-century male literati had numerous personal and professional incentives to embrace the gendered domestic ideology subtending genteel sentimentality, women did not. When they tried, their poetry became riddled, therefore, with precisely the kinds of self-contradictions and inner divisions that Walker and Prins describe. But to view women's poetry exclusively in terms of these self-effacing, self-contradictory texts is finally to let men have the last say, treating women only as they present themselves under the sign of lack. As a result, although I recognize the wealth of material women's genteel poetry represents, the remainder of this book will pursue another tack. Rather than elaborate on the disciplinary role that genteel texts played in the production of the female bourgeois subject—a subject handled with great competence by Brodhead, Loeffleholz, and others—my book examines those many, yet typically isolated, moments when, as in "To My Child," individual women writers resisted the pull of genteel conventions in order to construct subjectivities of their own.

Publicizing Charlotte's Sorrows: The Poetics of Female Resistance

"Is any one else in the Book?" (I knew
    She would ask me that.) Yes, Charlotte is there.
["]Then is it the Sorrows of Charlotte too?"
    No, child, for never a man would care
To write such a long sad story, you see,
    As the—cutting of bread-and-butter would be;
    And never a woman had time to dare!
—SARAH PIATT, "The Sorrows of Charlotte," 1872[29]

Without denying the genteel lyric's ubiquitousness in the first half of the century, one can still show that, like eighteenth-century women poets, many early-nineteenth-century women used their poetry to thrash through gender issues from a woman's point of view. What these poems reveal is their authors' intense subjective awareness of themselves as something other than/ more than their socially sanctioned roles—that is, their restriction to the Angelhood conferred upon them by men. Of the various strategies these poets employed to keep their gender options open, this chapter section concerns itself primarily with those that evolved directly from earlier eighteenth-century praxis. In particular, I trace early-nineteenth-century women's continued commitment to the eighteenth-century line of wit, focusing on their use of personae drawn from Enlightenment social topology, as in Magawley's "Coquets, Romps, Prudes" and "Women of Sense." By using masks such as the Old Maid, the Belle, the Seduced Maiden, the Woman of Wit, and the Coquette, early-nineteenth-century women were able to write poems in explicitly *un*sentimental, *un*domestic, *un*genteel voices. Tracking their poetic deployment of these personae in relation both to their poetry's expanding presence in print culture and to the rise of sentimental culture itself greatly problematizes bourgeois women's public praxis. Not least, it raises serious questions about these women's "real world" commitment to such Angel-defining qualities as modesty and purity, given the forwardness of the female speakers they are prepared to display on the public stage.

U.S. women's poetry between 1800 and 1850 breaks down into two distinct periods. For the first two-and-a-half decades of the new century, U.S. women poets continued to use newspapers and periodicals as their primary venues, publishing as few as forty-five books.[30] Stylistically also, their poetry has more in common with eighteenth-century verse than with the poetry penned by the following generation of "literary domestics" or "sentimentalists" (1826–50). It remains a poetry of wit and cultural debate, varied by odes to nature or poems dedicated to historical personages or events. After the mid-1820s, however the number of poetry volumes authored by U.S. women escalates rapidly, and the debate becomes more complicated, as women began to adopt the affect-based style enjoined on them both by sentimental literature and by their new roles as domestic saviors, incipient municipal housekeepers, and "Angel[s] in the House."

Only three poets with substantial name recognition in the second quarter of the century surfaced between 1800 and 1825. Sigourney, the best known and best paid woman poet of her day, published her first volume in 1815, the youthful *Moral Pieces in Verse and Prose*; Maria Gowen Brooks, intrepid author of *Zóphiël; or, The Bride of Seven*, published *Judith, Esther and Other Poems* in 1820; and Sarah Josepha Hale, best known for her editing of *Godey's Lady's Book*, published *The Genius of Oblivion and Other Original Poems* in 1823. But if major figures were scarce and books few in the early period, women poets themselves were everywhere, their productions enlivening the pages of newspapers and periodicals, not just in Boston or New York, but wherever communities were large enough to support such publications: Brattleborough, Vermont (*Brattleborough Reporter*); Marietta, Pennsylvania (*Ladies' Visiter*); and Lexington, Kentucky (*Kentucky Reporter*), for example.

Not yet burdened with the genteel aesthetic's (Victorian) scruples, or even with the late eighteenth century's cultivation of proto-Romantic sensibility, poets writing in the first few decades of the nineteenth century used personae to write freely on topics—seduction, rage, breast-feeding, illegitimate motherhood, disgust with men—that their literary daughters treated more gingerly (if they treated them at all). As a result, these poets could produce highly pungent verse. In the anonymously authored "Written by a Young Lady to Her Seducer" (1802), for example, the speaker, clearly no Angel herself, vents her rage in a tour de force of uninterrupted cursing ninety-four lines long and claiming, at least, to be straight from the heart:

Tainting pure air with your contagious breath,
And in a softened soul plant seeds of death.
And every breast, that beats with sacred fires,
You strive to level with your base desires;
To rob the sweetness of a virtuous mind
Has been the fellness of your black design:

. . . .

But I must stop and banish from my mind
All tender feelings of the human kind;
Borrow of Satan his infernal breath
To breathe on you the horrid chills of death.[31]

By blazoning the speaker's status as fallen woman in the poem's title, the author of this poem sets the stage for a direct expression of feminist rage. Yet, if this directness stands in striking contrast to the kinds of circumlocutions we associate with somewhat later women's verse, the poem itself, despite its high emotional quotient—or, maybe, because of it—feels blatantly staged. The speaker may claim to *be* a fallen woman but all the poem's formal elements—the iambic pentameter couplets, the conventional situation, elevated diction, and unstinting verbal excess—point to a persona poem, the poet adopting the mask of a seduced maiden in order to vent her or, possibly, his wrath at men who deceive.

If these early writers were ready to put women's fury on display, they were also ready, in the best Enlightenment fashion, to be witty at marriage's and men's expense. In a delightfully parodic response to "The Fop," a misogynistic ditty by "Dr. Caustick," editor of the *Weekly Inspector* (1806),[32] a woman signing herself "Volina" gives the editor a fair taste of his own medicine. "You Say We're Fond of Fops, —Why Not?" answers the male writer, all but line for line, in twelve biting stanzas that turn Dr. Caustick on his head: "You say we're fond of fops, —why not, / When men of sense cannot be got? / A woman, *something* must admire, / Or else with *ennui* expire" (*NAWP* 392). The speaker of "The Old Maid's Apology" (1801), is just as acidic, albeit considerably briefer. If, she observes, unmarried women are doomed to lead apes in hell after their death, better that "[t]han be led by a foolish ape now" (*NAWP* 388).

"The Bachelor's Soliloquy; or a New Puzzle in Praise of Women" (1822), by Anna Maria—possibly Anna Maria Wells, Frances Osgood's sister—ranks among the most successful examples of this kind of poem that I have found. Here the female speaker's retort is literally braided into the attack itself, cleverly twisting the long tradition of misogynistic rhetoric behind the bachelor's lines against itself. Read straight, "The Bachelor's Soliloquy" uses a bachelor persona to launch a conventional diatribe against women. Reading the first and third lines of each stanza and then the second and fourth, the poem reverses itself, extolling women instead. The very way in which the poem is constructed forces the reader to contemplate opposing perspectives, even as it deconstructs the diatribe from within, taking each canard and turning it back on itself. The result is a perfectly constructed rabbit/duck poem and, as such, a brilliant comment on the gulf dividing male and female perspectives:

> Happy a man may pass his life
> *When free'd from matrimonial chains*
> When he is govern'd by a wife
> *He's sure to suffer for his pains.*
>
> What tongue is able to declare
> *The failings which in women dwell*
> The worth that falls to woman's share
> *Can scarce be call'd—perceptible.*
>
> In all the female race appear
> *Hypocrisy, deceit and pride*
> Truth—darling of a heart sincere
> *In woman, never can reside.*
>
> They're always studying to employ
> *Their time in vanity and prate*
>
> Their leisure hours in social joy
> *To spend is what all women hate.*
>
> Destruction take the men I say
> *Who make of women their delight*
> Those who contempt to women pay
> *Keep prudence always in their sight.*[33]

Embellishing the poetry columns of magazines and enlivening the pages of local newspapers, the function of these poems was not to give personal expression to individual experience but to present a point of view. Indeed, the fact that these poems often evolve as parts of an ongoing debate suggests that personal expression was simply not the issue. Rather they were bits and pieces in a longer conversation, one that sometimes, as in the "bare elbows" debate in the *Boston Gazette* in 1803, might last for months at a time, defense and attack handed back and forth among various speakers. Set off by a male writer ("Trim"), who uses a dog persona ("Tray") to protest women's fashions, this particular exchange elicited nine poems by as many as six different poets, the women writing as bluntly and forcefully as the men. "And now poor 'curs' I'll not presume t'advise, / But print the evils which before you rise; / Your looks wont please us, neither will your clothes, / And as for honour, you have none, heav'n knows." So says "Clementine"—not to one man ("Tray") but to men generically ("curs"), who had nipped once too often at women's heels.[34]

Sometimes wittily, sometimes furiously, and sometimes, as in the following stanza on breast-feeding, tenderly, these early-nineteenth-century poets spoke up for what women knew, their pleasures as well as their "sorrows," their joys as well as their complaints:

> What! do thy little fingers leave the breast,
>   The fountain which thy small lip press'd at pleasure?
> Couldst thou exhaust it, pledge of passion blest!
>   Even then thou couldst not know my fond love's measure.[35]

Like the speaker of "To My Child," the speaker of "Verses to My First Born" deliberately pushes the veil aside "where," according to Frances Osgood, "feeling feeds the fire divine,"[36] allowing readers insight into one of the most intimate experiences that a woman can have. The speaker does so, moreover, without blushing, as if, in fact, this most private of experiences also had a right to public space. How different, then, from both the Nightingale tradition and from the much-touted ambivalences of those "private women" novelists who, as Mary Kelly has argued, would soon display themselves—presumably against their own belief in female modesty—on "the public stage."[37]

The spirited nature of the poetry just discussed—its impudence as well as its openness—clearly places it under the umbrella of the eighteenth century's poetry of wit, making it an extension of the kind of rational debate that Habermas identifies with the consensus-building public sphere of the late eighteenth century. Stylistically speaking, this poetry also has little in common with the soft romanticism—so heavy with propriety as well as with affect—that characterizes the poetry U.S. women began publishing in the mid-1820s, when the conventions of genteel sentimentality finally took root in U.S. soil. Reading the poetry garnered by Griswold, Read, and May, it is hard not to wonder sometimes where all the pleasure went—the fun as well as the fury and the logic. And it could be because the new ideology was so very heavy-handed that many middle-class women sought to perpetuate eighteenth-century personae even after literary sentimentality's emergence in or around 1825. A young Julia Ward Howe might, at the height of the

mid-1840s, entertain a poignant hope to *be* a woman as the dominant ideology of the Angel defined her:

> A vestal priestess, maid, or wife—
>   Vestal, and vowed to offer up
> The innocence of a holy life
>   To Him who gives the mingled cup;
> With man its bitter sweets to share,
>
> .   .   .   .
>
> His prayer to breathe, his tears to shed.

However, even as Howe wrote these lines, she knew better, as her conclusion
indicates: "Alas! I would that I were she" (*NAWP* 83). Between the mid-
1820s and 1850, not just Howe but many of the same writers whose genteel
poems can be found, like flowers, pressed between the pages of Griswold,
May, and Read, wrote other poems that questioned their new roles, keeping
their eighteenth-century precursors' feisty spirits alive. Of these latter poems,
none is more important or various than the Belle/Coquette poem, to which I
now turn.

When Howe evoked the vestal-priestess figure in "Woman," she was invoking
an ideological construct that was designed to reinforce in women those qualities constitutive of the domestic ideal: modesty, purity, and so forth. Once
introjected, this construct functioned, as Richard Brodhead has persuasively
argued, as an internalized set of behavioral norms or "disciplinary regime"
to which bourgeois women to *be* bourgeois women were obliged to conform.[38]
Not surprisingly, women of wit and fashion, like the speaker of "The Belle's
Philosophy," published in *Knickerbocker* in 1833, wanted nothing to do with
such regimes. Spoken in the voice of a Belle whom the *Knickerbocker* editor
ruefully identifes as, "the only one now extant," "The Belle's Philosophy"
defends the Belle's right to life, by attacking the very values of utility, dutiful-
ness, and fidelity that were, she believes, rendering her type extinct.
    Like Emily Dickinson, the erstwhile "belle," as well as "wayward nun," of
Amherst,[39] the *Knickerbocker* Belle rejects the doctrine of domestic usefulness
informing her period's advice book literature—a doctrine conflating proper
behavior in the parlor with duty to God—in favor of a pagan "philosophy"
of self-generated pleasure.[40] In three parallel stanzas, the Belle makes her case.
First, she argues, some beautiful things are meant to be enjoyed for themselves. Second, she claims that marrying her off will turn her into "common"
coin, fit only to bear her husband's name—or, as she sourly puts it, "the
stupid impress of a foolish king." In the third and last stanza, she raises her
most serious objection: marriage annuls her right to flirt, that is, her status
as a sexual free agent. Succinctly, flirting is what makes Belles Belles. Without it, as she chillingly points out, the sex game will come to an end

("drown[ing] / In the rights of one mortal, the hopes of all"), and then where will we be:

> There's another shrine where the votary sues
>> To the glorious life of that sculptured form;
> And where in the light that her smiles diffuse,
>> The iciest bosoms grow soft and warm.
> Shall the fatal spell of the parson drown
>> In the rights of one mortal, the hopes of all.
> Shall the queen of the belles lay the sceptre down,
>> And yield to a homely domestic thrall.
>>> Oh no, philosopher, no.
>> Utility must not mislead us so.
>>> We must always strive
>>> To preserve alive
> A little romance in this world below.
>> (*NAWP* 403)

At the risk of overreading, let me suggest that there is a good deal more at stake in this last stanza than mere flirtation. Like Shakespeare's Cleopatra—a charismatic figure for many nineteenth-century women writers, including Dickinson and Piatt—the Belle warms "the iciest bosoms," identifying her sexual power, that is, her "scepter," with the life principle itself. Without her, there would be neither hope nor life; rather, all would be frozen and dead—another way to understand her allusion to "the hopes of all." Playful the point may seem, but behind it lay a serious issue. As epitomized in Howe's absurd formulation—the vestal-priestess wife—domestic ideology's commitment to sexual purity, if taken literally, would have jeopardized the species. As in Shakespeare's *Antony and Cleopatra*, the vestally virginal Octavia may look like the "ideal" wife, on her knees praying the entire time her husband is away, but, as Antony admits, his "pleasure" lies elsewhere (2.3.41). Without the possibility of pleasure, there can be no desire for either husband or wife. That is, domestic ideology set up not only unattainable expectations for women, as Howe acknowledges, but self-defeating ones for the race. The purity it demanded was not just marital fidelity but a concept of passionlessness *in* marriage that, even on the face of it, made no sense, and that certainly would not be an inducement to sex, "passion blest" or otherwise, between husband and wife. If no sex, however, then, logically, no babies either.

"A Belle's Philosophy" is one of many poems by antebellum women that preserved well into the next century the sophisticated erotic awareness usually associated with eighteenth-century elite women. As signaled by the title, the Belle is a woman of wit ("Philosophy")—no simple, mindless flirt—and her arguments are those of reason. From the perspective enjoined by her philosophy, domestic ideology's emphasis on purity put the human race at risk, precisely because, *pace* Lord Acton, it took all pleasure from sex—in particular, the teasing forepleasure so necessary to stimulate desire in the first place. In a long poem, titled simply "Stanzas," published in the *Louisville Daily Journal* in 1857, the young Sarah Bryan (Piatt), who was at the time one of a number of young poets, male and female, carrying on their flirtations in the *Journal's* pages, says much the same thing in a more experientially oriented way:

> Wherefore said the world I loved him—
> *And could love no other one?*
> Wherefore heard I this believing?
> Ah, my former faith's undone:
>
> Love *but one?* The world is crowded—
> Many glorious rivals breathe—
> Love but one? Ah, love will wear out
> Striving round *one* form to wreathe.[41]

However youthful these verses, they indicate that in the late 1850s, the eighteenth-century erotic attitude of the *Knickerbocker* Belle was still extant in the urban centers of the Southern tier of the nation's "heartland," now introjected as part of an elite young woman's subjective consciousness of herself. Belle poems, and their darker double, Coquette poems, can, in fact, be found ubiquitously throughout the century, key sites where women put images of female sexual power on display. As we shall see in chapter 7, despite domestic ideology's cult of passionlessness, nineteenth-century women poets themselves never lost sight of the joys of sex nor of the agency free sexual choice offered them, placing their Belle poems among their first lines of defense against the potentially fatal power of domesticity itself.

The Belle of Broadway: Fanny Osgood's Public Life

Of all the antebellum woman poets who wrote Belle poems, Frances Sargent Osgood best illustrates how this persona could be used as a site for resistance to the domestic construction of women. Osgood is the period's most elusive and intriguing female literary figure, at least among poets, and I have no wish to pluck out the heart of her mystery here. Indeed, I don't think it can be done. Rather, I want to examine how recent scholarship on her salon poetry and on her newspaper and periodical publishing practices challenges us to qualify our views, not just on Osgood, but on nineteenth-century bourgeois women's relation to print culture generally. Specifically, I want to look at what freedoms women poets still possessed, even at the height of the "Sentimental Years," to express their distance from the idealized construction of themselves as household Angels upon which sentimental culture had in many ways been founded.

One does not need much exposure to the recent turns and twists in Osgood scholarship to know that this is a poet who cannot be safely contained either within the eighteenth-century line of wit or within the genteel-sentimental line that presumably supplanted it. Despite the enormous gulf existing between these two poetic modes, Osgood herself exploited both in equal measure, with, moreover, equal success. Strikingly like Dickinson, who often seems to echo Osgood's voice in her numerous naughty-child poems, Osgood is a Janus figure. Conservative in social attitudes but with a subversive writing style and an equally subversive view of herself as poet, Osgood is among the first U.S. women poets to build a full-blown persona out of ironizing sentimentality. At the same time, as with Dickinson, her protest against domesticity owes little or nothing to the politically progressive movements of her day, the women's rights movement included. Rather, this protest stems from her own, idiosyncratic, Belle-based aesthetic. That is, like Dickinson's, Osgood's radicality is a matter of personal taste, a desire for personal, not social, freedom. As such it aligns her with the Amherst poet among the century's most progressive women writers and at the same time among its most regressive.[42]

After Sigourney, Osgood has attracted more critical attention than any other antebellum woman poet, for the very good reason that she was a highly skilled writer, not just an immensely popular one. Her idealized portrait as youthful "poetess" adorns the title pages of May's and Read's anthologies. In a classic homosocial triangle, Griswold and Edgar Allan Poe acted out their personal and professional rivalry over the body of her work, vying to praise her while visiting contempt upon each other. When not blatantly satiric, her poetry, produced with great facility, is the epitome of the literary sentimental at its playful best: redolent with flowers, young love, childish enthusiasms, delicate wit, and whimsical fancy. Dying of consumption at forty, Osgood departed the world as she entered it: young, beautiful, and immemorially a flirt, but such an ingenuous flirt, it hardly seemed to matter. She was the ultimate Belle as the nineteenth-century male wanted her: an ideal fantasy object, but at the same time, so childlike, one had—or thought one had—nothing to fear from her. Put another way, she was or seemed to be the Belle who was also—wonder of wonders—the vestal priestess, the "True Woman," the Angel for whom men could nonetheless sensuously yearn.

"We look in vain, throughout her writings, for an offence against taste, or decorum—for a low thought—a platitude of expression. . . . A happy refinement—an exquisite instinct of the pure—the delicate—the graceful—gives a charm inexpressible to everything which flows from her pen," gushed Poe, falling all over himself with enthusiasm, in his 1845 review of Osgood's

Poems for the *Broadway Journal*.[43] Her "later poems are marked by a freedom of style, a tenderness of feeling, and a wisdom of apprehension, and are informed with a grace, so undefinable, but so pervading and attractive, that the consideration to which she is entitled is altogether different in kind, as well as in degree, from that which was awarded to the playful, piquant, and capricious improvisatrice of former years," oozed the somewhat more guarded Griswold (*FPA* 273). As another woman and another poet to boot, May was probably less easily won over by Osgood's flirtatious ways than her male admirers had been; but the anthologist quotes Dr. Davidson to make up for her own lack, and the good reverend has no similar reservations. Comparing Osgood to "that exquisite creation of Fonqué, Undine," Davidson exclaims, "There is nothing mechanical about her. . . . all is buoyant, overflowing, irrepressible vivacity, like the bubbling up of a natural fountain. . . . The great charm of her poetry is its unaffected simplicity. It is the transparent simplicity of truth, reflecting the feeling of the moment like a mirror."[44] For an antebellum woman poet, there could be no higher praise. The reviews of post-bellum women poets do not come close.

In her dissertation on the Poe circle, Eliza Richards has persuasively argued that the key to Osgood's success in her own period was her ability, indeed, genius, at performing femininity. As Richards succinctly puts it, Osgood was as "hard-nosed in her business dealings as she was flirtatious in her writing,"[45] but what she presented to the world was the performance. As was true of many writers in this period, Osgood was forced into this stylistic "double life," by her economic circumstances. Unlike Dickinson, who did not have to submit to the "Disgrace of Price" (P788), Osgood wrote for money. Her husband, the society painter Samuel Osgood, was a feckless provider, given to philandering and travel. Although Osgood came from a solid middle-class background, she had herself and three young daughters to support. She did so, as Richards demonstrates, in good part by projecting herself as the erotic dream of the nineteenth-century bourgeois everyman, marketing at literary soirees, as well as in her poems, a childlike persona: playful, fantastical, angelic, sentimental, knowing, innocently perverse, always promising, never giving. Only the recent work of Richards and of Joanne Dobson has put shadows into this picture, shadows suggesting that Osgood's persona, far from being transparent, as Davidson claims, was an entirely self-conscious strategy which she used to sell herself and her work, the two being, in this case, virtually identical and both equally manufactured.

The first major breakthrough in the reading of Osgood came in 1993 when Joanne Dobson announced the discovery of three "salon verses" which, she rightly believed, gave a deeper dimension to Osgood's poetry than the poet's well-honed child persona had allowed. Dobson describes her find as skillfully written "verses of sexual teasing and heterosocial satire" and speculates that they were probably produced "for salon gatherings of the 'New

York Literati' in the 1840s and definitely not for publication."[46] As Dobson clearly recognized, the poems' discovery was important on a number of grounds, well beyond the impact on our reading of Osgood herself. In particular, the three poems, "Won't you die & be a spirit," "The Wraith of the Rose," and "The Lady's Mistake" raised serious questions regarding Cott's model of the "passionless" Victorian woman.[47] The raciness of these poems represented, Dobson claimed, "the 'wild card' of nineteenth-century American poetry. . . . reveal[ing] an irrepressible female *joie de vivre*, a cosmopolitan grasp of the implications of heterosexual attraction, and a mastery of poetic form in which to embody its dilemmas and its absurdities. . . . In these poems," Dobson asserts, Osgood "wrote consciously and deliberately from what has previously been perceived as the repressed sexual unconscious of mid-nineteenth-century women: of sexual limitation, yes, but also of desire, enticement, and transgressive sexual autonomy."[48]

Dobson was right on every count but one. As she recently discovered, at least one "manuscript" poem was published. Under the title "The Maiden's Mistake," "The Lady's Mistake" appeared in the *Ladies' Companion* in November 1839. Racy it might be, but it was eminently publishable also.[49] What makes Osgood's salon verses unusually important, consequently, is not their raciness per se but their authorship and date. If domestic ideology and the Victorian propriety of the genteel aesthetic can ever be said to dominate women's poetry, it was between 1830 and 1850; and if any woman poet has come down in literary history as epitomizing the nineteenth-century "poetess," it is Osgood. What Dobson's discovery suggests, therefore, is that Osgood's sweetly sentimental persona may have been no less fraudulent than that of the salon male whom she mercilessly deconstructs in "The Lady's Mistake," a male whose "eyebrows were false," whose "hair / Was assumed," whose "moustache of a barber was bought," and whose "elegant calf by his tailor was sold" (*NAWP* 64). And if this poet of "unaffected simplicity" was not in fact "transparent," and could not be trusted, then who could one trust?

In her 1993 article, Dobson, who appears somewhat uncomfortable with her own discovery, asks us to accept the sincerity of the sentimental domestic values which Osgood espouses elsewhere. One can understand why. Especially when writing of her children, Osgood can be a deeply moving poet. But if one reads her poems on men and on heterosexual attraction with the "salon poems" in mind, Osgood's image as a sincerely sentimental poet, even if a highly flirtatious one, becomes difficult to sustain. On the whole, Osgood's style is more compatible with the nineteenth century's rhetoric of sensibility than with the eighteenth century's poetry of wit, and her appeal is more affective than rational. But these stylistic "facts" must, where Osgood is concerned, be weighed against other "facts" having to do with her publishing practices that deeply trouble the image to which Dobson would cling. Most notably, as Eliza Richards has demonstrated, Osgood used her access to the periodical press to carry on a highly public "affair" with Edgar Allan Poe in the pages of the 1845 *Broadway Journal*.[50] To some Poe biographers, albeit emphatically not to Richards herself, this affair has seemed so real that they have fantasized a child came of it. As Richards argues, in taking Osgood's flirtations so literally, the biographers have confused an embodied poetic practice for the bodies themselves. Nevertheless, Osgood, however teasingly, led them into this error.[51] In light, then, of the verifiability of Osgood's ideological and stylistic "double life," which of her styles—the chastely sentimental style of "A Reply" ("Ah! woman still / Must veil the shrine" [*AWP* 133]) or the bold, cynical, even whorish, style of "The Lady's Mistake" represents her "true" voice? Both? Neither?

In "The Lady's Mistake," Osgood, adopting the persona of a fortune-chasing coquette, takes aim at the artificiality of the New York City cosmopolitan male: false hair, false teeth, false calf, and false fortune and European title. The poem is very funny, but its hints as to what Osgood's social world was actually like draw a very different and far more brutal picture than her more sentimental verses suggest. Looking closely at Osgood's—sometimes truly vicious—poetry on heterosexual relationships and the sex game, another Osgood emerges, one far more suited to survive on Broadway than in the nursery. Like Piatt's high-visibility courting in the pages of her hometown newspaper, Osgood's "salon verse" destabilizes Cott's model of the "passionless" Victorian Woman. But it also does a great deal more. It opens up the possibility that Osgood, and by extension any number of other women poets, may also have been "posing"—to use Austin Dickinson's memorable term for his sister's praxis—with respect not just to their commitment to domesticity but also to their commitment to privacy.

Were these women committed to private domestic life? Or did they, in fact, view their domestic personae—the loving wife and mother, the sanctified bride, the mournful widow—as so many public "poses," masks thrown up by the ideological waves of change in precisely the same way eighteenth-century rationalism threw up, say, the figure of the Belle? Can we assume because they claimed these personae in their verse that they also subscribed to them as living reality? Or does their use of them simply point to the role fashion plays in the evolution of subjectivity? (I think here of the host of roles adolescents go through on their way to maturation.) What happens then to the sincerity, the transparent truth, without which sentimentality was, as Douglas claimed it was, bad faith, at best? And what happens to "home" as the place where subjectivity is formed? And, indeed, what happens to the bourgeois female sentimental subject herself if her "being" rests on such slippery performative grounds?

As far as is known, there is only one private U.S. woman poet of any importance in the nineteenth century, Emily Dickinson, and even her poetry's privacy was deeply compromised by her decision to bring it to the attention of two of the most public literary figures of her day, Thomas Wentworth Higginson and Helen Hunt Jackson. For the rest, these women's private lives cannot be separated from the publicity they gave their writings. Theirs was a poetry of interiority but an interiority shaped and informed by public concerns and placed on public display even when the authors themselves were physically barred from many public spaces.[52] Far from being silenced by domestic ideology, they used their access to print culture to critique it publicly. They were not simply the victims of its "intimate discipline." Their safety, one could say, lay in their numbers and in their very contradictions, contradictions which left spaces open for change.

In the next chapter, I will turn to these women writers' exploitation of antebellum sentimentality's other, and far more obviously, "public" form, "high sentimentality," as a specifically public, and profoundly political, discourse. If antebellum women turned the interiority of literary sentimentality into a platform publicizing the dilemmas of their own feminine subjectivity, including their discontent with Charlotte's lot, they used the lyric of high sentimentality to turn the world, in Angelina Grimké's words, upside down.

❊ 2 ❊

High Sentimentality and the Politics of Reform

> Prof. I. D. Peck . . . said . . . he thanked Heaven, these sad
> ebullitions of mistaken fancy (Woman's Rights,) have cre-
> ated scarcely a ripple upon the calm wave of the divinely
> created instincts of the women, (mark instincts not intel-
> ligence,) of our day. . . . If the subject be so contemptible
> and ridiculous. . . . [w]ould the *Knickerbocker, Harper,*
> *Putnam* . . . bend them from their high estate to satirize,
> caricature and repel an "ebullition of fancy" . . . ? We
> think not.
> —FRANCES D. GAGE, Letter to the *Una*, 1854[1]

> The emergence of subjectivity as a fundamental category
> of feminist discourse must be understood in relation to the
> development of the women's movement as a whole.
> —RITA FELSKI, *Beyond Feminist Aesthetics*[2]

When, in July 1848, the women of Seneca Falls issued "The Declaration of Sentiments," U.S. women, both white and of color, had been actively protesting their oppression in letters, poems, vindications, plays, novels, public lectures, and impromptu speeches for over one hundred years. What the Seneca Falls convention did was stamp paid on these efforts. The convention organizers, their mandate clear, borrowed the rhetoric as well as the format of the Declaration of Independence and put women's complaints in a form that men were able to recognize as a serious political threat, possibly for the first time. Not surprisingly, their action hit local and regional newspapers from one end of the country to the other. If, like the *Cherokee Advocate*, in Tahlequah, Oklahoma, a newspaper missed out on the July convention, it did not ignore the follow-up meeting that August in Rochester, New York.[3] After a hundred years or more, the complaints of women had finally become news.

Focus on official nineteenth-century woman's rights organizations and their quest for suffrage has largely obscured nineteenth-century feminism's fundamentally grass-roots character. Woman's rights rallies, such as that at Seneca Falls, were a key part of the picture, but women had been advocating their views in public from the late eighteenth century on. By the mid-1830s, women like the socialist/free thought advocate Frances Wright, the Northern black orator Maria Stewart, and the South Carolinian Grimké sisters had all actively challenged the taboos limiting women's public speech. Transmitted by newspapers as well as by word of mouth, the reports of their activities brought increasing numbers of women into the fold. "The whole land seems roused to discussion of the *province of woman*," Angelina Grimké wrote excitedly to her friend Jane Smith in 1837, "& I am glad of it. We are willing to bear the brunt of the storm, if we can only be the means of making a breach in the wall of public opinion. . . . What dost thou think of some of *them* [women attending a talk given by Sarah Grimké on woman's rights] walking 2, 4, 6, & 8 miles to attend our meetings?"[4] In 1845, a similarly optimistic Margaret Fuller confidently predicted that now that women had the free agency of the pen, agency of the rostrum would soon follow.[5]

At the same time, as one would expect of subjects multipositioned along differing social axes—class, race, religion, region, etcetera—early-nineteenth-century women were deeply at odds with each other over what they wanted and how they should go about getting it. By 1850, women had made enormous gains: the first women's institutions of higher learning, the first women's medical schools, and the first woman-owned and edited newspapers and periodicals were all up and running. Even more important, married women's property rights legislation had started making crucial breaches in the principle of coverture, inroads that would eventually bring down the legal barriers to women's professional advancement. But as the list of achievements grew, so too did the tensions between different groups of women. Angelina Grimké wanted to believe that the woman's rights movement that she and her sister, Sarah, had helped spark would turn the world upside down. In some ways it did. However, the conflicts on which the nineteenth-century woman's rights movement eventually foundered, in particular, those of race and class, were present from the beginning, even as they persist to this day.

This chapter explores how one of the most basic conflicts dividing nineteenth-century feminists from each other, that between "equality feminists" and "difference feminists," informs women's political poetry in the antebellum period and the role that sentimentality played within it.[6] For nineteenth-century equality feminists—Julia Ward Howe, for example—the effect of feminism was to demystify domestic ideology. Thinking back over her long life, Howe claimed that the woman's rights movement gave her a new understanding of women as "free agent[s], fully sharing with man every human right."[7] Difference feminists, on the other hand, took a much less straightforward path to female empowerment, attempting to theorize a gender-specific form of female political power from within domestic ideology itself. Keenly aware that virtually all forms of social engagement other than the domestic itself were off-limits to women as domestic ideology defined their sphere, difference feminists rationalized their transgressions by claiming them as women's duties rather than, as the woman's rights movement did, a matter of their rights.

It is the profound difference between these two basic forms of feminism that accounts for the equally profound difference in the two kinds of political poetry this chapter explores, one an explicitly feminist poetry of equal rights, the other the far more complex and internally contradictory poetry of high-sentimental sympathy politics. Genealogically speaking, both kinds of poetry had their roots in the eighteenth century, but they sprang from vastly different strains of social and political thought as well as of rhetorical practice. Equality feminist poetry drew on the line of wit already touched on in the introduction and chapter 1. Invoking liberal political arguments derived from the thinking of men like the British philosopher John Locke (1632–1704) and the Anglo-American political theorist Thomas Paine (1737–1809), equality feminists used their verse to argue rationally, if often satirically, for women's natural rights, that is, for their political status as civic and juridical equals of men. Their poetry functioned in the Habermasian public sphere in precisely the way that Habermas describes, and the limitations of their political thinking—an elite class bias, in particular—were those of the late-eighteenth-century public sphere itself. In terms of subjectivity as well as in terms of rights, equality feminists presented themselves as the equals of men, with similar needs for freedom and intellectual stimulation. Theoretically, at any rate, their thinking was gender and race blind.

Rhetorically compatible with literary sentimentality, but a world apart in emphasis, high-sentimental poetry derived its social politics from the Scottish enlightenment philosophers, theorists like Adam Smith who specifically routed morality through feeling, rather than through reason. Far more conservative than equal-rights feminists on most issues, difference feminists were attracted to Scottish Enlightenment thinkers because the latter's approach to morality allowed women to legitimize their public interventions without violating their sense of what, as women, it was appropriate for them to do. Difference feminists argued that women's power to feel and their socially sanctioned role as nurturers not only fitted them to intervene in certain public matters, for example, Indian removal and slavery, but mandated that they do so. It should not "be deemed unnatural that the cause of the helpless should excite commiseration in a sex whom nature has taught both the *need* and the *value* of protection," Sigourney declared in an 1830 memorial for the Cherokee. "Yet when the subject that prompts, and the motives that actuate us, are candidly balanced, we trust to be acquitted of having unwarrantably transgressed the bounds of that subordinate sphere, where our duties and felicities centre." Given that women themselves by *nature* stood in need of protection, their "commiseration" with "the helpless" and unprotected Cherokee could hardly be faulted as "unnatural," nor were the petitions they sent to Washington on the Indians' behalf an unwarranted transgression, therefore, of their sphere. Sigourney, you could say, was trying to have her cake and eat it too.[8]

As the product of conservative bourgeois women's anxious response to the various social upheavals occurring around them, equality feminism not least, the difference feminism that women like Sigourney espoused to justify their reform activity never served as a platform for a free-standing political movement. Rather, like Sigourney in her memorial, most individual high-sentimental difference feminists invented their politics as they went along, shaping their rationales to fit their behavior and their immediate needs. In ways equality feminism could not, nineteenth-century difference feminism was able, therefore, to register the struggles of individual women as they tried to come to grips with their changing social roles in the new republic. Precisely because these struggles were individual, high-sentimental poetry, strikingly unlike the equality feminists' poetry of wit, became in itself a site for multiplicity and change, as individual women tried to adjust their desires to the ideologically defined limits of their sphere. Before turning to this poetry, however, I will first sketch out equality feminist poetry, to clarify how very different these two kinds of feminisms were, not only in their stances and goals but also in the poetry they produced.

Equality Feminism and the Poetry of Wit

No better example of how nineteenth-century women used their poetry as a vehicle for public suasion could be asked than their participation in the debate over women's rights itself, a debate that ultimately did lead to profound social change. In "The Rights of Man and Woman in Post-Revolutionary America," feminist historian Rosemarie Zagarri has provided a stunning amount of evidence for just how influential women's literary participation in this debate, occurring during the early republican period (1790–1825), was. Taking advantage of the centrifugal nature of rights talk, its tendency, as Zagarri puts it, to "spin out of control,"[9] the women who took part in this debate were trying in various ways to reposition themselves within a republican form of government which, having proclaimed all men equal, made no provision for women whatsoever. So blatant was this slight to the fair sex that men themselves were casting about to find ways to remedy it. Those concerned to solve the problem without at the same time disrupting male rule believed they found their answer in the concept of "passive rights" advanced by the Scottish common-sense philosophers. While male rights were defined as Lockean freedoms and were political in nature, women's rights, they argued, should be defined passively in terms of the responsibilities or duties of their "sphere." From this split between two competing definitions of rights, the split between equality feminism and difference feminism would develop, as well as the many, often disturbing, contradictions to which high-sentimental difference feminists would fall heir.

The turning point for the discussion of women's rights in the United States came with the 1792 publication of Mary Wollstonecraft's feminist manifesto, *A Vindication of the Rights of Woman*, a text that put the issue of women's rights on the table in ways, Zagarri argues, that neither men nor women could ignore. That U.S. poets would respond vigorously to Wollstonecraft's articulation of the issue was a given. "Let Woman have a share, / Nor yield to slavish fear. / Her equal rights declare. . . . See Wollstonecraft, a friend, / Your injur'd rights defend, / Wisdom her steps attend, / The cause maintain," boldly declared "A Young Lady of This City" in a poem printed in 1795 New York in the *Weekly Museum* and reprinted in the *Philadelphia Minerva*. Publishing in the *Ladies' Monitor* in 1818, Thomas Fessenden took the opposite position: "Dame Nature tells us Mary's rights are wrong. / Her female freedom is a syren-song," he opined, cannily alluding to the sexual scandal that had tarnished Wollstonecraft's name in the late 1790s, making her a difficult model for many middle-class women to follow.

Zagarri's evidence suggests that both men and women worried about the possibility of role reversal should women get their rights as Locke and Paine defined them, that is, politically. After women voted in a New Jersey congressional election in 1797, "versifiers," Zagarri writes, "direly predicted: 'To Congress, lo! widows shall go, / like metamorphosed witches! / Cloath'd in the dignity of state, / and eke! in coat and breeches!'" Similarly, in 1802, a "Miss M. Warner" published a poem in the *Boston Weekly Magazine* admonishing women: "But know ye not that Woman's proper sphere / Is the domestic walk? To interfere / With politics, divinity, or law, / A much deserv'd ridicule would draw / On Woman." But if some women demurred at stepping outside their sphere, some men supported their doing so. "Let us not force them back with brow severe, / Within the pale of ignorance and fear, / Confin'd entirely by domestic arts: / Producing only children, pies and tarts," one author chided his brothers, in a poem published in 1801 in the *Weekly Museum*.[10]

Given that some men did support political rights for women, one cannot be sure whether a man or a woman authored the most literarily ingenious of these early poetic defenses of women's rights, "Epitaph on a Bird," which appeared in the *Lady's Magazine and Musical Repository* in 1801. Drawing, as did Wollstonecraft herself, on the venerable association of women with caged birds, "Epitaph"'s author combines the eighteenth-century convention of the mock epitaph with the universalistic rhetoric of the Declaration of Independence to produce a moving—and at the same time marvelously satirical—plea for birds' (women's) "natural rights":[11]

> closely confined in a grated prison,
> and scarcely permitted to view those fields,
> to the possession of which he had an undoubted charter.
> Deeply sensible of this infringement of
> his natural and unalienable rights,
> he was often heard to petition for redress,
> not with rude and violent clamours,
> but in the most plaintive notes of harmonious sorrow!
>
> (*NAWP* 387)

Certainly, for women readers of this magazine, which also published a "Plan for the Emancipation of the Fair Sex" and extracts from Wollstonecraft's travel writings, it was a short hop from a bird's "natural rights" to their own; and the pathos of its plight undoubtedly touched more than one female heart.

While Zagarri's discussion of the women's rights debate ends in 1825, the debate itself did not; but beginning in the mid-1820s, a poetic divide opens between the two sides, as difference feminists shifted to the new, affect-laden rhetoric coming into fashion, while equality feminists continued to employ the eighteenth-century line of wit. The reason for equality feminists' rhetorical conservatism was probably the obvious one: if women were to get out from under male guardianship, they first had to prove that they were rational creatures capable of self-government. The "Young Lady of This City" put the case eloquently in 1795: "Why should a tyrant bind / A cultivated mind, / By reason well refin'd / Ordained Free."[12] For such an argument, appeals to feeling simply would not work.

This stress on reason had, however, another advantage as well. Namely, it allowed women to point out just how irrational men's response to their demands was. Could it be that men were afraid of women? In 1829, "Ada" penned a very witty defense of Frances Wright in a poem that, first published in New York City, eventually circulated in newspapers as far west as Kentucky. Wright was not only the first woman in the United States known to speak on political matters before mixed audiences but an early advocate of socialism, abolition, and free thought; and the press, as was its wont with transgressive women, pummeled her for it. Interpreting Wright's transgressiveness as a demonstration of women's intellectual power, the feisty "Ada" turns the tables. Titling her poem "The Panic," she wittily hits Wright's male maligners just where it will hurt most—in, precisely, their fear of smart women:

What a panic has seized all the men!
    How scared that we women should know—
Something more about handling a pen,
    Than our grandams some ages ago!

. . . .

The dear fellows have taken affright;
    And forsooth, not without a good cause;
For the Lectures of Miss Frances Wright,
    Are received with unbounded applause.

She tells us we women possess
    An intellect equal with them;
But this the poor souls wont confess
    And that part of her doctrine condemn.[13]

If women were intellectually equal to men, then how justify confining them permanently to the narrow rounds of "housewifery"? And if they were not and never could be equal, what were men so "scared" of? Why, that is, did men find the idea of educated women so threatening? Why, indeed.

One of a core group of elite women who made the shift from abolition to woman's rights in the antebellum period,[14] Maria Weston Chapman was equally witty at men's expense. Confronted with the opprobrium heaped upon herself and other women activists, Chapman lets "the Other Sex" have it in "The Times That Try Men's Souls," a poem read at the Seneca Falls convention and reprinted both in *Littell's Living Age* and in Frederick Douglass's *North Star*: "Confusion has seized us, and all things go wrong, / The women have leaped from "their spheres," / . . . / They've taken a notion to speak for themselves, / And are wielding the tongue and the pen; / They've mounted the rostrum, the termagant elves, / And, oh horrid, are talking to *men*" (*NAWP* 416, 417). The poem keeps this up for ten devastating stanzas, with Congregational ministers among its chief targets—Chapman's payback, possibly, for the ministers' heavy-handed attempt to gag the Grimké sisters in 1837.[15]

What makes these poems notable, along with their stress on women's intellectual capacity, is their humor and aggressiveness, qualities going hand in hand with their wit. Informed by a strong sense of entitlement, these are, one could say, "power poems." "Humor's inherent posture of superiority," Nancy Walker comments in *A Very Serious Thing*, "even aggression—is in conflict with traditional notions of female submissiveness and passivity."[16] It is this "inherent posture of superiority"—so at odds with "female submissiveness and passivity"—that these poets use their wit to project, affecting a nonchalant indifference to the anger they knowingly arouse. The Congregationalist ministers may have wanted to keep women in their place—"'vine[s] whose strength and beauty is to lean upon the trellis work'"[17]—but women like Chapman were having none of it. However oppressed equality feminists may have felt themselves to be as women, they asked for no sympathy. Indeed, they could not, since to ask would merely confirm their need for male support—a need, as Sarah Grimké said of the ministers' vine image, "inconsistent with the dignity of a Christian body,"[18] and, therefore, one these women could least afford to project.

This last cannot be stressed enough. Equality feminists used humor not just to put men down but also to distinguish themselves from other women, especially those women who accepted what tradition and the law said of them, willingly ceding free agency (or what the Grimkés referred to as "the dignity of a Christian body") for security—so many birds in a cage. In a culture dominated by essentialist views of gender, from whose assumptions even the most militant equality feminists were not entirely immune, this meant running against a very high tide. The private letters and memoirs of women in the movement, from leadership figures like the Grimké sisters, Chapman, and Howe to those who participated only from the margins, make clear that nineteenth-century feminist thinking on gender questions was constantly in flux and often profoundly contradictory. Yet to be effective in their mission, these women had to keep their doubts and insecurities out of their public self-representations. Insofar as humor allowed them to model for themselves and others new forms of female subjectivity, it was one way they could solve their dilemma. As humorists, they could present themselves as what they hoped to become: women who did not need men to support them, women without lack. They could imagine such women, I would suggest, precisely because the Lockean concept of human rights, which ineluctably brought the possibility of free agency with it, was, at least in theory, gender blind. In theory, women no less than men had the ability, right, and duty to stand alone. Using humor, they did.

Rooted though nineteenth-century equality feminist poems were in the conventions of eighteenth-century newspaper poetry, they were also, therefore, very much of their times. As such, they contributed to an ongoing public conversation, flowing back and forth between men and women and among women with themselves, a conversation to which they contribute to this day by their inclusion here. Significantly, as "Ada"'s poem on Fanny Wright in the *Kentucky Reporter* indicates, even as early as 1829, if not earlier, poems were carrying the news of the struggle for women's rights wherever newspapers and periodicals were published.[19] If we are to believe a report printed in the *Irish Nationalist*, a virulently anti–woman's rights newspaper published in San Francisco, by 1873 Grimké's "wall of public opinion" was breached. Reviewing "the changes which [had] taken place in modern times in the legal status of married women" as a result of married

women's property rights legislation, a judge on the supreme court of the
State of Illinois informed a woman accused of libel that she was now fair
game. Man's "legal supremacy is gone," he mournfully intoned, "and the
sceptre has departed from him."

> She, on the contrary, can have her separate estate; can contract with refer-
> ence to it; . . . can sue in her own name for injury of her person and
> slander of her character, and can enjoy the fruits of her time and la-
> bor. . . . The chains of the past have been broken by the progression of the
> present, and she may now enter upon the stern conflicts of life untram-
> meled. She . . . [can aspire] to battle with [man] in the contests of the
> forum, to outvie him in the healing art, to climb with him the steps of
> fame, and to share with him in every occupation. Her brain, and hands,
> and her tongue are her own, and she should be responsible for slanders
> uttered by herself.

"Our opinion," the judge concluded, "is, that the necessary operation of the
statutes is to discharge the husband from his liabilities for the torts of his
wife which he neither aided, advised, nor countenanced."[20] In short, if
women were legally free to sign contracts, to compete with men in the professions, and to "share with him in every occupation," women were also free
to be sued. To this judge, if not to suffragists, the battle that mattered had
been fought and women had won. Where coverture once protected the married woman, she now stood before the bar of justice, as she would, presumably, one day stand before her God, a full, or almost full, civic person in her
own right, accountable for her own words and deeds.[21] One could say both
the vine and the wall had come down together. Although women still had
(still have?) a long way to go to achieve full civic parity with men, the principle of parity was established. In this sense, the nineteenth-century women's
rights movement, so often called a failure, was in fact an impressive success.

Women's grass-roots feminist agitation in the antebellum period, of which
their poetry was a vital part, presents, therefore, a serious challenge to those
literary theorists who have treated nineteenth-century domestic ideology as
uniformly and seamlessly hegemonic. Scholars relying on prescriptive literature have drawn, and redrawn, nineteenth-century women as the interpel-
lated subjects of a classed and gendered ideology. Most recently, this
Althusserian-Foucauldian approach has taken the form of Brodhead's arguments for domestic ideology as a disciplinary regime, wherein the subject
learns to receive and express love by submitting herself to and internalizing
domestic norms. Central to such arguments is a view of the social subject as
discursively produced and without agency.[22] But the women whose poetry I
have just discussed were not only, like the *Knickerbocker* Belle, resisting the
loss of agency or, like Fanny Osgood, slyly asserting it through public play;
by acting collectively, they got it. However grudging the judge's concession, it

shows that by the 1870s women in courtrooms across the nation had become legally accountable for their words. They may not have had the vote; but they could be sued, and this latter "right" may, finally, have been the more important. Married or not, and over 90 percent of these women were, women had become persons before the law. They could sign contracts; they could keep their wages. Sooner or later, they would vote.

High-Sentimental Politics and Poetics

Why, then have so many literary scholars—many of them, like Brodhead, highly skilled and knowledgeable readers—presented nineteenth-century women as the passive victims of Foucauldian disciplinary regimes? Part of the problem, I think, lies in the failure of historians to value "ordinary" women's newspaper contributions at their full worth. Using traditional models for the writing of history, scholars of the nineteenth-century woman's rights movement have focused on the trials and tribulations of its leadership and on divisions between competing rights organizations, creating the impression, among other things, that the movement stood apart from ordinary women's lives.[23] But there is also a significant body of literature that supports and justifies a Foucauldian approach and it is to this body of work that I now want to turn.

Like equality feminists, difference feminists used newspapers and magazines to promote their ideas, but they justified their exercise of this very public agency in a very different way, namely, by grounding it in women's role in the private sphere. Like the Push-me-Pull-you beast in the *Dr. Dolittle* books, difference feminists faced in two opposite directions at once. On the one hand, they embraced the domestic as the essential site for the production and staging of female values, both their difference and their power. On the other, they argued that this difference was what legitimated their own interventions into public affairs. "A lady hardly thinks her life complete, unless she is directly aiding in some work of reform or charity," Ednah Cheney commented in *Women of Boston*.[24] Committed to a much more conservative set of values than those to which equality feminists appealed, these women defended their public interventions by paradoxically disclaiming women's right to publicity itself. What they saw themselves bringing to the public arena was precisely those virtues that they most closely associated with their confinement within the home, but confinement to the home was, they believed, the only right and appropriate place for women—a paradoxical position that many prominent conservative women entertain to this day.

Read in these terms, the current scholarly debate over domestic feminism and high-sentimental sympathy politics–often referred to as the Douglas-Tompkins debate—appears to derive almost entirely from deeply embedded contradictions within difference feminism itself.[25] Prescriptively, difference feminists advocated a disciplinary domestic regime of precisely the sort that Brodhead identifies, one that, as I noted earlier when discussing Rosemarie Zagarri's work, followed the Scottish common-sense philosophers in identifying women's "rights" passively with their "duties." As one female authority, Hannah Mather Crocker, put it in *The Real Rights of Women* (1818): "to shine in the domestic circle," "to keep calm and serene under every circumstance in life," "to soothe and alleviate the anxious cares of man," and "to partake with [their husbands of] the cares, as well as pleasures, of life"— these were women's "Appropriate Duties" (i.e., "Real Rights") *as* "Scripture, Reason and Common Sense" defined them, or, at any rate, so the subtitle of Crocker's book declared. For this descendent of Cotton Mather, having the freedom to manage a well-run home was both the female equivalent to voting and a duty owed to God.[26]

At the same time, when difference feminists—whether conservatives like Catherine Beecher and Sarah J. Hale or activists like Sigourney and Stowe— sought to justify their public interventions, they did so in the name of this same gender ideology, calling it their duty. Thus, for example, in "Petitioning Congress," published in the *National Enquirer* and in the *Liberator* in 1837, the feminist abolitionist poet, Eliza Earle first acknowledges that women's proper station is "To pluck life's thorn and strew its path with flowers," but then goes on to defend women's right to petition anyway. Defining herself specifically as a "female christian," Earle's speaker claims that she is duty-bound to invoke this right in the face of the great social evil that slavery represented. Earle is also anxious, however, that her gesture not be misread. Taking a sharp swipe at Wollstonecraft, she makes an absolute distinction between her rationale for activism and the rationale invoked by equality feminists: "Ours be the 'Duty,' not the 'Rights of woman,' / Knowing the strength of nature's dearest ties, / May we yet 'prove that ours are feelings human,' / Holy affections, kindly sympathies" (*NAWP* 408). For Earle, as she puts it in another poem, "this *is* woman's work, / Her own appropriate sphere; and nought should drive / Her from the Mercy seat, till Mercy's work / Be finished" (*NAWP* 406).[27] In doing "Mercy's work," women did God's, and doing God's work, they did woman's. It was a self-denying and self-aggrandizing position at once and, logically speaking, untenable; but this did not prevent it from proving, as Jane Tompkins argues, an enormously potent social force.

A good deal of evidence suggests that difference feminists were pushed into this illogic by their need to respond to equality feminism's critique of traditional gender ideology, a critique, as Zagarri points out, to which Mary Wollstonecraft had given new life. On the one hand, difference feminists justifiably distrusted the Lockean tendency to put individual rights over the needs of others, a tendency that, unhappily, helps account for the woman's rights movement's failure to address the concerns of black women.[28] On the other hand, most difference feminists also recognized that the combined effect of coverture and domestic ideology, taken to extremes, was to leave women utterly vulnerable to the tyrannical whims of men. An epistolary exchange between two "Boston teenagers" makes the basics of the difference feminist's dilemma clear, as well as the confused, contradictory thinking to which it gave rise.

"I think you are a *ninny* to call yourself a slave," wrote fifteen-year-old Caroline Healey [Dall] to her best friend, thirteen-year-old Ednah Dow Littlehale [Cheney], in 1837. Ednah had written Dall renouncing marriage "until [women] are allowed [their] full political rights, the rights of free women." Dall, a future journalist, wanted nothing to do with such unwomanly freedoms. Nevertheless, when Dall decided to expand her thoughts in an essay published in the *Casket* the following year, she backtracks considerably, producing a blatantly unstable compromise that yields more to Cheney's side, as Dall herself admits, than she would like. "I do not deny that woman may have the right to vote; the right of legislation, for I am very tenacious of my sex's privileges, and am not prepared to argue, *as I could wish* [italics mine], to the contrary:—but what *lady* would claim the right?"[29] Well bolstered by God, Felicia Hemans, and the prescriptive authorities of the day, Dall never abandoned her stand on "difference." According to Margaret McFadden, who recovered this exceptionally interesting correspondence, Dall did, however, eventually broaden her concept of ladyship enough to include the vote.[30]

In various ways and over a variety of issues, Dall's inability to escape the net of her own contradictions is repeated throughout difference feminist texts. As in Dall's essay, the presence of these contradictions reflects the attempts of a wide range of women to adapt difference feminism's ideologically generated conundrums to their own values, desires, and needs. Significantly, even race was no barrier to confusion. No less than difference feminism's best-known figures, such as Hale and the Beecher sisters, high-sentimental poets like Sigourney and Earle, who were white, and Sarah Louisa Forten, Charlotte Forten Grimké, and Sarah Mapps Douglass, who were black, all sought to negotiate the space between the Scylla of undiluted oppression and, as they saw it, the Charybdis of Lockean individualism. These writers were not about to abandon a position that made helping the afflicted an appropriate, indeed, mandatory, spheric responsibility for WOMEN. "The cause of bleeding humanity is always, legitimately, the cause of WOMAN. Without her powerful assistance, its progress must be slow, difficult, imperfect," Garrison had written in the *Liberator*.[31] But what exactly did this mandate allow women to do? What were the true "bounds of [their] subordinate sphere"?

Precisely because high-sentimental difference feminists were pushing domestic power well beyond where it was supposed to go, they ended up deploying their gender ideology in some remarkably individualized ways, both sustaining and dismantling the notion of womanhood that gave and denied them power at once. If ideology seems to swallow some up—Earle and Forten Grimké, for example—others, like Forten, Douglass, and Sigourney, were able, at least at times, to distance themselves from it. Playing in powerful and interesting ways on the ironies to which difference feminism gave rise, these latter writers exhibit a keen sense of high sentimentality's own very problematic limits. I will begin, however, with the orthodox position.

No high-sentimental poem sheds more light on the conundrums of difference feminism's sympathy politics than does the oft anthologized "Lines suggested on reading 'An Appeal to [sic] Christian Women of the South' by A. E. Grimké." Long attributed to the African American poet Sarah Louisa Forten, who published a handful of abolitionist lyrics in the *Liberator* between 1831 and 1835 under the name "Ada," this poem was actually the work of Eliza Earle, a twenty-nine-year-old Quaker from Leicester, Massachusetts.[32] As Todd Gernes, who first discovered the mix-up, argues, the misattribution was possible because Forten and Earle, as feminist abolitionists, belonged to the same discursive, ideological, and political community. For all their different backgrounds—one a young black Episcopalian from Philadelphia, the other a mature white Quaker from Massachusetts—they shared the same venues, readerships, and, unfortunately, pen names. Even more important, they wrote for the same reason: to inspire readers with their own fierce desire to bring slavery to an end. As with abolitionist poetry generally, that is, whether authored by blacks or whites, their poems were not intended as revelations of unique inner lives. Rather, they were part of the collective voice of all those laboring, as Earle puts it, "in the moral field," and what these poets produced, therefore, is, despite stylistic differences, close to interchangeable as a result.

Precisely because this is true, however, Earle's poem to Grimké takes on special interest, for it deals specifically with the complexities of individual choice. Positioned as, effectively, a born-again feminist abolitionist, Earle's speaker wrestles with the legitimacy of her call, a call that her basically conservative gender ideology prima facie should prevent her from responding to. Whatever else "Lines, suggested on reading . . . A. E. Grimké" is about, it is about the contradiction that antislavery difference feminists confronted in choosing to become politically transgressive; and in the description the poem gives of its speaker's anguished decision-making process, Earle's own struggle to find a way between conflicting cultural and religious imperatives can be heard. Determined to do her part, the speaker achieves a détente cordiale between the twin poles of her subjectivity as bourgeois Christian woman and as feminist abolitionist—one pole formed by the edict to be still, the other by the injunction to do good. If she cannot speak aloud in public, her pen, the speaker declares, will speak for her in "Mercy's sacred cause."

As Earle explains it, reading Angelina Grimké's "An Appeal to the Christian Women of the South" had an effect on her not unlike God's revelation to Paul on the road to Tarsus. By redefining the scope of the traditional woman's sphere to include certain active forms of public opposition, Grimké had found a way to make domestic ideology compatible with a limited or situational form of female agency. At least in this cause, Earle's speaker concludes, it is not only permissible to be a "female politician" but obligatory, if she is to fulfill the conflicting behavioral and moral norms in which she deeply believes:

> My spirit leaps in joyousness tow'rd thine,
> My gifted sister, as with gladdened heart
> My vision flies along thy "speaking pages."
> Well hast thou toiled in Mercy's sacred cause;
> And thus another strong and lasting thread
> Is added to the woof our sex is weaving,
> With skill and industry, for Freedom's garb.
> Precious the privilege to labor here,—
> Worthy the lofty mind and handy-work
> Of Chapman, Chandler, Child, and Grimké too.
> There's much in woman's influence, ay much,
> To swell the rolling tide of sympathy,
> And aid those champions of a fettered race,
> Now laboring arduous in the moral field.
> We may not 'cry aloud,' as they are bid,
> And lift our voices in the *public* ear;
> Nor yet be mute. The pen is ours to wield,
> The heart to will, and hands to execute.
>   (*NAWP* 405–6)

As Earle presents it, Angelina Grimké's enormous accomplishment had been to show bourgeois women how to reconcile duty and desire, bondage and freedom, silence and speech. In this sense, Earle's poem is powerfully liberating, even visionary, in precisely the way that Jane Tompkins describes when speaking of "sentimental power" in *Uncle Tom's Cabin*. Indeed, the poem's proudly self-reflexive identification with a specifically female literary tradition—"Chapman, Chandler, Child, and Grimké too"—goes well beyond anything one finds in equality feminist poetry itself, if only because the latter had a vested interest in not encouraging any form of gender segregation, even literary.[33]

In legitimating women's political activity as a function of their spheric duty rather than as a matter of their political/human rights, Grimké had abandoned, however, essential aspects of her own position. Evidence suggests that unlike most of the feminist abolitionist leadership—Elizabeth Chandler and Lydia Maria Child, for example—both Grimké sisters were equality feminists, for whom the issues of agency extended well beyond their participation in the abolitionist movement.[34] However, Angelina Grimké was also deeply committed to bringing women into abolitionist ranks, this despite the fact that most of the women who answered her call were not only personally racist but unalterably opposed to women's rights as equality feminists defined them. Following the urging of her future husband, Theodore Weld, who feared she was undermining her credibility with talk of women's rights, Angelina ceded ground, turning to difference feminism's arguments instead.[35] As a political move, the concession worked, at least for a while; but, as Earle's poem suggests, it locked feminist abolitionism into a politics whose legitimacy rested on the singularly unstable base of bourgeois women's interpretation of their moral duty. Political free agency—a principle to which the Grimkés themselves were deeply devoted—played, as the Earle poem makes painfully clear, no part in the argument. What thrills Earle's speaker is not finding out that she has rights but discovering that she can be a "female politician" without them. As with so much female-authored social reform literature of the period—from tracts on temperance to memorials on Indians—the concept of female agency that this poem advances requires a victim if it is to exist at all.

Read thus, "Lines, suggested" is anything but liberatory. Rather, like so many difference feminist texts, including, most notoriously, *Uncle Tom's Cabin*, the poem stunningly supports Karen Sánchez-Eppler's argument that "domestic and sentimental antislavery writings [were] implicated in the very oppressions they [sought] to reform."[36] For the putative white speaker of the Grimké poem, her "right" to speak was structurally dependent on, and could only emanate from, the slave's silence. As Sánchez-Eppler argues, laying the blame squarely, if, in my opinion, quite unfairly, on Angelina Grimké, "[t]he bound and silent figure of the slave . . . grants the white woman access to political discourse denied the slave."[37] For difference feminists to engage in this discourse required that someone somewhere suffer—a lot. But was the claim to access that Earle asserts in this poem more than local, as Sánchez-Eppler also suggests? That is, did feminist abolitionist women, Angelina Grimké included, actually come to ground a doctrine of women's rights generally on the foundation that abolitionism provided? Or even worse, consciously or unconsciously, use abolitionism as a cover for furthering their own (feminist) cause, as Sánchez-Eppler also seems to imply?

The evidence supports neither inference. Rather, those women, like Stanton and Chapman, who made the shift from abolitionism to woman's rights did so using equality feminist arguments, largely dropping out of abolitionism as they began to put their energy into their own cause instead. They may have referred to their own "slavery" metaphorically, but they did not use their concern for slaves as a cover to gain access to public speech. They did not need to, since their rationale for political activism came from the Declaration of Independence, not from God. Women like Earle, on the other hand, who founded their abolitionism on women's *duties, not* their *rights, not* did use slaves as Sánchez-Eppler describes but not in order to liberate themselves beyond the local moment. Indeed, it is very probable that, like Hannah Mather Crocker, these women did not think of themselves as without rights. What they wanted to be free to do was their duty.

Although Sánchez-Eppler is right in arguing that appropriativeness—and, therefore, complicity—lies at the core of feminist abolitionists' sympathy politics, it did not do so, then, as a covert equality feminist gesture. As June Howard insists in "What is Sentimentality?" appropriativeness is the basic dynamic of sympathy politics, whoever practices it, white or black, male or female, Euro-American or Native American, Christian, Muslim, or Jew. In "The Two Voices," published in the *National Anti-Slavery Standard* in 1859, and "The Angel's Visit,"[38] Charlotte Forten Grimké, Sarah Louisa Forten's niece, is just as appropriative as Earle, albeit in a more personally inflected way. Suffering from severe, possibly suicidal, depression, Forten Grimké's speaker is admonished by God—and her long-dead mother—to think about other people's misery instead: "Canst thou see the souls around thee / Bravely battling with the wrong, / And not feel thy soul within thee / In the cause of Truth grow strong?'/ . . . / Thou forgettest other sufferers, / In thy selfish prayer for peace. / Live for others; work for others; / Sharing, strive to soothe their woe, / Till thy heart, no longer fainting, / With an ardent zeal will glow."[39]

For the highly sensitive and psychologically fragile Forten Grimké, political action on the slave's behalf was a way to give meaning to a life otherwise hollowed out by the combination of her mother's early death and her own daily battles with racism. Forten Grimké's sense of identification with slaves and her use of this identification as a means to remedy her own situation permeate her antebellum poetry. But this is hardly less appropriative than Eliza Earle giving meaning to her life by "[b]ravely battling with the wrong" and committing herself to "Mercy's" work. Nor is it that different from any other standard abolitionist appropriation of the slave's voice and situation, where the political aim is implemented by stirring compassion in the reader, as in, for example, "The Slave Girl's Address to her Mother," written by Forten Grimké's aunt, Sarah Louisa Forten: "Think of me, mother, as I bend / My way across the sea; / And midst thy tears, a blessing waft, / To her who prays for thee."[40] All such poems exhibit "[t]he difficulty of preventing moments of identification from becoming acts of appropriation," which Sánchez-Eppler calls "the essential dilemma of feminist abolitionist rhetoric," but which, as Howard argues, is the essential dilemma of sympathy politics—or what Howard calls "benevolence"—itself.[41] Quite simply, to invoke compassion requires imagining—that is, identifying with—someone else's pain and then passing that sense of identification on to others.

My point here is not to put the castigation of black women abolitionists along side Sánchez-Eppler's castigation of white women, but rather to suggest that appropriation is inevitable wherever sympathy serves as the basis for political reform. "Expose thyself to feel what wretches feel," cries King Lear at the moment of his greatest moral enlightenment (3.3.34). Shakespeare repeats the idea with slight variations three more times in the play while parading one form of wretchedness after another across the stage.[42] Euripides uses virtually the same strategy in *Trojan Women*, placing sentimentality's most trusty chestnut, the dead child, at the center of his tragedy. Committed to passive, not to Lockean rights, difference feminists wanted to find some way to live up to the tenets of their (Christian) morality without violating at the same time the gender norms Christianity also bequeathed them. High sentimentality's sympathy politics, with its emphasis on traditional female values of caring and nurturing, made this possible. "[W]e place ourself [*sic*] in [the victim's] situation, we conceive ourselves enduring all the same torments," Adam Smith wrote in *Theory of Moral Sentiments*, "we enter as it were into his body, and become in some measure the same person with him, and thence form some idea of his sensations, and even feel something which, though weaker in degree, is not altogether unlike them."[43]

As a rhetoric and politics of social reform, high sentimentality began here, not in the identification or disidentification of white women's bodies with the bodies of slaves, as Sánchez-Eppler theorizes, but in an epistemology of suffering that made a feeling imagination the primary source of moral knowledge and, hence, of civil action. If there is a problem with nineteenth-century sympathy politics, moreover—which there is—it also lies here: not in the exploitation of black bodily suffering, but in the substitution of feeling for a recognition of rights. When Euripides and Shakespeare used sympathy politics, a concept of natural rights had yet to be articulated; they had nothing else but pity and a utopic sense of civil justice to fall back on. But the nineteenth century—that was another matter. "[A]s soon as abolitionists demanded for the oppressed American the *very same treatment* upon the high ground of *human rights*," Angelina Grimké wrote bitterly in an open letter to Catherine Beecher in 1837, "why, then it was instantly withdrawn, simply because *it had never been conceded on the right* ground. . . . the principle of *equal rights*, irrespective of color or condition, instead of on the mere principle of '*pity and generosity.*'"[44] No one, I would submit, understood the problem better than Angelina Grimké, but the racist tide she fought against was simply too strong.

Critiquing Sympathy Politics from Within

In concluding this chapter, I want to turn to three poets, Sarah Louisa Forten, Sarah Mapps Douglass, and Lydia Sigourney, all of whom in one way or another critique high sentimentality's sympathy politics from within. These writers did not escape the problem of vicariousness or the "appropriation" of another's pain altogether. They could not, since, as Howard points out, vicariousness is structural to sympathy and winning sympathy was their desire. But, as Adam Smith himself clearly recognized, there were set limits to how effective such acts of imaginative identification could be. How much, for example, can one really feel of what another experiences? And how successfully can one speak for them on this basis? Finally, even if one can speak successfully, how far will this take you in the actual achievement of your desired political goal? These are the questions that, I believe, these three poets ask us to consider.

Of the thirteen poems that Sarah Louisa Forten published in the *Liberator*, her 1834 "An Appeal to Woman" is the best known and most impressive. What makes it impressive is that it does not address slavery. It addresses racism among white female abolitionists; and it stung sufficiently to elicit at least two poetic responses, one from James Scott, cheering Forten on, the other by "Augusta," swallowing the "shame."[45] As the daughter of James Forten, the *Liberator*'s principal financial backer, and as the sister-in-law of Robert Purvis, another highly influential black abolitionist, Forten was personally familiar with the upper echelons of the abolitionist movement and knew whereof she spoke.[46] Many female antislavery societies explicitly excluded blacks from membership. Sarah and Angelina Grimké's own Arch Street Meeting House hardly did better. To the sisters' intense chagrin (although apparently to no one else's), black Quakers like Grace and Sarah Mapps Douglass had to sit on segregated benches in the rear of the hall during meetings.

When Forten asked white women abolitionists to summon up the courage to resist their own prejudice, therefore, she was addressing a very real problem, one severely compounded by the fact that, however limited these women's social vision, they were still exhibiting considerable courage in their willingness to advocate for abolition at all. As in William Cullen Bryant's vicious "Ode to Frances Wright" (1829), so throughout the 1820s and 1830s, opponents of abolition made it clear that there would be no separate peace for white women who chose to walk this road. On the contrary, any protection their sex and class might have afforded them was forfeited by their political activities. Bryant's accusation that Wright, "with our watery blood would blend / The richer blood of Congo's race" is typical of the sort of charge leveled at abolitionist women, who also had to endure having their speeches interrupted, their words twisted, their bodies threatened, and their halls burned.[47]

Given this, it is not surprising then, that Forten framed her pleas to white women in terms of courage: "Oh, nobly dare to act a Christian's part, / That well befits a lovely woman's heart! / Dare to be good, as thou canst dare be great; / Despise the taunts of envy, scorn and hate; / Our 'skins may differ,' but from thee we claim / A sister's privilege, in a sister's name" (*NAWP* 80). As white female abolitionists' discriminatory behavior toward free blacks all too clearly demonstrated, despite their claim to sisterhood and their ardent desire to get the sin of slavery off their own and the nation's soul, white women's sense of "sisterhood" barely ran skin deep. But if so, how could these women possibly feel what wretches feel, when they so self-evidently feared or outright despised the wretches themselves, slave or free? The poem's implicit answer is that they cannot, at least not without a good deal of conscious effort.

The fundamental gulf making true sympathetic understanding between whites and blacks difficult, if not impossible, is even more explicit in the theme of "The Mother and Her Captive Boy," published in the *National Enquirer* in 1836 under the name "Ella" probably, Sarah Mapps Douglass. Douglass's point of departure is a stanza from an anonymous abolitionist lyric "The Negro Mother to her Child, the Night before their Separation," which had appeared in an earlier issue of the *Enquirer.* "Wilt thou, when long years roll o'er thee, / Years of toil, and woe, and scorn, / Still remember her who bore thee? / Still when thou art most forlorn?" To this conventionally sympathetic query, probably, albeit not necessarily, penned by a white hand, Douglass's speaker gives a resoundingly unsoftened reply: "No, he will not!" She then lays out the ugly facts of a slave child's rearing with uncompromising rigor: "[T]hey who can rend apart / The strongest chords that bind the human heart, / . . . / Will crush his feelings,—pois'ning as they wound."

The poem becomes a lecture educating readers item by item on the ways in which "[e]ach tender, generous impulse of [the slave's] soul," will be systematically twisted or destroyed. Nothing good that he does will be honored, he will be immersed in evil, "[w]itness of darkest crimes, while yet a child." Under such oppression, he will "soon forget the pure, the mild, / Unsullied feelings of a 'sinless child,' / And turn to bitterness."[48] In light of Douglass's litany of horrors, the facileness of the original stanza seems profoundly trivializing of slavery's brutal consequences, wringing maximum pathos from mother love instead. Douglass's rage burns through the page; but this rage is directed as much toward do-gooding Northern abolitionist poets as it is toward Southern white slaveholders. High-sentimental poetry was simply not an adequate discursive vehicle for the communication of slavery's evils. Rather, in oversimplifying (sentimentalizing?) slavery's brutalities and romanticizing the slave-victim himself, it verged on precisely the kind of bad-faith politics that Sánchez-Eppler, for different reasons, said it was.

Although it hardly fits with the way that literary history has chosen to "invent" Lydia Sigourney, as Nina Baym puts it, I would suggest that by the last years of her career—if not before—Hartford's sweet singer came to a similar conclusion respecting some of her own high-sentimental efforts.[49]

Sigourney spent a sizeable chunk of her career protesting the government's Indian removal policies, writing poem after poem in which Indians figured as noble warriors, venerable patriarchs, grieving mothers, and chaste maidens. These poems enjoyed enormous popularity and were reprinted everywhere, including in Indian newspapers such as the *Cherokee Phoenix* and its later incarnation, the *Cherokee Advocate*. Some of the poems, like "Indian Names," are both powerful and moving. Paeans to a lost culture, a lost people, they are always utterly sympathetic. Indeed, they probably epitomize the best high sentimentality could do in this particular vein. As such, they had, at the least, to have been a thorn in the government's side.

However, in a little-known narrative poem, "The Lost Lily," published in *Western Home* in 1854, Sigourney, of all people, gives them the lie. "Lost Lily" is, one might say, a captivity narrative turned inside out. Having vowed on their father's deathbed never to abandon their search for their long-lost younger sister, Lily, an elderly and exceedingly pious pair of siblings make the long trek to visit a white woman who reportedly is living among the Miami in a remote area of Wyoming. The woman is Lily all right, but no longer the delicate "Saxon" child whom they remember, and she rejects their offer to return to "civilization" out of hand. From the poem's apparently Christian perspective, the "Lily" who, effectively, tells her siblings to "get lost," is "lost." She looks "with the stony eye of prejudice" on those who love her; and Sigourney leaves this reading open in the poem's final lines: "And so they left / Their pagan sister in her Indian home, and to their native vale of Wyoming / Turn'd mournful back. There, often steep'd in tears, / At morn or evening, rose the earnest prayer, / That God would keep in their lost Lily's soul / The seed her mother sow'd."[50]

But if Sigourney allows a Christian reading for this sad conclusion, she offers an autonomous "pagan" reading as well, one supplied by Lily herself, wherein prejudice meets prejudice and the Indians take the higher as well as the more sophisticated moral ground. The "coarsely-mantled," pipe-smoking crone who speaks these lines has long since abandoned Christian culture. When Lily responds to her siblings' entreaties, she responds as, presumably, any Indian woman might:

> Upon my head
> Rest sixty winters. Scarcely seven were past
> Among the pale-faced people. Hate they not
> The red man in their heart? Smooth Christian words
> They speak, but from their touch we fade away
> As from the poisonous snake.
> Have I not said
> Here is my home? And yonder is the bed
> Of the Miami chief? two sons who bore

His brow, rest on his pillow.
                    Shall I turn
My back upon my dead, and bear the curse
Of the great Spirit?[51]

Coming from the pen of nineteenth-century U.S. poetry's high priestess of sentimentality, this cameo portrait of an elderly, enraged Indian woman is odd indeed, and made even odder not just by its irony but by its multiple ambiguities. Is Sigourney, and not just Lily, suggesting that Christians can go to hell, that being "lost" is a matter of perspective, that the father's word is not law, that white civilization is something one can not live with but can live very nicely without? If so, then she—that is, Sigourney, not just Lily—is turning her back on a good deal that she once believed and that, presumably, justified much of what she did and wrote.

I would like to suggest that this is in fact what Sigourney is doing, if only within the space of this speech. By 1854, more than "Lily" was lost. Only the Civil War would stave off for a few decades the new nation's complete victory over surviving indigenous peoples. With "Lost Lily," Sigourney, now over sixty-three years old, threw in the towel. However morally correct high-sentimental politics might be, sympathy's tears made no headway against guns and greed. Those grave and graying patriarchs, fierce freedom fighters, and so on who peopled her earlier protest poetry and were meant to win sympathy from whites had not. The brutality of the government's genocidal policies continued unabated—indeed, if anything, accelerated—pushed on by each new wave of immigration and westward expansion. *Ramona* notwithstanding, no Indian *Uncle Tom's Cabin* would turn the tide. Indians were simply not an aspect of "bleeding humanity" for whose sake most Euro-Americans were prepared to sacrifice. From an economic and expansionist perspective the price tag for sparing them was simply too high.

Sigourney's poem marks an effective end, I would submit, to high-sentimentality as a political discourse used by white bourgeois women poets on behalf of racial minorities in the United States. As I discuss in the next chapter, high-sentimental sympathy politics continued to be employed by minority poets themselves, either because they still hoped to win support from the dominant population or because they found such sentimentality useful in building solidarity in their own communities. After 1860, with some exceptions, most notably Helen Hunt Jackson and Elaine Goodale Eastman, the poetry of white, Christian, middle-class women no longer interested itself in the "cause" of bleeding humanity, at least not if those who bled were of another race. When, after the war, issues of social oppression reemerge, as they do powerfully in Sarah Piatt's poetry, they are, as we shall see, thoroughly ironized and focus largely on issues of gender and class. At least where white women's poems were concerned, Indians did indeed "dis-appear" and blacks also, taking with them much of the political sympathy that white women had once generated on their behalf. What one finds instead is poetry of denigrating stereotypes in which hyperracialized speakers, often using dialect and addressing themselves to child readers, wax nostalgic about the Old South or try vainly to keep up with the white man's mysterious ways. Read against these poems, some of which I will discuss in the next chapter, the poetry of high sentimental sympathy politics, for all its obvious internal contradictions and failures, may still seem a preferable alternative to the poetry of outright hate or silencing obliteration that took its place.

3

The Politics and Poetics of Difference

[The American Jew] is made aware . . . that the Anglo-
Saxon is the only native American, and that all other races
are aliens. Then he reflects that perhaps the soil of his
birth . . . does not claim him as her veritable child—he
has no share in her motherhood.
    —NINA MORAIS COHEN, *The Menorah*, 1892[1]

If we follow the badge of color from "African" to "Negro"
to "colored race" to "black" to "Afro-American" to "African-American" (and this ignores such fascinating detours
as the route by way of "Afro-Saxon") we are thus tracing
the history not only of a signifier, a label, but also a history of its effects.
    —K. ANTHONY APPIAH, *Color Conscious*, 1996[2]

When, in the 1770s, J. Hector St. John de Crèvecoeur's European-born
farmer looked about him at the "modern society" evolving in his adopted
homeland of America, he saw two things "different from what he had hith-
erto seen." First, there were no great lords, no landed families, and, he believed, no class tensions between rich and poor as a result. Second, there was
a new "race" in the process of formation: "They are a mixture of English,
Scotch, Irish, French, Dutch, Germans, and Swedes. From this promiscuous
breed," Crèvecoeur reports, "that race now called Americans have arisen."[3]
    Writing three-quarters of a century after Crèvecoeur, Sarah Margaret Fuller
also describes Americans as a new "breed," one produced, however, not just
by the melding of nationalities but by the impact of differing cultural institutions and environmental circumstances. Of the growing distance separating
the United States and its "mother-country," Fuller observes: "What suits
Great Britain, with her insular position . . . limited monarchy, and spirit of
trade, does not suit a mixed race, continually enriched with new blood from
other stocks the most unlike that of our first descent." The "genius" of
Americans, Fuller predicts, will be as "wide and full as our rivers, flowery,
luxuriant and impassioned as our vast prairies, rooted in strength as the
rocks on which the Puritan fathers landed."[4]

Last, but never least, in the 1855 preface to *Leaves of Grass*, Whitman also links racialized genius to nation, culture, and geography, defining America's "greatest poet," as he who absorbs all that the continent has to offer, "incarnating" it in flesh as well as text: "The American poets are to enclose old and new for America is the race of races. Of them a bard is to be commensurate with a people. To him the other continents arrive as contributions . . . he gives them reception for their sake and his own sake. His spirit responds to his country's spirit. . . . he incarnates its geography and natural life and rivers and lakes."[5]

Similar conflations of an "American race" with American nationality, not to mention with the American landscape, can be documented indefinitely in nineteenth-century U.S. literature, but one hardly need do so.[6] With the science of genetics still in its infancy, most people, both in the United States and in Europe, identified race with nationality and nationality with the sum product of the biologically embedded effects of a people's language, culture, and environment: you "are," or become, where you live. Even today, long after geneticists have thoroughly discredited the idea that nationality or ethnicity is genetically transmitted, popular lore still appeals to an "American people" with the same gusto that it invokes "the spirit of America," an "American way of life," or, bringing it very close to home, an "American literary tradition." As Benedict Anderson argues, the sense of national solidarity or "community" to which these patriotic shibboleths give rise may be imaginary, but the phrases remain politically potent nonetheless, their power testifying to the fact that the juridical status of citizenship is only one of many sites where national identity is formed, and, possibly, not the most important.[7]

When understood thus, as a signifier for successive, historically contingent versions of national identity and purpose, the designation "American" can be seen to function politically, in much the same way that "white" or "black" or "man" or "woman" or "Irish" or "Jew" do in their respective ideological fields: race, gender, and ethnicity. These identifiers or labels represent shifting coalitions of competing ideological investments. They do not point to entities so much as create them, through the meanings we give them and the "effects," as Appiah puts it,[8] that they produce; but as Anderson argues of national identities generally, this has never stopped people from believing in them fiercely, or killing or dying for them. By no means mere air, these labels represent belief systems that have proved astonishingly plastic over time, multiplying and surviving, as Crèvecoeur might say, by "promiscuous" breeding.

What makes labels of nationality, ethnicity, and race so dangerous is also what makes them so useful: at any given point, they provide possibilities for categorical stabilization, retarding what otherwise would be the constantly undoing flux of experience itself. They mark, that is, those moments of coalescence when identity comes, or appears to come, into being, as, for example, it did most dramatically in the various "pride" movements of the 1970s.[9] But if for writers like Fuller and Whitman, being "American" was neither a mere label nor a fixed civil or juridical status, if, rather, it meant being physically, not just nominally, part of a shifting conglomerate, a "new race," a "new breed of people," then just how mixed was this "new race" going to be? Whom could the national body safely incorporate, and how and on what grounds should their title to inclusion be proved? Given the period's conflation of race and nation, these were pressing questions for most nineteenth-century writers, whether mainstream or minority, and their answers continue to impact American lives today.

In this chapter and the next, I look at how these questions were raised and answered in texts by Anglophone women poets from four of the United States' principal minorities: African American, Jewish American, Irish American, and Native American. Ranging from the unknown (a Louisa Anna or Lily Lee) to the well known (an Emma Lazarus or Frances Harper), the poets to whom I now turn had on the whole very little in common beside their location outside the nation's putative Anglo-Saxon mainstream and their use of Anglo-American literary conventions in their verse. Starting with their outsider status and addressing themselves to the "counter-public spheres" to which their own communities gave rise,[10] these authors created poems positioned very differently from those of their mainstream peers—women of whom even the most critical, a Lydia Sigourney or Sarah Piatt, for example, never questioned their right to incorporation in the national body at large.

Minority writers did not have this same confidence, and their insecurity affected everything they wrote. Coming from communities that were treated at best with suspicion, these poets tried to remain faithful to their minority constituencies even while proving that they too had a rightful place in the United States' evolving mainstream. Positioned between these needs, their poetry became a fraught balancing act wherein a thematics celebrating the specifics of minority identity was mediated by conventions that largely occluded the identifiably "different" in their work. Indeed, it would be fair to say that the tension between these two impulses, the one toward community cohesion, the other toward assimilation, pervasively structures their writing, dictating the roles both literary and high sentimentality play in it.

In *The Spirit of the Ghetto* (1902), a book describing life among turn-of-the-century Russian Jews living on New York City's lower East Side, Hutchins Hapgood provides a striking if, from the perspective of this study, belated illustration of how this tension played itself out in the lives of one particularly forward-looking group of immigrant minority women. For these women, who began their movement toward assimilation in Russia, taking up their new identities as American Jews and as "modern" women (that is, shedding their traditional roles as Jewish women) were to all intents and purposes the same thing. "As we ascend in the scale of education," Hapgood writes, "we find women [who]. . . . have lost faith completely in the ortho-dox religion, have substituted no other, know Russian better than Yiddish, read Tolstoi, Turgenef and Chekov, and often put into practice the most radical theories of the 'new woman,' particularly those which say that woman should be economically independent of man. There are successful female dentists, physicians, writers, and even lawyers by the score in East Broad-way."[11] Already exposed to feminism in Russia in the 1880s, largely through the auspices of socialism, these Jewish women were already well on their way to Western-style female modernity by the time they reached the United States. Their daughters, like their sons, would finalize their break with their parents' ghettoed past by abandoning Russian for English and socialism for security and the opportunity to "make it" in the New World, becoming doctors, writers, lawyers, and even politicians somewhere else beside on East Broadway.

But as these women shed Yiddish for Russian and Russian for English, so they also shed their previous cultural/ethnic identities, irrevocably separating themselves from the kinds of people their parents and grandparents had been. Although the specifics of generational conflict that Hapgood describes differ among minority groups, this shifting positioning between a minority past and a "progressive" present/future characterizes the subjectivities of most nineteenth-century Anglophone minority women poets, and their os-cillation between positions of sameness and difference is, therefore, the most striking aspect of their verse. In this chapter, I will look at how these poets used the rhetorical strategies available to them, in particular, those of ante-bellum literary and high sentimentality, to negotiate the conflicted terrain of their "hyphenated" identities as Americans. In the next chapter, I will ex-plore the work of four poets—Frances Harper, Fanny Parnell, Emma Laz-arus, and E. Pauline Johnson—whose very difference from the people for whom they spoke was, ironically, the source of their effectiveness as spokes-persons for them.

Rethinking "American": Mrs. Mary E. Ashe Lee's "Afmerica"

In a rare departure from its usually conservative approach to racial and so-cial questions, Hampton Institute's *Southern Workman* reprinted a lengthy excerpt from "Afmerica" in its October 1886 issue. A long narrative poem by the black educator Mary E. Ashe Lee, "Afmerica," as its title boldly an-nounces, confronts one of the nineteenth century's most controversial social issues, "amalgamation," or the sexual mixing of whites with peoples of color. Even more controversially, the poem treats this explosive topic at the level of the nation, not just as a matter of personal choice. In "Afmerica," Lee hy-pothesizes for the United States—as, indeed, for the entire continental land mass—a racial presence that embraces not only the unmixed descendants of the original European colonizers but also those whom the colonizers produced through their interbreeding with non-Caucasian peoples, in particular, Africans, initially brought to this continent as slaves.

Like the idealized portrait of America's multiracial future featured on *Time* magazine's cover several years ago,—a computer-generated composite face of a vaguely Asiatic young woman with light brown skin, gray-brown eyes, and straight, brownish hair—Lee's symbolic figure for this made-in-America American is a young woman of ambiguous coloring.[12] Future incubator of others like herself, Afmerica by her very existence gives new racialized significance to the great democratic experiment that the United States had become. In her poem, Lee rewrites Crèvecoeur's answer to the question, "what is an American?" specifically in terms of color, a mixing Crèvecoeur himself abjures.[13] Not just Italians, Germans, French, and Swedes were promiscuously mixing in what became the United States, but peoples of varying shades and hues. Like *Time* magazine after her, Lee asserts that this mixing was producing a new, peculiarly American physiognomic type:

> With cheeks as soft as roses are,
> And yet as brown as chestnuts dark;
> And eyes that borrow from a star
> A tranquil, yet a brilliant spark;
> Or face of olive, with a glow
> Of carmine on the lip and cheek;
> The hair in wavelets falling low,
> With jet or hazel eyes, that speak;
> Or brow of pure Caucasi[a]n hue,
> With auburn or with flaxen hair;
> And eyes that beam in liquid blue,
> A perfect type of Saxon fair,—
> Behold this strange, this well-known maid,
> Of every hue, of every shade!
> (*NAWP* 466–67, ll. 1–14)

Part prophecy, part jeremiad, part special pleading, part historical lecture, part celebration, "Afmerica" imagines a nation that has incorporated into itself peoples as diverse as the land on which they settle, a "turbulent" nation, as Lee describes it, "So mixed and intermixed" that "[a]ll nationalities at will / Become [its] own, [its] legal heirs" (ll. 144–45). Afmerica, Lee argues, has a rightful place among these nationalities, guaranteed by her contributions of love and labor, from nursing the infant George Washington, the first U.S. president, to harvesting cotton and cane, to felling forests and clearing land. As much the result of the joint efforts of blacks and whites to build the nation as of the actual couplings of white and black bodies or the mingling of black and white cultures, Afmerica has a legitimate share in the national identity. Neatly inverting the rhetorical cant that to this day maintains the Puritans' grip on national identity, this late-nineteenth-century black woman insists that Providence has ordained her presence here, even as she categorically rejects the idea that Americans of African descent "belong" somewhere else:

> Her destiny is marked out here.
> Her ancestors, like all the rest,
> Came from the eastern hemisphere:
> But *she* is native of the *west.*
> . . . .
> No one has power to send her hence;
> This home was planned by Providence.
>   (ll. 173–76, 1181–82)

Precisely because Lee's stance on America's amalgamated national identity is so radical, however, her equally passionate embracing of Afmerica's bourgeois/genteel values is likely to disappoint readers hoping for a radical social politics from the author as well. Even in the midst of slavery's cruelties and deprivations, Lee's speaker avers, "In many of [Afmerica's] homes . . . / Refinement true, and some degree / Of culture" (ll. 135–37) could still be found. Forced to acculturate to white ways, Afmerica, it seems, goes her masters one better, fully introjecting "white" bourgeois values and making them her own. No nomad, like the gypsy or "the savage red-man's child" (l. 24), Afmerica turns out to be the very exemplar of True Womanhood and the genteel life-style: "Of home and civil habits mild" (ll. 26). Like Hapgood's immigrant Jewish women who found in education a way out of oppressive ghetto life, Afmerica, having come into "independent womanhood" (l. 38), can now be found "[i]n any sphere of busy life, / . . . though in numbers few," making music, painting, sculpting, orating, practicing medicine, teaching, working in the temperance movement, missionizing, or else, "[i]n her own home, a blessed queen" (ll. 184 and 196). "Whatever other women do" (ll.183–84), Lee confidently asserts, here, where Providence has led Afric's daughters, we find black women making the most of the opportunities around them. Now that 'Afmerica' has demonstrated her capacity for civility, as well as civilization, Lee's speaker asks, how can the nation continue to reject her?[14]

> But now, a child of liberty,
> Of independent womanhood,
> The world in wonder looks to see
> If in her there is any good;
> If this new child, Afmerica,
> Can dwell in free Columbia.
>   (ll. 37–42)

From Lee's perspective, not only is Afmerica, as the "daughter of futurity" (l. 27), where she belongs, but the future—in all its figurative, if not literal, whiteness—belongs to her.

Yet uncomfortable as Lee's advocacy of this white bourgeois social agenda makes us today, from the perspective of the newly emancipated black women whom she addressed, Lee was no Judas goat. On the contrary, the program of social "uplift," as it was called, that Lee, as a black educator and civic leader, espouses here was itself a form of political resistance. As Louise Newman puts it, it was a repudiation of the notion of fixed biological inheritance and, even more crucially, an assertion that black women also had "rights."[15] Among these "rights," as another *Southern Workman* author put it—sounding remarkably like Hannah Mather Crocker—"the right to your children, the right to your husband, the right to labor for your loved ones, the right to a pure and serene home."[16] Whatever equality feminists, then or now, may think of such "rights," for the formerly enslaved women whom Afmerica represents, they were, as Crocker says, "*real.*" Uplift, Barbara McCaskill explains, had the power to "bleach blackness of its dehumanizing, satanic, objectified, and exotic connotations. Having memorized the litany of uplift virtues, and assimilated bourgeois, white, middle-class norms and aspirations and moral and civil codes of conduct, African-American people would loom legitimately as peers of and equals to white Americans."[17] Via uplift, black women, so sorely mistreated in the past, could finally lay claim to the same respect and dignity nineteenth-century bourgeois white women assumed as a matter of course, unaware of the privileges they enjoyed.

Lee's insistence on "uplift's" "civilizing" values no less than her extrusion of gypsies and "wild" Indians can certainly be read as colonizing moves, ones that undoubtedly help explain her otherwise radical poem's appearance in a periodical as unilaterally dedicated to cultural colonization as the *Southern Workman.* But the poem must also be read in terms of the needs of the postbellum African American community to whom it is addressed. As we saw in Caroline Dall's rebuttal of Ednah Cheney's equality feminist arguments, for a white middle-class woman to adopt the values of ladyhood meant voluntarily sacrificing rights that even Dall admits were by nature hers; it set, that is, self-chosen limits on her freedom. For a black woman like Lee's Afmerica, fresh from enslavement, where she had no rights even to her own body, and had been forced into centuries of killing physical labor, enjoying the perquisites of ladyhood could be, and undoubtedly was, a valid definition of what freedom was all about.

But were black women the only minority women promoting uplift? What I want to consider now is whether, given the particular nature of the nineteenth century's racist environment—an environment which, among other things, made no distinction between race and nationality or, just as crucially, between national culture and bourgeois class values—most minority women poets did not feel compelled to adopt similar "litan[ies] of uplift virtues." As far as mainstream white Americans were concerned, to be an "American" was not just a matter of white skin. On the contrary, what constituted the latter, as Matthew Frye Jacobson has demonstrated, was itself a highly manipulatable point of debate. Being an "American" also meant conforming to "white," middle-class, behavioral norms—or, at any rate, showing that a critical mass in one's ethnic or racial group could live up to these norms, however much poverty, lack of education, or lack of English hampered the rest. "To enter the white race," Noel Ignatiev observes in *How the Irish Became White*, "was a strategy to secure an advantage in a competitive society."[18] As Ignatiev uses "white-ness" here, the term was a signifier of caste and of an entire set of assumptions about those whom the dominant class considered inferior to itself; and it was these assumptions that minority writers needed to contradict if they were to prove their own community's "fitness for self-government" and right to inclusion in mainstream culture at large.[19]

Of the four minority groups I treat here, the women writers of all but one—Native Americans—voluntarily took uplift, that is, assimilation to the dominant class's bourgeois social and gender values, as a desirable end in itself, supporting women's traditional role as caretaker rather than demanding their rights. Even more than Lee, who clearly was prepared to embrace certain elements in the equality feminist program, other minority women's poems are often strikingly conservative as a result. After 1850 mainstream women poets, as we shall see in part 2, increasingly ironized the sentimental strategies they used, but minority women both before and after the war, continued to employ these strategies with little or not critique. Blending the moral goals of antebellum high-sentimental poetry, with the aesthetics, class, and gender assumptions of literary sentimentality, they produced versions of minority women's subjectivity that are in consequence every bit as historically contingent as the poetic strategies they deployed. Far from expressing some sort of timeless, incorruptible, minority essence, their poems are, as a result, eminently political texts, and, as Richard Brodhead argues generally of literature, they must be read in terms of the cultural environment in which they were produced and to which they respond.[20] My discussion will begin with a brief overview of the minority political situation itself and in particular with an examination of the kind of systematic racist stereotyping to which these women and their communities were subject and to which, with great courage and persistence, they gave the lie.

Racial Typology in the Postbellum Period

> Race [is] a consummate biological fiction which is also a
> social fact.
> —ALDON NIELSEN, *Reading Race*, 2000[21]

To understand why U.S. minority women poets might have felt a compelling need to demonstrate "uplift" virtues, one need look no further than the racist environment that prevailed during the century itself. Despite the efforts of U.S. literary and cultural historians over the past few decades to do justice to this material, it remains difficult to appreciate just how extensive, vicious, and, at the same time, absolutely casual, racism was until one actually immerses oneself in the newspapers and periodicals of the day. Deployed by minority groups against each other, as well as by the Protestant white majority against everyone else, a fully elaborated discourse evolved around what the period frankly and ubiquitously defined as racial types: German, British, Jewish, Chinese, Mexican, and so on. Among minority groups, Jews, the Irish, blacks, Native Americans, and belatedly, the Chinese, were subjected to the most persistent and abusive stereotyping. Periodicals and newspapers as diverse as the *Irish World*, the humor magazine *New Varieties*, the *Monthly Jubilee*, the pro-labor magazine put out by "the Daughters and Sons of Toil," the *Youth's Companion*, the *Continent*, *Harper's Weekly*, and the *Springfield Republican* routinely gave space to racist articles, cartoons, poems, jokes, and stories, much of the material, like the following "miscellaneous" news item from the 1860 *Springfield (Mass.) Republican*, presented with a gratuitousness that boggles the mind:

> A big buck nigger eloped from Boston, a year or two since, with a white woman, leaving his black wife and children behind; and now, after living with this woman at Carbondale, Pa., he has again eloped, taking this time her white niece. The negro [*sic*] is 50, the girl 17. The deserted aunt has a little milk-and-molasses baby by which to remember her sin and shame.[23]

Since the behavior of an anonymous black man and an equally anonymous white woman from Boston, Massachusetts, could not possibly have direct relevance to anyone anywhere in the country, including most people in Boston itself, the *Republican*'s only justification for printing this "news item" is its cleverly salacious wit. The tidbit was published, that is, because someone—presumably, Samuel Bowles, the *Republican*'s philandering publisher—found it funny.

In fairness to Bowles, who is much admired by some Dickinson scholars, he did moderate his views on blacks once the Civil War began or, at any rate, he chastened his newspaper's speech. Up to that point, however, the daily version of the *Republican* remained (for a Northern newspaper) one of the ugliest I encountered in the antebellum period, with terms like "niggers," "darkies," and "Sambo" dancing attendance on a reportage of hate.[23] Yet even when newspaper and periodical writers were "sympathetic," racist stereotyping typically went hand in hand with their discussions of minority affairs. For example, Anna Brackett's "Indian and Negro," published in *Harper's New Monthly Magazine*, purports to provide thoughtful commentary on black and Indian students' differing responses to their schooling at Hampton: "The characteristics of this race [the Negro] we know sufficiently well. They are light-hearted and happy, easily impressible, ambitious to be better than they are, and as willing as a child to let that ambition be seen." Indians, on the other hand, Brackett finds sullen and relatively untrainable, true to their "proud" and reserved natures and their general unwillingness to be seen doing anything at which they did not already excel.[24] Given Brackett's commitment to education, it is not surprising that she writes of her charges in the uninflected language of Caucasian superiority, but the constitutive biases of this language undermine nonetheless any effort she makes to project empathy and respect.

Most often, however, as in the vicious anti-Semitic cartoons published in the *Irish World* in the 1870s or the anti-Catholic, anti-Irish, anti-Chinese, and antiblack cartoons swamping *Harper's Weekly*, the motivation behind racist attacks was the obvious one: the desire to put and keep the Other in his or her place by sanctioning and promoting discrimination against targeted groups. Among the most disturbing pieces of this sort that I have run into is "The Heathen Chinee," possibly the work of Bret Harte, whose highly popular "Plain Language from Truthful James" famously used the same epithet with much the same intent, albeit in not quite so vicious a setting. Two stanzas are enough to convery the poem's flavor:

> They hash up the gristle and bones when you've dined,
> And wear a long *cue* that's suspended behind,
> Like the tail of a monkey, and *him* they will eat,
> Pronouncing the morsel exceedingly sweet.
> The Hottentot people are bad, we'll agree.
> But they never can equal the Heathen Chinee.

> They scrape all the money they can on the sly,
> Then back to the "Flowery Nation" to die.
> A dollar's a fortune to last a whole life—
> Tobacco will buy a John Chinaman's wife.
> Oh, filthy is "John," and not better is *she*—
> For "bummers" and "beats" are the Heathen Chinee.[25]

The best one can say of the "The Heathen Chinee" is that it is rather cleverer than most of its kind, creating a witty picture of the strange and arbitrary ways of the Chinese. Discursively self-contained, as this kind of material typically is, the poem bears no relation to the complexities of Chinese culture either in the United States or in the "Flowery Nation." That is, however, neither here nor there. The poem's perspective is strictly Western, the behavior of the Chinese conveyed entirely through unsympathetic and uncomprehending Western eyes, the poem's stereotyped images acting as a lens whose very distortions block all other possibilities out.

Writers and artists had, in fact, an impressive array of strategies at their disposal by which to mediate racist attitudes. Speech patterns, for example, were conventionalized into various forms of identifying dialects, with Southern black dialect, in particular, reaching the height of its popularity among white readers in the fin de siècle. Even more potent were those specific sets of pictorial conventions that were used to represent individual "racial"/national types. These conventions functioned not only to make each minority readily identifiable but also to ground "difference" in the presumptive "specifics" of physical bodies, along with such accidental qualities as ethnic manners and dress. Thus cartoonists denoted the Irish not just by top or bowler hats and tobacco pipes but by snub noses and square, simian jaws. Jews are distinguished by satanically narrow faces, huge hooked noses, uncombed beards, elf locks, and gabardines. Chinese have slanty eyes and grotesquely long pigtails. Blacks have thick lips, bulging eyes, wooly hair, and ragged clothing; and Indians have feathers, blankets, tomahawks, large noses, and rigidly wooden faces. As with the *Springfield Republican* squib, these denigrating images are often presented as "humorous," but they fed prejudice nonetheless; and even highly sophisticated magazines such as *Harper's Bazar* gave them space, albeit typically only in their "humor" pages (figs. 1–3).

Equally depressing one even finds children's literature saturated with this material, with some of the most offensive matter appearing in *Youth's Companion*, an extremely long-lived children's periodical that treated all social/racial groups except Protestant Euro-Americans as exotica. Like cartoons generally, racial stereotypes are, if nothing else, easy to "read," helping explain, perhaps, why authors of children's books continue to deploy them even today. As a form of shorthand for difference, stereotypes spare authors the labor of putting the complexity of "Otherness" in terms still comprehensible to the young. But this use carries a price of its own. When Lizzie W. Champney attempted to move from stereotype to heroic image, in "That Small Piecee Boy from China," the weight of the preexisting literature—that is, the racism already embedded in the representational conventions she deploys—confounded her. Trying to give her small protagonist a voice to explain why he wants so desperately to fly home, she turns him, intentionally or not, into a miniature heathen Chinee, blotting out his particularity together with his fundamental humanity:

> "Speakee you too much fool pigeon,
>   Better China home than here.
> Me no likee English junkee,
>   English chowchow too no nice.
> Why no can some roasted monkey?
>   What for not some piecee mice?"[26]

If, as I think she did, Champney wanted her young readers to sympathize with this little boy, who braves white folks' mockery to make a kite that will

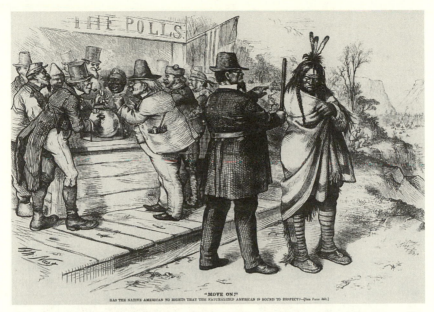

Fig. 1. "Move On!" Has the native American no rights that the naturalized American is bound to respect?

take him back to China, her use of dialect and her reliance on stereotyped details subvert her intention, introducing condescension, even mocking contempt, into the description itself. This same problem, far more famously, plagues Twain's portrait of Jim in *Huckleberry Finn*. The author may want to invest his or her character with a more complicated humanity, but once invoked, the racist stereotype has a signifying power of its own. At the least, the stereotype's presence will muddy any positive message that the author seeks to convey—as the large body of scholarly literature devoted to Jim's status in Twain's novel makes clear.[27]

Most seriously for this study, racist stereotypes of one sort or another appear in the writings of the majority of postbellum white woman writers, Emily Dickinson included. Whether because she enjoyed their gimmicky appeal or because she was, in fact, consciously racist, Dickinson, whose use of language was never careless, invokes a number of conventional stereotypes, making coy references to "Bridgets," "Jews," and "Malays," the latter of whom she willfully conflates—presumably, because both are "colored"— with "Negros." Precisely because these references are so brief, they are also irredeemable. That is, their very brevity signals that Dickinson is trading on, not interrogating or challenging, the racist assumptions they encode. Thus, "Bridget" in "The Spider as an Artist" is typed and classed by both name and

Fig. 2. "Them Steers," *Irish World* (1880)

Fig. 3. "Now, General Washington, you jes' cum an' put on your shoes dis minit. De idea of you bein' out-doors barefoot on de Lord's Day! Why, folks will think you're Irish!"

broom (F1373), while in "I Came to buy a smile - today," "Jew" is used, as in "to Jew someone down," to stand for a rapacious bargainer, slimily intent on getting the best deal: "'Twould be 'a Bargain' for a *Jew*! / *Say* - May I have it - Sir?" (F258).

Equally disturbing, Dickinson's tone in her early letters to her brother Austin when she tells him to whip his Irish students comes uncomfortably close to that of the *Springfield Republican* in its moments of gratuitous cruelty: "So far as *I* am concerned I should like to have you kill some—there are so many now, there is no room for the Americans," she declares with mock ferocity, "I don't think deaths or murders can ever come amiss in a young woman's journal" (L43, see also L44).[28] How much was Dickinson influenced by Bowles's racism, this man some believe to have been her adored "Master"? In particular, could "The Malay - took the Pearl -," dated by Franklin late 1862, represent Dickinson's conscious or unconscious reworking of the miscellaneous news item Bowles's *Republican* had published a few years before? "The Swarthy fellow swam - / And bore my Jewel—Home - / Home to the Hut! What lot / Had I - the Jewel - got - / Borne on a Dusky Breast - / I had not deemed a Vest / Of Amber- fit - / The Negro never knew / I - wooed it - too" (F451). Obviously, short of harder evidence, it is impossible to say. Just as obviously, however, one cannot rule the possibility out. Both the poem and the squib play on white anxieties around amalgamation—the poem, with its gratuitous substitution of a "Negro" for the opening line's "Malay," even more than the squib. Both depict the black man stealing the prize and bringing her/it home to his "Hut." Both reduce the black man to a symbol of animalistic sexual desire and primitive display—that "Dusky Breast -."[29] And, finally, both present the union as a "sin and shame," degrading that which should have been revered. Did Dickinson find in the squib, then, a suitable "objective correlative" for her frustration at having lost "Sister Sue" to a—as she saw it—undeserving brother, a brother who, not that long before, had tried to rival her in poetry writing as well?

Whether one turns to casual cartoons or to major writers, racist attitudes and imagery pervade late-nineteenth-century U.S. literature from bottom to top, with minority writers themselves as likely as anyone else to indulge in them. The period was, as Peter Gay notes, distinguished by its cultivation of hatred.[30] Remembering that the nineteenth century identified the national body with a racialized body, one can appreciate why the need to keep the Other in their place would have been felt so intensely on all sides. Nevertheless, this made racism no less ugly or destructive. The "Pearl" at stake was one of very great price, and, as in Dickinson's ever-so-loaded poem, ethnic/racial rivalry drove each group to claim possession at some Other's expense, sometimes, as in *Harper's Weekly* cartoons, with a viciousness that can take one's breath away. Engaged competitively with her brother Austin for Susan Gilbert Dickinson's love, Dickinson casts her classic sibling triangle in specifically racial terms; but this same sibling dynamic underlay, I would suggest, racism within the society as a whole. If, as in the *Republican*'s news-item, it was woe unto the white woman who took a black man for her mate, finally all this material came down to controlling who came home to dinner, and, once invited in, who got the largest slice of the great American pie. In saying, "So far as *I* am concerned I should like to have you kill some—there are so many now, there is no room for the Americans," Dickinson with unimpeachable accuracy was summing up the way many, perhaps most, white Protestant Americans of the period felt, if not with respect to one group, then with respect to another.

Minority Women's Resistance

Confronted with a constant barrage of negative material, minority women poets did what American women poets had done from the late 1720s on. They used their access to the public press, especially community newspapers and periodicals, to counter negative stereotypes and take charge of their own representation. Inflecting the conventions of antebellum True Womanhood in such a way as to make them compatible with their own communities' values, these poets put the discourses of sentimentality to work in service to their own group needs. Like Mary E. Ashe Lee, what they sought to prove was not their superiority to the dominant class but their right to be part of it, thereby reclaiming the cultural territory and the human dignity racist stereotyping denied them. The result is poetry that is as much situated "between worlds" as the authors themselves: Anglocentric in form, bourgeois and assimilationist in stance, yet ethnically individuated at the same time. It was antebellum sentimentality's very appropriative potential—in particular, its universalizing moral sentiments—that allowed these minority women to twist it in this way, undoing the distance between subordinate and dominant on which high sentimentality's sympathy politics and genteel notions of refined culture both depended. In these women's poetry, one could say, the subaltern is able to speak precisely because she uses the dominant culture's discourse, even while addressing herself to the alternative or counter-public sphere that her community readership represents.

Take, for example, the following poem by Louisa Anna, published in 1868 in the generally progressive *Cincinnati Israelite*, mouthpiece for Reform Judaism in the Midwest. In this poem, the anglophonic author's use of the lyric conventions of sentimental poetry renders her heroine, Zuleika, all but indistinguishable from the many Christian female martyrs inhabiting poems by Victorian women from Felicia Hemans on. Indeed, Zuleika's death comes complete with angels and generous hints of an afterlife that are modeled so closely on the way these constituent elements appear in Christian poems as to obliterate any significant difference between Christian and Jew: "With stately and majestic grace, / The scaffold plank she trod, / Then cried: 'O, Israel hear! / The Lord alone is God.' / With that cry her young life fled / Beneath the swordsman's blow; / Her pure, bright soul the angels bore / From suffering here below."[31] Zuleika's cry to Israel may echo Jewish ritual prayer, but like the archetypal Christian martyr, her heroism lies in suffering for her faith, and her reward is firmly situated in the hereafter. Zuleika dies, moreover, with such nobility that, as with Christian martyrs, she spiritually transforms her oppressor. Since Judaism is not a proselytizing religion, the would-be-lover-turned-executioner does not, as he might in a Christian poem, abandon his own religion; but filled with remorse, he erects a statue in Zuleika's memory, "a shaft of beauty rare." Jewish though Zuleika is, she is also the epitome of the self-sacrificial "True Woman," and the power coursing through her veins is the power of the sentimental, a power, like Little Eva's, supremely realized only through self-abnegating death.

In the final stanza of "Zuleika," however, Louisa Anna does give her poem an explicitly community-oriented twist. Addressing Jewish women directly, the speaker pleads with the modern "daughters of Jerusalem" to be worthy of their glorious past and like the hard-pressed Zuleika, resist all temptations to forsake the faith. She then reinforces this plea with a second one to the "Mothers of Israel," bidding them make sure their daughters toe the line. As Mary Ryan observes in her study of women and the nineteenth-century public sphere, for ethnic minorities generally it was crucial that women—the bearers of the next generation—remain loyal.[32] But for Jews, who do not increase their numbers through conversion and who trace tribal membership only through the mother's line, this fidelity has special urgency, as women's failure to commit could, quite literally, bring the tribe to an end. From a Jewish perspective, therefore, a great deal more is at stake in this poem than the testing of one woman's faith, however glorious her martyrdom as a testimony to faith's power.

Louisa Anna uses sentimental conventions, then, not only to demonstrate the sublimity of Jewish women, who rival their Christian counterparts in the art of dying, but equally important, she uses them to create the emotional bonding and "racial" pride needed for group cohesion within the community itself. Like Rebekah Hyneman, whose paeans to Jewish womanhood, "Female Scriptural Characters," appeared in the *Occident* in the late 1840s and early 1850s, and like most other nineteenth-century Anglophone Jewish women poets with whom I am familiar, Louisa Anna is no equality feminist. (Hyneman's one poem explicitly on woman's rights defines them as Hannah Mather Crocker does.)[34] Rather, as in "Zuleika," she makes the idea of woman as conduit of "sentimental power" central to her thinking about ethnic experience. Insofar as women carry Israel's seed, they are the key to tribal survival. Like Zuleika, all Jewish women must be ready, therefore, to resist the blandishments of the dominant population—be it Muslim, as in "Zuleika," or Christian—sacrificing themselves, if they must, to insure the continuation of the community as a whole. However paradoxically, this very assimilated poem is about the dangers of assimilation, dangers whose reality, I would add, and speaking very personally, my own experience as a second-generation American of Jewish descent largely confirms.

If Jewish women writers were prepared to exploit the heroic/high-sentimental tradition of the "True Woman" as "martyr to the faith" to achieve group solidarity, Irish Roman Catholic poets were hardly loathe to do so. In "St. Agnes," the popular Irish poet Mary McMullen Ford ("Una") creates a figure of sublime Christian femininity that is virtually identical to Louisa Anna's Zuleika in most respects. "With clear eyes raised to Heaven she kneels in silent prayer, / And hears triumphal music resounding through the air; / She sees the glorious city whose portals open stand, / Revealing to her vision the noble martyr band / That she so soon shall follow, while angels trooping down / The sky, are twining lillies (*sic*) around her palm and crown." Like Zuleika, Agnes is beheaded, and her sacrifice is also not in vain. The two poems substantively differ only in their conclusions. Since "St. Agnes" is a Christian poem, the "conversions" that the saint works are not a matter of renewed commitment such as Louisa Anna sought. Rather, Agnes's body becomes a veritable baptismal font, its "warm, bright currents gushing from out her pure heart's tide / Baptize a thousand Christians where she for Christ has died."[34]

No less striking than the narrative similarities between these two poems are the ways in which the poets themselves are situated with respect to their communities at large. If, in the closing stanzas of "Zuleika," Louisa Anna's speaker takes on the biblically sanctioned role of the female prophet—a role that Hyneman also exploits in her series on biblical women—Ford after death was treated as if she were the sainted Agnes herself. Thus the memorial issue of *Irish World* dedicated to Ford (May 6, 1876) not only reprints "St. Agnes" but devotes its front page to a portrait bust of the poet surrounded by the various symbols of her nationality, faith, and art: an Irish harp, an American Flag, an angel, and a very angelic-looking muse (fig. 4). Above Ford's head floats what appears to be Agnes's own crown. In that passionate conflation of religion and nationalism that characterizes nineteenth-century Irish American patriotic thinking and about which I will have a good deal more to say in the next chapter, Ford is thus made one with her subject. No less than Agnes, it seems, she redeems souls, if not through her blood, then by the "warm, bright currents" of her verse. Just as Jews had female poet-prophets, who, like so many Jeremiahs, pointed the hard road to truth, so Irish Roman Catholics had female poet-saints who through their sacrifices kept faith in nation and God bright.

As with antebellum high-sentimentalists, the kind of power that these two minority women poets exercise in their poetry has nothing to do with the kinds of public agency that equality feminists sought. On the contrary, had Louisa Anna or Ford adopted an aggressively feminist platform, it is doubtful that either would have had an audience inside their own communities for long. Rather, the power they wield derives, as it did for the antebellum high-sentimentalists, from their willing subordination of self to community needs and to the qualities of purity and spirituality that their speakers project—their sentimental high-mindedness and self-abnegation in service to a greater cause. In postbellum minority communities as in antebellum society gener-ally, that is, women were voices of conscience, not agents with a vote. As in Ford's "Unite," their greatest contribution to politics, like Earle's in "On Reading . . . A. E. Grimke," was to urge men on:

Fig. 4. The Poetess Una, *Irish World* (1876)

No; brothers, friends, no more apart
    Like foes or strangers stand;
Unite, a noble brotherhood,
    To raise our trampled land;
No longer let the shameful taunt
    Upon our race be thrown:
"You fight the stranger's battles well,
    But can not fight your own."[35]

For Ford, it was only by inspiring men ("brothers, friends") that she could enact her political will.

As we shall see in the next chapter, the supporting role that Ford plays in "Unite" did not always fit comfortably when taken up by strong-minded women, but most minority poets appear to have accepted it willingly, proudly exploiting such power as it gave them. Given the gulf between traditional religious/cultural values and the progressive, "modern" social values with which assimilation into U.S. culture was associated, these women may well have believed themselves sufficiently "liberated" as it was.[36] At the same time, however, the fact that they did take this (indirect) route to power seriously compromises any argument for the counter-public sphere as a site for progressive opposition. On the contrary, at least where Western-style female modernity is concerned, the more opposed a particular counter-public sphere was to the dominant culture, the less likely it was to open itself to women's emancipation, and the fewer women its press was likely to publish as a result. The counter-public sphere was one solution to the exclusions of the dominant culture's public sphere, but it was a solution that carried with it exclusions of its own.

The vast majority of nineteenth-century U.S. minority women had no way to separate their political progress from both assimilation and genteelization. Genealogically speaking, the U.S. liberal subject was inherently the bourgeois subject, whether female or male, whether immigrant or native-born. To become a full-fledged member of U.S. society also meant, as Jacobson, Ignatiev, and others have argued, to become middle-class. If minority women were to share in the economic and social advantages life in the United States offered—from higher education to well-paid (and respectable) employment—they, like Bernard Shaw's Eliza Dolittle, had to recreate themselves. As Ignatiev puts it, they had to become white. It is no wonder, consequently, that in the postbellum period women like Louisa Anna and Ford declined the full leap, clinging to antebellum sentimental strategies their mainstream peers had largely abandoned, strategies that gave them power, but, as it were, not too much. In this context, both "Zuleika" and "St. Agnes" can be seen as way-stations along the same path, and we should not be surprised, therefore, that despite all the differences separating Christian and Jew, in their handling of their "True Woman" subject, these two poems are so very much alike.

The Poetry of Native American Difference

For reasons that seem fairly obvious, Native American writers' handling of the conventions of antebellum sentimental poetry takes a very different and more complicated course than that taken by the minority poets discussed thus far. No matter how closely associated antebellum literary conventions were with the dominant culture's values, its exclusionary tactics included, the Jewish and Irish women who employed these conventions did so by choice. They could have risked—as, indeed, some did—community rejection by writing in more explicitly feminist ways or, conversely, they could have remained true to the traditional forms of verse extant in their own communities. Although some might disagree, there is plenty of evidence to suggest that African American women poets also used these conventions by choice, taking substantial pride in the aura of gentility they brought thereby to their verse. Mrs. Mary E. Ashe Lee, "a graduate of Wilberforce University," writes Mrs. N. F. Mossell in *The Work of the Afro-American Woman* (1894), "has, by her intelligence and sympathy, done much to inspire the students . . . with a love for broad culture, true refinement and high moral aims." Of "Afmerica," itself, Mossell writes that the poem's thoughts are "expressed in a most chaste and exquisite style."[37] Mrs. Mossell basks in the light of Mrs. Lee's achievements, knowing that these achievements were, whatever else, proof positive that black women did have a right to their rights—to an education, culture, and a morally respectable life. For not only would they take advantage of these opportunities, they would excel at them.

As Anna Brackett's piece on Hampton Institute makes clear, however, Native American students were far less enthusiastic when it came to education in the white man's ways—not surprisingly, since their primary motivation for assimilation came from the barrel of a gun. When the young Cherokee schoolgirl, Qua-Tsy, published an essay entitled "Female Influence" in her school newspaper, *The Wreath of Cherokee Rose Buds*, in 1855, one simply cannot be sure, therefore, how much she actually believes what she says and how much she is merely "parroting" what she has been told she should believe. Citing Madame de Staël as a modern example of female power, Qua-Tsy lays out a program all but indistinguishable from the doctrine of True Womanhood at its ideological worst: "The elevation of the Cherokee people," she opines, "depends upon the females. . . . How necessary it is that each one of us should strive to rightly improve and discipline our minds . . . so that when we are called to other stations and our field of effect widens, *our influence* may have an elevating and ennobling effect upon all with whom we come in contact."[38] It is possible that Qua-Tsy really believed this stuff; but in the same issue one also finds wicked Lily Lee's "A Literary Day among the Birds." In this mock school assembly, the students—"Eight pretty green PARROTS" who speak their little parts "with art"—are the only bits of color around (*NAWP* 426). The remaining speakers are all parodic versions of whites: drab, pompous, long-winded, and male. It's a very funny poem if you get the joke, but one wonders what Lily Lee's teachers made of it and also what Qua-Tsy did.

The same problem arises far more somberly thirty years later when one tries to evaluate the sincerity of Indian student writing in the *Southern Workman*. Describing the changing situation for women in her own Dakota community, Zallie Rulo, a young Hampton graduate, expresses pride that old ways were breaking down, especially where gender roles were concerned. The men no longer sit around and let the women do all the work, Rulo explains in a speech delivered to her "sisters" at Hampton, but now "many of them live differently. . . . many of the Indian men carry the wood and water for the women and they never think now to ask the women to plow or cut hay."[39] This again sounds "good," but then one remembers Sitting Bull's plea to Alice Fletcher, made not long before he was murdered in 1890, a plea that puts Rulo's assertions in a very different light:

> Take pity on my women, for they have no future. The young men can be like the white men, till the soil, supply food and clothing; they will take the work out of the hands of the women, and the women to whom we have owed everything in the past, will be stripped of all which gave them power and position among the people. Give a future to my women.[40]

Granted that Rulo probably spent years in an Indian boarding school, would even a young woman so sequestered (brainwashed?), have been utterly blind to what was happening to women on her reservation or to the abysmal failure of the government's Indian policies? What did she really see when she returned to the reservation? How did she really feel?

I raise these questions because the high-sentimental political poetry written by Native American women at the end of the century manifestly positions itself very differently from that of the minority poetry discussed thus far. As the work of E. Pauline Johnson (Tekahionwake, Canadian Mohawk) and Zitkala-Sa (Gertrude Bonin, Sioux) suggests, lessons in "female influence" were not wholly lost on Indian women, but they did not necessarily absorb them in the name of "uplift" or assimilation. On the contrary, insofar as Johnson and Zitkala-Sa deploy the rhetorical strategies of high-sentimental sympathy politics, they do so as did white and black women abolitionists in the antebellum period. That is, they use them to make those who oppress aware of what they do. Thus, for example, in "A Cry from an Indian Wife" (1885), the poem whose recital initiated Johnson's career as an "Iroquois poet-entertainer," the power lies in the speaker's weaving back and forth between expressions of sympathy for each culture. As half-British herself, Johnson may well have felt real sympathy for British losses in the Northwest rebellion. But in this empathic presentation of the Indian side, she also uses her dual perspective to force white audiences into understanding what it feels like to be on the wrong end of someone else's gun. The result is a chiasmic structuring of the rhetoric that reverses the poem's viewpoint almost line by line.

> One pleads her God to guard some sweet-faced child
> That marches on toward the North-West wild.
> The other prays to shield her love from harm,
> To strengthen his young, proud uplifted arm.
> Ah, how her white face quivers thus to think,
> *Your* tomahawk his life's best blood will drink.
> She never thinks of my wild aching breast,
> Nor prays for your dark face and eagle crest.
>
> (*NAWP* 328)

By crisscrossing the thoughts of a white and an Indian woman in this way, Johnson forced her white audience to confront the narcissistic element in its own ethnocentrism. Try walking in the Indian's moccasins for a mile, the poem seems to say; then you will understand our rage. The explosive audience response that greeted "Cry" when Johnson first recited it before the Young Liberal Club of Toronto in 1892 argues strongly for the strategy's success.[41]

If Johnson uses the sufferings of young soldiers, and of wives, mothers, and daughters, to create sympathetic identification between Indians and her white audience, in "A Sioux Woman's Love for Her Grandchild," Zitkala-Sa uses one of the most reliable weapons in the high sentimentalist's arsenal, the figure of the aged grandmother, to bring the horror of genocide home.[42] In this poem, an Indian grandmother gives up her life rather than abandon her granddaughter to General Custer's marauding troops. Appearing in 1917 in the *American Indian Magazine*, Zitkala-Sa's poem is pure nineteenth-century verse despite its off-rhymes and choppy rhythms, a high-sentimental poem published almost sixty years after the style went out of vogue: "'Gainst the sudden flashing, angry fires, a figure / Stood, propped by a cane. A soul in torture / Sacrificing life than leave behind her lost one. / Greater love hath no man; love surpassing reason."[43] In such lines with their echoes of the New Testament, Christianity's chickens come home to roost. Like the abolitionist poets before her, Zitkala-Sa turns Christian culture's deepest moral sentiments against it, compelling whites to understand what they have done by appealing to presumptively shared values between otherwise radically disparate cultures. That is, like the antislavery writers, Zitkala-Sa manipulates the ironic gap between what the dominant culture says it believes and how it actually behaves, giving the Indians thereby the high moral ground, and leaving whites to choke on their own hypocrisy. The same twist appears in hundreds of abolitionist poems also.

Yet, even as one says this, the problem confronting nineteenth-century minority women writers, whether they chose to embrace or criticize the dominant culture's values and behavior, also becomes painfully clear. Unlike the other poets discussed in this chapter, Johnson and Zitkala-Sa addressed their poems to the dominant population, using the latter's own faith in the universality of its "moral sentiments" against it. But this strategy no more escapes co-option finally than does the outright adoption of bourgeois values by other minority writers. As Sacvan Bercovitch observes in what could de-scribed as a negative spin on the Habermasian public sphere, the liberal democracy of the United States survives because its internal mechanisms enable it to swallow up all forms of resistance. As a site for the working through of differences, the U.S. public sphere is, finally, a one-way street. To achieve full parity within it, the intransigence of minority difference must be sacrificed for membership in a greater whole. For minority communities, as Native Americans had, perhaps, the best reason to know, assimilation thus carried with it a terrible price, potentially, the yielding up of identity itself. As a friend of mine put it when speaking of our identity as Americans of Jewish descent, it is only a matter of time before Orthodox Jews will be the only "American" Jews left, the only group within U.S. Judaism, that is, for whom being Jewish is something more than having bagels and lox at Sunday brunch.

In the next chapter, I will look at how the dream of ethnic purity, or group cohesion, and the tensions around assimilation and difference played out in the lives and poetry of four minority women poets of exceptional— indeed, historically unique—visibility: Frances Harper, Fanny Parnell, Emma Lazarus, and E. Pauline Johnson. As poets, these four women enjoyed iconic status in their own communities and/or the society at large, a status that has helped to obscure many of the painful ironies of their situations. As I have insisted, the values embedded in sentimental poetry were class values even more than they were gender or racial values. Especially when used on behalf of those in the community who bore the brunt of inequalities—typically the uneducated and the poor—high sentimentality's sympathy politics was therefore problematic from the start. The evocation of sentimentality by strong minority women poets on behalf of the subjugated in their own com-munities only repeated this problem in a different key. The question then becomes how one evaluates the role such poets played, whether for good or ill, in trying to lead others to where they themselves already were; and the answers to this question may prove as slippery as the role(s) themselves and the discourses these minority women evolved in order to perform them.

4

Harper, Parnell, Lazarus, and Johnson

> Invited to the houses of individuals of wealth and distinc-
> tion (which frequently happened), [Phillis] would eat at a
> separate side-table, modestly apart from the rest of the
> company.
> —MARGARETTA ODELL,
> *Memoir of Phillis Wheatley, 1834*[1]

Building on chapter 3, I now want to look more closely at four poets who, despite vastly different backgrounds, were situated with respect to their constituencies in strikingly similar ways: Frances Ellen Watkins Harper (1825–1911), Fanny Parnell (1848–1882), Emma Lazarus (1849–1887), and, in Canada, E. Pauline Johnson (Mohawk) (1861–1913). Harper, Parnell, Lazarus, and Johnson were intensely passionate poets who used high-sentimental rhetorical strategies on behalf of those whom they identified as their "race," "people," or "nation." Yet for different reasons, none of these poets fully belonged to the community she served. On the contrary, each led the equivalent of a "double life," free to move with more or less ease between the dominant population and her minority subculture. "Race women," these poets dedicated themselves to creating solidarity in their own communities even while representing them to the outside world. Precisely because they could speak the oppressor's language so well, they, like the first U.S. minority poet to walk this path, Phillis Wheatley, were invited into homes where, except as servants, their "people" would not otherwise be found.

In this chapter, I want to examine what it was about these four poets' lives, their poetry, and the social circumstances under which they wrote that let them become such charismatically compelling spokespersons for people in many ways fundamentally unlike themselves. That is, I want to examine what it was about their positioning within and without their own communities that allowed them to function as representative when manifestly they were not—indeed, when it was their exceptionality that enabled them not just to write but to be heard. In order to keep faith with the substantial differences dividing these poets from each other, I will treat each one separately before returning to a more general consideration of what it might mean when the politics of minority communities are mediated by female figures whose importance for their people rests all but entirely, as we shall see, in their power to dream.

Frances Ellen Watkins Harper and Moses

Over the past few decades, African American scholars have increasingly stressed the role that a quasi-religious commitment to community building has played in the evolution of nineteenth-century black women's literature. In *Doers of the Word*, for example, Carla Peterson argues that women like Maria Stewart, Sojourner Truth, Harriet A. Jacobs, and Frances E. W. Harper, patterned themselves on the model of the itinerant evangelical preacher, "insisting on their right to preach the gospel, to lecture, and to write on such topics as religious evangelicism, abolitionism, moral reform, temperance, and women's rights." Deeply imbued with "faith in the performative power of the word," these women, Peterson believes, understood speaking and writing as constituting "a form of doing, of social action continuous with their social, political, and cultural work."[2] In *Spiritual Interrogations*, Katherine Bassard writes similarly. Of the spirituals, she argues that far from passively reflecting some hypothetical African essence, they should be viewed as forms of "community building."[3] By "*performing community*," they encode "the means by which boundaries of self/other, insider/outsider become negotiated, as a challenge to racial proscriptions and definitions" that served the society at large.[4]

In 1873, the black poet and novelist, Frances Harper describes her sense of vocation along the same quasi-religious lines: "I hardly know what I shall succeed in doing, but I want to be a living loving force, not a mere intellectual force, eager and excited only for my own welfare; but a moral and spiritual force. A woman who can and will do something for a woman, especially for our own women because they will need me the most."[5] If Harper's stress on "moral and spiritual force" suggests the religious basis of her community-building efforts, her use of "loving" suggests that creating the affective ties of communal bonding was her principal concern, whether in writing or in her life. "My race needs me," Harper wrote from Alabama in 1870, "if I will only be faithful."[6] For Harper, being "faithful" meant making her political, social, religious, and artistic goals one; and this is precisely what this free-born, middle-class black woman did, committing herself to a lifetime of unrelenting labor on behalf of those less fortunate than herself.

But are those like Harper, who seek to build community, part of that community at the same time, or are they, for all their dedication, sacrifice, and zeal, located somewhere else, some Archimedean point, as it were, outside the society that they want to "uplift"? According to her editor, Frances Smith Foster, Harper, unlike most women reformers of her period, left no diaries or journals at her death, nor did she write an autobiography. But a comment on Harper by the white political activist Phebe A. Hanaford, cited by Foster in *Daughters of America* (1882), is telling: "Frances E. W. Harper is one of the most eloquent women lecturers in the country," Hanaford declares. "She is one of the colored women of whom white women may be proud, and to whom the abolitionists can point and declare that a race which could show such women never ought to have been held in bondage."[7] Not typicalness, but exceptionality, gives Harper representational authority among abolitionists, the same exceptionality that, as she herself understood, allowed her to speak for those who "need[ed her] the most."

There is other evidence suggesting that Harper knew she was an anomaly. During an 1870 lecture tour in the South, for example, she wrote to a friend: "you would laugh if you were to hear some of the remarks which my lectures call forth: 'She is a man,' again 'She is not colored, she is painted.'" "Still," Harper comforted herself, "I am standing with my race on the threshold of a new era, and though some be far past me in the learning of the schools, yet to-day, with my limited and fragmentary knowledge, I may help the race forward a little" (126–27). Harper did stand with her race, working assiduously throughout her life to improve its lot. But her modest framing of her desire—"my limited and fragmentary knowledge"—should not obscure the driving literary ambition behind it, an ambition that issued in hundreds of poems, short stories, essays, lectures, and letters, along with several novels— an impressive output even by nineteenth-century standards. Having produced this literature, a good bit of which deals with humanitarian concerns not specific to any one race, how could Harper not know that much as she wanted to stand with her race, she also stood apart?

Harper's awareness of the problematic aspects of her positioning—inside and outside at once—is nowhere more evident than in her blank verse epyllion, or little epic, "Moses: A Story of the Nile" (1869), a poem which, according to Carla Peterson, deals with "the problematics of leadership under conditions of slavery."[8] In retelling the story of the great Jewish leader— a charismatic figure for nineteenth-century blacks—Harper valorizes the voluntarism of Moses' gesture, and the isolation that results, an isolation whose fullest expression is his unattended death on Mount Nebo. As Harper tells it, Moses' heroism lies in his willing decision to "be" what he is not, throwing in his lot with an oppressed people with whom he has, in terms of situation and expectations, nothing in common. Challenged by his foster mother, the pharaoh's daughter, to explain why he would "rather choose / The badge of servitude and toil" than remain with her, surrounded by royal comforts, Moses replies with words that reverberate throughout Harper's career. "I feel an earnest purpose binding all / My soul unto a strong resolve, which bids / Me put aside all other ends and aims, / Until the hour shall come when God—the God / Our fathers loved and worshipped—shall break our chains, / And lead our willing feet to freedom" (139).

If, as Harper suggests, Moses' heroism lies here, in his willing renunciation of his own privilege in order to wear the badge ("chains") of another's oppression, it was a heroism that his own "restless and rebellious race" appreciates tepidly at best: "Born slaves, they did not love / The freedom of the wild more than their pots of flesh." The true evil of slavery, Harper's narrator observes, is not the affliction of the flesh, which is "curse" enough, but what it does to the soul: "For when the chains were shaken from their limbs, / They failed to strike the impress from their souls." Moses, who, despite all he gave up, "ne'er turned regretful eyes upon / The past," finds his "saddest trial" in leading people who, as he painfully discovers, want only to go "back where they might bind anew / Their broken chains" (162–63). When Moses dies at the poem's end, he dies alone: "not one / Of all that mighty throng who had trod with him / In triumph through the parted flood was there" (164), a sad conclusion indeed for a man who sacrificed so much to redeem his people.

Peterson argues that Harper modifies the bleakness of this picture in the Aunt Chloe sequence in *Sketches of Southern Life* (1872), a volume inspired by the same 1870 lecture tour mentioned earlier. But while both Chloe's identity as a former slave and her southern speech mark her in Peterson's words as one of the "common folk," even Chloe does not escape Moses' fate.[9] On the contrary, the more this elderly ex-slave woman functions as the moral/political/spiritual voice of her community—the one who holds firm when others quail—the less like those around her she seems. "Some of our people remind me of sheep without a shepherd," Harper wrote confidentially in the same 1870 letter in which she describes her audience's confusion (127). Representing a rare moment of discouragement in Harper's writing, this comment casts its shadow on the sunny optimism of the Aunt Chloe sequence also.

The great appeal of Harper's Aunt Chloe poems lies first and foremost in Chloe herself. As a singularly tough-minded critic of Southern slaveholders, Chloe feels authentic to the bone. Ironically named, as Barbara McCaskill has noted, after Tom's wife in *Uncle Tom's Cabin*, Harper's "Aunt Chloe" is hardly the ideal slave-victim populating the white abolitionist imaginary.[10] On the contrary, far from passively suffering all, Aunt Chloe expresses just the kind of anger one would expect from someone so abused. Having seen her own children sold to pay debts, Chloe, for example, has no sympathy for "old Mistus" when the latter's only son dies fighting for the Confederacy. Once Chloe is reunited with her son, Jakey, after the war, she gleefully chortles: "I'm richer now than Mistus, / Because I have got my son; / And Mister Thomas he is dead, / And she's got 'nary one" (208). Certainly not a "Christlike" observation, nor a turning of the other cheek; but by that token, a good deal more plausible—and probably infinitely healthier—than Uncle Tom's Christlike refusal of any and all vindictive desires. There's no letting white folk off the hook here.

It is not just whites who get the sharp edge of Chloe's tongue, however. Like Moses, Chloe, too, is determined to bring her erring flock in line. She is especially hard on the men, who, from her perspective, were failing dismally to appreciate the value of their newly won vote—a real sore point for Harper, one of a small group of black women highly prominent in the women's suffrage movement.[11] Far from embracing their new freedom, Chloe complains, men were letting local politicos "honey-fugle" them out of it. "And if any man should ask me," she sanctimoniously declares, "If I would sell my vote, / I'd tell him I was not the one / To change and turn my coat; / If freedom seem'd a little rough / I'd weather through the gale; / And as to buying up my vote, / I hadn't it for sale" (202–3). Worse, these men were trading their votes for the equivalent of the biblical mess of pottage: "three sticks of candy" or sugar mixed with sand. However, even exchanges for solid food earn Chloe's disapprobation: "You ought to seen Aunt Kitty raise, / And heard her blaze away; / She gave the meat and flour a toss, / And said they should not stay" (203).

It is, of course, neither impossible nor even improbable that an elderly former slave woman like Chloe would take such a high-minded position, but it does set her apart from the many whom she berates. Insofar as Chloe understands the need to delay gratification—"If freedom seem'd a little rough," etcetera—she exhibits precisely the kind of future-oriented insight one wants in a leader; but the need for such people derives precisely from their rarity. The leader is one who fills the social niche that, left unfilled, would put the entire community at risk. Nevertheless, at this point, the distance between Chloe and her flock begins to look suspiciously like that between Moses and those who "Born slaves . . . did not love / The freedom of the wild more than their pots of flesh."

Harper's own recorded position on the vote supports this conclusion: "I do not believe in unrestricted and universal suffrage," Harper declared at a post–Fifteenth Amendment woman's rights convention. "I believe in moral and educational tests. I do not believe that the most ignorant and brutal man is better prepared to add value to the strength and durability of the government than the most cultured, upright, and intelligent woman. I do not think that willful ignorance should swamp earnest intelligence at the ballot box."[12] Stanton and Anthony used the same argument in their fulminations against the amendment; and it was this argument that opened the doors wide to racism in the women's suffrage movement, as "expediency" ended the divide between Northern and Southern white women.[13] Yet is Chloe all that far from the Stanton-Anthony position?

Drawing on the license permitted old age, Chloe, now "rising sixty," presents herself as the model for how newly emancipated slaves should behave and how they should take advantage of their new-won freedoms: voting, taking action in the community, learning to read, getting their own homes. "So I got a pair of glasses, / And straight to work I went, / And never stopped till I could read / The hymns and Testament. / Then I got a little cabin—/ A place to call my own—/ And I felt as independent / As the queen upon her throne" (206). But no matter how valuable these very bourgeois attainments are in themselves, their net effect makes Chloe a singularly hard act to follow. Harper's very commitment to community building compels her to make Chloe the ideal, the ideal as Harper—herself an unusually proud, intelligent, hard-working, and courageous woman—wanted it to be. But admirable as this ideal is, by that very token, it is not one to which many ex-slaves, especially those suffering direst poverty in the deep South, could easily relate.

Although throughout the Chloe poems, Chloe exhibits strong bonds with other women—using phrases like "we women radicals" (204)—Harper is telling the ex-slaves' stories her way. "If we have had no past," she wrote in 1867, "it is well for us to look hopefully to the future" (124). But African Americans did have a past, just as they had a present. They were not one but many; and like Moses' stiff-necked Hebrews, they were given to straying, not behaving as those who led them thought that they should. Insofar as Harper, like other promoters of uplift, wanted to transform her constituency into people like herself, with the same bourgeois values, one could say that her poetry testifies less to community building than to the deeply entrenched class divisions that characterize the politics of difference in the African American community to this day. These were divisions embedded in the class structure of uplift itself. Despite shared color and all that brought with it, Harper and her constituency lived in some respects in different worlds, as her comment on sheep and her position on the vote both suggest. To say this is not to criticize Harper, who gave all she had to a cause in which she deeply and rightly believed, but to accept the finite limits of leadership in an imperfect world. Each in her own way, the three other poets whom I discuss next fared no better, their idealism—an idealism to which, as a rule, only the entitled have access—rendering their enterprise, not to mention, their representativeness, problematic from the start.

Fanny Parnell's Funeral(s)

Distant though Harper was from the former slaves she viewed as her race, this distance shrinks to nothing compared to that separating Fanny Parnell from those for whom she spoke. A granddaughter of the American naval hero Charles Stewart, Parnell, who had been born in Ireland, was of mixed Irish and Irish American descent and, like her illustrious brother, Charles

Parnell, a Protestant. As a woman, let alone a member of the ruling Anglo-Irish Ascendancy, Parnell could have remained apolitical and suffered no disapprobation, at least in her own elite set. Like her far more famous brother and like her sister, Anna, she became an activist instead, bringing her wealth, education, social prestige, and sense of entitlement to the Irish cause. If Charles Parnell was dubbed Ireland's "uncrowned king" for his efforts on behalf of Ireland's impoverished peasantry, his sister was Ireland's (exiled) Princess Di. When she died prematurely on July 20, 1882, "the whole Irish race" mourned—at least so claimed the Boston *Pilot*, mouthpiece for the flamboyant John Boyle O'Reilly, poet, patriot, and journalist.[14] In its grief the Irish American community gave Parnell what may be the most elaborate funeral ever held for a poet in U.S. history. What I will ask here is, why? Beyond the obvious gratitude Irish Americans felt toward the Parnells generally, what led a community of highly political, hard-nosed men to mourn with such extravagance the passing of a young woman so utterly unlike themselves in every conceivable way except their shared passionate commitment to Ireland? What were they to Fanny? What was Fanny to them?

To answer these questions, let me begin by describing Parnell's funerals, for there were in fact two, and both, according to the *Pilot*, were stirring affairs. The first, held immediately after Parnell's death, took place in the New Jersey home of her widowed mother, with whom she had been living at the time. In attendance were a multitude of Irish and Irish American Land Leaguers, plus assorted other male notables, including Ernest Longfellow, Wendell Phillips, and several direct descendants of Thomas Jefferson. Surrounding Parnell's coffin were multiple gifts, plus four huge harps, donated by individual Land Leagues. Mlle Rosa d'Erina, a member of one of the Ladies' Land Leagues that Fanny herself had founded, sang "Angels Ever Bright and Fair." At a follow-up meeting, the Boston Land League passed a series of resolutions in Parnell's memory, this woman who "worship[ped] at the same political altar" as themselves. Her "heart," the Land Leaguers fulsomely declared, "could feel for the sorrows, the hardships and the miseries of [the Irish] people. . . . [her] pen and tongue, ever eloquent," burned "with the fire of patriotism and love of country."

Elaborate as these ceremonies were, however, they were also strictly preliminary. Parnell's remains were lodged in a receiving vault in Trenton, there to await repatriation to Ireland, where she expressed the wish to be buried. Unsympathetic with Fanny's desire, Charles Parnell blocked the transfer. After months of wrangling, his wishes prevailed. With great solemnity, Parnell was interred in Mount Auburn Cemetery in Cambridge, Massachusetts, instead, joining in death a host of American literary luminaries, Margaret Fuller, Fanny Osgood, Henry Wadsworth Longfellow, and James Russell Lowell, among others. The ceremonies bringing Parnell to Cambridge constitute her second funeral, an event unique in the annals of American literary history.

According to the *Pilot*, which gave a blow-by-blow description of the event for those who could not attend, Parnell's brother and grief-stricken mother included, the cortege went by train, ferry, and hearse, the latter "drawn by six beautiful white horses, accompanied by eighteen pall bearers . . . [and] preceded by an open barouche, containing a number of floral offerings . . . decorated with American and Irish flags on either side and surmounted by six white plumes." Thousands "of both sexes" waited along parade routes in Philadelphia, New York, and Boston itself. In Philadelphia, the procession included "some seven thousand persons." At the train depot "the body was taken to the second floor, where the coffin lid was removed," for viewing. (The face, we are told, was so well preserved it was "difficult to realize that Miss Parnell had been dead for nearly three months.") In New York City, the procession went "up Broadway from Twenty-third Street through Fifth Avenue and Forty-second to the Grand Central Depot," with dense masses of people in attendance the entire way. At Grand Central "the casket was reverently carried into the depot and placed in the special train for Boston."

In Boston, Fanny again went on display, this time at the Beacon Street mansion of relatives, the Tudors, in whose vault she would be buried.[15] Tickets were required to see her. Mlle d'Erina again sang "Angels Ever Bright and Fair," by a bier once more surrounded by offerings, including a huge harp made of flowers and a lyre sporting a broken string. Pronouncing her casket "one of the most elaborate of its kind ever manufactured in this country"—as doubtless it was—the *Pilot* describes it in lavish detail. Other than the ubiquitous Mlle. d'Erina, women are again all but absent from the *Pilot's* account, appearing only as semianonymous donors of gifts. Fanny Parnell's funeral(s) were overwhelmingly male affairs—but the question remains, why? Aside from the debt the Irish owed her brother, who clearly wanted no part in these proceedings, what led these hard-bitten, thoroughly chauvinistic men to bury Fanny Parnell with such extravagant pomp and ceremony that sad October day?

The excessive rituals of mourning characterizing Parnell's second funeral—like those accompanying the funeral of Princess Diana—suggest that the poet, like the Princess, was as much an emotional as a political symbol to those who mourned her. According to Hasia Diner's study of nineteenth-century Irish American women, Parnell was "one of the few women in the Irish nationalist movement."[16] Those remembered today—Constance Markiewicz, Maud Gonne, Lady Wilde, and Fanny's sister Anna—came, like Fanny herself, from Ireland's Anglo-Irish literary-intellectual elite. Unlike Fanny, however, they lived in Ireland and involved themselves directly in Irish political affairs. Companioning her widowed mother in the ancestral home in New Jersey, in what Anna called Ireland's "empire beyond the seas,"[17] Fanny had no such option. Practically speaking, her political activities on behalf of the Irish were confined to organizing Ladies' Land Leagues, auxiliary money-making groups whose existence, like that of their male counterparts, was abruptly terminated by Charles Parnell in 1883. Situated in a community that viewed politics as a male affair,[18] Fanny Parnell should have been no more than a miniscule footnote to history. And that is probably all she would have been, despite her family, had it not been for one thing: her verse. It was here, in her poems, that Parnell's extraordinary emotional bond to these men was forged.

Although Parnell's funeral was a tribute to her remarkable family, it was also, I would suggest, exactly what it claimed to be: a tribute to Fanny herself. In the two-year space between 1880 and her death in 1882, Parnell took her prodigious commitment to Irish nationalism and turned it into violent, angry, passionate, inspired poems, placing them, as the Boston Land Leaguers put it, with a certain ingenuous charm, on "the same political altar" at which they themselves worshiped. "Her lyre," O'Reilly declared, "would only respond to one breeze—nationality." The "magnetic and almost startling force" of her "noble heart-work," he opined, bringing nationalism, gender, politics, and high sentimentality squarely together, made her "that which crystallizes the efforts and aspirations of a popular movement—a Poet."[19] This is high praise indeed for a poet who mockingly referred to her work as "'varses,'"[20] and published perhaps forty poems in all. However, it is also the truth. Parnell's poems are stunningly, unforgettably, what O'Reilly says they are, poems of "magnetic and almost startling force," with militant rhythms and a heavy use of hypnotic repetition. In these poems, which at least one nineteenth-century reader judged too vulgar to be feminine, Fanny transformed the "noble heart-work" of female high sentimentality into expressions of raw power and "masculine" rage—no weak-kneed sympathy here.[21]

Parnell's poetry splits between two basic kinds: love songs to Ireland and tour de forces in the jeremiadic tradition, the latter melding high-sentimental moral/political goals with an emotional rhetoric of sheer outrage. Insofar as both kinds of poems fuse politics with religion, and erotic with patriotic desire, they are both extraordinary in their own way, creating a nationalistic discourse in which everything Irish is (at least in theory) good, and all that hurts Ireland is (no theory about it) demonically evil. In poems of the first type, like "She is not Dead!" Parnell speaks boldly as lover: "Who said that thou wast dead, O darling of my heart? / My fairest one amid the daughters, / My lily, brooding on the waters,—/ Who said that thou wast dead, and I from thee must part?" The biblical echoes are deliberate. Ireland is a reincarnation of the Queen of Sheba, semidivine, the chosen one. The roses that her "lovers strew before [her] shrine" are dipped in their own hearts' blood.[22] And if Ireland is the Promised Land, the lost Eden, the beloved Queen, then, as in "Michael Davitt," Ireland's champions are types of Solomon, Moses, and Christ. "Out of the slime and the squalor, / Out of the slough of de-spond, / Out of the yoke of Egypt, / Out of the gyve and bond; / . . . / Up to the heights of freedom, / Up to the hills of light, / Up to the holy places, / Where the dim eyes see aright,—/ . . . / [Davitt] has gone to tread the mar-tyr's way."[23]

If Ireland's defenders do no wrong, however, her enemies, including those Irish who fail Fanny's very high standard of behavior for them, can do no right. In "What Shall We Weep For?" the speaker bids her readers not weep for their own suffering but for the vengeance that God—and they—will someday wreak on Britain. The latter is no Queen of Sheba but "the Scarlet Woman" of Revelation, the Whore of Babylon, "that's drunken with the blood and tears of her slaves, / Who goes forth to slay with a psalm-tune, and builds her churches on graves."[24] In "To the Land Leaguers," perhaps Parnell's most powerfully visionary political poem, the speaker prophesies an ultimate worldwide Armageddon, pitting poor against rich. "From each far land whence echoes the heart-beat of our race, / Each home where labor's bondage has left its branding trace, / Each breast that feels the trampling of the iron hooves of caste, / And knows its cry is helpless to laws the rich have passed. / . . . / From every jail and brothel, from every death-bed ditch, / The cry is swelling—surging—*Now cursed be the rich!*"[25] Fanny, it should be noted, is energetically cursing her own caste and class here.

Nor was Parnell any easier on her gender. In "To My Fellow-Women," she excoriates Irish American women for their indifference to the plight of their starving "sisters" across the ocean: "But ye sweep in your silks and laces here, in your new found honors proud, / While over the stream the corpse lips call, from many a woman's shroud."[26] Last, not least, she excoriates Irish men also. Indeed, in "To the Irish Farmers—Hold the Harvest!" she all but flays them alive for failing to do their patriotic duty: "Now are you men, or are you kine, ye tillers of the soil? / Would you be free, or evermore, the rich man's cattle, toil? / The shadow on the dial hangs, that points the fated hour, / Now *hold your own*! or, branded slaves, forever cringe and cower / . . . / Let not one sordid churl pollute the Nation's natal hour."[27]

"Poetry," Parnell's biographer, Jane McL. Côté, comments, "offered a Vic-torian woman one of the few acceptable ways of expressing strong, even violent sentiments and emotions which would have been condemned as fa-natic, unseemly, or hysterical in prose."[28] Few Victorian women on either side of the Atlantic took greater advantage of this potential than did Parnell. Neither male, nor living any longer in Ireland, trapped thousands of miles from the land she loved and the people whose cause she embraced, Parnell produced awesomely powerful poems that rage against their own disem-powerment; and, I would suggest, it was precisely because Fanny wrote so blatantly from this position that the men whose cause she shared so loved her. Unable to confront their own impotence, trapped, as she was, in a land of exile, worshiping at "the same political altar" that she did, these expatriate Irishmen found their hungers mirrored in hers. Slipping the jesses of gender, Parnell flew straight into the molten core of her own frustrated desire, voicing their desire as well:

Vein of my heart, light of mine eyes,
Pulse of my life, star of my skies,
Dimmed is thy beauty, sad are thy sighs,
Fairest and saddest, what shall I do for thee?
          Ireland, mother!

Vain, ah vain is a woman's prayer!
Vain is a woman's hot despair;
Naught can she do, naught can she dare,—
I am a woman, I can do naught for thee,
          Ireland, mother!

Hast thou not sons, like the ocean-sands?
Hast thou not sons, with brave hearts and hands?
Hast thou not *heirs* for thy broad, bright lands?
What have they done,—or what will they do for thee?
          Ireland, mother?

Were I a man from thy glorious womb,
I'd hurl the stone from thy living tomb;
Thy grief should be joy, and light thy gloom,
Thy rose should gleam 'mid thy golden broom;
Thy marish wastes should blossom and bloom;
I'd smite thy foes with thy own long doom,
While God's heaped judgments should round them loom;
Were I a man, lo! this would I do for thee,
          Ireland, mother![29]

There is something terribly poignant as well as ironic here. Whatever these Irish American men thought they buried that October day, it was not Fanny Parnell, the historical personage, born, according to O'Reilly, "at Avondale, the family estate, in county Wicklow, Ireland," and dying in her mother's ancestral home in Bordentown, New Jersey.[30] As herself, Parnell had no connection to these men, explaining perhaps why they could treat her remains as they did. Fanny was not a woman to them, let alone a member of their "family" or community. Her poems had articulated their hopes and their despairs, their glimpses of the Promised Land, and their yearning for it, their shame, their rage, and their frustration, and that was what they buried: the voice that gave their passions tongue. What they mourned was themselves, their loss of home and manhood and the country of their desire. If

the intensity of Parnell's passion measures less her "Irishness" than the degree to which she romanticized an identity that she—a woman, well-heeled
and Anglo-Irish at that—never had, this was an identity which her
mourners could not claim either, not so long as they too remained in Ireland's "empire beyond the seas."

Emma Lazarus and the Jews

Unlike Harper, Emma Lazarus shared a good deal with Fanny Parnell: a
privileged childhood, early death, and posthumous mythologizing in her
own community. However, there are also striking differences. Most notably,
of the poets discussed in this chapter, Parnell is the most consistently political, her "lyre" vibrating, as O'Reilly put it, to only one "breeze," "nationalism." Lazarus, on the other hand, began her literary career outside the ethnic
pale, sensitive to Jewish issues but not emphasizing them in her verse. Born
into a wealthy New York family, Lazarus traced her roots to Sephardic Jews
expelled from Spain at the end of the fifteenth century. Her ancestors came
to North America early in the eighteenth century. Cocooned by her family's
wealth, Lazarus, until close to her thirtieth year, never seems to have seriously questioned her national identity as American. On the contrary, determined not to let minority status hold her back, she put most of her considerable energy into what might best be called, "making it" in the U.S. literary
mainstream.

Lazarus ranks among the most aggressive literary women of her generation.[31] At the tender age of nineteen, she kicked off her campaign for literary
recognition by sending Emerson her first book, *Poems and Translations,
Written between the Ages of Fourteen and Sixteen* (1867). To the well-bred but
provincial Emersons, Jews, it seems, were an exotic life form, and Emma
soon became something of a pet to the Concord sage.[32] By the mid-1870s,
when Emerson earned Lazarus's ire by not including her in his fashionable
anthology, *The New Parnassus*, she no longer needed him anyway. Her second volume, *Admetus and Other Poems* (1871), received good reviews, and
her circle of literary acquaintances included, or soon would include, some of
the best-known names in the business: Thomas Wentworth Higginson, Richard Gilder, Ivan Turgenev, Henry James, and John Burroughs. Her poems, no
better or worse than most genteel poetry, were appearing regularly in mainstream literary journals, the *Atlantic* excepted. At her death in 1887, Whittier
and Browning were among those mourning her loss in a string of testi-
monials proudly reprinted in the *American Hebrew*.

Lazarus's posthumous reputation registers little of this and rests instead on
her contribution to minority letters instead: she is remembered as the first
American Jewish woman poet with name recognition, a pre-Herzl prophet of
Zionism (the call for a Jewish "homeland"), an assiduous worker for the

betterment of East European Jewish immigrants, and the renowned author of "The New Colossus," undoubtedly the best-known sonnet in U.S. literary history. Nevertheless, as Bette Roth Young argues in *Emma Lazarus in Her World* (1995), Lazarus came to her minority writer identity relatively late and not without ambivalence.

> Emma Lazarus was never "radical," nor was she comfortably Jewish. She was more at home in the cultured milieu of New York, Newport, Concord, and London than in the Jewish world she so ardently embraced in the last years of her life. Said to have had a "conversion" experience upon meeting East European Jewish refugees at Ward's Island, she became their spokesperson in poetry and prose. Nevertheless, her world remained, as it had been, one of gentility and high culture.[33]

If Emma Lazarus was no Frances Harper, working tirelessly throughout a lifetime to uplift her people, neither was she Fanny Parnell, passionately and wholeheartedly identifying with those for whom she chose to speak.

Young's insight casts Lazarus's metamorphosis into ethnic poet in the last years of her life in a very different, and far more ambiguous, light than her myth allows. Until the Russian pogroms and the massive flight of East European Jewry to the United States, Emma Lazarus had never had to experience directly the full horror of anti-Semitism, whatever she knew of its history. Unprepared for and possibly emotionally overwhelmed by what she saw, she responded to this latest exodus, by vociferously identifying with a people whose persecution she had only known of from books.[34] Forsaking the vague universalizing idealism of the bourgeois genteel lyric, Lazarus began writing "Jewish" poetry instead, boldly titling her next—and last—volume *Songs of a Semite* (1882) to signal the change. But was this apparent transformation of Lazarus's literary identity real, or do her Jewish poems merely represent her adaptation of her earlier universalistic idiom to the Jewish cause?

Superficially, at least, Lazarus's "mainstream" poetry does seem very unlike her Jewish verse. As a genteel writer, Lazarus penned poems on such safely aesthetic subjects as fog: "Light silken curtain, colorless and soft, / Dreamlike before me floating! what abides / Behind thy pearly veil's / Opaque, mysterious woof?" and Canada's Thousand Islands: "Enchanted world! enchanted hour! / Hail and farewell, enchanted stream, / That hast the unimagined power / To make the real surpass the dream!"[35] Blending Emersonian nature mysticism with German romanticism, these poems implicitly position their author as mystic or seer, a view Lazarus fully develops in "Scenes in the Wood," inspired by the music of Schumann: "His soul found never vision too sublime, / Nor image too fantastic, to translate / Into a speech transcending word and rhyme / . . . / *Sorrow he maketh beautiful, and Fate.* / Within our world he opes a world of dreams / A realm of shadows fed by mystic streams" (italics mine).[36] This was a role to which Lazarus was deeply committed and had been for a decade or more—but could Emma Lazarus, "Semite poet," also make "Sorrow . . . beautiful, and Fate"? Could Jewish history be turned, that is, into a site for the genteel / romantic sublime; and, if not, how was Lazarus to reconcile her idealizing aesthetic with the ugly facts of diasporic Jewish life, facts whose ugliness the "wretched refuse" (*NAWP* 287) then pouring in from East Europe undoubtedly made all to vivid to her? These are the concerns, I believe, that dictated the particular swerve that Lazarus's "Jewish poetry" took.

As Young astutely points out, Lazarus found the answer to her aesthetic dilemma in George Eliot. In the ironically titled "Epistle to the Hebrews," Lazarus identifies Eliot as one of a handful of Christian writers who appreciated "the full beauty and grandeur of [Judaism's] past, the glory and infinite expansiveness of her future" more than Jews themselves did.[37] To take this position, Eliot effectively separated Judaism from Jews—or, rather, from the stereotyped flaws thought to characterize Jewish behavior: avarice, obsequiousness, and so on. Speaking through the persona of Theophrastus Such in "The Modern Hep! Hep! Hep!" (1879), Eliot, conflating nation and race, had blamed the more ignoble side of Jews not on Judaism but on Jews' forced "de-nationalization" (the Diaspora) instead: "An individual man, to be harmoniously great," Theophrastus propounds, "must belong to a nation of this order, if not in actual existence yet existing in the past, in memory, as a departed, invisible, beloved ideal, once a reality, and perhaps to be restored."[38] Without such a national past, replete with heroes, a people could not help but lack "some of the conditions of nobleness," Eliot opined, just as they would also lack a future.[39]

To have a future, what Jews needed, therefore, was a firmer grip on the glories of their past—that "departed, invisible, beloved ideal." In "Epistle to the Hebrews," Lazarus takes up where Eliot leaves off: "As long as every man respects the virtues and achievements of his ancestors, he is proud to claim his rightful lineage. Only when a deep and abiding sense of national humiliation has taken root, is it possible for men . . . to . . . shrink from acknowledgement of their descent."[40] To redeem Jews from self-hatred, and all the ignoble ways of behaving to which self-hatred gave rise, Lazarus need only recreate the "beloved ideal, once a reality, and perhaps to be restored." Beginning in the late-1870s, this is what she does, using her poetry to transform the Jews' long, sordid history of persecution, slaughter, and survival into occasions for martyred heroism and glory—her aesthetic idealism returning, as it were, through the back door of a reenvisioned past.

Serialized in the *American Hebrew* in 1882, "The Dance to Death," which Lazarus dedicated to Eliot, is exemplary. Based on Richard Reinhard's prose narrative *Der Tanz zum Tode* (1877), Lazarus's verse drama deals with the destruction of the Jewish community in Nordhausen, Germany, in 1349, when the entire Jewish population—"Jews, Jewesses, and Jewlings"—was burnt alive after an outbreak of the Black Death.[41] In a pattern that Lazarus would follow throughout her brief career as minority poet, she transforms this pathetic spectacle into one filled with acts of nobility and grace. The "defiant Jews," Diane Lichtenstein comments, "die proclaiming their devotion to God":[42] "Ours is the truth, / Ours is the power, the gift of Heaven. We hold / His Law, His lamp, His covenant. His pledge. / Wherever in the ages shall arise / Jew-priest, Jew-poet, Jew-singer, or Jew-saint—/ . . . / In each of these the martyrs are avenged!" (2:165). In a scene I suspect no Jew today can read without shuddering, the Nordhausen Jews not only voluntarily walk to the bonfire, but demand that a dancing platform be erected so that they can dance while they burn.

In her sonnet dedicated to the Jewish insurrectionist Bar Kochba—whom Lazarus identifies as "the last King of the Jews"—she again snatches victory out of the jaws of defeat. Indeed, both in the poem and in an essay she wrote on Bar Kochba's last battle, "The Last National Revolt of the Jews," Lazarus hectors readers on the unfairness of "the world's customary ingratitude towards the unsuccessful brave."[43] Bar Kochba never received the honor that was his due, Lazarus insists, even though his "heroic valor and endurance" represent "the very principle of revolt and independence upon which our present nation state is based."[44] Not only was the unhonored Bar Kochba a bold fighter, but a freedom fighter in the American mold, one who nobly resisted the armed might of the Roman empire (135 C.E.). "Weep, Israel!" Lazarus commands, "your tardy meed outpour / Of grateful homage on his fallen head, / That never coronal of triumph wore" (2:22). Similarly in "The Feast of Lights," Lazarus, sounding very much like Parnell, puts out a call for "the Maccabean spirit" of yore, the martial spirit of Judea's warrior past: "Where are the lion-warriors of the Lord? / Clash, Israel, the cymbals, touch the lyre, / Sound the brass trumpet and the harsh-tongued horn, / Chant hymns of victory till the heart take fire, / The Maccabean spirit leap new-born!" (2:19–20).

So far, so good, but what else? Lazarus's problem was that the bulk of the historical record simply would not support this particular recuperative strategy; and Lazarus, like Eliot, knew it. The age of Jewish martial heroism, such as it was, ended definitively with Rome's conquest of Judea in 135 C.E., and the beginning of the long migration west. Debarred from land and nationality together, Jews became the people of the book, questers, perforce, after knowledge and wealth, goods that were easily transportable, if nothing else. "De-nationalized" for close to two thousand years, they survived by fair means and foul, creating a historical record as long on ignominy as it is on martyrdom. This was not the kind of record with which Lazarus, genteel poet and heroic idealist, could be comfortable, any more than she could be comfortable with the "wretched refuse" currently washing up on America's shores. For Lazarus, these latest victims of age-old persecution did not confirm her dreams of Jewish heroism. They were the stuff of her nightmares. In section 4 of "By the Waters of Babylon," her last published work, she says as much:

1. Daylong I brooded upon the Passion of Israel.
2. I saw him bound to the wheel, nailed to the cross, cut off by the sword, burned at the stake, tossed into the seas.
3. And always the patient, resolute, martyr face arose in silent rebuke and defiance.
4. A Prophet with four eyes; wide gazed the orbs of the spirit above the sleeping eyelids of the senses.
5. A Poet, who plucked from his bosom the quivering heart and fashioned it into a lyre.
6. A placid-browed Sage, uplifted from earth in celestial meditation.
7. These I saw, with princes and people in their train; the monumental dead and the standard-bearers of the future.
8. And suddenly I heard a burst of mocking laughter, and turning, I beheld the shuffling gait, the ignominious features, the sordid mask of the son of the Ghetto.

(NAWP 286–87)

What this poem, easily the most controversial that Lazarus wrote, suggests is that she knew just how hollow her idealizations were. Young believes that behind Lazarus's "strident" attacks on the evils of anti-Semitism lay her father's indirect involvement in slaveholding. A wealthy sugar refiner, Moses Lazarus was the business partner of Bradish Johnson, owner of an antebellum sugar plantation in Louisiana and, to put it as my daughters might, a really sleazy crook.[45] Unable to take slavery on directly, Lazarus, Young hypothesizes, found "a safe social problem" on which to vent "her imprisoned passion,"[46] namely, her crusade against anti-Semitism. Perhaps. But to date no evidence has been found suggesting Lazarus was opposed to slavery. On the contrary, the one poem she wrote on the South leaves the moral question disturbingly open: "Was hers [the South's] a dream of empire? *was it sin?* / And is it well that all was borne in vain? / She knows no more than one who slow doth win, / After fierce fever, conscious life again" (*NAWP* 285; my italics). Given Lazarus's moral absolutism respecting anti-Semitism, I do not see how the moral indifference in these lines can fail to be deeply troubling.

There may, however, be another way in which Moses Lazarus's business associations help explain the stridency of his daughter's efforts on behalf of the Jewish people. Up until the Russian pogroms, Emma Lazarus, daughter of Moses, aspirant to New York society's most exclusive circles, had assumed that sooner or later her literary efforts would pay off, making her fully acceptable in the U.S. mainstream—at least that elite branch of it in which she swam. Then the Russian pogroms taught her what Hitler taught all twentieth-century Jews—namely, that for Jews, acceptance can never be taken for granted. If so, then, it is possible that Lazarus dealt with the anxiety this recognition produced by vociferously adopting an ethnic identity (label?) that was not really hers and then, just as loudly, insisting that the United States was one nation to which, as Mary E. Ashe Lee put it in "Afmerica," all "nationalities" were "legal heirs," even Jews. This was the vision—the immigrant "yearning to breathe free," not in the positive sense of having free political choice, but as in free from persecution—that Lazarus put into "The New Colossus" (*NAWP* 287). "Why, good my lords," says the Jewish community spokesman in "The Dance to Death," "the Jews are not a flock / Of gallows-birds, they are a colony / Of kindly, virtuous folk. Come home with me; / I'll show you happy hearths, glad roofs, pure lives./ . . . / Amongst them there be mothers, infants, brides, / Just like your Christian people" (2:146–147). Oh, yes.

But what if her father's business connections proved the reverse, and Jews unalterably "were" the ignoble folk that Eliot said the Diaspora had made them? What if those stereotypes—"the shuffling gait, the ignominious features, the sordid mask"—were in the blood, as anti-Semites averred? Then, in claiming her Jewishness, what was Emma Lazarus claiming? How far outside the "inside"—that mainstream to which she so longed to belong—did her identification with "her" people put her? And could she ever find her way back to where she wanted to be? It is possible that a young Christian woman in the United States, a white Southerner, say, might worry in this way; but it is almost a given that a young Jewish woman like Lazarus, so eager for acceptance, would. Jews had too long a history of being blamed not just for their own sins but everyone else's to allow them to shrug off even relatively modest paternal peccadilloes, not if the latter helped confirm what, thanks to centuries of persecution, they already half-believed about themselves.[47]

These were the questions that, I believe, Lazarus's loud insistence on heroes was meant to drown out, and couldn't. Without evidence of heroes— the patient, resolute martyr, the prophet, the poet, the placid-browed sage— the sordid reality that her father's business dealings represented left Lazarus no place to stand and no nation to call her own. Whichever way she chose, she chose against herself. To be at once American and Jewish, freedom fighter and smarmy practitioner of shady business dealings, "kindly, virtuous folk" and the shuffling product of ghettos, was from this perspective a contradiction in terms that only the complete undoing of the ties between nation and race and race and the behavior of specific individuals could resolve. And this undoing Emma Lazarus, Jewish poet, and acolyte of George Eliot, could not perform. Instead, taking her cue from Eliot, she romanticized (idealized/essentialized) the history and identity of the people with whom she had so impulsively thrown in her lot. On this slippery foundation, enabled largely by her personal distance from the realities of diasporic Jewish life, with its complex wealth of religious and secular cultures, she built her dreams of a Jewish state and of a Jewish people in whom all Jews, even Emma Lazarus, could unambivalently take pride.

Performing Indianness with E. Pauline Johnson

Of the poets examined in this chapter, E. Pauline Johnson is the only one to address herself all but entirely to the dominant white population, and, arguably, the one furthest removed from those for whom she spoke. Johnson's father, George Henry Martin Johnson, came from a distinguished line of Mohawk orators and chiefs. Johnson's mother, Emily Howells Johnson, came to the United States from Bristol, England, when she was eight. Henry Howells, Emily's Quaker father, was an ardent abolitionist and the great uncle of W. D. Howells, the well-known U.S. litterateur. Johnson, who was raised on her father's estate on the Six Nation reserve in the county of Brant, Ontario, only received seven years of formal education, but with the aid of maternal tutoring, she became very knowledgeable about literature, having read extensively in Scott, Longfellow, Byron, and Shakespeare by the time she was twelve.

Johnson's privileged childhood as the daughter of a highly respected Mohawk chief and a cultured British mother is symbolized visually by the two-story mansion which gave her father his adult Indian name: Onwanonsyshon, or "He Who Has the Great Mansion." George Johnson built this home ("Chiefswood") for Emily in 1853, situating it across the river from the reservation. Constructed along commodious European lines, Chiefswood featured two equally elegant entrances: the front door, which served a drive capable of accommodating the carriages of visiting whites, and a rear door, open to the river, used by Indians arriving by canoe. Although Johnson's paternal grandparents, John "Smoke" Johnson and Helen Martin Johnson, lived with the family, Johnson's rearing was "white." She and her siblings went to Anglo schools, wore Anglo dress, and spent childhoods surrounded by the material comforts of an Anglo lifestyle, from books and artworks to crystal and china. According to Johnson, her mother never learned more than six words of Iroquois[48]—nor did she need to, since both George and his father spoke fluent English. Later in life, A. LaVonne Brown Ruoff writes, Johnson deeply regretted "not tak[ing] the time to learn more of [her paternal grandfather's] rich knowledge of his people's culture."[49]

Following George Johnson's death in 1884, the financially strapped family rented out Chiefswood and moved to Brantford. There Pauline began to earn her living, publishing heavily in newspapers and periodicals, including numerous poems in Canada's two most prestigious literary periodicals, *This Week* and *Saturday Night*. A well-established poet by the time she recited "A

Cry from an Indian Wife" (1885) at the Young Liberal Club in Toronto, it was nonetheless this occasion that launched her adult career as an "Iroquois Indian Poet-Entertainer."[50] For two decades, Johnson traveled the length and breadth of Canada, publicly performing her poetry, typically dressed in Indian costume for one half of the evening and in an evening gown for the other. Like her father's mansion and like these performances, her life and career would always look two ways at once, with the "Indian" side ever the more problematic. To perform Indianness, Johnson took the Indian name of her paternal great grandfather, Tekahionwake ("Double Wampum" or "Double Life"), and designed an Indian costume for herself, modeling it, according to her biographers, Veronica Strong-Boag and Carole Gerson, on "an artist's rendition" of Minnehaha's in Longfellow's *Hiawatha*.[51] However, she lived with and performed before whites; and when she died prematurely of cancer in 1912, whites orchestrated her funeral, burying her ashes in a white site, Vancouver's Stanley Park, a federal reserve.[52]

Johnson used writing to bridge differences in race and culture, and insofar as she ranks among Canada's best-loved authors, she remains a bridge to this day. In her poems and fiction, however, Johnson employed exclusively European conventions, and her popular essays on Indian customs and history are aimed at white readers.[53] When putting together a collection of Native American tales, *Legends of Vancouver*, she drew on what anthropologists call "a native informant," the elderly Squamish chief Joe Capilano, whom she first met in London, in 1906. As a self-appointed explicator of Indian history and culture, Johnson was, in other words, closer to Elaine Goodale Eastman, the white wife of Charles Eastman, a Santee Sioux, than to, say, Juana Manwell, or "Owl Woman," the Papago shaman whose medicine songs Frances Densmore recorded in the late 1920s.[54] For Manwell, native culture was everyday life. Never departing from traditional ways, she created her art only by way of praxis, her songs were an integral part of a spiritual vocation. For Johnson, as for Eastman, poetry was an avocation turned vocation to meet perceived needs—the need to communicate, to preserve, and to arouse sympathy for the oppressed, but also to make a living by commodifying Indian culture for whites.

Despite Johnson's powerful Indian affiliation, therefore, her Indian poems must be read in terms of their origins in Euro-American and Euro-Canadian verse. Like her performances, Johnson's oeuvre splits in two, divided between genteel poetry of the sort standard in her day and poetry on Indian themes, the latter often engaging, as in "A Cry from an Indian Wife," imaginary Indian personae. Although Johnson's genteel poetry forms the greater part of her poetic oeuvre, like Lazarus's genteel poetry, it is not distinctive, certainly not strong, enough to have kept her name alive on its own. Johnson's Indian poems present a more complicated picture, further breaking down into two kinds: one, like "A Cry from an Indian Wife," geared for dramatic presentation, the other, to which I return in chapter 8, more contemplative and modern. I will address the dramatic poems now since they are the ones exhibiting the tensions I am exploring in this chapter.

As noted in chapter 3, Johnson made effective use of high-sentimental rhetorical strategies in her performance poems. However, in these same poems, as in many of her short stories about Indians, she also uses racial stereotypes identical to those found in so much white writing on Indians. Indeed, in "Ojistoh" (1895) the lead-off poem for her first collection, *White Wampum*, the Mohawk speaker, Ojistoh, describes her husband in terms that could come straight from a supermarket romance with an Indian hero—a twist on the bodice-ripper that has gained great popularity in these multi-cultural times: "Ah! but they hated him, those Huron braves, / Him who had flung their warriors into graves, / Him who had crushed them underneath his heel, / Whose arm was iron, and whose heart was steel."[55] The opening stanza of "As Red Men Die," the volume's second poem, is as simplistic as its title: "Captive! Is there a hell to him like this? / A taunt more galling than the Huron's hiss? / He—proud and scornful, he—who laughed at law, / He—scion of the deadly Iroquois, / He—the bloodthirsty, he—the Mohawk chief, / He—who despises pain and sneers at grief" (6). If Johnson were not the author of such poems, I doubt we would be reading them today. When performing them, Johnson, whose stage costume included two authentic scalps, along with wampum belts and feathers, accompanied herself with war whoops and tomahawk thrusts. Why not?

Taking such poems on their own, one could assume that Johnson knew no better or that her primary concern was giving her audience as much bang as possible for their buck. In other performance poems, however, not just "A cry from an Indian Wife," but, even more, "The Cattle Thief" (1894), she makes clear, as she does in her essays, that she knew how misleading, and therefore dangerous, the evocation of such stereotypes was.[56] Indeed, in "The Cattle Thief," her most powerful dramatic poem, she deliberately sets out to deconstruct them. Johnson opens this poem conventionally enough, her narrative told from the perspective of a group of vigilante whites who are tracking the fleeing Cattle Thief to his "lair": "That monstrous, fearless Indian, who lorded it over the plain, / Who thieved and raided, and scouted, who rode like a hurricane!"

The whites hold to this absurdly exaggerated image of male Indian ferocity until they arrive at the Cattle Thief's camp. When they only find a woman there, they immediately switch to another, equally exaggerated—and no less damaging—stereotype: "'The sneaking Indian coward,' they hissed; 'he hides while yet he can; / He'll come in the night for cattle, but he's scared to a face a *man*.'" This, of course, is an insult no self-respecting Indian brave could be expected to endure and, predictably, the "thief" reveals himself: "'Never!' and up from the cotton woods rang the voice of Eagle Chief; / And right out into the open stepped, unarmed, the Cattle Thief." A brief volley of insults follows; then the whites gun the Cattle Thief down.

It is at this point that Johnson's poem takes a remarkable swerve. Bold and bloody the Eagle Chief may have been, but the man who answers the whites' challenge, compelled to sacrifice life for honor, is no "monstrous, fearless Indian," if he ever was one. He is a pathetic old man, with a "fleshless, hungry frame, starved to the bone" and "hungry, hollow eyes that glar[e] for the sight of food." As Johnson zooms in on this description, the poem's "real" situation—a bunch of bloodthirsty whites chasing down a starving old man—emerges; and Johnson delivers the poem into the hands of the Cattle Thief's daughter. Standing over her father's crumpled body, this unnamed woman launches into a tirade fit to skin any white alive, in some of the angriest poetry that Johnson wrote:

> Go back with your new religion, we never have understood
> Your robbing an Indian's *body*, and mocking his *soul* with food.
> Go back with your new religion, and find—if find you can—
> The *honest* man you have ever made from out a *starving* man.
> You say your cattle are not ours, your meat is not our meat;
> When *you* pay for the land you live in, *we'll* pay for the meat we eat.
> Give back our land and our country, give back our herds of game;
> Give back the furs and the forests that were ours before you came;
> Give back the peace and the plenty. Then come with your new belief,
> And blame if you dare, the hunger that *drove* him to be a thief.
>
> (12, 13, 15–16)

In performance, the impact of this reversal must have been electrifying, especially given the way the poem opens. Nevertheless, if Johnson understood how dangerous these stereotypes were, as "The Cattle Thief," indicates she did, why did she use them, especially when her more tempered (more subtle? less overtly political?) Indian poetry eschews them altogether? It is not enough, I think, to attribute Johnson's stereotyping to her poems' intended use in oral presentations, the only possible explanation other than ignorance. Something drew her to these images, possibly against her own better judgment.

In a poem discussed in chapter 8, "The Corn Husker" (1896), Johnson makes brilliant use of the image of empty corn husks to suggest the way in which the substance of indigenous Indian cultures was hollowed out by colonization. Her dramatic poems are, I would suggest, these husks. That is, they are attempts to recreate in language images of a way of life that Johnson herself never knew, one whose substance, as she recognized in one essay, had been wiped out, leaving only trace memories behind.[57] As a child, Ruoff comments, Johnson "loved to hear [her father's] stories about Hiawatha, the Shawnee chief Tecumseh, and the Ottawa chief Pontiac," while her grandfather, Smoke Johnson, "thrilled [her] . . . with his wartime deeds and those of the Mohawks."[58] Although Johnson's portrait of Indian warrior society has much in common with that of white writers, her father and grandfather were, it appears, primarily responsible for shaping it. Without access to pre-reservation Indian culture, especially the female side (Johnson's Indian grandmother spoke no English), Johnson had only paternal tales of male Indian heroism to build on. Absorbed in childhood, their masculinist vision was what she recreated in her dramatic poems, attempting to give to others the thrill that her fathers' stories once gave her.[59] According to her thinly veiled autobiographical story, "My Mother," Johnson's parents raised their children "with pride of race and heritage, and . . . that peculiar, unconquerable courage that *only a fighting ancestry can give*" (italics mine). For better or worse, this was what their daughter passed on.[60]

What makes the dramatic poems' almost exclusive focus on North American Indian warrior culture truly sad is that Johnson did have a male hero in her own family about whom she wrote no known poems, although he certainly deserved one. George Johnson, Pauline's father, was something more than a hereditary Mohawk chief. As Johnson describes him in "My Mother," he was a man of strength, wisdom, and courage. Installed as warden on the reservation by Canadian authorities, George Johnson used his power (against his own father's advice) to stop the flow of whiskey into the reservation and to curb the illegal timber trade. Strictly speaking, Smoke was right. George Johnson's reward for these efforts was to be beaten twice by gangs of whites and once by fellow Iroquois, angry at his interference. He never fully recovered from the effects of these beatings, the first of which left "his skull so crushed that to the end of his days a silver dollar could quite easily be laid flat in the cavity." But he also refused to desist, pursuing his mission until the third and final beating permanently disabled him.[61]

However, one need only look at a photograph of George Johnson's mansion or that of his very British wife to understand why Pauline Johnson might have found it difficult to write an "Indian poem" about her Indian father. Rightly or wrongly, George Johnson, for all the stories he told, walked the path of assimilation and compromise. Either because he believed white culture superior to native culture (according to Strong-Boag and Gerson, he was part of a "Christian elite")[62] or because he was a realist, accepting what he could not change, he left traditional ways behind, working with, rather than against, whites, and raising his family apart from the very community for whose welfare he ultimately sacrificed his life. Believing, like Lazarus, that a heroic present required a heroic past, his daughter Pauline chose to use her verse to restore those ways as she had been led to imagine them. "The Cattle Thief" may be the closest that Johnson could come to an elegy for a man who deserved so much more.

Conclusion

There is something all too ironically appropriate in the fact that the words inscribed on the base of the United States' premier symbol of liberty are those of a woman who never condemned her father's complicity in slavery and that the voice of American Jewry is a poet who wanted nothing more than to make it in the mainstream. These contradictions are no more ironic, however, than that a poet as utterly devoted to her people's welfare as Harper should espouse a principle that was pivotal in the woman's suffrage movement's adoption of the racist expediency argument or that the male members of the nineteenth-century Irish American community should find in an upper-class woman of Anglo-Irish descent the voice that best represented their own desires, or even that scholars of Indian literature today identify as a Native American writer a woman whose knowledge of indigenous culture, like the Indian costume she wore, was a patchwork assembled from fragments she herself sewed together. Such contradictions characterize the literatures of any politicized minority seeking to make a place for itself in a society already burdened with more contradictions than one can count. As Terry Eagleton reminds us, when speaking of Charles Parnell and the ultimate failure of the pro-Irish Anglo-Irish Ascendancy, such contradictions are inevitable in political movements that as "forms of immanent critique" are "installed within the logic of what they oppose, and for just that reason are able to press that logic through to an outside or beyond which is political emancipation."[63] In such instances, impurity cannot be avoided.

What is also clear, however, is that the ethnic/racial absolutism and moral fervor these four poets displayed is nonetheless vital to the struggles of minorities if they are to emerge as unified political movements. Liminal figures within their own communities, both "inside" and "outside" at once and in both directions, these poets dreamed the dream of a people, a race. Each saw her community not as an incoherent bunch of strangers with diverse, contradictory, even opposing goals, held together by a label and, perhaps, by the knowledge that someone hated them, but as a coherent idea, a fantasy that they could write into existence. They dreamt the purity of their race/nation in a myth, like that of Moses, of origins: an Eden lost—be it mother Ireland, ancient Judea, or precontact Indian tribal culture—and a paradise regained, whether "community," nation, or merely a restored bonding of nationalist pride. High-sentimental women poets were ideally suited to be the vehicles for such a politics of difference—we call it "identity politics" today—because women's sanctioned role in political life, at least in Western societies, had always been symbolic anyway. Like the Statue of Liberty, with Lazarus's sonnet emblazoned on it, these women simultaneously voiced the dream and served as icons of it. Their ability and willingness to commit emotionally and publicly was the source of their power as well as of its limits, and their most fervent efforts were undermined by the hopelessly idealistic nature of the goals they set, the dreams they dreamed, the communities they imagined. They had, as John Boyle O'Reilly put it, "that which crystallizes the efforts and aspirations of a popular movement." But however necessary such dreams are to any emancipatory project, they should never be confused with the realities of political life, whose complexities are only matched by the impurities of its demands.

❧ PART TWO ❧

❧ 5 ❧

Domestic Gothic and Sentimental Parody

[T]he poet, who re-attaches things to nature and the
Whole . . . disposes very easily of the most disagreeable
facts.
—RALPH WALDO EMERSON, "The Poet," 1844[1]

[W]hile *the law* leaves thousands of women in the hands
of brutal husbands . . . the beauty and harmony of
woman's condition exist only in the imagination of the
poet.
—"MRS. SIGOURNEY ON WOMAN'S RIGHTS," 1854[2]

In 1854, in the unlikely person of Phoebe Cary, white bourgeois women
buried literary sentimentality, the principal rhetorical vehicle through which
nineteenth-century domestic ideology carried out its cultural work. Not that
literary sentimentality rolled over and died on the spot. On the contrary, like
other residual literary modalities—the Petrarchan, say, or the neoclassical—
literary sentimentality remains an available rhetorical option even today, to
be tapped whenever the idealization of the domestic or the affectional is
wanted. However, in *Poems and Parodies*, Cary's first volume, the cynical
Ohioan—a "disenchanter," her biographer, Mary Clemmer Ames, called her[3]—
did to literary sentimentality what no rhetorical mode can have done to it
and maintain its mystique: she made fun of it. In a series of poems mocking
the great worthies of the genteel tradition—all but one (Felicia Hemans)
male—Cary roasted literary sentimentality as a style and, to use Raymond
Williams's definition of hegemony in "Base and Superstructure in Marxist
Cultural Theory," as "a central system of [lived] practices, meanings and
values."[4] Specifically, the "practices, meanings and values" Cary targets in
Poems and Parodies were those through which gender difference in nineteenth-century bourgeois culture was literarily represented and socially
reproduced.

Although a heavy weight to put on such a slim volume of verse, the best
way to appreciate the importance of Cary's volume is to view its gender
critique in relation to Williams's discussion of hegemony in his well-known
essay. Williams's starting point is Antonio Gramsci's seminal reworking of

the Marxist concept of hegemony, a concept that, by Eagleton's account, originally addressed "how the working class could [noncoercively] win political authority over other radical movements."[5] According to Williams, Gramsci's contribution in *Prison Notebooks* was to apply this same idea of a noncoercive form of authority to bourgeois culture itself. In contrast to the "crudeness" of the earlier Marxist formulation of a base/superstructure model, in which economic forces (the "base") are totally determinative with respect to art and culture (the "superstructure"), the Gramscian model of hegemony, Williams argues, provides a dynamic and subtle way to understand how the middle class maintains its cultural dominance in the liberal state.[6] Succinctly, because bourgeois ideology operates inwardly rather than by the imposition of direct force, it is experienced as a matter of "lived" beliefs. Functioning as a set of "reciprocally confirming" cultural practices, Williams writes, hegemonic meanings and values "constitut[e] a sense of reality for most people in the society," rulers and ruled alike.[7] Addressing Williams's concept of hegemony, Eagleton calls such "lived systems"—usefully, for my purposes—"structure[s] of subjectivity."[8] Since these systems are tantamount to how people understand the world, their ideological status is, Williams argues, very difficult to recognize, much less oppose.

Resituating the Gramsci-Williams concept of hegemony within the structural framework of the Habermasian public sphere allows us to honor the power of domestic ideology's "intimate discipline" while still making room for agency and change. Most particularly, viewing hegemony as dynamic, not static, helps explain how a movement as diffuse and internally contradictory as the nineteenth-century woman's rights movement could nevertheless succeed, not only radically undermining the legal structures supporting male dominance but transforming—and politicizing—the subjectivities of bourgeois women themselves. "We have to emphasize," Williams writes, "that hegemony is not singular; indeed that its own internal structures are highly complex, and have continually to be renewed, recreated and defended; and by the same token, that they can be continually challenged and in certain respects modified."[9] It is my argument that in ironizing literary sentimentality as they did, mid-nineteenth-century women poets like Cary were offering such a challenge to the dominant gender ideology of their day. Stripping domestic ideology of its mystique, they revealed it for what they knew it was: a socially constructed system oppressive to women. Doing so, they helped facilitate bourgeois women's entrance into a modernity that was literary and social at once.

In *Sentimental Collaborations*, Mary Louise Kete argues persuasively for a gender-blind concept of sentimentality that defines it in terms of its antebellum role as a rhetoric of connection, reattaching bonds "severed by the contingencies of human existence," in particular, the death of loved ones.[10] That what I call literary sentimentality served antebellum middle-class U.S.

culture, especially in the Northeast, in this "utopic" way is inarguable. Indeed, as Kete points out, sentimental rhetoric still fulfills this mission today.[11] Nevertheless, an epigraph Kete takes from Emerson's "The Poet" suggests that this use of literary sentimentality was also problematic on a number of grounds, not least, "utopianism" itself—a term that puns on a "happy place" (*eu-topos*) as "no place" (*ou-topos*): "For," Emerson writes, "as it is dislocation and detachment from the life of God that makes things ugly, the poet, who re-attaches things to nature and the Whole,—re-attaching even artificial things and violation of nature, to nature, by a deeper insight,—disposes very easily of the most disagreeable facts."[12]

This is to say, confronting the ugliness of disruption, the poet, be he romantic or sentimental, makes things beautiful by restoring the "Whole," "re-attaching" what was sundered to a transcendent order or "God." Employed thus, literary sentimentality was, you might say, a stylistic form of cognitive dissonance writ into bourgeois culture at large, a sort of perverse *concordia discors* creating fictitious harmonies out of "disagreeable facts," even as coverture made one person of two.

But what happens when the gap between what is and what one wants to believe grows so great that the imposed harmonies of cognitive dissonance no longer work, where in the head or in the heart? In a remarkably angry essay on woman's rights, published, like *Poems and Parodies*, in 1854, that very wayward lady Lydia Huntley Sigourney, so pilloried by Ann Douglas and others as the high priestess of antebellum sentimentality, put it this way, when confronting the "dislocation[s] and detachment[s]" and other "disagreeable facts" of midcentury marriage:

> But while the laws and customs of society fetter woman in that very sphere which nature has assigned her, it is useless to prate of "contentment and diligence," of "gratitude and joy" in the performance of her task, while *the law* leaves thousands of women in the hands of brutal husbands, who can legally claim control over the persons of their wives, squander their hard earned property in debauchery and vice, and tear their children from the arms of maternal love and give them to strangers;—while these outrages on the name of humanity are known, the beauty and harmony of woman's condition exist only in the imagination of the poet or the dream of the idealist.[13]

Both as a "lived system of beliefs" and as a structure of subjectivity, nineteenth-century domestic ideology, as I observed in chapter 1, played out very differently in men's and women's lives, and women like Sigourney, who had her own marital problems, knew it. Much more deeply, these women also knew that being an "Angel in the House" meant nothing as long as the "practices, meanings and values" underwriting this image also supported laws that allowed "brutal husbands" to terrorize their wives and children at will.

Frustrated in their personal lives and professional ambitions by cultural assumptions wedding women to hearth, home, and heart, while leaving intact laws denying them protection on an individual basis, nineteenth-century women writers began attacking domesticity's internal ideological structure and the sentimental rhetoric encoding it. Uneven in their political positions, and without a clear operational base or constituency, most of these writers were not, strictly speaking, "feminists," let alone revolutionaries. But in using their poetry to test domestic ideology's myths against women's "life-world" experience, these writers collectively broke the Angel's grip on middle-class women's subjectivities, clearing the way for the polyvocal writings and multiple life orientations of modern women, women whose status as social and literary free agents led them to call themselves, with considerable justice, "new."

This chapter will focus on two of the primary ways in which mid- and late-nineteenth-century women poets participated in this very public process of ideological demystification. First, I will look at their literature of parodic excess or the "domestic gothic." Nothing if not morbid, this form of parodic sentimentality took women's literal and figurative vulnerability to death as its principal theme. By insisting on the sheer fatality of being female, the domestic gothic ironized the myth of woman as household "Angel" by taking it literally. Pious, passive, and physically attenuated, the wraithlike female subjects of these poems die without ever having had the chance to live. For all that such poems seem to honor their overly passive subjects and, indeed, do honor many of them, their excess of domesticity renders the gender ideology subtending them suspect. Reading these poems, it is difficult not to agree with their authors' oft-stated opinion that domestic Angels—passive, loving, and all-but-inevitably betrayed—are better off dead.

In the second, and far more direct, mode of attack, these same writers parody literary texts, especially men's, which cleave to the figure of the Angel nonetheless, ignoring the price paid by "living" women forced to "die" into this role. One of the more obvious puzzles of *Poems and Parodies* is how Cary could put together two such seemingly antithetical kinds of poetry, the morbidly sentimental and the overtly parodic, in one collection. Of the first thirteen poems in this volume all but one, an elegy for a dead male, are devoted to dead or dying women, while the remaining poems in the "Poems" section, present life as, largely, one misery after another. In the final third of the volume, however, Cary does a complete about-face. Not only does she parody well-known works—Poe's "Annabel Lee," Wordsworth's "She dwelt among the untrodden ways," Longfellow's "The Day Is Done," and so on— but she parodies the very themes over which her speaker waxed lachrymose in the first two-thirds of the book.

A disjunction this blatant, especially in a poet so closely associated with literary sentimentality as Cary was, cannot be ignored. Although Cary never gave her disenchantment with nineteenth-century domestic ideology such free rein again, at least in her books, the internal splits and self-contradictions of *Poems and Parodies* should warn scholars that where nineteenth-century female sentimentalists are concerned, things may not always be what they seem.[14]

Death and Domesticity in the Nineteenth Century

While this chapter argues that much of the apparent morbidity in nineteenth-century women's poetry is politically motivated, this does not mean that these women were not also—and quite legitimately—death obsessed. In her critically acclaimed biography of Emily Dickinson, Cynthia Griffin Wolff speaks eloquently of health conditions at midcentury: "The medical profession could not offer protection from the commonest killers: antibiotics were unheard-of; surgery was performed without anesthesia or any proper form of antisepsis; typhoid, pneumonia, smallpox, cholera, and malaria were all local threats to life; . . . even dysentery might prove fatal—Samuel Bowles's father died of it in 1851 at the age of fifty-four."[15] Under such conditions, a perfectly healthy child could be playing one day, come down ill that evening, and die one week later—as happened to Dickinson's beloved nephew, Gib, who contracted typhoid fever in 1883. When fatal illness struck a family, moreover, it was the women, typically, who dealt with it, performing most of the duties that today's society leaves to professionals—nurses, doctors, and undertakers. Women cared for the sick throughout their illness, sat watches by the bedside at night, and even prepared the corpse for burial, washing it and dressing and arranging it for viewing. As two Dickinson poems—"There's been a Death, in the Opposite House" (F547) and "The Bustle in a House" (F1108)—suggest, women also swept up afterward: disposing of the mattress on which "it died," cleaning the deceased's room, and airing it out. Yet even as they erased the tangible reminders of the dying process, women were also, as Kete reminds us, expected to memorialize the dead, whether by manufacturing sentimental artifacts or writing poems.[16]

In *Women of the South Distinguished in Literature*, Mary Forest (Julia Deane Freeman) comments on a poem by Rosa Vertner Johnson that sheds light on how nineteenth-century bourgeois women dealt with the trauma of loss. Speaking of "Angel Watchers," Johnson's elegy to two dead children, Forest, a devotee of spiritualism, asserts that having "passed from earth," these children nevertheless remained in "communion with [their mother's] loving spirit."[17] Forest means this literally. As the poem's first stanza tells it, Johnson's children were "communing" with her on a daily—or, rather, nightly—basis. "Angel faces watch my pillow, angel voices haunt my sleep, /

And upon the winds of midnight shining pinions round me sweep; / Floating downward on the starlight two bright infant forms I see, / They are mine, my own bright darlings, come from Heaven to visit me."[18] "A deep fountain was troubled" in Johnson, "at the death of her children," Forest explains, "and her songs only grew more low and tender—the mother's pang lost in the mother's hope."[19] From Forest's perspective, losing two children made Johnson a richer poet by effectively reconnecting her to the "Whole," the spirit life that lay behind the veil.

It would be wrong to dismiss the *unironized* link between women, poetry, death, and communion with spirits that Forest and Johnson forge here as so much spiritualist bunkum. At a time when so many died so young or simply disappeared (usually out West or somewhere below the border), spiritualism of one kind or another can be found cropping up across the entire range of U.S. women: northern, southern, eastern, western, black, white, Native American, rich, poor, educated and uneducated, immigrant and native-born, Jewish and Christian. Keepers of the domestic hearth, nineteenth-century women were also keepers of the family's household gods. Like the speaker in "Angels," by the Jewish poet Grace Aguilar, many undoubtedly felt "balmy pinions float around, with blessings redolent" while they sat watch at the bedside of dying loved ones.[20] Nor is it surprising that, as a result, so many women felt themselves "channels" for the spirits of those who had "passed to the other side." No less than the Papago shaman "Owl Woman," who claimed that all of her songs were given to her by the dead (*NAWP* 358), women like Forten Grimké, author of "The Angel's Visit," and Johnson, author of "Angel Watchers," dreamt of their dead regularly and recorded their dream visions in verse. Fueled, possibly, by the horrendous death toll of the Civil War, spiritualism, which posited a single continuum of living and dead, reached the height of its popularity in the final decades of the century (fig. 5). The comfort it gave believers is evident in Clara Longdon's "Spirit Josie," a poem originally published in the Springfield (Missouri) *Advertiser* and reprinted in the 1875 *Woodhull and Claflin Weekly*.

In this fourteen-stanza poem, Longdon's speaker recounts how Josie's spirit appeared to her one night as she sat half-dreaming by the fire. Startled to discover that her baby sister has grown into a beautiful young woman in paradise, the speaker enters into conversation with her, and Josie explains how readers can establish a similar comforting communion with their own dead family members. "But I want to tell you, sister, how we spirits watch and wait, / Patiently, to come back to you, but so seldom is the gate / Of your soul left open to us, that we oft times turn away / Almost sadly, hoping, praying, that there yet will come a day / And an hour when we can enter the recess of the heart, / And find ourselves remembered, of the household still a part."[21] For women like Longdon, keeping the "gate" open, or as Elizabeth Stuart Phelps, another authoritative speaker on the afterlife, put it, "ajar,"

Fig. 5. "One Year Ago"

was among the domestic Angel's most important duties. However perverse it may appear—at least to unbelievers such as myself—communing with the dead was one of the principal means by which the Angel could keep her family together, ensuring that its deceased members were "of the household still a part."

At the same time, this Angelic duty was not without ironies of its own. For in performing this particular aspect of her sentimental connective labor, the Angel made her home, in a singularly ironic gesture, a site for *das Unheimliche*—literally, the unhomelike—a play on words that Freud makes central to his discussion of the "uncanny" or "gothic" in literature.[22] And this irony was only deepened when, in the hands of the domestic gothic poets whom I now discuss, the Angel herself became the "spirit" most likely to be found haunting her own hearth. In returning the Angel to her literary setting, as I now do, I want to read this seemingly transparent sentimental gesture—the making of "home," as it were, into a "house of spirits"—with all the gothic literalism it deserves. Death was a major player in the lives of many, probably most, nineteenth-century bourgeois women. However, the rate at which women are killed off in these poems—and, equally important, the miserable lives they lead prior to their demise—suggests that we need to think twice before assuming that every elegy devoted to a defunct household Angel is merely, that is, transparently, "sentimental."

Gothicizing the Sentimental

That nineteenth-century fiction writers like Nathaniel Hawthorne, Harriet Beecher Stowe, George Lippard, and Louisa May Alcott introduced sentimental motifs into their gothic fantasies—and vice versa—is by now quite well known. Time and again, the gothic and sentimental are flip sides of each other in their texts, discursive modes of heightened emotional awareness and morbid excess, titillating or terrifying. But that nineteenth-century women poets—not just Dickinson but many others—persistently gothicized the sentimental has received surprisingly little recognition by anyone except Cheryl Walker, despite the fact that the corpses of women, children, and even men litter women's poems.[23] In these poems, the barriers that define "common sense" reality—in particular, those separating life and death, present and past, self and other, natural and supernatural, rational and irrational, and good and evil—are collapsed, and the familiar, as Freud argues in "The Uncanny," becomes *unheimlich*, unhomelike or strange. No longer located in the realm of the fantastic—some polar icecap, remote moor, or castle in Transylvania—the gothic, it turns out, dwells in the house next door, where, as Dickinson puts it, it populates the domestically confined woman's solitude "with awe" (F1743).

Given the way in which Dickinson's real-life seclusion has been generalized as if it were the plight of all nineteenth-century women writers, let me stress that aside from Dickinson, most of those who produced domestic gothic poems were professional writers who led, for women of their era, highly visible public lives. They did have what Phoebe Cary calls trials. They lost their mothers or their children; sometimes they lost husbands as well, as did Helen Hunt Jackson; and the latter loss could have devastating financial consequences. Like Sigourney, some probably had abusive husbands also. None, however, including Dickinson, was ever involuntarily incarcerated in the home or in an insane asylum, nor were they worked to death fulfilling household duties, the most common reason these poets give for the Angel's demise. On the contrary, they were often quite enjoyably employed, living here and abroad, raising children, acting as editors and journalists, engaging in political activism, and contributing to their communities in great ways and small, memorable and now forgotten. One particularly engaging poet, albeit more for her enthusiasms than for the quality of her verse, "Aunt Fanny" Gage (1808–84), is exemplary: a housewife, mother, grandmother, political activist, abolitionist poet, and, in her fifties, beloved Civil War nurse. Her "voice rang for freedom when freedom was sold," Clara Barton declared in her 1892 poem "The Women Who Went to the Field."[24] Both as a female abolitionist and as one of Barton's trained corps of nurses, Gage helped make women's history; but her personal success notwithstanding, she wrote poems like "The Maniac Wife" and "The Wife's Prayer in Agony."

However useful Freud is in unpacking the latent meanings behind gothic poetry's content, therefore, one must be cautious in assuming that this content is the product of *unconscious* conflicts either in the poet or in the text. With Freud and the repressive hypothesis as starting points, early second-wave feminist critics like Sandra Gilbert and Susan Gubar attributed the doublings, displacements, and high anxiety quotient of female gothic texts to various forms of intrapsychic dynamics—hysteria, in particular. For these scholars as for Freud, the eruption of the gothic signaled a return of the repressed—a something once known (*heimlich*, homelike) that comes back in the guise of the unknown (*das Unheimliche*), thus creating that distinctive frisson by which the uncanny announces its presence. From a phenomenological perspective, this interpretation is easily supported. Women's gothic poetry is filled to overflowing with the terrors of a known that returns as the unknown: ghosts of dead wives and dead children, lovers who transform into monsters, moments of (mis)recognition when female victims no longer know who they are, etcetera. However, as we shall see, the causes of these terrors are as much a part of this poetry's overt manifest content as are the terrors themselves.

Rather than situating the gothic within a psychoanalytic structuring of female experience, therefore, as earlier scholars did, I want to join those who, more recently, have begun to explore the gothic's social and political dimensions.[25] I will argue that nineteenth-century women poets self-consciously used the gothic for specifically political ends; like complaint literature generally, their gothic poetry calls attention to injustice. For these writers, who were all too aware of how oppressive nineteenth-century domestic ideology was, the mirror in which they could not recognize their face—Freud's classic instance of the uncanny—was gender ideology itself. By introducing the gothic into the literary sentimental—that is, into the very discourse that served as domestic ideology's rhetorical vehicle—these poets unsettled domesticity's hold over bourgeois female subjectivity and over the social construction of women generally. In their poems, bourgeois domestic space turns out to be the gothic mise en scène par excellence; and the displacements, doublings, and anxieties characterizing gothic experience are the direct consequence of domestic ideology's impact on the lives and psyches of ordinary bourgeois women.

Starting in the antebellum period with a trickle of poems, such as Mrs. L. L. Da Ponte's "The Dying Wife" (*Knickerbocker*, 1834) and Mary Hewitt's "The Bride" (*Knickerbocker*, 1837), domestic gothic poems achieved flood status, as Dickinson might say, by midcentury, appearing in every conceivable venue. The best place for me to begin, however, is with the somewhat belated "The Maniac Wife" (1866) by Fanny Gage. Precisely because Gage was neither a subtle nor a complex writer, her politicization of gothic themes could not be more stunningly clear. The psychic collapse of the wife in this poem is the direct result of her husband's having ceased to love her, and the consequence is an over-the-top descent into madness that any lover of the gothic should admire:

> There is a woe to deep for words,
>   An agony too strong for tears,
> When the warm, bleeding, quivering chords
>   Of love, which have been wrung for years,
> Are by the hand we trusted riven;
>   By one rude blow all swept apart,
> And hope and peace and home and heaven
>   Are shut forever from the heart!
>
> Then doth despair's wild, piercing shriek
>   Burst from the crushed and vanquished soul;
> And lips, used gentle words to speak,
>   Breathe curses forth beyond control.[26]

No eruption of the repressed, much less some elusive supernatural evil, makes the familiar strange in this poem. No, what creates the rift is the shattering of those very sentimental attachments or "quivering chords / Of love" upon which the wife depended for her connection to the "Whole," identified here as "hope and peace and home and heaven." Whatever the wife was before "one rude blow all swept apart," what emerges from the ruins of her domesticity is a monster with a woman's face, a being so violated by her husband's behavior that all her "gentle words" are turned to "curses." Transformed by rage and pain, this "Angel in the House" becomes, to steal a phrase from *Hamlet*, a "goblin damn'd" (1.4.40), her transformation a lurid mirroring of her marriage's transformation from heaven into hell. Far from producing the harmony of *concordia discors*, marriages such as this, Gage says in another poem (equally pessimistic about marriage) produce "discordant notes" only.[27]

A solid, unblinking distrust of men and marriage lies at the core of "Maniac Wife," as it does in scores of poems like it. Marriage is no pathway to bliss or a higher state of being, and certainly no Dickinsonian "blameless mystery" (F307). On the contrary, it is a soul-killing deceit, objectifying women, and then sucking life and desire out of them through years of misery, until at last death brings peace. In Mary Hewitt's exceptionally powerful "The Bride," marriage is a monster, one, however, that only reveals its true nature after it is too late, as the naïve young bride, "love[d] . . . for a season" and worn by her husband "like a festal robe," finds herself "flung careless by." Like the thirteenth Wise Woman at the celebration of Sleeping Beauty's birth, Hewitt's speaker warns her innocent heroine of things to come, perversely rewriting the fairy-tale script simply by taking it beyond the ending (that is, beyond the wedding):

> Wear broidered robe and costly gem—light be thy laugh and jest—
> Lead the gay dance—none look for wo beneath the glittering vest;
> Hide deep thy thoughts—yet thy young heart back from itself will quail,
> From all the hideousness which lies beneath its silver veil.

The "blissful vision" "will fade," the speaker sourly informs her subject in an apostrophe patently meant for other ears, and "thou wilt awake in tears!" No happy ending here, nor in the searing advice that the speaker gives in the poem's concluding stanza, advice that makes the Bible's "balm of Gilead" sound all too like a poisonous dram:

> Thou may'st not bend at other shrines—thy vow is on the first—
> Thou may'st not at another fount quaff to allay thy thirst:
> O drooping reed! no draught for thee may earthly hand prepare—
> Yet there is "balm in Gilead"—seek thy physician there!
>
> (*NAWP* 410)

Not only does Hewitt challenge the fairy-tale ending here, she treats—or seems to treat—marriage itself as some sort of divinely set trap, meant, perhaps, to swell the ranks of martyred female saints in heaven. For given that both divine law and its earthly reflection, coverture, forbade the bride "to allay [her] thirst" by quaffing "at another fount" (i.e., either to divorce or to have an affair), there is literally no way for this woman to separate herself from her misery except by dying.

Understood in these terms, the terms, that is, of coverture, marriage for women was little more than voluntary self-incarceration, a self-incarceration from which death was the only escape. And this is how poet after poet presents it. Thus Dickinson's well-known "She rose to His Requirement" (F857) buries the wife, with any talents she might possess, at the bottom of the patriarchal sea. In "Released," A.D.T. Whitney describes a housewife who lives and dies within "Four walls / Whose blank shut out all else of life"

(*NAWP* 131). In "A Woman's Death Wound," Helen Hunt Jackson, probably the most conservative on gender issues of all these writers, compares living in a marriage gone wrong to death by blood poisoning:

> Since then, the world has nothing missed
> In her, in voice or smile. But she—each day
> She counts until her dying is complete.
> One moan she makes, and ever doth repeat:
> "O lips that I have loved and kissed and kissed,
> Did I deserve to die this bitterest way?"
> (*AWP* 289–90)

Trapped by laws that worked entirely in the husband's favor, the best a woman caught in such a marriage could do was count the days "until her dying is complete"—not exactly the outcome domestic ideologues promised but certainly one likely to make death itself welcome to the female victim.

And this is, of course, precisely how that ultimate Wise Woman (or wicked fairy) among nineteenth-century women poets, Phoebe Cary, presents death, not once but over and over in *Poems and Parodies*. "I'm glad her life is over, / Glad that all her trials are past; / For her pillow was not softened / Down with roses to the last," Cary's speaker announces of the female protagonist in "The Life of Trial."[28] Cary's other female victims agree. The heroine of "Entering Heaven" comforts those watching by her bedside: "Never think of me as lying / By the dismal mould o'erspread, / But about the soft white pillow / Folded underneath my head" (3). After a lifetime of unremitting, unappreciated labor, this woman is more than ready to rest—a theme also underlying, albeit more subtly, Dickinson's great elegy to a dead housewife, "How many times these low feet staggered" (F238). Like many Dickinson speakers, although for different reasons, Cary's dying heroines in fact find death far more attractive than life. In "Death Scene," the female protagonist positively glows with rapture as she goes to God: "One moment her pale lips trembled / With the triumph she might not tell, / As the light of the life immortal / On her spirit's vision fell" (20). Morbid gothic excess doesn't get more gleeful than this.

For these speakers, dying is the only solution to the problem that living under coverture presented. Indeed, insofar as Cary draws her female victims generically, not even giving them names, they could be said to attenuate into spirit before one's very eyes, wraiths haunting their own poems just as their ghosts will haunt the houses in which they once lived. They are, that is, what coverture made them: nonpersons, beings without presence of their own, no/bodies, in more ways than one. What these poems suggest, in short, is that the nineteenth-century literary sentimentalization of domesticity was just what Sigourney said it was, a sentimentalization. Prescriptive literature, not to mention thousands of poems by male authors, identified the private sphere as a place where "ugly," "disagreeable facts" were swallowed up in the transcendent bliss of domestic comfort; but for the female speakers of these poems, home was its own kind of "ugly."

Among the poets I discuss, few wrote more pointedly of what domestic incarceration did to women than did the ever restless Elizabeth Stoddard. Published in *Harper's* in 1860, Stoddard's "Before the Mirror" is an unusually specific attack on domestic confinement. Looking into the ideological mirror supplied by texts such as Tennyson's "Lady of Shalott," the poem's speaker finds not "the beauty and harmony of woman's condition" but the phantasmatic images thrown up by her own frustration and despair. In this very gothic rewrite of male Victorian romanticism, Stoddard's speaker confronts her own nothingness, the "nobody" who she is and must be insofar as she lives the life men wished upon her—and wrote into their laws:

> And like the Lady of Shalott,
> 　　I look into the mirror wide,
> Where shadows come, and shadows go,
> 　　And ply my shuttle as they glide.
>
> .　.　.　.　.　.　.　.　.　.　.　.
>
> But weaving with a steady hand,
> 　　The shadows, whether false or true,
> I put aside a doubt which asks,
> 　　"Among these phantoms what are you?"

Confronted with her own attenuation into "shadow," Stoddard's speaker becomes one with the "phantoms" she weaves, the poet's re-vision of Tennyson's Arthurian fable reshaped into a modern woman's gothic horror story. This Lady of Shalott's destiny is not to die a vaguely idealized, but ever so romantic, death. Rather, it is to live a dark half-life of boredom, anger, and psychological enervation, doomed by the very protected status to which her Angelic "ladyhood" entitles her.

Like Piatt in "Charlotte's Sorrows," which also takes its cue from a male-authored version of the (sentimentalized) domestic woman, Stoddard is letting Tennyson's putative heroine write back, telling "the long, sad [real] story" of her life (*PB* 33). What "Before the Mirror" describes is what it feels like to have a self that is not a self but only some man's image of what you are, shaped to meet his needs and cut his bread and butter:

> And as my web grows darker too,
> 　　Accursed seems this empty room;
> I know I must forever weave
> 　　These phantoms by this hateful loom.
> 　　　　　　(*NAWP* 434)

In this uncanny nineteenth-century prefiguration of Sartre's existential drama *No Exit*, home is just another word for hell, at least for the women who are confined there.

That these poets were using gothic conventions to challenge domestic ideology as "a central system of practices, meanings and values" seems obvious to me; but as "Before the Mirror" suggests, marriage and home were not the only sites wherein the doublings and displacements of the gothic occur in their poems. Dickinson's most distinctive contribution to the domestic gothic was to relocate its mise en scène explicitly within the self, making her speakers' most important gothic encounters internal. In "It's [*sic*] Hour with itself" (F1211), it is "The Subterranean Freight" packed in "The Cellars of the Soul" that produces a "Terror" which "would enthrall the Street / Could Countenance disclose" (F1121). What need for a husband, when you can scare yourself to death?

Told by the culture at large that they were "Angels," "Doves," and so forth, how were women to deal with their dark side, their potential for rage and violence? And how were they to deal with the self-alienation such internal recognitions set off? "You call my soul a dove, a snowy dove," Piatt's speaker complains in "Shapes of a Soul." "But, take it from its sphere of bloom and dew, / And where will then your bird or blossom be?" (*PB* 8). Will she appear as a tiger or snake perhaps? These are the alternatives that Piatt's speaker offers. Like Piatt, Dickinson in "Civilization - spurns - the Leopard!" also uses feral animals to suggest the self-alienation women experienced when trying to understand themselves in relation to the ideological ideal. According to Dickinson, once a woman becomes aware of the poor ideological fit, this awareness cannot "be stifled - with Narcotic - / Nor suppressed - with Balm -" (F276),[29] and she longs for a freedom "Civilization" does not allow. Like Stoddard's "Before the Mirror" and Piatt's "Shapes of a Soul," that is, Dickinson's poem plays on the splits in subjectivity that literary sentimentality's self-alienating domestic tropes produced in women, rendering them strangers to themselves. Conscious of the fact that the Angel was, as Prins might say, an empty signifier as well as a signifier of emptiness, writers like Stoddard, Dickinson, and Piatt, each in her own way, entered into the darkness that this emptiness created to roust out what was lurking there.

Possibly the most consistently gothic, and disenchanted, of all these writers, including, Dickinson, Sarah Piatt could find intimations of gothic horror just about everywhere, inside and out—looking at a copy of Guido Reni's famous portrait of Beatrice Cenci in a shop window, for example, while out walking with a child: "Is it some Actress?" a slight school-boy said. / Some Actress? Yes— / The curtain rolled away, / Dusty and dim / The scene—among the dead." Dimly aware, perhaps, of his mother's dangerous plunge into the gothic imaginary, the child breaks the spell: "for a child's quick murmur breaks the charm, / Of terror that was winding round me so. / And, at the white touch of a pretty arm, / Darkness and Death and Agony crouch low" (*PB* 21–22).

For Piatt, who spent her childhood on her family's slaveholding plantation in Kentucky, the gothic was never far away. Waiting just behind the scrim of the conscious mind, it was a sort of internal theatre of the damned, projected onto and reflecting back the "real," if secret, life of women. The suggestion of possible incest in her Cenci poem is but one of a long list of possibilities for terror that her poetry offers up for contemplation, the most poignant being the ghosts of her own children, who return to haunt the family hearth: "No,—no, he is no ghost; he could not be; / . . . / Something whose moan we call the wind, whose tears / Sound but as rain-drops in our human ears" (*PB* 85). Unlike Longdon and Johnson, who found comfort in renewed contact with their dead, for Piatt such ghostly returns, like Freud's return of the repressed, had a destabilizing, anxiety-producing effect. Since her dead children exist only in memory, her yearning for them can never bridge that awe-filled gap in time that their deaths created. For Piatt, therefore, middle-class women's sanctioned role as channel to the dead was not, as Forest depicted it, a reconnection of severed attachments but, rather, a source of constant, unremitting pain.

Wherever one looks in domestic gothic poetry, one thing is clear: for women, the consequences of allegiance to domestic ideology were devastating. Taken in aggregate—not poet by poet but poem by poem—the poems in which nineteenth-century women rip the "veil," as Osgood calls it, from the "shrine," to disclose the "true" state of affairs in the private sphere, cover virtually every aspect of women's lives. Young women are seduced and abandoned; they sell themselves into marriage or turn prostitute to survive—and in the end they commit suicide. Married women are deceived, worked to death, bored, frustrated, or unfaithful. Mothers fare no better. God takes their children from them, or they lose their children to alcohol or prostitution or through divorce.[30] Some poets, like Rose Terry Cooke in "Blue-Beard's Closet," explicitly use the gothic to suggest that such miseries are women's inevitable fate: "Fasten the chamber! / Hide the red key; / Cover the portal, / That eyes may not see. / Get thee to market, / To wedding and prayer; / Labor or revel, / *The chamber is there!*" (*NAWP* 154). No matter what the addressee of this poem does, she is doomed. Even going to a nunnery won't save her. The story of Blue-Beard's closet, heaped high with the corpses of unnamed women, *was* woman's story, the "true," if gothic, "fairy-tale" that followed Sleeping Beauty's awakening.

In turning the domestic Angel into the universal female victim, unsafe at home and abroad, these poets confronted readers with bourgeois domesticity's self-splitting, soul-destroying effects. In Richard Brodhead's terms, that is, they confronted women with domesticity's status as an internally reinforced disciplinary regime or, put another way, its status as socially constructed performance. In so doing, they also worked to demystify it, making it possible for their readers to distance themselves both from the way things were supposed to be and the way things were. Going well beyond Sigourney, that is, they encouraged women to view the Angel herself as a fabrication of "laws and customs," *nomos* not *physis*. Once recognized as ideology, not "the way things were" or should be (Sigourney's position), the Angel could be disposed of, together with those laws that kept her in her place, "her sphere," even if it killed her.

No poem with which I am familiar, therefore, better illustrates the demystifying, deconstructive effect of domestic gothic poetry than Elizabeth Akers Allen's "Her Sphere," published in *Scribner's Monthly* the 1872. Ostensibly an elegy for a dead domestic Angel, "Her Sphere" is a singularly clear example of how political this entire discourse was when taken up by this extremely angry group of writers. In this sixteen-stanza poem, with its bitterly ironic title, Akers presents her deceased protagonist—with no apparent irony—as the ideological ideal: "No outward sign her angelhood revealed / Save that her eyes were wondrous mild and fair,— / The aureole round her forehead was concealed / By the pale glory of her shining hair." What more could one want? Beautiful, gentle, serene, good, clearly this woman should have the very best that bourgeois domesticity, which is to say, "her sphere," has to offer. Should. In fact, she does not. Rather, having taken up "the yoke and . . . name of wife," what she gets for her goodness is a life sentence at hard labor, working herself to death, serving others in that alternative definition of "her sphere" which the poem with brutal clarity offers. Married to a man "who made her tenderness and grace / A mere convenience of his narrow life / And put a seraph in a servant's place," she keeps her husband's house, rears "his" children, and nurses him back to health when he falls dangerously ill:

> She cheered his meager hearth,—she blessed and warmed
> > His poverty, and met its harsh demands
> With meek, unvarying patience, and performed
> > Its menial tasks with stained and battered hands.
>
> She nursed his children through their helpless years,—
> > Gave them her strength, her youth, her beauty's prime,—
> Bore for them sore privation, toil and tears,
> > Which made her old and tired before her time.
>
> And when fierce fever smote him with its blight
> > Her calm, consoling presence charmed his pain;
> Through long and thankless watches, day and night,
> > Her fluttering fingers cooled his face like rain.

When the husband finally repents—as she lies dying—it is, of course, too late. Like the protagonist of Cary's "Entering Heaven," Allen's Angel is already well on her way to some much-deserved R & R in paradise.[31]

Ostensibly, "Her Sphere" uses sentimentality to celebrate the beauteous self-sacrifice of female Angels, but it does so by focusing unrelentingly on the pain and suffering that are the Angel's lot, subtly, or maybe not so subtly, trashing domesticity as a "lived body of meanings and values" in the process. Not only is this woman killed by her unpaid labor but she is thoroughly alienated from it also, and alienated from herself as well, despite the fact that ideologically speaking she was fulfilling her "natural" role in "her [natural and divinely appointed] sphere." As Allen carefully establishes, this is in fact the husband's sphere, not hers. Under coverture, which, I would suggest, is the poem's primary target, everything is "his"—the home, the hearth, the children, the woman herself, together with her services. Against this legally constituted set of domestic arrangements, a woman on her own had, as we saw in "To My Child," no chance.

What Allen is talking about here, that is, is not simply one individual male's isolated indifference and brutality. Like Sigourney, she is indicting a system that was tantamount to state-supported murder, no matter how complicit the woman made herself through her own submission. If domestic ideologues assumed that women's fulfillment of their duties would guarantee them happiness and security in this world as well as in the next, coverture insured that this "dream" would fall, as Sigourney insisted, very far short of fulfillment, at least in this world, whatever might happen in the next. Going beyond Sigourney, Allen's poem also suggests that coverture itself produces the Angel. Empty as the life she leads, this wife has no raison d'être except as an extension of her husband's desire. Both her misery and her death are written into "her sphere," and into her as well, by virtue of her Angelhood, her gender.

Killing the Angel I: Literary Parody and the Sentimental

Precisely because domestic gothic poems are ironic, however, one can never be absolutely certain, even in a poem as seemingly blatant as "Her Sphere," of the author's intentions. Irony, of all literary figures, is the slipperiest, the most difficult to detect. "You will read or you will not read," Piatt declares in "An After-Poem" (*PB* 18). Put into today's vernacular: you'll "get it" or you won't.[32] The use of literary parody to ironize the sentimental is another matter and makes Cary's *Poems and Parodies* central not just to this chapter but also to this entire study. Cary's volume is a Rosetta Stone, allowing us to translate from one "language"—or set of signifying practices—to another. Without the parodies, Cary's *Poems* is indistinguishable from a multitude of seemingly similar volumes, its inclusion of an occasional deviant poem notwithstanding. As reviews make clear, however, one's entire sense of Cary's volume and of Cary herself changes radically on reading the parodies. From a trite but true sentimentalist, Cary suddenly looks more like a blasphemer, perpetrating "wanton" burlesques on the genteel literary tradition, or at least so said an anguished review in the *Southern Literary Messenger*:

> We cannot say . . . that either the poems or the parodies greatly please us. The subjects of the former are serious even to the deepest sadness— ten of the first fifteen . . . are death-bed scenes—and Miss Carey's [*sic*] melancholy muse seems a *memento mori* whose eyes are a fountain of tears. Parodies we have ever held in detestation, especially such as Miss Carey gives us on page 192, in which the exquisite verses of Aldrich are so wantonly burlesqued. We ask the reader what is to be thought of a parodist who seeks to turn into ridicule such a gem . . .? We cannot give Miss Carey's profanation of these stanzas even for the sake of illustration. We suppose she is so fond of describing death-beds herself, that she is unwilling any body else should do it.[33]

The reviewer's use of the term "profanation" is telling. In not only subjecting Aldrich's sacred hymn to dying womanhood ("A Death-Bed") to ridicule but doing so in the crudest possible way, Cary was striking at the heart of domesticity's empire, challenging simultaneously both the quasi-religious mystique that hedged the "Angel" in *and* the language of hyperrefinement and delicacy that kept this mystique alive: its quintessentially genteel "vagueness." Understood in these terms, Cary's satirizing of the genteel jeopardized the very foundations of bourgeois cultural hegemony—its gender expectations and its literary expectations alike; and Cary did so in ways so patently obvious that Victorian readers could not ignore them. If irony is subtle, parody is not; and for a poet so closely associated with the sentimental to mock the very themes she promoted elsewhere put all she wrote in doubt. Indeed, as another, equally outraged, reviewer said, speaking of Cary's hatchet job on Bryant's "The Future Life," the parodies put Cary herself in doubt also, for what "woman of sentiment," that is, what "True Woman," would take such a poem "for the exercise of her humor"?[34]

A few examples from Cary's 1854 volume and from A.D.T. Whitney's *Mother Goose for Grown Folks* (1860) will suffice to show how writers like Cary and Whitney used parody to undermine the disciplinary power of domestic ideology and genteel sentimental literature alike. As noted earlier, except for the British poet Felicia Hemans, Cary's parodies are all aimed at the best-known *male* writers of the mainstream tradition. I will look at "Samuel Brown," a parody of Poe's "Annabel Lee," and two poems mentioned by reviewers, "The City Life," parodying Bryant's "The Future Life," and "The Wife," a reworking of Aldrich's "A Death-Bed." What interests me in these, as in other, parodies, is the way Cary uses crass, hard-nosed, imagery to puncture the ideality of the genteel style and its Wertherian perspective on women, love, and marriage. In "Samuel Brown," for example, no vague death divides the young lovers; greed does. Seduced by a woman with a carriage and assorted "high-bred kinsmen" (Poe's phrase), Samuel abandons his first beloved (the speaker) for life "uptown." Not entirely, however. By means of secret letters, nighttime meetings in the park, walks down Broadway, and liaisons in the speaker's house "down town," the "love that was more than love" goes on, all but undeterred by Samuel's selling himself to another woman. Even Samuel's name brings Poe's romantic balderdash down to earth: the melodious "Annabel Lee" is exchanged for the singularly unmelodious, not to mention utterly plebian, Sam Brown.

In "The City Life," Cary debunks Bryant's reverential ode to a dead wife in similarly crude ways, turning it into a morally twisted variant of the city mouse/country mouse fable. According to Bryant's speaker, what he lost when his wife died was the services of the domestic Angel incarnate: gentle, serene, tender, meek, and so on—a woman effectively identical to Allen's Angel in "Her Sphere," right down to the same woes. She "meekly with my harsher nature bore," Bryant's self-reproaching speaker confesses, the belated admission presumably getting him off the hook. In Cary's version, on the other hand, the male lover is the one to suffer: he must put up with the speaker's uncouth country ways. Now that he has moved to town, she worries that he will no longer acknowledge her or teach her what she needs to know:

> Yet though thou wear'st the glory of the town,
>   Wilt thou not keep the same belovèd name,
> The same black-satin vest, and morning-gown,
>   Lovelier in New York city, yet the same?
>
> Shalt thou not teach me, in that grander home
>   The wisdom that I learned so ill in this,—
> The wisdom which is fine,—till I become
>   Thy fit companion in that place of bliss?
>   (*NAWP* 101)

To turn heaven into the Big Apple is bad enough. To identify heavenly "bliss" with knowing how to behave and dress fashionably could only have struck many nineteenth-century readers—not just reviewers—as blasphemous, allowances for humor notwithstanding.

Yet the *Southern Literary Messenger* reviewer was probably right in singling out Cary's parody of Aldrich's "A Death-Bed" for special condemnation. A thoroughly conventional treatment of one of Cary's own favorite themes, the dying woman, Aldrich's poem gives neither the cause of death nor—significantly, in light of Cary's handling of the poem—information on the woman's marital status. Whoever the woman was, and whatever her history, her dying is all we know: "Her suffering ended with the day, / Yet lived she at its close, / And breathed the long, long night away / In statue-like repose." That is stanza one. Stanza two of this blessedly brief poem goes: "But when the sun in all his state / Illumed the eastern skies, / She passed through Glory's morning gate / And walked in Paradise!" (*AAA* 197). In Cary's hands, or at the mercy of her pen, this poem, now provocatively titled "The Wife," becomes: "Her washing ended with the day, / Yet lived she at its close, / And passed the long, long night away, / In darning ragged hose. / But when the sun in all his state / Illumed the eastern skies, / She passed about the kitchen grate, / And went to making pies" (*NAWP* 101). "If there is any kitchen in Parnassus, my Muse," Sigourney observed, summing up her career in a moment of ironic self-deprecation, "has surely officiated there as a woman of all work and an aproned waiter."[35] Call it Paradise or Parnassus, women's place was the kitchen, and there she labored until forever done with making pies and darning hose.

By firmly identifying the woman in her parody as a "wife," whether or not the protagonist of Aldrich's poem was, Cary is not only able to suggest a real cause for her death—exhaustion—but to deromanticize what Aldrich deliberately and genteelly leaves vague. Like Poe, Aldrich treats the death of a beautiful woman as the sublime object of aesthetic contemplation. The Angel is glorified, basically, for dying with pizzazz, "statue-like" in her "repose." Against this thoroughly spiritualized and completely unnatural image of marmoreal passivity, Cary gives us a wife who is up all day—and night—washing laundry, mending hose, baking pies. The juxtaposition could not be cruder or—at least from a woman's perspective—more on target. In "How many times these low feet staggered" (F238), Dickinson makes a similar juxtaposition—the corpse's monumentality on the one hand, her lowly labor in life on the other—to similar, if far more subtle, effect. More ironic than parodic, her poem, as I have discovered many times when teaching it, is susceptible to misreading. Cary's is not.

Like Cary's parodies, A.D.T. Whitney's *Mother Goose for Grown Folks* (1860), is also bent on demystifying the romanticism of the genteel tradition: its love of vagueness, its glorification of the noble and sublime, and its obsession with the aesthetically objectified woman. In the person of that "rampant hag," Mother Goose, Whitney gives herself the freedom to be as down-to-earth as she wants; and earthy she is, bitterly mocking the myths that identified greatness with men and treated "delicate" women (even poets) as maids of all work. If men are great, Mother Goose suggests, in a somewhat off-color treatment of that woefully named youth Jack Horner, it is because they take unto themselves the privilege of defining "greatness":

> And again it is his luck
> To be just in time to pluck,

By a clever "operation," from the pie
    An unexpected "plum";
    So he glorifies his thumb,
And says, proudly, "What a mighty man am I!"

Jack may think getting the plum is a sign of his "might," but Mother Goose thinks otherwise. Not only was it sheerest good luck that Jack got the plum, but whether or not he did, the pie itself was not of his making, so he cannot take credit for it, only for eating it, which is hardly the same thing: "For the fruit of others' baking / So a fresh diploma taking, / Comes he forth, a full accredited Professor!" As David Leverenz has shrewdly pointed out of Emerson, "Professor" Horner, too, seems blissfully unaware that his vaunted self-reliance is structurally dependent on women's work (pie making),[36] just as my students today are blissfully unaware that Thoreau's mother did his laundry. Like other men, from Emerson, Thoreau, and Whitman to Freud and Lacan, Jack, you could say, inflates the value of size and what it entitles him to: "Or he's not too nice to mix / In the dish of politics; / And the dignity of office he puts on: / And he feels as big again / As a dozen nobler men, / While he writes himself the Honorable John!" (*NAWP* 125). In "Brahmic," Whitney credits Mother Goose as the true source of the knowledge men claim, while in "Missions," we are told that women with the courage to change the world will only receive *their* credit in heaven. Mother Goose, in short, depicts a male imaginary in which women have no separate existence and no role except as the anonymous servicers of men (even as the Angel in Allen's poem has no name). And that, of course, is Whitney's point. Whatever women might contribute, male stars shine alone in the male sky. Only the latter's efforts count or are visible, just as, under coverture, only men were visible before the law.

Insofar as humor involves making fun of something, even if it is only an idea or a set of codes, the line between comedy and aggressive anger is, notoriously, difficult to discern. Indeed, joking is generally recognized as a relatively benign way of relieving one's anger toward someone. Are the poems in *Mother Goose* good-natured, if mildly salacious, fun, a venting of steam, not to be taken seriously, or are they the not-so-subtle expressions of one woman's rage? Although in life, as in *Mother Goose*, Whitney disclaimed feminist sympathies—"I don't stand up for Woman's Right," Mother Goose declares in "Missions" (*NAWP* 128)—her disgust with male self-aggrandizement is palpable. Poems such as "Jack Horner," with his very phallic thumb, and "Missions" suggest that, whatever Whitney preached publicly, privately she recognized that women were socially oppressed by men who benefited directly and indirectly from oppressing them. Through their power to control discourse as well as to ascribe value, men mystified their privilege, like the three wise men of Gotham (the target of "Bowls"), throwing a veil of "mute signification" over their failures or claiming them as successes: "Was it, perhaps, a railroad speculation? / Or a big ship to carry all creation, / That, by some kink of its machinery, / Failed, in the end, to carry even three? / Or other fond, erroneous calculation / Of splendid schemes that died disastrously?" (*NAWP* 127–28). From the speaker's perspective, human history was pock-marked with "splendid schemes that died disastrously." By cutting the men responsible for them down to size, Mother Goose, if nothing else, creates breathing room for women.

The particular poems touched on in this chapter represent pressure points where nineteenth-century bourgeois women and nineteenth-century bourgeois gender ideology clashed head on and where, ultimately, the latter gave way to new ways of thinking, new forms of subjectivity, new systems of "lived" beliefs. More than anything else, I would argue, it is the uninterrogated commitment to political purity, epitomized in the stark binaries of the Douglas-Tompkins debate, that has obscured the actual dimensions of these nineteenth-century women's achievements and the revolution—however uneven, however compromised by racism, imperialism, and class bias—that they wrought. As scholars from Douglas to Brodhead and Berlant have argued, bourgeois women generally were undeniably complicit in their own oppression, just as many joined bourgeois men in oppressing others; but collectively, as Tompkins argues, they were also powerful, if self-conflicted, agents of progressive reform to whom women living today owe a sizeable debt.

As Williams insists, hegemonic belief systems, even the most entrenched, are not rigid, uniform, and eternally fixed. They are constantly obliged to respond to pressures from within and without and to modify themselves accordingly. They are, therefore, processual, not static, and because they are, they are also unavoidably unstable. The liberatory task confronting nineteenth-century mainstream women, like that confronting their minority peers, could not be consummated in a day, nor could it occur without giving rise to deep new divisions among women themselves, given the differences of class, faith, race, and region dividing nineteenth-century women as a whole. But precisely because this is true, this is also why Habermas is so useful. Through the passionate intersubjective exchanges which constitute political debate in the Habermasian public sphere or in the numerous counter-public spheres into which it may be subdivided, nineteenth-century women, both white and of color, were able to carry out their emancipatory projects and because of their efforts the so-called "New Woman" came to be. But the revolution that these women wrought was not an overnight affair, nor did it proceed from the top down. Rather, it worked through evolution, that is, through piecemeal changes unremarkable in themselves and never less than compromised as a result. Given the complexity of social relationships among these women and the various factors dividing them, it would be not merely utopic but absurd to expect the kind of profound social transformation that they made possible to come about in any other way.

❧ 6 ❧

Irony's Edge: Sarah Piatt and the Postbellum Speaker

> [Paul de Man's] idea of textuality forecloses the possibility
> of his being able to show that "literature" is as much a
> "communicative action" (to borrow Habermas's term) as it
> is a discipline of "reading."
> —JEROME McGANN, *Social Values and Poetic Acts*, 1988[1]

In a long poem inspired by an 1871 engraving of the execution of a *pétroleuse* ("petroleum thrower" or "palace-burner"), Sarah Piatt's speaker, a bourgeois mother, takes up the fate of the Paris Commune, Europe's first experiment in communism, and of the women who, with no alternative but starvation, took their protests into the streets. Uncannily reminiscent of the opening scene in Virginia Woolf's *To the Lighthouse*, the mise en scène of Piatt's poem is quintessentially middle-class domestic. A mother and son are perusing clippings from some old newspapers, *Harper's Weekly* among them. Against his mother's objections, the boy returns to one clipping in particular, the execution of a woman by a firing squad of uniformed French soldiers. The woman's hands are bound behind her back, her face is ravaged, her black hair, long and tangled. But power as well as desperation emanate from her figure, which, with its voluminous black skirt, takes up a good share of the weekly's folio-size page (fig. 6).

In his innocence, the boy asks his mother if, like the pétroleuses, as the female Communards were known,[2] she too would "burn palaces." The mother does not respond, sending him off to play instead. After he leaves, however, she mulls over what her answer would be. In the following internal dialogue, the mother confronts the yawning gulf between herself and the nameless creature whose fate the *Weekly* has put before her. In the mirror the pétroleuse provides, Piatt's speaker measures who and what she herself is:

Would I? Go to your play. Would I, indeed?
I? Does the boy not know my soul to be

Languid and worldly, with a dainty need
  For light and music? Yet he questions me.

Can he have seen my soul more near than I?
  Ah! in the dusk and distance sweet she seems,
With lips to kiss away a baby's cry,
  Hands fit for flowers, and eyes for tears and dreams.

Can he have seen my soul? And could she wear
  Such utter life upon a dying face,
Such unappealing, beautiful despair,
  Such garments—soon to be a shroud—with grace?

Piatt's "Palace-Burner" appeared in the November 1872 issue of the *Independent*, a socially progressive New York City weekly to which she contributed, over the course of three decades, some sixty-nine poems, one-sixth of her mature output. The *Harper's* article appeared a year and a half earlier, on July 8, 1871, little more than a month after the Commune's fall. Like the poem, the article exhibits an ambivalent sympathy for its subject, expressing horror at the palace-burner's putative deed—putting the torch to "some of the finest buildings in Paris"—but acknowledging the legitimacy of the grievances driving her to it. From an "industrious, well-behaved woman, with a husband and children," *Harper's* explains, desperation and hunger transformed the pétroleuse into a being who had nothing to lose and acted accordingly.

However, as was Piatt's practice when using such sources, she gives the *Harper's* account a twist without precedent in the story itself. According to the newspaper, responsibility for the civil insurrection lay with the French politicians, whose "miserable jealousies and ambitions" dragged out the situation in Paris for a year, bringing untold suffering on Paris's working poor. Had the government done its job, the Commune women would never have gone to such extremes. From *Harper's* perspective, utter hopelessness alone could drive those "belong[ing] to what is emphatically styled the gentler sex" to behave so badly. "Can we not imagine," the newspaper asks, "that such a poor creature, demoralized by want of work, and with her brain weakened by slow starvation, would hail the establishment of the Commune as a sort of millennium which would cure all her troubles, and would therefore burst into a fury of uncontrollable mania upon its violent suppression?"[3]

Perhaps. But Piatt's speaker arrives at a different conclusion about the palace burner and, more significantly, about the "well-behaved woman, with . . . husband and children" who serves as the *Weekly's* unstated (bourgeois) female norm. Turning her thoughts back on herself, the speaker explores her own complicity and, by inference, that of other women, whose "dainty need for light and music" has left their souls too "languid and worldly" to risk the righting of a wrong. Surrounded by material comforts, women like the

Fig. 6. The End of the Commune—Execution of a Pétroleuse

speaker are also part of the problem, infecting the domestic interior, even the nursery, with their passive acquiescence in evil. Viewed thus, the mother, whose lips "are fit," as Piatt puts it, "to kiss away a baby's cry" is no fit guardian for this same child as it seeks to grow into moral—and political— maturity.

Consigned to literary oblivion for over a hundred years, "The Palace-Burner" is now Sarah Piatt's most frequently reprinted poem and given both its political insight and its strategy of ironic reversal—the way it twists back upon itself as the speaker interrogates her own political bad faith—justly so.

As the poem opens, the maternal speaker of this poem, like Allen's Angel in "Her Sphere," seems the ideal bourgeois type, a woman with "hands fit for flowers, and eyes for tears and dreams," an "Angel" of "light and music," a good Christian and a loving parent, who has taught her son "to respect the laws":

> You wish that you had lived in Paris then?
>   You would have loved to burn a palace, too?
> But they had guns in France, and Christian men
>   Shot wicked little Communists, like you.
>
> You would have burned the palace? Just because
>   You did not live in it yourself! Oh! why?
> Have I not taught you to respect the laws?
>   *You* would have burned the palace. Would not *I*?

But then her son's question turns this pretty bit of Victoriana inside out. Breaching the wall that presumably insulates the private from the public sphere, the question leads the mother to resituate herself historically and socially with respect to the very kind of class divisions that produced the pétroleuse in the first place. Not the palace-burner's morality, but that of this genteel bourgeois woman, is on trial in this poem. Her inactivity and moral indifference not only help perpetuate the status quo but encourage a similar passivity in her son. Most importantly, they instill noncritical obedience to authority, muddying the child's innate sense of justice—his readiness to burn palaces also.

If, as some have argued, antebellum high sentimentality's sympathy politics encouraged white bourgeois women to empower themselves by appropriating others' pain, then Piatt's postbellum mother can cry, "Not guilty." However, this is only because she has refused all social responsibility whatsoever. In the split consciousness that controls this poem, the speaker testifies against herself, as Piatt gives formal shape to her ironic awareness of the blatant gulf between sentimentality's social and its domestic vision. In particular, this poem challenges female high sentimentality's bedrock assumption that domestic virtue automatically translates into social virtue. To domestic ideology's idealized elevation of female morality, "The Palace-Burner" holds up a mirror wherein bourgeois domesticity reveals itself as a pernicious form of apolitical narcissism instead:

> Would *I* burn palaces? The child has seen
>   In this fierce creature of the Commune here,
> So bright with bitterness and so serene,
>   A being finer than my soul, I fear.
>
>   (*PB* 39–40)

On this enigmatic and mordantly self-ironizing note the poem ends.

Piatt's ability, so powerfully displayed in "The Palace-Burner," to engage in politically grounded self-ironization makes her the single most important poet in this study. Like almost all nineteenth-century U.S. poets who came of age after 1830, Piatt wrote a great deal of genteel poetry. To judge by her acceptance rate in the nation's leading literary magazines, she was unusually skilled at the genteel style, placing thirty poems in the *Atlantic Monthly* alone. Including 250 pieces of juvenilia, which she published principally in the *Louisville Journal* and the *New York Ledger*, some 500 of her poems appeared in over thirty newspapers and periodicals during her lifetime, a record only the best-known women poets matched and, possibly, only Sigourney exceeded. Nevertheless, a surprising amount of this output does not, in fact, conform to the period's idealizing genteel aesthetic. In these latter poems, Piatt deploys a set of rhetorical strategies—direct and indirect dialogue, parody, fragmented speakers, ambiguity of perspective—in ways that rank her among the century's most distinctive U.S. poets. In this chapter, I will focus on these poems and on Piatt as the poet whose writing has the most to say about the complicated relationship between irony, sentimentality, politics, and modernity in late-nineteenth-century women's poetry.

Of postbellum poets, Dickinson included, Piatt most consistently addressed the issue of "woman's place" in the modern world, making the formation of middle-class women's subjectivity—or, put another way, the ironic deconstruction of the Angel—her principal subject. In taking up this theme, Piatt treated women's role both in respect to itself and with respect to the larger political, social, and literary issues at stake. At the same time, however, because Piatt did rely so heavily on irony, she introduced a level of ambiguity into her writing that, as in "The Palace-Burner," constantly risks setting her very morally attuned poetry morally adrift. Despite Piatt's deep commitment to her poetry's political role in the public sphere, she, no less than Dickinson, contributed, therefore, to an emergent form of female textuality that left more directly engaged political writers, of the kind discussed thus far, all but entirely out in the cold.[4] In her poetry's split aims—political on the one hand, textual on the other—one finds adumbrations of the "great divide" that, according to Andreas Huyssen, was foundational to the making of modernism itself.[5]

Piatt's reliance on irony as the organizing principle of her verse makes her poetry, especially for a nineteenth-century writer, an unusually difficult read. To "get" her at all requires concentrating self-consciously on how her poems are put together, both what they put in and, even more important, what they leave out, their gaps, twists, and evasions. As contemporary reviews complained, this strategy wrought havoc with the high moral idealism that was the lifeblood of the genteel tradition and the foundation of genteel—as opposed to modernist—aesthetics. For Piatt, this was probably the point. All the evidence suggests that she found both the romance culture of the ante-bellum South and the sentimental bourgeois culture of the North equally problematic. Having avoided the oversimplifications of worldviews she, with very good reason, distrusted, however, Piatt, like many another ironist, had nothing but irony to put in their place. In "The Palace-Burner"'s self-reflex-ive yet nonetheless politically passive speaker—a woman who has no way out of the complicity she despises in herself—Piatt, with searing self-knowledge, was writing of herself. How she came to this position and the impact that it had on the poetry she produced are among the primary issues I will concern myself with here.

Irony's Origins: Sarah Piatt's Civil War

Piatt's awareness of female complicity's narcissistic foundations is inseparable from her response to the Civil War. Any analysis of her political poetry must therefore start here. A native Kentuckian and the daughter and granddaugh-ter of slaveholders—she listed Boones, Bryans, and Spiers among her imme-diate forebears—Piatt brought to the Civil War a political subjectivity formed and articulated in the borderland separating North from South. Born on her maternal grandmother's plantation outside Lexington, Ken-tucky, in 1836, she moved north in 1861 after her marriage to the Ohio poet John James Piatt. She and her husband spent the war years in Washington, D.C., where J. J., as John James signed himself, held a minor patronage position in the Treasury Department. Aside from a few brief visits, Piatt never returned to the South. Politically speaking, for her, the war became a geo-temporal watershed instead. On one side stood the South, a childhood "fairyland" of myth and romance, which, as she says in "A Hundred Years Ago," hid snakes in its "bright sands" (*PB* 13). On the other side, stood the postbellum North, a nightmare of industrial pollution and urban poverty where, according to another poem, "A Neighborhood Incident," the home-less froze to death in full view of commuters taking the trains into Cincinnati (*PB* 106–7). In neither of these worlds could Piatt escape the consequences of her class and race privilege, and it is from this bitter realization that the majority of her most powerful poems come. One of these poems is "Giving Back the Flower," the pivotal poem in the evolution of her writing.

Published in the 1867 *Galaxy*, but never collected in any of Piatt's books, "Giving Back the Flower" takes the form of a married woman's address to a dead lover. Even for a Piatt poem, it is unusually dense with intertextual links not just to numerous other poems she wrote but to an entire phalanx of texts, beginning with the *Iliad*, in which women, as symbols of the "goods" over which men quarrel, are linked to desire, war, and betrayal. As in "The Palace-Burner," "Giving" opens in medias res with the speaker re-sponding to what someone else has said, here the former lover:

So, because you chose to follow me into the subtle sadness of night,
　　And to stand in the half-set moon with the weird fall-light on your
　　　glimmering hair,
Till your presence hid all of the earth and all of the sky from my sight,
　　And to give me a little scarlet bud, that was dying of frost, to wear,

Say, must you taunt me forever, forever? You looked at my hand and you
　　knew
　　That I was the slave of the Ring, while you were as free as the wind is
　　　free.
When I saw your corpse in your coffin, I flung back your flower to you;
　　It was all of yours that I ever had; you may keep it, and—keep from
　　　me.

Ah? so God is your witness. Has God, then, no world to look after but
　　ours?
　　May He not have been searching for that wild star, with trailing
　　　plumage, that flew
Far over a part of our darkness while we were there by the freezing
　　flowers,
　　Or else brightening some planet's luminous rings, instead of thinking of
　　　you?

Or, if He was near us at all, do you think that He would sit listening there
　　Because you sang "Hear me, Norma," to a woman in jewels and lace,
While, so close to us, down in another street, in the wet, unlighted air,
　　There were children crying for bread and fire, and mothers who ques-
　　　tioned His grace?

Or perhaps He had gone to the ghastly field where the fight had been that
　　day,
　　To number the bloody stabs that were there, to look at and judge the
　　　dead;
Or else to the place full of fever and moans where the wretched wounded
　　lay;
　　At least I do not believe that He cares to remember a word that you
　　　said.

So take back your flower, I tell you—of its sweetness I now have no need;
　　Yes, take back your flower down into the stillness and mystery to keep;
When you wake I will take it, and God, then, perhaps will witness indeed,
　　But go, now, and tell Death he must watch you, and not let you walk in
　　　your sleep.

　　　　　　　　　　　　　　　　　　　　　　　　　　(PB 7–8)

Like many Piatt poems, "Giving Back the Flower" has a double time frame: *time when*, in this case, the moment when the lover vowed his faith, taking God as his witness, and *time now*, in which the poem itself occurs. In *time when* the speaker stood in a garden, amidst "freezing flowers," listening to her lover sing a melody from Bellini's opera *Norma*. Hearing him, the speaker was moved by feelings she had never experienced before, causing "all of the earth and all of the sky [to be hidden] from [her] sight." In a scene not unlike that between Clarissa Dalloway and Sally Seton in Woolf's *Mrs. Dalloway*, the lover gives the speaker "a little scarlet bud, dying of frost," a bud symbolizing, that is, not just mutual passion, but the specific state of the speaker's sexuality: tipped with frost. The man calls on God to witness his faith as he speaks.

From the speaker's perspective, in *time now*, the lover has kept his vow but not as he intended. Not only has the speaker remained "a slave to the Ring," that is, married, but the lover himself has died, leaving her, if anything, worse off than she was before. For having been given this brief glimpse of erotic possibility, the speaker now finds herself tormented by desires she cannot fulfill. Instead of providing closure, the lover's death has, that is, insured that their story will remain always open, always unfinished, always turning back on itself. This is what gives the lover's vow its terrible irony. Whatever else God was doing on the night these two came together, he was not concerned with them or with insuring that their story came out right. But in the bitterest of reversals, death has made it possible for the lover to keep his word anyway, if only in the most perverse of ways.

I have paraphrased "Giving Back the Flower" at length because even at the simplest narrative level, it is a manifestly difficult poem. Set within the context of Piatt's other poems to dead lover(s), most of whom are Southern, and set within the context of the romantic love tradition to which it belongs, as signaled by the allusion to Bellini's opera, this poem's meanings become even harder to unpack. This is true, I believe, because for Piatt, there was nothing simple about her speaker's situation either as a historical or as a literary subject. In terms of both subject locations, this married woman's loyalties are divided, her love an act of betrayal.

While the dead lover's identity as a soldier is not made clear in "Giving Back the Flower," other Piatt poems specifically address a Southern soldier-lover: for example, "One from the Dead" (1871), and "A Ghost at the Opera" (1873). In these latter poems, which appear to deal with the same individual, the salient features constituting the lover's "identity" include a rose geranium, a breast wound, his musical ability, the "glimmering" beauty of his presence, his fervent defense of the "lost cause," and the waste that is his death. "He looked at me across the fading field. / The South was in his blood, his soul, his face. / Imperious despair, too lost to yield, / Gave a quick glory to a desperate grace" ("Ghost at the Opera" [*PB* 44]).

If, however, such lines seem to represent stereotypically the magnetic attractiveness of Southern romanticism, the romanticism is one Piatt herself refuses to endorse. The Old South may have been a "fairyland," as she suggests in a number of poems, but, by that token, the soldiers who fought and died in her defense are "dead fairies." Unreal as their illusions of glory, they are "scorched to death with lightning" ("Dead Fairies" [*PB* 19]). Their dream dies with them. As Piatt's speaker declares in "Mock Diamonds," one of her bitterest poems and one that deconstructs not just the myth of the Southern Chevalier but that of the Southern Belle, those soldiers who survive the war do so only to metamorphose into brigands and Ku Klux Klansmen. And what they become becomes the underwriting signature of what they were: "'One of the doubtful chivalry, / The midnight-vengeance meetings, / Who sends, from ghostly company, / Such fearful queer-spell'd greetings!'" Wearing false masks before the war, they become self-mockeries afterward (*PB* 29).

But while Southern romanticism ends up betraying itself, concluding in outlawry or, as in "Giving Back the Flower," with death, the North offers nothing better. The *time when* location of this poem is Washington, D.C., in wartime, where Piatt could easily have attended Bellini's opera or heard a concert at which "Here me, Norma," was sung.[6] This is not a romantic setting, however, despite the flower-filled garden and the illicit meeting between lovers. On the contrary, in neighboring streets, women and children, pauperized by the war, are crying for bread and shivering in the cold. The death-infected hospitals, described so vividly by Whitman, are also nearby, as are the fields where soldiers were fighting and dying. Against this backdrop, the gratifications of romantic love seem selfish at best. In the homosocial triangle structuring this love affair—a triangle which replicates the war itself—the speaker, like the land fought over, is nothing but a prize for which men compete, and die.

If, like the titular heroine of Bellini's opera, the speaker has chosen a lover from among the enemy, there is, therefore, nothing transcendent, let alone "sublime," in her gesture or in her subsequent destiny or, finally, in the drama in which she figures. And having apprehended just how shabby this overwritten story is, the speaker is no longer willing to hold up her part. The price is too high, the reward, fraudulent. For Piatt, writing on the romantic tradition from a specifically woman's point of view and gazing at its idealism from the other side of a war in which death occurred on a scale unimaginable at the time, Western culture imploded here. As a thinking human being and a moral one, Piatt's *time now* speaker wants out, saying, like Robert Graves of World War I—a war whose disillusioning effect occurred on a far vaster scale—"good-bye to all that." In particular, she is saying good-bye to the time-honored literary role that women from Helen and Dido to Cleopatra and Norma played as the objects of heroic male desire and the prizes for which men fought.[7]

It is against the ironized position that Piatt adopts in this relatively early poem that her later, far more realist, critiques of domestic ideology and both literary and high sentimentality must be read. Although fragments of "Giving Back the Flower"'s romance appear in later poems, Piatt never wrote another poem quite like it. It was in truth a "valedictory," a farewell to the melodramatic Byronic posturing of her juvenilia and to her own naïve faith in glimmering illusions. In other poems published at the same time, she began moving toward her mature poetic instead, a stripped-down kind of writing in which multiple speakers and direct and indirect dialogue give her thinking the hard, if typically subtle, edge of "The Palace-Burner." What Piatt took from the Civil War was the recognition of narcissism's dangers, especially when underwriting or underwritten by the romance of war. After "Giving Back the Flower," she extended her critique of narcissism to its impact on marriage and domestic life as she experienced them in her new subject position as Northern bourgeois matron. If Piatt shed one ideologically informed "identity"—that, as it were, of the heroine of Southern Romance culture—the poems to which I now turn suggest that she found her next incarnation—that of the Angel in the House—no less problematic.

Killing the Angel II: Parody Reprised

When the twenty-five-year-old Sarah Morgan Bryan married the Ohio-born John James Piatt at her Aunt "Annie" Boone's home in New Castle, Kentucky, in June 1861, she married a man who, if we believe his poetry, deemed "Home" another word for "Heaven." In this Heaven-Home, the Angel-wife dedicated herself entirely to meeting her husband's needs and those of their "blithe children." Within this Angelically created "circle [of] warmth," the husband found refuge and reward for his labors, while, "enchanted still," the Angel went about her daily chores—cooking, cleaning, darning hose, and making pies—shedding rose petals everywhere. Possessing her, the husband, otherwise doomed to "dusty work-day toil," possessed the summa of human life. At least, so John James presents domestic life in "Firelight Abroad" (1878), a poem whose central figure, the alighting bride, Sarah would parody in "The Descent of the Angel" (1879), her own, much less enthusiastic, poem on marriage. First, however, here is J. J.:

> By my lone casement so I love to watch
> That halo of the fireside shed abroad
> Into the world—Home's holy breath of light—
> Dreaming of spirits in its inner glow.
>
> There the young bride alights from charmed air
> Into the real air, enchanted still,

Breathing a bower of roses evermore
Over the husband's dusty week-day toil—

. . . .

      There the mother smiles
Her patient days away in daily love,
With gentle lips and tender-touching hands.
There her blithe children, asking for her knees,
(Illumined by the climbing, dancing blaze,)
Cling warm forever. . . .

Given the benefits conferred on the husband in this very Wertherish vision of family life, one should hardly be surprised to find John James calling home "The world's first good, the earth's last happiness." Having an Angel who "smil[ed] / Her patient days away in daily love,"[8] who could wish for anything more?

In "Charity at Home," J. J.'s speaker compares himself and his wife to two children looking out a window on a stormy night: "[W]arm within, from our sweet rooms we gaze / Into the dark, and see—our Fireside-blaze!"[9] The power of this home-based contentment is so great that, like the firelight reflected in the windows, it blocks all else out— darkness, storms, other people, the need to mature, you name it. In "The First Fire," which J. J. wrote not long after he and Sarah took up residence in the Washington, D.C., area in 1861, the speaker is even more narcissistically complacent, disturbingly so. Standing by the window yet again—for J. J., the ideal site for poetically contemplating one's domestic good fortune—the speaker suddenly remembers that there is a war going on. So, lest his "gay conceit[s]" seem "[i]ll-timed," he brings the war in. Nearby, he says, "Stand battle-tents, that, everywhere, / Keep ghostly white the moonless air. / The sentinel walks his lonely beat, / The soldier slumbers on the ground." But the somber mood does not last long: two and a half stanzas, to be exact, in a fourteen-stanza poem. Then "hark!'" the speaker exclaims, "the cricket's song / Within!—the Fairy's minstrel sings / Away the ghosts of saddest things!"[10] So much for the Civil War.

Although J. J. probably hoped to make money with these poems—and needed to, given the brood he and Sarah were jointly creating—he continued to produce similar paeans to domestic bliss long after the fad for literary sentimentality ended. Whether a true believer or not, this was how J. J. chose to represent marriage, suturing over all that his own marriage taught him of the less than ideal, from economic woes to the searing pain of child death. Indeed, possibly because he was such a weak poet even by genteel standards, he insisted on this idealizing vision with a fierceness that stripped away all inessentials. Here was the ideological line, sans any significant internal development. To a parodist, he was a sitting duck—and parody him Sarah did, not kindly either.[11]

"The Descent of the Angel" (1879), is among the most specific parodies that Piatt wrote of her husband's verse. In this poem, whose title turns on a homophonic pun with "dissent," Piatt repeats the same Aristotelean pattern of *peripeteia* (reversal) followed by *anagnôrisis* (recognition) that structures her Civil War poetry. Here, however, it is the realities of wifehood, not war, that bring ironic enlightenment. No longer the "enchanted" bride of "Firelight Abroad," but merely a "pretty" one, Piatt's domestic Angel is every bit as naïve as the speaker of J. J.'s poem and just as unprepared to meet the hard realities of married life: "With satin sandals, fit alone / To glide in air, she touched the stone. / A thing to fade through wedding lace." More ignorant than innocent, this Angel-Bride expects "Romance and travel." Instead, she lands "[w]here life must be an earthly thing," and her reward, as Hewitt's "Wise Woman" might have told her, is "earthly tears" (*PB* 95). Angels, Piatt reiterates throughout her later career, belong nowhere but in heaven. Satin sandals were not made for walking.

In "Hearing the Battle" (1864), a poem set in the same time period as J. J.'s "The First Fire," Piatt's attack on J. J. is even more up close and personal, aiming straight at the narcissistic cocoon that allowed him to trivialize the pain of war while waxing eloquent on his own good luck in not having to fight it. Banishing J. J.'s sanitized "white" tents and slumbering soldiers, Sarah gives us instead a battlefield where "things with blinded eyes / . . . stared at the golden stillness / Of the moon in those lighted skies; / And . . . souls, at morning wrestling / In the dust with passion and moan, / So far away at evening / In the silence of worlds unknown." "I shall never know," the speaker concludes, handing her lover/husband a sprig of "snowy jessamine-flowers" (the Piattian equivalent of a white feather?) "How the hearts in the land are breaking, / my dearest, unless you go" (*PB* 2–3). Like Elizabeth Stoddard, who also married a man of lesser talent, Piatt had a mordantly cynical sense of humor where male obtuseness was concerned.

Piatt's most interesting and complex parody of J. J.'s vision of the Angel-Wife, however, is "Shapes of a Soul," which I have already discussed, albeit briefly, in chapter 5 and elsewhere. I will not repeat those discussions here, but the poem is too important to pass over entirely.[12] Like "Giving Back the Flower," "Shapes" was published in *Galaxy* in 1867, but where the former poem looks backward, "Shapes," which parodies J. J.'s "The Birthdays" (1864), looks forward toward things to come. In "The Birthdays," which J. J. dedicated to Sarah, he speaks of her in offensively infantilizing terms: "My fancy, love-created, goes / Lightly from passing year to year: / My little fairy maiden grows / To tender girlhood dear. / A dreaming girl, as shy as dew / In dells of Fairyland apart, / Within your soul a lily grew—/ A rose within your heart."[13] From "Shapes," it is clear that Sarah was not impressed. As she says repeatedly in later poems, the Civil War destroyed whatever "faith in fairyland" she had, and her postbellum married life, with all its pain and shattered expectations, did nothing to revive it.[14] Whatever was growing in her heart, it was not a rose.

But in 1867, Piatt had yet to settle on a way to counter these tropes outside a romantic framework. Instead, as we have already seen, she uses feral animals to identify those aspects of her subjectivity she could not reconcile with the male sentimental view: "a tiger, fierce and bright / Among the trembling passions in its path"; a snake, "drag[ging] its colors through the dust . . . / And hiss[ing] its poison under foot" (*PB* 8). In chapter 5, I identified these figures as part of Piatt's gothic, and she repeats them frequently in relatively early poems like "The Lily of the Nile" and "Her Rescue." But while such poems resist the speaker's interpellation as Angel, they do so only by appealing to another set of equally unrealistic literary conventions, as Piatt seems to acknowledge when the speaker tells her interlocutor in "Shapes of a Soul" not to smile—that is, laugh—at her comparisons.

If Piatt was to get around the oversimplifications of both romantic and sentimental versions of female subjectivity, she needed new grounds for self-representation. As "The Palace-Burner" suggests, she found them in her biographically grounded subject position as a Northern bourgeois matron. Taking the complicity of her subject position as given, that is, the lack of Angelhood, Piatt's speaker began to explore both the complicity of the society in which she lived and what I can only call the complicity of God. Two poems, both literarily and psychologically dense, will help clarify what I mean: "A Funeral of a Doll" and "We Two." In both these poems, Piatt does indeed kill the Angel, but, as we shall see, at some cost.

"A Funeral of a Doll" (1872) is one of a sizeable group of poems in which Piatt's speaker qua bourgeois mother confronts her helplessness to protect her children from grief. At the same time, "Funeral" offers, as does "We Two," a scathing critique of sentimental culture's own rituals of comfort. Unfolding in slippery exchanges between child and adult perspectives, "Funeral"'s subtlety and complexity justify quoting it in full:

> They used to call her Little Nell,
>   In memory of that lovely child
> Whose story each had learned to tell.
>   She, too, was slight and still and mild,
>   Blue-eyed and sweet; she always smiled,
> And never troubled any one
> Until her pretty life was done.
> And so they tolled a tiny bell,

That made a wailing fine and faint,
As fairies ring, and all was well.
Then she became a waxen saint.

Her funeral it was small and sad.
    Some birds sang bird-hymns in the air.
The humming-bee seemed hardly glad,
    Spite of the honey everywhere.
    The very sunshine seemed to wear
Some thought of death, caught in its gold,
That made it waver wan and cold.
Then, with what broken voice he had,
    The Preacher slowly murmured on
(With many warnings to the bad)
    The virtues of the Doll now gone.

A paper coffin rosily-lined
    Had Little Nell. There, drest in white,
With buds about her, she reclined,
    A very fair and piteous sight—
    Enough to make one sorry, quite.
And, when at last the lid was shut
Under white flowers, I fancied——but
No matter. When I heard the wind
    Scatter Spring-rain that night across
The Doll's wee grave, with tears half-blind
    One child's heart felt a grievous loss.

"It was a funeral, mamma. Oh,
    Poor Little Nell is dead, is dead.
How dark!—and do you hear it blow?
    She is afraid." And, as she said
    These sobbing words, she laid her head
Between her hands and whispered: "Here
Her bed is made, the precious dear—
She cannot sleep in it, I know.
    And there is no one left to wear
Her pretty clothes. *Where did she go?*
    ——See, this poor ribbon tied her hair!"
                              (*PB* 32–33)

As is frequently the case in Piatt, this poem, purportedly describing a little
girl's grief over the "death" of her doll, is not what it seems. True, the doll of
the poem, like its literary original, "Little Nell," the juvenile heroine of
Charles Dickens's *Old Curiosity Shop* (1841), reeks of Victorian cuteness. No

less than its namesake, it is, you might say, a perfect doll, always smiling, never a bother, sweet and mild. In "life," this doll was a domestic Angel-in-training. Dead, it is a "waxen saint." Since, like Little Eva's death scene in *Uncle Tom's Cabin*, that of Little Nell in *The Old Curiosity Shop* was a cultural watering hole for artists, playwrights, and poets to exploit when catering to bourgeois culture's sentimental cravings, one can easily imagine sincere Victorian readers wiping away the tears as they read Piatt's poem.[15] Undoubtedly, many did cry when they read it, assuming it dealt with the pain children suffer at the loss of a beloved toy, and never giving even the possibility of irony a second thought.

However, as with so many Piatt poems, one must reckon with more than one perspective in "Funeral," and that of the narrator, the child's mother, has a nasty way of muddying the sentimental response the child's perspective would otherwise straightforwardly elicit. Take, for instance, the description of the doll. Not only does the speaker sentimentalize the doll, she animates it, making it uncannily alive—a gothic trick. She gothicizes the toy in other ways as well, describing it, first to last, as a "waxen saint," a living dead-thing or a dead living-thing, not life itself but its imitation, mechanical in her fixed smile and imperturbable stillness, soulless in her blue-eyed sweetness. When the narrator says the doll never troubled anyone, is she praising this miniature Angel in the House, therefore, or is she mocking it? Is this doll, like Dickens's Little Nell, too good to be true? (One of the striking features of Piatt's poetry on children is her absolute insistence on the trouble living children are, with its corollary acknowledgment that only dead children are "good.")[16] How can lines like "And *never troubled* any one / Until her *pretty* life was done" (italics mine), be anything but sarcastic, especially given Piatt's use of "pretty" elsewhere?

And if "the Doll now gone" is ironized, what about the funeral? It was, the narrator informs us, "A very fair and piteous sight—," then adds the edgy, "Enough to make one sorry, quite." What weight does "quite" get? At how great a distance does this word place the narrator from the child's naïve pain, so soon to break out in genuine anguish? Indeed, why does the narrator offer no consolation to her child? The little girl's anxieties as she imagines her doll in a paper coffin—outside, alone on a stormy night, afraid, in the dark—are precisely those that the sentimental cult of death, nourished by texts like *The Old Curiosity Shop* and *Uncle Tom's Cabin*, was supposed to help the bereaved surmount. Little Nell is now an Angel, safe in heaven. But of course, this "Little Nell" is a doll, an inert bit of wax, cloth, and straw. Is she in heaven also? Where is she? What does she feel? And why does this now-dead-and-buried doll seem so much more real as the vessel for the child's fears than she did as the Perfect Polly of stanza one? Why does the poem come so brutally alive in its final, pain-filled moments?

By ending the poem so inconclusively, Piatt, like Dickinson, who employs similar tactics, leaves the question of the afterlife open, forcing readers to confront the epistemological conundrum that death is. In light of what we do not know, the rituals constituting the doll's funeral begin to look not just pathetic but useless. Without a God there to respond to them—is there a God for dolls?—they have no power; and there is no God in this poem, just birds singing bird-hymns in the air and a preacher with a broken voice. As a "keepsake" of the sort in which sentimentalists set great store, the ribbon fails also. Little more than a tattered bit of fabric, it represents the irreparability of loss, not the preservation of connection. As one reviewer complained, Piatt's speakers give us "hints and innuendoes," nothing more.[17] Neither the child nor we get the comfort we need—no glib endings here, no "closure."

Read thus, "A Funeral for a Doll" is anything but cute. Far from living up to its genteel promise, it is a ruthless attack on bourgeois sentimental culture, especially its naïve rituals of consolation—so like the hymns birds sing in the air. This "Little Nell" may have a beautiful death, but that is no compensation for the half-life she led before "dying" as always-smiling "waxen saint." Nor does her death resolve any of the questions it raises. As the last line indicates, this poem has no answers. The child is not comforted. The mother is isolated in her bitter recognition of her own failure and that of the social rituals evolved to heal pain. The narrator has done what Woolf said women writers must do: she has killed the Angel.[18] She has not offered false comfort; she has not reconciled the irreconcilable; she has not made things better than they are; she has not joined in the pretense that a half-life is life. But having stripped herself of lies, she has nothing but a dark, alienating intelligence to put in their place, another kind of emptiness where the emptiness of falseness had been.

There is a good deal of anger in "A Funeral for a Doll," and a great deal of distrust. Sentimental culture claimed to reverence human connectedness. It was supposed to be about feeling; but it made no allowance for anger, alienation, or fear. One had to be attached to "the Whole," not separated by "disagreeable facts" or by disagreeable feelings either—rage, pain, despair. In the brilliantly titled "We Two," Piatt splits female subjectivity in two, dividing self from other in order to exorcise, ironically, the "better half"—the Angel who would kill her unless she kills it first. Nowhere does Piatt come closer to Dickinsonian apostasy than in this poem, complaining at the top of her lungs against a universe arranged for the narcissistic self-aggrandizement of an uncaring God:

God's will is—the bud of the rose for your hair,
    The ring for your hand and the pearl for your breast;
God's will is—the mirror that makes you look fair.
    No wonder you whisper: "God's will is the best."

But what if God's will were the famine, the flood?
  And were God's will the coffin shut down in your face?
And were God's will the worm in the fold of the bud,
  Instead of the picture, the light, and the lace?

Were God's will the arrow that flieth by night,
  Were God's will the pestilence walking by day,
The clod in the valley, the rock on the hight—
  I fancy "God's will" would be harder to say.

God's will is—your own will. What honor have you
  For having your own will, awake or asleep?
Who praises the lily for keeping the dew,
  When the dew is so sweet for the lily to keep?

God's will unto me is not music or wine.
  With helpless reproaching, with desolate tears
God's will I resist, for God's will is divine;
  And I—shall be dust to the end of my years.

God's will is—not mine. Yet one night I shall lie
  Very still at his feet, where the stars may not shine.
"Lo! I am well pleased" I shall hear from the sky;
  Because—it is God's will I do, and not mine.

(PB 50–51)

Published in the *Independent* in September 1874, "We Two" appears to belong to a series of poems, most explicitly elegiac, in which Piatt responded to the deaths of two of her children: an unnamed infant in 1873 and her oldest son, Victor—probably the boy in "The Palace-Burner"—in July 1874.[19] These poems, which include "A Butterfly's Message," "The Favorite Child," "Answering a Child," "Comfort—by a Coffin," and "Sad Wisdom—Four Years Old," run the gamut of emotions one might expect from a woman who had lost two children within a single year and whose religious faith was not strong enough to handle the pursuant crisis. To a greater or lesser extent, all the poems are blasphemous, with "We Two," perhaps, at the furthest extreme. What makes "We Two" especially relevant here, however, is the way Piatt uses it to turn the "good" woman (the Angel/the "waxen saint") into a diabolical double, a parody of goodness, not goodness itself. Narcissistically invested in the Angel's ideological position, the speaker's interlocutor has only Christian platitudes to offer—"not my will but thine" was the formula—where intersubjective exchange should be.[20] Without the empathic connection true comfort demands, like Job's "comforters," she passes judgment instead.

Piatt's blatant inversion of biblical tags in "We Two"'s ninth and tenth lines, may, therefore, not be accidental.[21] All the positions in this poem are inverted, are parodic, not just the comforter incapable of comforting, but a "God of life" who wills death, a "God of love" who wills suffering, an omnipotent God who does not intervene. Like Dickinson, Piatt could not forgive God his perversions; and she attributes divine indifference to a divine narcissism every bit as cocooning as the genteel/sentimental narcissism in which her husband indulged. No less than J. J. in his Home, the Almighty in Heaven is, it seems, outside human reach and outside human suffering. Giving nothing, he nevertheless demands all. As Dickinson so brilliantly lashes out in "Behind Me - dips Eternity" (F743) and "Sang from the Heart, Sire" (F1083), so Piatt lashes out in "We Two" and other elegies against a universe in which Garrison's "bleeding humanity" is left to heal itself in any which way it can. Like the law in "The Palace-Burner" and Victorian gender ideology in "A Funeral of a Doll," religion in "We Two" functions to preserve the status quo, only rewarding those who, like the ideologically correct interlocutor in "We Two," deny the protester's right to protest, telling her to accept God's will instead. Poem after poem, Piatt sweeps her decks clean. What was left was only darkness and her own long howl.

Toward Modernism: Irony and the (Un)sentimental Speaker

If the critique of domestic ideology and bourgeois Christianity gave substantial depth to Piatt's poetry, however, it also signals her problematic status as a practitioner of high sentimentality's "sympathy politics." As a political thinker, Piatt recognized all too well the degree to which the domestic vision of bourgeois ideology was itself complicit in the evils high sentimentalists decried. But in killing the Angel as she did, she also undermined, willingly or no, the grounds for her own moral authority as bourgeois woman. Given the concerns driving Piatt's political complaint poems—in particular, her commitment to social justice—her protest poetry should have fit comfortably within the high-sentimental tradition; but it does not, precisely because in killing the Angel, Piatt had ironized her speaker throughout. Although she thereby escaped the dilemma of narcissistic appropriation, especially its insulating self-righteousness, her escape came at the cost of sympathy itself. For Piatt, this was the conundrum of sentimental politics, and it was one that, for all her passion, she could not solve. In chapter 8, I will suggest that the pervasive moral confusion in early-twentieth-century women's writing— the hard edge, the bitter cynicism of a Djuna Barnes or a Mina Loy— was the ultimate price that women writers paid for using irony as their instrument of choice when rooting out in themselves the self-destructive values for which they believed the Angel—that is, their mothers—stood.

Although, as we shall see, Piatt had sound political reasons for using irony rather than appeals to sympathy in her political writing, I do not think her decision can be separated from the postbellum guilt she carried as the daughter of slaveholders. Unlike antebellum high sentimentalists, who, with the striking exception of the Southern-born Grimké sisters, stood well outside the circle of the sins they condemned, Piatt could not claim a virtue of her own, let alone don God's mantle, as Harriet Beecher Stowe felt called to do. On the contrary, Piatt's was a legacy of guilt: "I . . . think of it with shame," her speaker says of cruel words she spoke to a "dusky playmate," a slave child, on her grandmother's plantation ("A Child's Party," *PB* 114). Piatt lost her innocence long before she could have known she had it, and her poetry is everywhere and always informed by this recognition.

But precisely because Piatt regrounded the moral authority of her speaker in her recognition of guilt, her social-protest poems lack the kind of overt, overwhelmingly passionate conviction that could make the antebellum high-sentimental poet such a powerful spokesperson for reform. The product of a highly idiosyncratic and ironic sensibility, Piatt's "protest" poems are complex and ambiguous instead, as befit an author writing in the postbellum period. I will look at two: "His Mother's Way" (1880) and "A Night-Scene from the Rock of Cashel, Ireland" (1889). In the first, Piatt legitimates her use of irony in the poem itself, presenting it as the only viable alternative to the sentimental female speaker's naïve emotionality and to the emotional unavailability of her antithesis, the socially indifferent and supremely self-interested bourgeois male. In the second poem, "A Night-Scene," irony dominates the poem entirely, giving Piatt complete control over its emotional and intellectual content. Successful as this strategy is, however, in securing the speaker's credibility (she's no "weeping Nelly"), it crucially weakens the poem's activist thrust. Read together, these two poems make clear just how precarious a tightrope Piatt's political poetry walked, as she sought to adjust the moral principles and goals of antebellum sympathy politics to the ironizing complexities of a modern female subjectivity all too aware of its own sins along with others'.

First published in 1880 in the *Independent,* "His Mother's Way" is a sustained critique of the feminization of sympathy politics that occurred during the earlier part of the century. While, as we have already seen, one can trace the roots of sympathy politics back to the writings of male eighteenth-century thinkers, by 1850 the "cause of bleeding humanity" had become closely associated in the United States with women or, more properly, with psychic and moral qualities women were believed to possess in significantly larger quantities than did men. But given such gendering, could women be effective advocates for those whom they saw it as their spheric duty to succor and protect? In "His Mother's Way," Piatt provides a close-to parodic answer to this question. Told until the final stanzas from the limited perspective of a young boy, "His Mother's Way" presents a woman whose excessively sympathetic reaction to a passing tramp does no more to solve the problem he represents than does her husband's macho reaction. Where the latter's response is to use brute force (he will "sleep to-night / With both his pistols at his head"), hers is tears—the same tears, her disgusted son reports, that she sheds over keepsake treasures ("old glove[s]" and "ring[s]"), and over clothing she cannot afford to buy and really ought not want to buy anyway ("the shabbiest shawl").

If the child is confused by his father's absolute determination *not* to feel —he would not even cry at his own death, the boy says, speaking of the father—his mother's emotional excesses are equally off-putting. Both parents are locked into their stereotyped gender roles, leaving the child—and the reader for whom in some sense he stands—no room to maneuver. Whether the mother's concerns are serious or trivial, she does nothing but weep and wail, while the father does nothing but posture. Meanwhile, the poet tells us in the final stanzas, in a rare Piattian voiceover, the tramp himself goes unhoused, unfed:

> So the boy babbled. . . . Well, sweet sirs,
>   Flushed with your office-fires, you write
> Your laugh down at such grief as hers;
>   But are these women foolish quite?
>
> . . . .
>
> . . . there are prisons made for such,
>   Where the strong roof shuts out the snow;
> And bread (that you would scorn to touch)
>   Is served them there. I know, I know.
>
> Ah! while you have your books, your ease,
>   Your lamp-light leisure, jests, and wine,
> Fierce outside whispers, if you please,
>   Moan, each: "These things are also mine!"
>   (*PB* 101)

Insofar as the mother's tears call attention to the tramp's needs, rather than simply obliterating them with cannon fire, she has the moral high ground over her rather bullish mate. Her capacity to feel another's pain and her desire to relieve it bring her closer to her society's normative Christian values—the values, for example, of the Sermon on the Mount—than are the men who, with their "lamp-light leisure, jests, and wine," laugh her to scorn. But Piatt's adult speaker, the poem's adjudicating voice, calls the mother "foolish" nonetheless, not because she feels—she should feel—but because that is all she does. Action was left to men, and since men had no particular investment in feeling—at least when it came to feeling for others—they were unlikely to compromise their own position to benefit those less fortunate than themselves. Far from remedying social indifference, the mother's exces-sive tearfulness makes it, if anything, more likely that the next generation of males, represented by her son, will behave precisely as their fathers did, rather than risk the contempt that a cross-gendered expression of sympathy might evoke.

In a thoughtful article on the keepsake tradition, Joanne Dobson argues that nineteenth-century sentimentality celebrates the preservation of human bonds, the affectional bonds that hold society as well as individual families together, and which sentimentalized artifacts such as keepsakes symbolically embodied.[22] When directed, as the wife's sentimentality is, toward asserting the ties of obligation and common humanity binding the rich and the poor, the privileged and the oppressed, the impact of nineteenth-century senti-mentality could indeed be a force for good. As is famously the case with *Uncle Tom's Cabin*, sympathy politics could be an effective instrument of progressive social change. Barring that, it could at least make life difficult for oppressors—as, for example, Sigourney did with her Indian poems. Simply standing witness to crime may help keep governments in check. Otherwise, why castigate those Germans who, through their silence, tacitly consented, to the atrocities of the Nazi era?

But precisely because high sentimentality had been relied on so heavily by women to rationalize their own transgressions, it had also become a risky road to take in a society largely run by hard-nosed and indifferent men. For Piatt, as, I might add, for Margaret Fuller in *Summer on the Lakes in 1843*, sympathetic expression was, therefore, a difficult balancing act at best. "I have not wished to write sentimentally about the Indians," Fuller declares in chapter 6, after outlining the fate of America's indigenous peoples, "however moved by the thought of their wrongs and speedy extinction."[23] In the prac-tical world of reality-based politics, too much "caring for" made you look, as we put it today, "sloppily sentimental," "a bleeding-heart liberal." Too little, however, and one became insensitive to the affective values presumably mak-ing humans "human," that is, the ability to love, to care, to feel for another's pain. In this latter scenario, "might" would indeed "make right," as Fuller observes in "Governor Everett Receiving the Indian Chiefs," and then neither Indians—nor tramps—would stand a chance (*NAWP* 57).[24]

For Piatt, the belated high sentimentalist, the difficulty with high senti-mentality was not that it lacked serious purpose or good faith but that as a political strategy, it was likely to rebound against those who used it. As high sentimentalists like Sigourney and Fuller discovered, to those in power, high sentimentalists were naïve glamorizers of a humanity not worth "extricat-ing," as Dickinson so famously put it, "from [its] hopeless ditch" (L380). In "His Mother's Way," Piatt, who, whatever else she was, was never naïve, saw the dilemma for what it was: a product of the gendered distribution of power that put men's self-interest on one side of the ledger and women's putative need to protect the helpless on the other. Like Fuller, she chose to adopt a distancing neutrality instead, blocking in her speaker's voice the very emotions that she wished to encourage in her readers. No longer a moral authority, the (un)sentimental speaker became an ironic observer instead, both of her own sins, as in "The Palace-Burner," and those of others, as in "His Mother's Way." With this speaker carrying the burden of her political verse, Piatt, I want now to suggest, the quintessential border poet, wrote her poetry into a no-woman's-land between the outmoded practices of ante-bellum high sentimentalism and its emerging aesthetic and political antithesis, the irony-based modernism to come. An examination of "A Night-Scene from the Rock of Cashel, Ireland" (1889) will clarify how she did this, and the price she paid.

Between 1881 and 1892, Piatt and her husband lived in Ireland, where J. J. held patronage positions in various consulates. Piatt's response to what she called "exile" was, to put it mildly, mixed. With her Southern background no longer a bar sinister, she received a warmer reception from the Irish and British literary establishments—especially writers associated with the Irish Renaissance—than she ever got in the States. But living in famine-racked Ireland, where scenes of horror were enacted daily, could not have been pleasant, even to one inured to human misery. For someone like Piatt, already burdened with her own family's sins, it brought the double pain of present and past guilt. In her poems, she grapples both with her own conscience and with Ireland's sorrows, even while struggling to keep her writing under tight emotional control. No poem better illustrates the aesthetic power she achieved thereby—or the interpretive risks she incurred—than "A Night-Scene from the Rock of Cashel, Ireland," one of her most carefully wrought social protest poems. In this poem, as Pamela Kincheloe argues in her dissertation on Piatt's Irish poetry, Piatt uses the ironizing framework of a sentimental tour guide to Ireland's ancient monuments and rural beauties in order to—figuratively, if not literally—bring the situation of the present-day Irish peasantry home.[25] The result is a poem whose difficulty and intent are, unless one reads very carefully, all too easy to miss, or, to put it another way, a poem that doesn't quite fit into either the high-sentimental or the modernist mold.

Piatt opens "Night-Scene" by locating her speaker at the rock of Cashel, "legendary" home of Ireland's kings, but now, as she notes with deliberate vagueness, "of—certain other things." From this site, safely above Matthew Arnold's "darkling plain," she conducts the reader on a guided tour of the rock's modern habitations and inhabitants. No castles or churches now, but the sod huts of Ireland's peasant poor and the open graves of the dead:

Come, look by this blurred moon, if you would know.

From darkness such as hides the happier dead,
    On the wet earth-floor grows a ghastly flame;

A woman's wasted arm, a child's gold head,
   Shrink back into the wind-stirred straw for shame.

Through the half-door, down from the awful Rock,
   The death chill from some open grave creeps in—
The skeleton's fixed laugh is seen to mock
   The cry for bread below. Oh, shame and sin!

Warm only with the fire of its starved eyes,
   In one grim corner, crouches a black cat.
   . . . Night moans itself away.

The description is high gothic, complete with starving women and children, black cats, and skeletons. Yet, despite all the gothic paraphernalia and even the speaker's cry, "Oh, shame and sin!" the description is at the same time weirdly objective. This is, after all, a tour. The guide shows us what we have come to see, and Piatt is at some pains to emphasize the voyeuristic aspects of our engagement, bidding us to "Come, look," while she tells us, from this distance, what there is to be seen in this "scene."

Because Piatt holds to this tour-guide approach, there is very little disruption, therefore, despite the evils her pen has recorded, when she shifts the scene in the penultimate stanza with the rising of the sun. One wants one's tour to be at least reasonably comprehensive, to show the beautiful as well as the ugly, and certainly famine-stricken Ireland had its fair share of both. "And look!" the speaker exclaims, without missing a beat,

   . . . In meadows beautiful, knee-deep
   In bloom for many a shining mile around,
The undying grass is white with lambs and sheep
   And wandering cattle make a pleasant sound.
                (*PB* 130–31)

However horrific Cashel's "night-scene" may be, its picturesqueness by day is above reproach and, for virtual tourists like us, quite redeems it. We can now pack up our bags and go home. Our tour has been successful. We have seen what there is to see.

Or have we?

What makes this poem so tricky to read is precisely what it leaves out. As I learned when guiding Kincheloe through her first encounters with it as a graduate student, even trained readers, including the Irish studies specialist on her graduate committee, were likely to take the poem at face value, making no connection between the two views it presents: the "day-scene" of tranquil natural beauty, the night-scene of human misery and horror. To paraphrase lines from one of Piatt's favorite plays, *Hamlet*, from this poem's very Swiftian perspective, your fat sheep and your lean beggar were "variable service—two dishes but to one table" (4.2.23–24), and that table did not belong to the Irish themselves. Highlighting the gap between the poem's two perspectives by simply juxtaposing them without comment, Piatt dropped herself as author out of the poem's outrage, leaving readers to make of it what they will. Aesthetically speaking, this is a powerful strategy, allowing for that golden "shock of recognition," that can leave one in awe of a particular writer's skill, their ability to withhold where a lesser writer—or your sincere high-sentimentalist—would say all. But as my colleague's misreading (not just my student's misreading) suggests, insofar as this strategy relied on the head, not on a straightforward appeal to the heart, it had limitations of its own. The result is a protomodernist poem that hangs suspended between two antithetical literary modes, contributing involuntarily to the demise of one even as—just as involuntarily—it helped give rise to the other.

By the late 1880s, Piatt was in fact but one of many women writers trying to avoid displays of excessive emotion in art. The age of Sigourney, Whittier, and Stowe was over. Whitman would soon be dead. Emily Dickinson—in the public mind, at any rate—was on the verge of being born; and Henry James had one very large foot in the door. Too ironic to be part of the old dispensation, and too political to be part of the new one, Sarah Piatt stood where others went their separate ways, her poetry no less an anomaly of the border state than she herself—both poet and poems sites where antitheses met and undid each other.

Sex, Sexualities, and Female Erotic Discourse

Whitman seems to understand everything in nature but woman. . . . He speaks as if the female must be forced to the creative act, apparently ignorant of the great natural fact that a healthy woman has as much passion as a man, that she needs nothing stronger than the law of attraction to draw her to the male.
    —ELIZABETH CADY STANTON, *Feminist Papers*, 1883[1]

[S]he . . . knows nothing of it.
    —JACQUES LACAN, "God and the *Jouissance* of Woman," 1972[2]

In the *Dial's* first issue (July 1840), Margaret Fuller, New England transcendentalism's most prominent female advocate, published a brief, and in most respects conventional, dialogue poem between a dahlia and the sun. The noted Americanist Perry Miller, who reprinted the poem in his 1950 anthology, *The Transcendentalists*, did not, on the whole, find Fuller's poetical "effusions . . . memorable." However, he thought this poem intriguing enough to preserve, letting it stand for an entire set of poems in which transcendentalists used "highly charged sexual imagery." Whether or not Fuller knew how "highly charged" her imagery was, Miller cannily leaves "students . . . to resolve":

DAHLIA   My cup already doth with light o'errun
             Descend, fair sun;
        I am all crimsoned for the bridal hour,
             Come to thy flower.

THE SUN   Ah, if I pause, my work will not be done,
             On I must run,
        The mountains wait.—I love thee, lustrous flower,
             But give to love no hour.[3]

Miller's unwillingness to overread Fuller's intention in "A Dialogue" is understandable. Steven Marcus's paradigm-shattering study of sexuality and pornography in Victorian England, *The Other Victorians* (1964), could only have been a gleam in the author's eye in 1950, if that. *My Secret Life,* with its massive documentation of one man's sewage, real or imagined, was still secret.[4] Nothing was known of Austin Dickinson's and Mabel Loomis Todd's secret lives either, or of the coded record Mrs. Todd kept of her sexual activity with husband and lover, orgasms included.[5] In the popular mind, Victorians, and Victorian women in particular, were people who put frills on piano legs and did not know where babies came from. Certainly, given their "Victorian" inhibitions, they took no pleasure in creating them. Look at Queen Victoria. Ah, yes, look at Queen Victoria. Who knew then of Mrs. Brown?

Popular opinion aside, Miller had more serious reasons to hesitate as well. In theorizing dreams as a symbolic language, originating in the unconscious, Freud's *Interpretation of Dreams* (1900, trans. 1913) had opened new horizons of interpretative possibility for literary scholars. However, the much remarked-on similarity between sexual images in dreams and those in literature cut two ways. Scholars now had far greater liberty to identify images as sexual; but they were much less free to assume conscious authorial intent. For if the unconscious could generate sexual images in dreams, who was to say it could not do so in poems also? Since "A Dialogue"'s author was a Victorian woman to boot, and Victorian women's poetical "effusions" were, as everyone knew, "flowery" (i.e., sentimental), not erotic, Miller undoubtedly felt that the case for conscious intent could not be made. Technically, he was right. Although Fuller is obviously using sexual imagery, no literary historian of Miller's period would have credited what he saw. Too many assumptions—about Victorians, about women, and about women's poetry—stood in the way.

Given the role that women played in purging U.S. poetry of sentimentality, it is more than a little ironic that scholars have blamed them for sentimentalizing it anyway. However, that is next chapter's subject. Here I want to look at something else: namely, the evolution of a nineteenth-century female erotic discourse *within* the sentimental. We now know that the image of the "Victorian" Victorian is a myth created, largely, by early-twentieth-century writers. Male and female Victorians, like ourselves, were obsessed with sex, wrote about it constantly, and engaged in it frequently. There were sex manuals one could read, offering a wide range of contradictory, often bad, advice. Doctors who specialized in various forms of sexual dysfunction abounded. By the end of the century, Rachel Maines's *Technology of Orgasm* reports, sexually dysfunctional men or women could even buy relief, via electrical vibrators and assorted other gadgets, at the doctor's office or at home.[6] Highly sexualized images of women were widely circulated both as pornography and as "fine art," and there was a lively market in sex and sensation thrillers. Vaudeville, girlie shows, and prostitution all flourished. Given all this, not to mention women's role in childbearing, it is impossible that nineteenth-century women could *not* have known that they were sexual beings, whether they discussed the fact openly or not.

At the same time, Victorian ideas about sexuality were often monumentally confused, allowing self-serving professional advice givers, from ministers to quack physicians, to manipulate those in need. Anxieties over the physical and moral degeneration of the race gave rise to myriad fads in medical thinking, some relatively harmless, like graham crackers, and some incredibly destructive, like the campaign against masturbation. The medical notion that "good" women did not want sex was among these fads. According to feminist historian, Nancy Cott, the "cult of passionlessness" originated in early-nineteenth-century attempts to rethink women as moral and spiritual beings. "[B]etween the seventeenth and the nineteenth centuries," Cott writes, the traditional "view of women as *especially* sexual . . . was . . . transformed . . . into the view that women . . . were *less* carnal and lustful than men."[7] It was the British gynecologist William Acton who, in 1857, made passionlessness literal by somatizing it. In a move that neither the British nor the U.S. medical community supported, Acton, who was more concerned with morality than medicine, took the concept of women's superior spirituality and turned it into the medical conviction that good women did not want sex. "I am ready to maintain that there are many females who never feel any sexual excitement whatever," he wrote in *Functions and Disorders of the Reproductive Organs.* "Love of home, of children, and of domestic duties are the only passions they feel."[8]

According to most medical historians, Acton's version of passionlessness was never adopted by physicians at large. But the cult of passionlessness did a great deal of mischief nonetheless, both among bourgeois women, whom it targeted, and among working-class women, prostitutes, and others, whom it effectively condemned. Even as bourgeois women began making substantive gains toward equality in the professions and in education, the identification of female virtue with low libido gave a new and powerful twist to the separate-spheres argument. Male physicians like Harvard's notorious Edward Clarke, for example, declared off-limits a host of activities—from riding bicycles to attending college—that, they claimed, would overstimulate bourgeois women sexually even while interfering with their ability to bear children, thus endangering their physical and moral health and the health of the nation (see fig. 7).[9] At the same time, these authorities used passionlessness to essentialize the moral inferiority of those women who, because they came from the "wrong" race, class, or ethnic community, were thought to indulge their sexuality freely, thus placing themselves outside the magic circle of the "Anglo-Saxon" bourgeoisie.

Fig. 7. The Wife of the Period: "Suffer *No* Little Children to Come unto Me"

Bourgeois women were not slow to recognize what was at stake, at least as it pertained to themselves. "In these rough and troubled days," Rebecca Harding Davis wrote in 1863, "we'd better give [women] their places as flesh and blood, with exactly the same wants and passions as men."[10] Women physicians like Elizabeth Blackwell denounced the idea of passionlessness, with its insistence on sexual gender inequality, as "a false assertion of the facts of human nature."[11] According to the historian Charles Degler, even some members of the Social Purity movement, Ida Craddock, for example, "entertained no doubt that women's sexual feelings need expression and resolution."[12] Equality feminists like Elizabeth Cady Stanton agreed, calling women's sexual desire both "natural" and "healthy."[13] Phoebe Cary took the same position. In a poem called "Archie," in *Poems and Parodies*, Cary's speaker declares: "We have been fashioned for earth, and not heaven; / Angels are perfect,—I am a woman; / Saints may be passionless,—Archie is human" (54). Nor was Cary the only woman poet to hew this line. While I have yet to find a nineteenth-century U.S. woman's poem celebrating passionlessness, I have found scores of poems in which women celebrate their passion. In fact, I know of few subjects on which women writers lavished more attention.

It is against the background of these highly public and contested issues that I will treat women's erotic poetry in this chapter, that is, as a body of consciously wrought verse in which authors explored and defended their desires, their status as "flesh and blood." Although I have no way to prove that every writer knew what she was doing, I think it likely that most did. The erotic discourse that these women deployed was indeed "sentimental," unavoidably so, since from the late eighteenth century on, sentimentality was the rhetoric of choice for the bourgeois expression of romantic love. But this sentimental discourse itself had deep roots in the broad history of Western erotic expression, roots traceable to the Bible's Canticles, on the one hand, and to Sappho's lyrics, on the other. Given how often these poets appeal to Sappho by name and how directly they deploy Canticles' imagery in their verse, it is inconceivable that they could have been uniformly ignorant of the tradition in which they wrote or of the erotic component in their own writing.[14]

However, the scandal-plagued histories of Mary Wollstonecraft, Frances Wright, Adah Menken, and Victoria Woodhull also suggest that women had far more than men at risk in expressing erotic desire. Confronted with the burgeoning medicalization of traditional female stereotypes—the Angel on the one hand, the whore on the other—nineteenth-century women poets needed to find some way to represent sex and their sexualities that would avoid bringing opprobrium down upon them. They found it, I argue, by using Canticles' nature imagery to represent their sexuality as natural, healthy, and free from sin—as, indeed, they believed God intended it to be. Before discussing this "third way," however, and why, ultimately, it failed, I want to digress briefly to look at Harriet Prescott Spofford's short story "The Amber Gods," which appeared in the *Atlantic Monthly* in 1860. Better than any other work I know, this story suggests the impressive amount that nineteenth-century women could say using the putatively "sentimental" erotic codes of their day.

Parlor Games

> A bad woman as well as a pure woman might love roses,
> but a bad woman does not love the small and hidden wild
> flowers of the field.
> —David Robinson, *Sappho and Her Influence*, 1924[15]

Employing literary sentimentality's "language of flowers," the characters in Spofford's "The Amber Gods" engage in a dining-room conversation about sex. The dining room belongs to Mr. Willoughby, an old-line New Englander, whose wife, an Italian by birth, died some years before. His daughter, Giorgione (nicknamed Yone), and Yone's orphaned cousin, Louise, live with him. Like Mr. Willoughby, Louise comes of old New England stock. A model "True Woman," she is chaste, dutiful, and self-sacrificing. The half-Italian Yone, who narrates the story from beginning to posthumous conclusion, is none of these things. Named after a sixteenth-century Italian artist best known for his nude, "Sleeping Venus" (see fig. 8), Yone glories in her

Fig. 8. Giorgione (finished by Titian), *Sleeping Venus*, c. 1510. Gemäldegalerie, Dresden.

female sexuality's rank "superabundance": "I'm a golden blonde. . . . not slight, or I couldn't have such perfect roundings, such flexible moulding. Here's nothing of the spiny Diana or Pallas, but Clytie or Isis speaks in such delicious curves."[16] Raised by a beauty-adoring father to adore herself, Yone is transcendently self-absorbed: "I'm not good," she unabashedly cries, "I wouldn't give a fig to be good. So it's not vanity. It's on a far grander scale; a splendid selfishness" (39). Convinced by male figurations of the female body that physical desirability trumped "goodness," Yone associates herself with those, from Isis and Venus to Circe and Cleopatra, who were "bad" women all.

But what Yone does not understand is that just because men fantasize about such women does not mean they prefer them. Certainly, the man whom Yone wants, the painter of "feminine" sensibility Vaughan Rose—or "Rose," as he is called—does not. Of some early-blooming, mayflowers with which he showers cousin Lu, Rose declares, "there's nothing like them, nothing but pure, clear things; they're the fruit of snow-flakes. . . . When one thinks how sweetly they come from their warm coverts and look into this cold, breezy sky so unshrinkingly, and from what a soil they gather such a wealth of simple beauty, one feels ashamed." "Climax worthy of the useless things!" Yone exclaims, with a double entendre in no way beyond her (58). "Shame" is not the sort of "climax" Yone wants to inspire.[17] However, Rose and the two other participants in this very proper Victorian debate over flowers, Louise and Louise's mild-mannered suitor, Dudley, do not agree.

In a before-dinner conversation, Dudley had already expressed his preference for pure women, when remarking on Yone's amber beads. Carved into the grotesque shapes of pagan gods, these beads once belonged to an "Asian imp" who had served Yone's mother. After the servant's death, the beads came down to Yone, who finds in them a mysterious, primeval eroticism that she associates with her own sexuality. Dudley also seems to see them this way: "I can imagine there is something rich and voluptuous and sating about amber, its color, and its lustre, and its scent; but for others, not for me" (56). Ominously, Rose concurs, finding amber's smell, in particular, distasteful, even "hateful" (55).

The chaste Lu, on the other hand, wears aquamarine beads. Amber, she observes, "'is warm and smells of earth; but this [aqua-marina] is cool and dewy, and—' 'Smells of heaven,'" Yone concludes, finishing Lu's sentence for her, and highlighting the gulf between them (54). Yone is the mistress of the quick retort, the barbed word. However, in the end she is outnumbered three to one. She does snag Rose and marries him—to her misfortune. "[F]rom the slave of bald form, I enlarged him to the master of gorgeous color," Yone brags (80). But helping Rose become the peer of the Renaissance "master" after whom she was named kills her. Still in her early thirties, she dies of consumption, sucked dry by a man who wanted her for his art but not as his wife. The cool and dewy mayflower, cousin Lu, whose soul is as limpid as her aquamarine, and who had secretly loved Rose and been loved by him all along, gets him in the end.

That "Amber Gods" draws heavily on late-nineteenth-century orientalist stereotypes associating hypersexuality with darker or "Southern" peoples, whether Italians or "Asians," hardly needs pointing out. However, precisely because the association of oriental images with sex was so fixed in Victorian society, it makes "The Amber Gods" an unusually good example of how nineteenth-century women writers could talk about sex and about variant styles of sexuality without using the word. As noted earlier, "Amber Gods" appeared in the *Atlantic*, that bastion of genteel taste, as did Spofford's long poem of autoerotic fantasy, "Pomegranate-Flowers." Both story and poem were safely importable into bourgeois parlors because they were written in a widely employed code that readers could decipher or not as they chose. But how explicit can one's decodings get?

For example, could one say that "Amber Gods," among other things, is "about" oral sex or, better perhaps, about men's discomfort with women who might want it?[18] Not only does a good chunk of the debate over flowers occur at the dining-room table, but, as Yone sarcastically observes, the conversation keeps reverting to the "culinary" (58). The amber-producing tree is said to have fruits "bursting with juice" (55); the mayflowers are called "delicious" and "sweet" (57); they and their odor are associated with strawberries, apple blossoms, and blackberries (57, 58, 59). If mayflowers are the "fruit of snowflakes," amber is identified with "poison" (56). Even more telling, since it is not true, we are told many times that amber has a disagreeable smell—at least to men. Yone and, significantly enough, Lu, are not bothered by its odor, but Rose, apparently conflating amber with vile-smelling ambergris, compares its "perfume" to the stink of St. Basil's jawbone, presumably after it had been buried in the earth for a while. The smells and tastes associated with the pure and chaste Lu, on the other hand, are as chilling as they are sweet. These sexually uptight men may feel uncomfortable around Yone's hypersexuality, but they clearly find the desexualized and sanitized Lu pleasant to have around.

Given Yone's "nick-name"—which in Italian is pronounced "yoni," the Sanskrit term for the female genitalia—it may even be that she is the pudenda, speaking in their own voice and in their own defense. Certainly, this kind of word play was not beyond Spofford, who delighted in rare words. Would her readers have known what she was doing? According to the Oxford English Dictionary, "yoni" entered the English language in 1799, at a time when comparative philologists began scouring Sanskrit for evidence of a single Indo-European language system. Thanks to these efforts, knowledge of the *Kamasutra* was in circulation by the time Spofford wrote. But even if readers missed Spofford's pun, most would have known of Giorgione's famous Venus, and hence, Yone's explicit association with a powerful icon of female sexuality.[19] The blatant orientalism of "Amber Gods," its allusions to the "darker/Southern" races, its references to juices, saps, rank smells, and so forth, and its multiple allusions to male representations of hypersexualized female bodies, all point inescapably to Yone as a figure for female sexuality, alive, aware, and seeking pleasures "over-civilized" males like Rose might indeed find difficult to stomach.

At the same time, however, Spofford's story also provides a wealth of evidence on the conflicts shaping nineteenth-century bourgeois women's thinking about sex. One need only browse through art history books like Bram Dijkstra's *Idols of Perversity* or Joseph Kestner's *Mythology and Misogyny* to know that, whether taken figuratively or with Actonian literalness, the cult of passionlessness in no way put an end to the production and circulation of hypersexualized images of women. Nor did the ascension of domestic ideology's "Angel in the House." On the contrary, by associating the female sex drive so closely with prostitutes, both Acton and the domestic ideologues of purity had breathed new life into the age-old split between "good women" and "bad." Read with respect to this history, Yone, though the product of a woman author's pen, is as much the product of male anxieties over autonomous female sexuality as is her antithesis, the chaste and chilling Lu. If Lu is the woman nineteenth-century men wanted to marry, Yone is the one they fantasized about when making love to their wives. Transformed into an objet d'art by the end of the story, Yone returns to where she began: an image created by men for their own gratification. Like her chaste double, Lu, she has, in this sense, no life apart from the male script she inhabits. Women either only wanted sex, or they did not want sex at all. For men historically enmeshed, as Maines says, in their own androcentric view of female sexuality, there was nothing in between.[20] A woman was a fantasy figure they used to unleash their own pleasure, or she was the mother of their children and ever-nurturant caretaker of themselves. Neither script gave women freedom of sexual choice or acknowledged them as legitimate agents of their own desire.

But did nineteenth-century women also view their sexuality in these terms? Were they, too, limited to a perspective that defined their sexuality as men did, as an extension of male needs, casting themselves as either Angels or whores, wanting no sex or too much? Or does the dark, bitter, and strikingly ironic humor with which Spofford treats Yone's fate suggest that nineteenth-century women's approach to their sexuality was a good deal more complicated than what men served up—and more diversified as a result? I now want to examine the various ways in which U.S. women poets, ranging from the well known to the unknown, used the poetic codes available to them to articulate sexualities and sexual desires that self-consciously diverged from both the "chaste sex" program of domestic ideologues and the hypersexuality of the Angel's opposite, the whore.

In approaching this material, let me stress again that multiplicity, not homogeneity, governs nineteenth-century women's self-representations. If this multiplicity further fragmented bourgeois women's subjectivities, it also testifies to these writers' determination to pursue ways of understanding and representing themselves that lay outside the conventions of male representation. With a few exceptions, most notably the historian Carl Degler, those purporting to speak authoritatively about nineteenth-century women's sexuality—be they literary scholars, sexologists, or psychoanalysts—have ignored what women themselves had to say about sex. Indeed, as was blatantly the case with Freud (not to mention his modern avatar, Lacan), male authorities, in particular, used women's putative ignorance of their own bodies as the ground on which to stake their own professional claims. They knew what women, presumably, did not.[21] No less than in the 1960s, women in the 1860s understood that their ability to act as agents on their own behalf had of necessity to include free sexual agency, an agency neither pole of the Angel/Whore binary allowed. To get outside this male symbolic required, therefore, that they reconceptualize not just marriage (as did the women active in the free-love movement) but the very nature of their own sexual needs. How they did this is the subject to which I now turn.

Re-Visioning Canticles

If nineteenth-century bourgeois women's erotic writing differs significantly from that of their male peers, it does so largely in its focus on autoeroticism.

For nineteenth-century women, the body was, it seems, a source of pleasure independent of love relationships. The reasons for women going this route are undoubtedly multiple, but coverture is the most obvious, as it gave women no right of refusal where their husbands were concerned. With coverture hanging over them, many women may have found the sexual relief gained through autoerotic practices far more satisfactory than that obtained through marital intercourse, burdened as the latter was with male demands and with women's own anxieties over conception. But whether or not this is the case, what is clear is that the poets—poets like Harriet Prescott Spofford in "Pomegranate-Flowers"—made self-pleasuring a principal motif of their works.

Originally published in the *Atlantic* for May 1861, Spofford's "Pomegranate-Flowers" devotes twenty-seven stanzas to a young woman's ecstatic response to a pomegranate tree, a gift from a now absent lover. Spofford's protagonist, a seamstress by trade, lives in a garret room, overlooking a "narrow, close, and dark" street, in a shady section of a "sea-board town" (ll. 1, 22). Whether this location is meant to suggest that she is also a prostitute is left moot. What is beyond question is that despite her garret and her poverty, this young woman has impressive resources of her own, resources that, because they are experienced alone, are also, as Spofford depicts them, pure. Taking the pomegranate tree as her focus, the sometime seamstress weaves her sensual response to the flower into the wedding veil she sews. By means of her fantasies, she not only escapes the ugliness of her surroundings but also experiences directly the bursting power of female sexuality itself, a sexuality that Spofford conveys through the conventionalized code of flower language. Fully open to her own sensuality, the seamstress converts her daydreams into a source for "daedal" art, art that gives her, like the mythic labyrinth maker, Daedalus, the freedom and power of imaginative flight:

> Bent lightly at her needle there
> In that small room stair over stair,
> All fancies blithe and debonair
> She deftly wrought on fabrics rare,
> All clustered moss, all drifting snow,
> All trailing vines, all flowers that blow,
> Her daedal fingers laid them bare.

> . . . .

> Now, she said, in the heart of the woods
> The sweet south-winds assert their power,
> And blow apart the snowy snoods
> Of trilliums in their thrice-green bower.
> Now all the swamps are flushed with dower

Of viscid pink, where, hour by hour,
The bees swim amorous, and a shower
Reddens the stream where cardinals tower.
Far lost in fern of fragrant stir
Her fancies roam, for unto her
All nature came in this one flower.
                    (ll. 93–99, 122–32)

Rich, indeed, excessive, as this passage is, it is also awash in erotic clichés, clichés in no way different from those heating up much woman-authored soft porn—and much great literature as well. From the ocular to the olfactory to the gustatory, every sense is indulged as the "glad girl" (l. 121) contemplates—gets aroused by—her flower. With its dark, glossy outer leaves and its swelling, rosy bud, the pomegranate flower is clearly a surrogate for her genitalia or, rather, for the pleasures her genitals provide; and it is the contemplation of these pleasures that arouses her, leading her to don the white lace veil on which she works and effectively marry herself before her mirror.[22] Possessing all Yone's narcissistic sensuality, with none of her petty, confused discontent, the seamstress plays Solomon and Sheba to herself: "Out of some heaven's unfancied screen / The gorgeous vision seemed to lean. / The Oriental kings have seen / Less beauty in their daïs-queen, / And any limner's pencil then / Had drawn the eternal love of men" (ll. 191–96).

Yet precisely because this "marriage" is fantasized, Spofford can also present the seamstress's eroticism as sin-free. Indeed, the poem's narrator explicitly excludes the phallic—the "white snake" and the "humming-bird" with his "ebon spear"—from the seamstress's experience (ll. 250, 253, and 255). She does mention a "bacchanalian" fling in the last stanza (l. 289), to be sure, gesturing toward the pomegranate's own long-standing association with female fertility rites. Similarly, an allusion to the "moresque" (l. 286) glances at the darker Mediterranean peoples—North African and Middle Eastern—taking the poem back to its "oriental" origins. But the girl's orgasm then breaks, and she falls back into dream-laden sleep. The pagan atavism unleashed by sexual fantasy is recontained, and the seamstress is left in post-climactic contentment, her sexuality again conveyed in flower-inspired terms:

The sudden street-lights in moresque
        Broke through her tender murmuring,
And on her ceiling shades grotesque
        Reeled in a bacchanalian swing.
        Then all things swam, and like a ring
        Of bubbles welling from a spring
        Breaking in deepest coloring
        Flower-spirits paid her minist'ring.
Sleep, fusing all her senses, soon

> Fanned over her in drowsy rune
>   All night long a pomegranate wing.
>   (ll. 286–96, *NAWP* 215–22)

However risky, neither the seamstress's sexual play nor her fantasies have corrupted her. On the contrary, they liberate, integrate, empower, and restore. Unlike Yone, Spofford's seamstress is in truth the author of her own story; her marriage is with herself, her own power, outside all masculinist paradigms, Lord Acton's (and Lacan's) included.

With the exception of Maria Gowen Brooks's *Zóphiël*, which I discuss later, few nineteenth-century U.S. women's poems approach the lush, superabundant sensuality of Spofford's "Pomegranate-Flowers." But, like Spofford, many women poets probe female sexuality's autoerotic component. In these poems, autoeroticism often appears, as it does in many Dickinson poems, as a preferred alternative to "adult" heterosexual relationships. In the very Dickinsonian "My Heart" (1879), for example, published anonymously in *Frank Leslie's Popular Monthly*, the author explicitly assumes the perspective of a young woman still in the bud, that is, still in what Freud called the clitoral stage of female psychosexual development, before the transition to "mature" heterosexuality—with its mythical vaginal orgasm—set in.[23] Identifying this latter stage as the "rose that knows a blooming hour," "My Heart"'s speaker specifically links her willed immaturity to her fear of being dominated by "[s]ome master, powerful and passionate," a domination that coverture all but insured.

While "My Heart"'s speaker acknowledges that her clitoral sexuality—the bud, as opposed to the full-blown flower—yields a "lesser" form of sexual satisfaction, she also views the latter, by that very token, as the more pleasurable: "'Tis true some little, wordless fantasie / May have been wakened by a toying hand; / Some genial breeze have oped a little bud / . . . / The music, burdened with grand words, awaits / Some master powerful and passionate; / And dreaming of the royal-hearted sun, / The rich red rose sleeps in her vailed state." But, "My Heart"'s speaker says, she is "happy of this hush, / So like the silence of that hour ere dawn."[24] In her famous 1852 "man of noon" letter to Susan Gilbert (Dickinson), Dickinson takes a similar position, noting that the flower-wives are "*satisfied* with the dew," until "the mighty sun . . . scorches [and] scathes" them. For both these poets, the seemingly ineluctable option of marriage is one they dread more than look forward to: "Oh, Susie, it is dangerous, and it is all too dear, these simple trusting spirits, and the spirits mightier, which we cannot resist! It does so rend me, Susie, the thought of it when it comes, that I tremble lest at sometime I, too, am yielded up" (L93).

Despite "My Heart"'s deployment of "highly charged sexual imagery," its sexual theme may be hard to credit because of the speaker's almost childlike tone and stress on innocence. "Only a Shadow," by Collette [Loomis], published in the *Springfield Republican* in 1859, admits no such doubt. Possibly a response to Whitman's twenty-ninth bather, as well as to Tennyson's "Lady of Shalott" (1833), Loomis's poem opens with a situation suspiciously like that in both these well-known male poems: A "lonely" lady looking out her window, "high and dreary," becomes erotically aroused—not by nude male bathers or by Sir Launcelot, but by the night. Falling into a dream state, she feels someone near her and "unbidden" clasps his hand in hers. From here things get increasingly sticky: "The hand of the night is very dear to her, / The arm of the night is about her form, / The lips of the night are very near to her, / And the breath of the summer night is warm." With the night's "unseen locks . . . upon her forehead, / . . . humanly waving soft and light," the woman gets so "warm" that "a sudden resistless impulse carried / Her lips to the lips of the shadowy knight!" Her reward for this odd form of love-making is "three white roses," which drop into "her hands when she loosed her hair."[25] Are these full-blown roses symbols of orgasm or (why not?) three orgasms? Sometimes a rose is not a rose, whatever Gertrude Stein said.

If Loomis's protagonist finds the night arousing, the speaker of Sara Jane Lippincott's "Siri, The Swimmer" (1851) uses the ocean to cool herself off. Like "Only a Shadow," "Swimmer" seems to respond to Tennyson's "Lady of Shalott" and the choice she is given of half a life or none at all. In Tennyson's narrative, the Lady of Shalott's desire for Sir Launcelot destroys her. When *she* looks out her window, "the shadowy knight" (night) who comes is death. As Elizabeth Stoddard pointed out in "Before the Mirror," Tennyson's view put women in a double bind from which there was no escape: to yield was to die; to protect oneself meant giving up life. Like Loomis, Lippincott rejects this prescripted fate, constructing a fantasy engagement with a potent, masculine aspect of the natural world instead. Within the safety zone erotic fantasy supplies, Lippincott's speaker is able to fully experience the physical pleasures that the Lady of Shalott is denied. Swimming, she relieves herself, just as, according to Maines, many nineteenth-century women relieved themselves by means of physician- and machine-aided orgasms: "I hear his gentle, wooing tone,— / I come, my lord, I haste! / Now are his arms about me thrown, / They circle round my waist!" "O, what delicious coolness," she exclaims, "flows / Through every quivering vein!"

No more than in the preceding poems is there any hint of transgressiveness in these lines, no breaking the "Father's Law." Rather, the poet writes outside the patriarchal framework altogether, her speaker's fantasies sanctioned, however ironically, by the Bible itself, albeit not that part of the Bible to which "moral purity" advocates were likely to appeal: "I will rise now and go . . . in the broad ways," says the Shulamite of Canticles, "I will seek him whom my soul loveth. . . . I found him whom my soul loveth. I held him and would not let him go" (3:2, 4). Biblically enabled, Lippincott's speaker can satisfy her desires without endangering herself:

A new and glorious life is mine,—
    I seem to float through heaven,

. . . .

On the billowy swell I lean my breast,
    And he fondly beareth me;
I dash the foam from his sparkling crest,
    In my wild and careless glee![26]

If Dickinson "ro[ws] in Eden" in "Wild Nights - Wild Nights," Lippincott's speaker "swims" there. "[W]ild," yet safe, she experiences the same pleasure for which Dickinson yearns: "Might I but moor - tonight - In Thee!" (F269).

Published in the *Overland Monthly* in January 1893, Eleanor Mary Ladd's "The Waiting Rain," takes full advantage of California's reputation as a lush physical paradise to produce a poem that makes all the poems discussed thus far look oblique. Succinctly, "The Waiting Rain" is a fantasy on morning sex. The poem opens as the "armored sun," with "His shining lance of gold," rests "His brazen shield . . . / Upon the mountain's breast." Under him lie the "bare, brown hills" of California, which the speaker describes as "A bronze-brown goddess rare, / . . . [with] gleaming limbs and sun-dried hair." No less "naked" than the light itself, California's hills, "Flash back the . . . light / Of fervid southern skies."

As one might expect of such a "bronze-brown" beauty, at least in this kind of poetry, California's response to the sun's "hot ministry" is sexual. Aroused by the sun's actions, dusky-skinned California begins to throb to the "murmured secrets, deep" of her own highly responsive body, her occulted reservoirs of sensual life and power:

The slumbrous eyelids' droop;
Belies her heart's hot beat;
Her throbbing pulses leap
To murmured secrets, deep,
Of teeming life in hidden cells,
Where occult forces meet.

"[T]eeming" with "life in hidden cells," and "Bathed in the sunlight's glow," California begins to secrete juices through her veins, the vintage of the grape and "The secret of the lily's bud." When orgasm comes, it is identified in the specifically Edenic floral terms of "blooming." However, in a nice touch obviously pointing to the poem's parched geographical setting, California's orgasm peaks only with the coming of the long-awaited rain:

Her ear against the earth,
She knows the season's birth,
The stir of Eden's gifts renewed,
The still of Nature's alchemy.

.   .   .   .

She calls the waiting rain,
And bids unlock the cells of life,
And make the brown earth bloom.

Ladd concludes her poem by insisting that California is uncorrupted by the pleasure she has just experienced. Her "girdle" of "virgin light" is intact; she wears her "robe, the morning's purple sheen." Day, it seems, has come.[27]

Like all the poems cited thus far, beginning with Spofford's "Pomegranate-Flowers," Ladd's poem is a tissue of erotic clichés—the sun's lance, the hotly beating heart, the throbbing pulse, the bronze-brown goddess, etcetera—most of them still in use today. Edith Wharton uses similar clichés in her posthumously published pornographic fragment "Beatrice Palmato": "As his hand stole higher she felt the *secret bud* of her body *swelling, yearning, quivering hotly* to *burst* into *bloom.* Ah, here was his subtle fore-finger pressing it, forcing its tight *petals softly* apart, and laying on their sensitive edges a circular touch so *soft* and yet so *fiery* that already *lightnings* of *heat* shot from that *palpitating centre* all over her *surrendered* body, to the . . . ends of her *loosened hair*" (italics mine).[28] Written after the turn of the century and not intended for publication, Wharton's fragment mingles the language of flowers with explicitly pornographic detail (e.g., the forefinger), providing the link—if any is needed—between nineteenth-century women poets proper and later female erotic writers. From "My Heart"'s anonymous author to Edith Wharton, these writers take for granted women's capacity for sexual pleasure and do so in a discourse men and women used from biblical times. Given how close Wharton's vocabulary is to that of these other writers, it seems ludicrous to insist that other women of this period did not know what they were "actually" writing about. It is also condescending.

At the same time, however, in using Canticles to construct their sexuality as natural and pure—in effect, as a biblical *hortus conclusus* or enclosed garden—what these poets won in the freedom to celebrate their pleasures, they paid back in taking a model for their sexuality that precluded sexual relations themselves. We now know that Canticles began life as an erotic poem or poems, composed in the third century B.C.E.[29] As such, it is a veritable cornucopia of sexual metaphors for men speaking of women, and for women speaking of men. For nineteenth-century women poets specifically, Canticles was a supremely important precursor text on two grounds. First, because in it male and female voices enjoy parity, the lovers alternating their songs while using the same densely figurative, sexually charged language. Second, because as an eastern text itself, Canticles is suffused with an "oriental" sensibility that is neither racist nor Eurocentric, investing positively through the Shulamite in racial and sexual difference instead. As part of the biblical canon, Canticles thus provided women poets with an unimpeachable source for an erotic discourse that was as much female- as male-authored and which valorized what would otherwise have been the dangerously exotic (i.e., the "southern" or "eastern") in themselves. But the value that Canticles found in women's sexuality was also dependent on enclosure: "A garden inclosed is my sister, my spouse, a spring shut up, a fountain sealed. Thy plants are an orchard of pomegranates, with pleasant fruits; . . . with all trees of frankincense, myrrh and aloes, with all chiefest spices: A fountain of gardens, a well of living waters, and streams from Lebanon" (4:12–15). What would happen, then, when the gate was opened? The fountain unsealed?

The difficulties presented by this conundrum are on display everywhere in nineteenth-century women's poetry but nowhere more spectacularly than in Maria Gowen Brooks's six-canto epic, *Zóphiël; or, The Bride of Seven* (1833), which is built entirely on the orientalizing/naturalizing trope of woman as gated or enclosed garden. Indeed, it is doubtful that any garden in the long history of this particular trope has ever proved harder to access than does that of Brooks's Jewish heroine, Egla, the "bride of seven." When Zóphiël, the fallen angel, first encounters her, Egla is napping in "a woody shade" where she "[l]oved to retire." The description that follows makes Egla an indivisible part of the lush but tranquil grove in which she rests, a grove clearly meant to mimic her own "enclosed garden," that is, her genitalia:

> . . . Acacias here inclined
>   Their friendly heads, in thick profusion planted,
> And with a thousand tendrils clasped and twined;
>   And when, at fervid noon, all nature panted,
>
> Inwoven with their boughs, a fragrant bower,
>   Inviting rest, its mossy pillow flung,
> And here the full cerulean passion-flower,
>   Climbing among the leaves, its mystic symbols hung.

But while Egla is able to rest in this "fragrant bower," complete with "passion-flower," there's no rest for Zóphiël once he happens upon her. Rather, like Satan, catching his first sight of "sweet Eve," Zóphiël is filled with "purpose fell":

> He caught a glimpse. The colors in her face,
>   Her bare white arms, her lips, her shining hair,
> Burst on his view. He would have flown the place,
>   Fearing some faithful angel rested there,
>
> . . . .

. . . But what assailed his ear?
A sigh! Surprised, another glance he took;
Then doubting, fearing, softly coming near,
He ventured to her side, and dared to look;

Whispering, "yes, 'tis of earth! So, new-found life
Refreshing, looked sweet Eve, with purpose fell,
When first Sin's sovereign gazed on her . . ."[30]

Only the appearance of Egla's maid, Sephora, saves Egla from rape. However, at a rather steep price, since it leads directly or indirectly to the deaths of six men before the seventh, her divinely ordained husband, the Hebrew Helon, gets her. Up to this point, the love-maddened Zóphiël, who is determined that if he cannot have Egla, no one else will, insures that this nominal "bride of seven" is never touched, making her, one suspects, the most virtuous femme fatale in the history of Anglophone poetry. Throughout the entire epic, she remains what she was: "a fragrant bower, / Inviting rest," a "passion-flower" whose "mystic symbols" only Helon gets to read, her great value to all these men apparently directly proportional to the difficulty they encounter in trying to get—literally—inside her.

By associating Egla's sexuality with the natural, flower-bedecked setting that, literarily speaking, Canticles established as female sexuality's appropriate mise en scène, Brooks keeps her heroine pure. No more than Spofford's seamstress is Brooks's Hebrew maiden tainted by her own desire or by the desire she arouses in others. However, this is only true because beginning with Zóphiël himself, no man is able to breach her. When one does (Helon), the epic ends. Finally, that is, the purity achieved through the trope of the enclosed garden could not extend beyond its own state of self-enclosure. Autoerotic desire was compatible with the latter, but alloerotic desire (the love of another) was not. What happens, then, when women turn from enjoying themselves to writing of their desire for another? To answer this question, I want to look at the second, alternative strain in nineteenth-century women's erotic poetry, that derived from Sappho (early sixth century B.C.E.). Written from the perspective of the desiring subject, this poetry yields a much darker, more complex, if equally embodied, vision.

Sappho's Sisters

Although Joan DeJean's *Fictions of Sappho, 1546–1937* has reduced the life of classical antiquity's most famous female poet to a series of successive cultural scripts, all fictitious, and Yopie Prins has added insult to injury by questioning the ontological status of "Sappho"'s texts as well, what interests me here is Sappho's literary contribution, which is not fictitious at all. Whoever, if anyone, Sappho was, and whatever, if anything, Sappho wrote, one fragment attributed to her by the Greek rhetorician Longinus and enshrined by him in

On the Sublime, has set the principal representational conventions for the Western love lyric, from Sappho's day to our own. Devoted in its entirety to the lover's interiority, this fragment describes how it feels to *be* in love. Written and rewritten by generations of lyricists—mostly male, at least until the nineteenth century—the lines that Longinus cited have had, as a result, an afterlife in cultural history every bit as complicated as Sappho's own, the more so since the conventions themselves functioned quite independently of any allusion to Sappho herself.[31] In this fragment, the speaker articulates what Longinus identifies as the "natural effects and living reality . . . of love," expressing in physical terms its delicious yet maddening mixture of pain, desire, and fear:

> Peer of immortals he appears to *my* mind,
> Who before *thy* face sitting is enchanted
> With the soft voice-tones, and the merry peals of
>   Loveliest laughter.
>
> How they make *my* heart flutter in my bosom,
> Timidly cowering: when I look upon thee,
> Voice and all living faculty of language
>   Sinks in confusion.
>
> All through my veins a subtle flame of passion
> Glides in its swift course, and a pall of darkness
> Falls on mine eye-sight, while reverberating
>   Murmurs assail me.
>
> Down the chill sweat pours, tremor seizes on me
> Breathless and blanching to a hue more pallid
> Than the pale-green grass, and the gates of death seem
>   Closing upon me.

Yet we must dare all, since unto the poor man, &c.[32]

Far more than the Ode to Aphrodite, the only complete Sapphic poem extant, let alone Ovid's apocryphal "Sappho to Phaon," the source for Prins's Victorian Sapphic tradition, the lines composing the Longinian fragment are Sappho's legacy to later poets. In them, the speaker depicts being in love both as a state of mind oscillating between heaven and hell, desire and frustration, ecstasy and despair, and as a set of physical symptoms, including, as the translator or imitator wills, palpitations of the heart, speechlessness, flames of passion, cold sweats, and so on. Mary Hewitt's "Imitation of Sappho" (1853), with its apostrophe to a silent beloved and its graphic description of inner turmoil, is an excellent example of a nineteenth-century U.S. woman's poem explicitly using the Sapphic conventions: "If to list breathless to thine accents falling, / Almost to pain, upon my eager ear; / And fondly when alone to be recalling / The words that I would die again to hear— / If at thy glance my heart all strength forsaking, / Pant in my breast as pants the frighted dove; / If to think on thee ever, sleeping—waking— / Oh, if this be to love thee, I do love!"[33] However, if this is a Sapphic "imitation," then so is Fanny Kemble's 1844 sonnet, which makes no direct reference to Sappho at all. Indeed, if anything, Kemble's poem does a better job of capturing Sappho's tone and vision of love than does Hewitt's, with its very Victorian panting dove: "There's not a fibre in my trembling frame / That does not vibrate when thy step draws near, / There's not a pulse that throbs not when I hear / Thy voice, thy breathing, nay, thy very name" (*NAWP* 48). Both of these poets are writing Sapphic poems, although only one acknowledges it.

It is on these grounds that I would argue, therefore, that no U.S. woman poet imitated the Sapphic love lyric more fully or wrung more changes on it, than did Dickinson, although she only mentions Sappho once in her poetry, and even then, slightly (F569). Taking interiority as her principal subject, Dickinson wrote endlessly of the agonies and sublime heights of a passion that could never be fulfilled and which she did not wish to see fulfilled, yet which she fantasized fulfilling, all at the same time: "The Apple on the Tree - / Provided it do hopeless - hang - / That - "Heaven" is - to Me!" (F310).[34] Like Petrarch, another great manipulator of the Sapphic lyric, Dickinson found the "extravagancies" of longing better served her muse than the realities of having if only because having brought longing, and hence the motivating force behind writing, to an end.[35] This was, in fact, the basic dynamic of the Sapphic love lyric, and probably the principal reason male and female poets continue to engage it to this day. Its situation is so basic, one can play with its constituents endlessly.

But would this poem of desire still work for nineteenth-century women should they turn from longing to having and actually try to write about sex? In concluding this chapter, I want to look at two poets whose crossing of the Sapphic desiring subject with an explicitly non-innocent use of imagery drawn from Canticles helps clarify the limits of the "sentimentalized" eroticism—the erotics of flowers, as it were—that I have explored here. Both "Cleopatra," by Helen (Burrell) D'Apery ("Olive Harper"), and "Antinous," by Annie Fields, invoke the "language of flowers" in extended fantasies of transgressive desire based on the lives of two well-known erotic figures from classical antiquity. But where "Cleopatra," embraces transgression with problematic warmth, Fields's poem on Antinous, the catamite of the Roman emperor Hadrian, ends up rejecting desire in equally problematic ways. Taken together, these poems suggest just how flexible nineteenth-century women's erotic discourse was and at the same time establish its limits, in particular its inability to deal with transgressive desire.

To my knowledge, D'Apery's "Cleopatra" is the only even minimally pornographic, as opposed to erotic, poem published by a nineteenth-century

U.S. woman poet. In a plain pamphlet bearing no publisher or date, her poem appears with an identically titled poem by the sculptor William Wetmore Story, and "Antony's Farewell to Cleopatra," by Brigadier General Lyttle, the latter found on the author's body after his death at the Battle of Chickamauga. Lyttle's poem is so tame one wonders how the poor man would have felt discovering his work in such posthumous company. D'Apery's and Story's poems, on the other hand, are of a piece, both written in ways clearly designed to stimulate readers erotically. The similarities between D'Apery's and Story's descriptions of Cleopatra's intense sexual frustration as she awaits Antony's return from Rome suggest that the poems have been written together, possibly in some sort of friendly rivalry or possibly as joint fantasy building in an ongoing sexual relationship (if they had one).

Mixing Canticles with Shakespeare's *Antony and Cleopatra*, D'Apery introduces us to Cleopatra as she lies on her couch, her "hot throbbing bosom" bathed "in the moon's silvery flood." Unable to sleep and tired of "tossing" about, Cleopatra leaves her "hot couch of purple" and goes into an adjacent garden, "to the crystalline fountain, / There my hot body to lave." The scene is a standard one: "I dipped in the sparkling waters / Beneath the broad light of the moon, / And the air was oppressive with fragrance / Of flowers, that hung folded at noon."[36] But, unlike Lippincott's swimmer, Cleopatra is not cooled off by her dip. On the contrary, she intensifies her torments by recalling a dream in which she watched Antony make love to another woman. D'Apery describes the scene graphically: Antony lies "Stretched at a woman's feet." He lifts "the hem of her garment." He presses "it long to [his] lips; / And, as if her mouth was her raiment, / [He] kissed as the honey-bee sips" (7). Whether D'Apery is suggesting voyeurism, fetishism, cunnilingus, or, possibly, all three is, as Perry Miller might say, for the reader to decide. What counts is that D'Apery's Cleopatra is indistinguishable from Story's and from woman as desiring subjects in the male pornographic imaginary generally. She is woman-panting-for-her-man:

> Ah! where is a king like my Roman,
>   With his royal, godlike form,
> With arms strong as steel from Damascus,
>   And his voice as grand as the storm?
> Whose shoulders are broad, snowy mountains,
>   Whose lips like the pomegranate bud;
> Dark eyes, like the deep pools in forests,
>   But stirred with his hot, jealous blood.
>   (6–7)

Canticles may have inspired the imagery in these lines—see, for example, "Thy temples are like a piece of pomegranate within thy locks. / Thy neck is like the tower of David / Builded for an armoury, whereon there hang a thousand bucklers, all shields of mighty men" (Canticles 4:3–4)—but the spirit is Greek.[37] As another Sapphic fragment puts it, the praise is for a "bridegroom" who "approaches like Ares," who is "much bigger than a big man."[38] We are back with the hypersexual woman again, positioning herself where men have always put her. She is once more an object, begging, as in Story's poem, to be taken: "Come to my arms, my hero, / The shadows of twilight grow, / And the tiger's ancient fierceness / In my veins begins to flow. / Come not cringing to sue me! / Take me with triumph and power, / As a warrior storms a fortress! / I will not shrink or cower" (20). Apparently neither D'Apery nor Story could imagine a sexualized woman who was not also an object to be conquered, a fortress to be taken, by the "biggest" of "big men." Both poets worship, that is, at the same phallic shrine, and either Cleopatra could have been created by either poet.

In this sense, Fields's poem, while about a young man, has much more complex things to say about female sexuality than does D'Apery's. Fields published "Antinous" in 1881 in *Under the Olive*, her second volume of verse. This same year also saw the death of her husband, James T. Fields, the *Atlantic Monthly's* esteemed editor, and marked a dramatic intensification of her intimate relationship with Sarah Orne Jewett, esteemed *Atlantic* writer. "Antinous" is one of a number of poems in this volume that suggest that Fields was using classical material to negotiate a same-sex relationship with Jewett, one that would not conflict with Fields's own Christian morality or with her sense of social duty. Taking the homosexual relationship between Hadrian and his famous catamite as given, Fields treats the beautiful youth as if he were, in fact, a woman, situating him in the flower-filled erotic setting of female sexuality itself: he lies "[s]tretched on the happy fields that view the sea, / Pillowed on beds of cyclamen, violet, rosemary," at a time when "lusty spears" of ripened corn reach to his "pillared throat."[39] Here his "rounding limbs . . . seem to grow and curve / Into more perfect life; [his] eyes to swim / With languor born of music; and these silent lips to rest in joys beyond the realm of thought" (100). "Clothed . . . with youth," Love's "child," as Antinous calls himself, watches "the eager bee, / Half drowned in his own bliss, while sleepy birds / Are calling drowsily in the summer noon" (101).

But Fields gives this lengthy autoerotic idyll a real life twist in line with Antinous's putative history. For, we learn, having been told that Hadrian "must part from . . . / His chosen joy, ere [his] fame he won," Antinous is contemplating suicide, though "[h]e nothing knew, save that his life was sweet / And death was bitter" (102). Since Fields devotes forty-seven lines to Antinous's ecstatic pleasure in his own sensuality, the "life" the youth is sacrificing seems to be specifically his sexuality, that is, his erotic pleasure in sensory experience, suppressed in the name of a higher love: "The jewel of my youth is mine to give; / Behold I bend me to the yellow stream, / And offer up this gift to my beloved" (102). Isn't it better, the poem seems to be asking Jewett/Hadrian, that I advance your career than that I give you sex? It was, of course, the kind of question the Angel could be expected to ask.[40] As chaste in the end as D'Apery's Cleopatra is oversexed, Fields's boy whore takes on the role that Annie Fields took on in life: sacrificing her own plea-sures and desires in service to esteemed others. This is a Sapphic lover who walks away from sex in the end, whether because she is afraid of its pain or because she feared its innate transgressiveness or because her own sense of duty was incapable of encompassing the idea of healthy pleasure as some-thing to be embraced for its own sake. Behind her, however, she leaves intact the hierarchical arrangements which led her, like her classical model, to sac-rifice herself in the first place and which, at least in this writer's opinion, are the primary source for difficulties in sexual relationships, whatever the sexual orientation of the couple involved.[41]

Written within a few years of each other, D'Apery's "Cleopatra" and Fields's "Antinuous" mark the outer boundaries of the female erotic discourse I have explored in this chapter, even as they, with no small irony, reconstitute its conventional limits, the binary of the Angel and the whore. But if these poems set limits to nineteenth-century women's eroticism, they also confirm that women did have an erotic discourse. Where Cleopatra and Antinuous are concerned, the subject has to be sex, since both poems engage historical figures whose iconic status, like Sappho's own, is the direct result of their association with transgressive sexual behavior. To deny the erotic content of such poems flies in the face of simple logic no less than to deny the erotic content of Ladd's "Waiting Rain."

Like cigars, fire hydrants, and guns, flowers, buds, and jewels remain part of the vast web of imagery on which writers and artists draw to signify male and female sexualities. But where the former (masculine) symbols are viewed as hard and their sexuality taken for granted, female symbols are viewed as soft and their sexuality is dismissed as vague, genteel romanticism or senti-mentalism. Like anger and irony, the erotic is supposed to stand outside the "sentimental," despite the fact that any open-minded reading of nineteenth-century poetry, whether written by men or women, shows that sentimental tropes regularly served for erotic expression as well. As we shall shortly see, however, women poets themselves must bear a good part of the respon-sibility for the delegitimation or "unwarranting," as Suzanne Clark calls it, of their own erotic discourse.[42] In turning wholesale against sentimentalism, fin-de-siècle women writers effectively cut themselves off from the pool of images through which female sexuality had been represented in Western lit-erature and art from biblical times. As a result, the unique and positive con-tribution nineteenth-century women's erotic discourse made to women's literature was lost, clearing the way for the "rosy snout / Rooting erotic garbage" of Mina Loy's "Pig Cupid" (1914) instead, and with it, a female-authored discourse on sexuality that, for better or worse, is all but indis-tinguishable from the way men talk about sex.[43]

8

Making It New in the Fin de Siècle

> If I smoked cigarettes, I have no doubt I should like cigars
> better. Doesn't a hookah take hold of your imagination?
> —MARIANNE MOORE to Bryher (Winifred Ellerman),
> January 16, 1923[1]

Between July and October, 1897, *Penny Magazine*, one of many sprightly new
little magazines dotting the U.S. literary landscape in the 1890s, published
two poems that, in all likelihood, would not have found a venue a decade
before. Mary Sebastian Lawson's "Realism" was one:

Out to-day upon the mall
I spied an August Lily tall—
A Tiger Lily—that was all.

Now you thought a lady fair,
Red-brown eyes and auburn hair,
Slim and stately, I spied there?

Nothing is two ways but lies;
Only facts can make us wise;
I *never* orientalize!

Out to-day upon the mall
I spied an August Lily tall—
A Tiger Lily—that was all.[2]

The second was "A Biography," by C.E.L.:

Born, welcomed, caressed, cried, fed, grew,
Amused, reared, studied, examined, graduated, in love,
engaged, married, quarreled, reconciled, suffered, deserted,
taken ill, died, mourned, buried and forgotten.[3]

Typical of the myriad "ephemeral bibelots" vying for attention in the century's last decade—also known as the "gay nineties," the "mauve decade,"
and the "fin de siècle"—*Penny Magazine* prided itself on its up-to-date so-
phistication and wit.[4] Smart as they are brief, these two poems fit the maga-

zine's self-image in both particulars. C.E.L. boils the generic story of a woman's life down to a string of twenty-three verbs, carrying her female subject from birth to death, but otherwise taking her nowhere. Lawson's flippant put-down of romanticism administers a sharp slap on the wrist to seven preceding decades of women's flower poetry. Speaking to and for the incoming generation of writers and readers, both poets present their bona fides as members of the United States' emerging literary avant-garde by, as Pound might say, "making it new."[5]

"Realism" and "A Biography" are not great works of art, but they are clever ones; and it is the quality of their cleverness that concerns me here, their breezy, in-your-face self-reflexivity and wink-of-the-eye antisentimentality. These poems push the envelope, going where they should not go, saying what they should not say, and keeping their "cool" at the same time—a kind of *sprezzatura* of affect or carefully calculated appearance of nonchalant unconcern.[6] Although both poems are too shallow to be "modernist," their liberatory aesthetic and highly self-conscious refusal to assign transcendental meanings take a big step in the direction of Modernism. In twenty-six words or less, "A Biography" drives a stake right through the Angel's heart, without wasting a single tear. Subtending "Realism" is a new view of the world, stripped of symbolic resonance: "Nothing is two ways but lies." Flowers, it seems, had lost their metaphoric value for bourgeois women writers, and so, apparently, had faith in domestic Angelhood. Facts had won out. As Lawson puts it, "that was all"—but an "all" that was, in fact, a very great deal.

Even in their brevity, these two poems suggest an enormous sea change in cultural attitudes respecting language, nature, art, the emotional life, and women. Cynical in attitude—cheerfully so, in Lawson's case—and boasting a diction purged of poetic archaisms, both poems are about as far as you can get from the densely metaphorical, heavily affect-driven poetry favored through most of the century. While Lawson's demystification of nature lacks the complexity of Robert Frost's or Wallace Stevens's, it is at an equal distance from Spofford's lushly romantic verse. Although C.E.L.'s "Biography" narrates a tragedy that earlier poets treated with great seriousness, albeit also with gothic panache, its own sardonic clippedness makes it a dress rehearsal for Dorothy Parker's wit. Looking backward to the poetry that preceded them and forward to the poetry to come, "Realism" and "A Biography" balance on a moment of transition. They are poems seeking a "new" which now knew itself to be "new" but at the same time did not know what that "new" was. Not with any security, at any rate.

By 1897, when "Realism" and "A Biography" appeared, the idea of "newness" as an honorific signifying end-of-the-century modernity had been in circulation in the United States for approximately three years, attached first, significantly enough, to the emergence of the "new" bourgeois woman. In France, both the *femme nouvelle* and the *art nouveau* had arrived somewhat earlier (according to Deborah Silverman in *Art Nouveau in Fin-de-Siècle France*, around 1889). In the United States, as abroad, the forces propelling society into twentieth-century modernity—from urbanization and the rise of mass-market technologies to radical shifts in gender values—were, by 1890, well on their way to convergence. What remained was for members of the incoming generation to take "newness" itself as their project, as, for example, Walter Blackburn Harte does in 1896, when he subtitles his new "little magazine," *Fly Leaf*, "A Pamphlet Periodical of the New—the New Man, New Woman, New Ideas, Whimsies and Things."

For avant-gardists like Harte, no less than for the early modernists who would follow him, terms such as "new" and "modern" were not just about change in fashion. According to Rita Felski in *The Gender of Modernity*, they incorporated "an exhilarating sense of liberation from the tyranny of the past, a leaving behind of outmoded and irrelevant values and traditions."[7] In the mission statement for *Fly Leaf*'s inaugural number, Harte, like Ezra Pound after him, legitimizes his literary efforts by blasting once-honored literary periodicals like the *Atlantic* and *Century* as so much dead wood. Newness for its own sake was "in." Harte embraces the revolution:

> The day is coming when [the respectable domestic] periodicals now devoted to the dissemination of the platitudes and ideas of two or three generations ago will have to awaken to the fact that the Young Man and Young Woman of this era demand the heart of life in their literature or they will be compelled to give way to bolder spirits, such as are now gathering strength in every modern literature. Already the tide has set in. Hence the *Fly Leaf*.[8]

Although Harte had no idea how much the tide he welcomed would sweep away, with himself among the sweepings, still he had caught the essence of what would be. In this sense, Mina Loy's 1913 manifesto, "Aphorisms on Futurism," a quintessential early-twentieth-century document, does little more than reframe Harte's assertions in capital letters: "DIE in the Past / Live in the Future, / . . . / . . . the Future is only dark from outside. *Leap* into it—and it EXPLODES with *Light*."[9] The British-born Loy was a bona fide early modernist and a woman of the world, but it was the 1890s generation in the United States as elsewhere that first valorized the "leap" she describes here, making newness for its own sake an aesthetic first principle. Both Harte and Loy project forward in the same direction, with the same "revolutionary" ardor and the same desire to be rid of the past, to make it NEW. But if early modernists cannot be credited with forging this first principle of their own aesthetic, they can be credited with something else, namely, making bourgeois women responsible for virtually everything in nineteenth-century art and culture that they chose to reject: timidity, conventionality, sentimentality, in fine, the genteel.

The gynophobic component in early modernist aesthetics, which continues to adversely affect the reading of nineteenth-century women writers today, has been so well documented that there is no need for me to rehearse the arguments here.[10] Writing of women's emasculation of nineteenth-century verse in a 1927 issue of *Poetry* (a woman-edited journal, I might note), H. L. Davis claims that any reader "with a little time and a copy of, say, Stedman's American anthology on his hands" could prove it for himself simply by counting. "It will be found that, whereas the harmonious numbers of the earlier part are uttered in a voice at least approximately male, if not masculine, the lyric asseverations of the later half are couched in an almost unmitigated soprano."[11] That men, in fact, substantially outnumber women first to last in Stedman's anthology made no difference to Davis. In his mind, nineteenth-century male poets were women, that is, pace Douglas, they were "feminized." Pound's friend T. E. Hulme was no less forward in putting the blame where he thought it belonged: "Imitative poetry springs up like weeds," he wrote in 1914, "and women whimper and whine of you and I alas, and roses, roses all the way. It becomes the expression of sentimentality rather than of virile thought."[12] Committed to being "new"—that is, *not* sentimental, *not* feminized—early-modernist women writers agreed. "[N]one of you has any word for me," Amy Lowell announced in "The Sisters," her backward glance at Sappho, Barrett Browning, and Dickinson. She may even have believed it.[13] She was a "New Woman," after all.

In recent years, this early-modernist narrative has been unsettled, at least from the twentieth-century side, by various scholars in different ways, most prominently by Gloria Hull, Alicia Ostriker, Suzanne Clark, Cheryl Walker, and Karen Kilcup. I now want to add to their work by exploring the substantial contribution that fin-de-siècle women poets' own rejection of sentimentality made to the emergence of U.S. literary modernism. In *The Gender of Modernity*, Felski astutely observes that the temporal replaces the spatial in late-nineteenth-century female modernity as the primary category of subjectivity. Women no longer identified themselves by their positioning along an axis running from private to public but rather along one running from old-fashioned to "new."[14] The New Woman knew herself to be new by virtue of her wholesale rejection of the past, including her rejection of the way in which women had traditionally been represented and represented themselves. Far more than a simple matter of style, for fin-de-siècle women writers, therefore, to write as a New Woman was to exhibit a new form of female authorial subjectivity, one that spoke to the life choices that women, now freed from their mothers' ideological burdens, were able to make: "I *never* orientalize."

In disavowing "orientalism"—here, more properly, romanticism—Lawson was speaking not just for herself but for an entire generation of young women eager not to be what they thought their mothers were, be that tiger lily or domestic Angel. Chauvinist males who tried to keep them in their mothers' place soon found that they could not do so with impunity, even in their own periodicals. When Harry Thurston Peck, editor of *The Philistine: A Periodical of Protest*, averred that women would always "be, at the most, somewhere down in the second or third ranks of the undistinguished," Sarah Norcliffe Cleghorn, snapped right back. After listing the varied accomplishments of the likes of Elizabeth I, Sappho, Heloise, and Florence Nightingale, all "Peckt to death by a bantam's pen," Cleghorn concludes her mock "Ballade of Queens and Great Ladies" with an "Envoi" that is no less unladylike than Peck's original comment was unchivalrous: "Herald, shall not even He, / Like all these ladies, wax and wane? / O let his piping memory be / Peckt to death by a bantam hen."[15]

Similarly, when William D. Forest published a bracing set of aphorisms putting women down in *Chips from Literary Workshops* (e.g., "Man is a brute—woman is the cause of man," and "Woman has no conception that there is aught else"), Marjorie R. Johnson's rebuttal comes two issues later: "Man is a fetish worshipper. His fetish is himself," "Man's pet amusement is to lay the blame of his failures on women; it never occurs to him to ascribe his successes to her," and so on.[16] "The Manners Tart," a prose piece of sorts, by Clara Cahill Park of Detroit, Michigan, published in the *Philistine* in September 1895, suggests that by the turn of the century there was very little off-limits to the new "Young Woman of [Harte's] era." Playing on the double meaning of tart (pastry/prostitute), Park's piece begins:

> An old and worn out Tart once sat on the pantry shelf and as it dried and stiffened, thus it soliloquized: "In my youth men fought over me, not to possess me, but that each should pass me to his neighbor. . . .
>
> "The cook, having made many of my brethren, cared not for me, so I, created to rejoice the soul of man, sit here, a cold and cheerless thing at which the rats gnaw nightly."

"But alas!" the Tart mourns, "I am a failure, and all because I move in a circle that makes a merit of self-sacrifice. I do not understand such things." The moral of the story? "If," says the narrator, the Tart "had understood it would have said—'there are many joys in the world that die unrejoiced over because no man will have the courage to do what he wants to do.'"[17] Given Park's obscurity, not to mention her Detroit address, one can only assume that clever plays on off-color material were "in" by the end of the century even in the most unlikely places. How giddy these young women must have felt with all their new freedoms. How little time was left before "Pig Cupid" took over the Angel's domain, and women like Loy would indeed "have the courage to do what [they wanted] to do," not just at home or in Detroit but wherever in the world they chose to be and horses, bicycles, balloons, boats, trains, airplanes, or their own two good feet could take them.

At the same time, stylistically and intellectually, fin-de-siècle women's writing, especially their poetry, is filled with inconsistencies and contradictions, perhaps necessarily so, since not only was newness as an aesthetic category still largely without content in this period but the "New Woman" herself was still largely unformed. From my perspective, however, this is also what gives fin-de-siècle women's poetry its particular interest. Across caste and class, race, faith, political and regional affiliation, fin-de-siècle U.S. women knew that they faced a host of opportunities never open to women before. No longer there on sufferance as Griswold's "poetesses" had been, large numbers of women were now full-fledged literary workers, contributing directly to the making of a U.S. literature at the national level, as editors, publishers, writers, reviewers, teachers, printers, illustrators, anthologists, and so on. If, as Mina Loy's biographer, Carolyn Burke, says, Loy "was the first to chart the sensibility of the 'new woman,'" it was her fin-de-siècle women precursors who made it possible for her to do so.[18] Early-modernist women, embracing a future that was exploding around and within them, could pour their energy into the challenging and complex forms of early-twentieth-century avant-garde art, sure of both who they were and what kind of art they wanted to produce or, at any rate, infinitely surer than their predecessors had been. My concern throughout this book has been to map how women writers reached this point, and it is now time to bring this narrative to an end.

Evolving towards Modernism

As I noted at the beginning of this chapter, the distinguishing feature of the "new poetry" that New Women began producing in the 1890s was a dissembling "coolness" or, since ultimately they amount to the same thing, an emphasis on emotionally restraining craft. No longer a platform for doing good or an effusion (i.e., the spontaneous overflow of feeling), poetry, as late-nineteenth-century women practice it, had become a way of shaping or making, and those who wrote it were artists first—not women, not preachers, not social workers, and certainly not poetesses. Thus deeply committed to artistic control, even in their most political writing, fin-de-siècle women evolved a form of stylistic, or what I call "affective," irony that, this chapter will argue, was their single most important contribution to the emergence of literary modernism as a whole.[19] As both "Realism" and "A Biography" suggest, behind women writers' development of this "cool," lay their determined need to separate themselves as completely as possible from the sentimental, exclusively "domestic" image of women that men had thrust upon them for the preceding one hundred years.

As we have already seen, genteel poetry had always had a strong aesthetic bent, but by the late 1880s, the overriding concern with formal excellence for its own sake becomes truly striking, especially in women's nature poetry. No poem better illustrates this than Margaret Deland's exquisitely crafted "Noon in a New England Pasture." In this poem, Deland, who is best known as a novelist, focuses entirely and unapologetically on the world as her senses knew it. The result is a poem as vivid today as it would have been a hundred years ago, a brilliant verbal record of a typical New England hillside pasture in midsummer. Deland brings the pasture to life through a careful choice of detail and by the accuracy of her language, as, for example, in the following descriptions of a stone wall and of mullein, a flowering weed ubiquitously inhabiting New England's waste areas:

With *soft, thick, wilted* leaves the mulleins grow,
   Like *tall straight candles* with *pale yellow* glow,
Their stalks *star-flowered* toward the cloudless west.
The crooning cricket with an endless song
   Jars the hot silence. The *crumbling* fence is grayed
   By the slow-*creeping* lichen, held and stayed
By arms of *wandering* rose, that, tough and strong,
Bind firm its *slipping* stones. The rusty brier
   And scarlet fingers of the bitter-sweet
   Cast a light shade that shelters from the heat
A thousand voiceless little lives.

To anyone familiar with mullein, each of the qualifiers I have highlighted is absolutely right, Deland perfectly capturing both the look and feel of this plant, whose leaves are so broad and soft Native Americans used them for diapers. Deland's description of a stone wall—among rural New England's most distinguishing features—is equally precise and evocative, consisting of a string of participles reinforcing the tension between the wall's permanence and its constantly slipping stones. "Natural" symbols of stasis and change, New England's stone walls are, as Frost observed, always in need of "mending," serving simultaneously as testaments to those who first cleared the land and as sites for new life: not just moss, lichen, and roses, but chipmunks, snakes, and assorted other creatures, who live in the crevices between stone and stone.

Published in *Harper's New Monthly Magazine* in 1887, "Noon in a New England Pasture" has more of an objective Frostian spirit to it than do the poems that Frost himself published in his first book, *A Boy's Will*, in 1913, a volume Karen Kilcup describes as "resolutely floral and often unapologetically sentimental."[20] "My November Guest," for example, opens on the following lugubrious note: "My Sorrow, when she's here with me, / Thinks these dark days of autumn rain / Are beautiful as days can be; / She loves the

bare, the withered tree."[21] Pound, who was committed throughout his career
to speaking through the voices of ages past, was doing no better in 1912:
"No, no! Go from me. I have still the flavour, / Soft as spring wind that's
come from birchen bowers. / Green come the shoots, aye April in the
branches."[22] "Birchen bowers"? "aye"? Admittedly, Frost's and Pound's early
work is uncharacteristic of their oeuvre as a whole, but their initial publications, at least, are still no match for Deland's poem in verbal control. Nor,
interestingly enough, was youth or inexperience a factor here, since Deland
was thirty, Frost thirty-eight, and Pound twenty-seven when they severally
published their poems.

While the early poems of Frost and Pound sound all too like the "senti-
mentalistic, mannerish" Victorian verse Pound would later despise and Frost
dismiss as "sissy" poetry, Deland concludes "Noon" with a stanza that
sounds remarkably like the final stanza of Wallace Stevens's "Sunday Morning" (1923), a poem of impeccable modernist credentials, thirty years off.[23]
Stevens famously uses images of bird flight and encroaching darkness to
bring his poem to an end: "Sweet berries ripen in the wilderness; / And, in
the isolation of the sky, / At evening, casual flocks of pigeons make / Ambiguous undulations as they sink, / Downward to darkness, on extended wings."[24]
Deland ends her poem with a hawk:

>   Poised in the brooding blue, on speckled wings,
>   A hawk hangs motionless: so straight he flings
>   His shadow to the earth, like plummet-line
>   It drops through seas of air. As in a swoon
>   Of light, the great world lies, and life stands still,
>   Wrapped in a breathless hush; till up the hill
>   Drift dappled shadows of the afternoon.
>   (*NAWP* 472)

Where Stevens's meditation on nature-without-God—or any other form of
transcendental meaning—ends with "pigeons" sinking into "darkness, on
extended wings," Deland ends her (very similar) meditation with a hawk's
shadow dropping "like plummet-line / . . . through seas of air." Both images
do the same work. Both are images of suspension, a momentary stay before
time moves on, like "a calm darken[ing] among water lights," as Stevens puts
it, or, as in Deland, till "dappled shadows of the afternoon" drift up the hill.
Both poets poise speakers and readers alike in a moment of stasis between
the fullness of life now (the flight of pigeons, the poised hawk) and the
acceptance of the darkness that inexorably follows, Stevens's "old catastro-
phe," death.[25]

Read in these terms, the aestheticization of nature that Deland shares with
modernists like Frost and Stevens goes much deeper than verbal precision,
touching on a commonality of worldview. In engaging the local specifics of

sensory experience, free of any metaphysical reading of nature itself, Deland, like the twentieth-century poets, places the full burden of her poem's
"meaning" on its ability to capture and recreate the aesthetic order of the
world. Art shapes and reproduces the natural world, becoming synonymous
with it. In this sense, "Noon in a New England Pasture" represents a vision
of nature that, however hauntingly beautiful, is also empty of transcendent
signifying power, a nature/world, in other words, very much like the one
that, in different ways, Frost and Stevens inhabited throughout most of
their careers.

With its points of contact to Frost and Stevens, "Noon in a New England
Pasture" is an unusually powerful example of the swerve that women's nature
poetry made in the final decades of the century toward a modernist poetic,
one that found in art itself the only reality in a world otherwise emptied of
meaning. Like Dickinson, who produced multiple poems on thunderstorms
and sunsets, each a self-contained sketch of the phenomenon it describes, no
more and no less, many fin-de-siècle women poets, not just Lawson and
Deland, used words to capture sensory experiences that never go beyond
themselves. As in Deland, the consequences of this swerve are most apparent
in their poems' conclusions. In nineteenth-century genteel nature poetry—
Emerson's "The Rhodora" or Bryant's "To a Waterfowl," for example—the
poem's final lines are usually reserved for a moral, often a religious sentiment, that gives readers closure on the experience the poem describes. Thus,
Emerson observes of the rhodora he finds blooming in the woods, "The self-
same Power that brought me there brought you."[26] Women's fin-de-siècle
nature poetry, on the other hand, often ends by leaving the reader hanging.
One can interpret Deland's final lines in "Noon," for instance, as pointing
toward death, but only inferentially. The speaker leaves the whole thing
open, anticipating the hallmark "indeterminacy" of modernist art, its preference for ambiguity over direct statement.[27]

Although the seasons are anthropomorphized in Lucy E. Tilley's "The
Touch of Frost" (1890), her poem concludes neutrally, with a personified
"Summer," lifting "an aster's drooping stem / And smitten corn leaves from
her garment's hem" (*NAWP* 485). We can, if we wish, project sadness into
these images—the drooping stem, the smitten leaves—but neither sadness
nor any higher meaning is thrust upon us. Similarly, Katherine T. Prescott's
"A November Prairie" (1891) concludes its unsettling and unsettled description of a coming storm, without resolution presenting the event strictly as a
thing observed: "A writhing, seething mass of angry clouds / Sweeps on with
fearful force and snowy breath; / The ghostly grass bows down with one
great moan of pain, / And all the shuddering air is filled with strife" (*NAWP*
489). Both these poets put ambiguous but figuratively charged descriptions
in the spot where earlier genteel nature poets put their moral or comforting
sentiment, thereby relating the observer to the thing observed. The final lines

of Maude Morrison Huey's 1897 "A Wintry Night" are so enigmatically evocative and, at the same time, so completely self-contained that they could be read as an "imagist" poem in themselves: "Strange fingers tap / My broken lattice-slats,—a frozen vine / That angry winds have loosed; a straggling stem, / Ice-burdened, that the trellis bars entwine" (*NAWP* 504). The image here is crystal clear; its meaning, if it has one, is not. It simply is the there that is there.

Unlike their forebears, from Cotton Mather to Emerson, the women who wrote these poems are not treating nature as a veil through which eternal meanings can be glimpsed, nor are they looking for lessons in running brooks, as does Shakespeare's Duke in *As You Like It*. For them, nature qua nature was sufficient. If, as Cynthia Griffin Wolff complains, Dickinson's late nature poetry made the world a "diminished thing," the vacuum left by God's disappearance—the disappearance of the transcendental or, as Emerson called it, the "Whole"—is filled not just for Dickinson but for all these poets by art itself.[28] The descriptions of the material universe they offer are no more or less than what their worldview led them to see. The telling of it, therefore, becomes an end in itself, in the absence of other possibilities. And perhaps for this reason, the privileging of craft began to demand not just close observation and moral neutrality but brevity. After almost a century of highly expansive writing, verbal elaboration was on the way out. The "new" generation wanted ease, grace, and flexibility ("naturalness") instead, the very dissolution of the old metaphysical and social orders, including gender order, demanding a stripped-down style. As the elite young women flooding the nation's newly established women's colleges had quickly found out, one could not climb mountains, ride bicycles, play tennis, or go swimming in Grandmother's clothing, nor could one write "modern" poetry using Grandmother's overdressed writing style (see fig. 9).[29]

The first major sign that verbal excess in poetry was no longer "in" took the form of the quatrain craze of the 1880s. As a form, the quatrain was nothing new, but the production rate for the quatrain in this period is another matter. *Current Literature* reprints twenty-eight, for example, on a single page in its March 1889 issue. Traditionally, poets wrote quatrains to give epigrammatic force to clever ideas, as, for instance, in S. S. Cohen's "False Kisses," a fresher-than-average presentation of a popular theme in nineteenth-century women's poetry: male narcissism. "Love came. I took him on my knee; / He stood tiptoe mine eyes to see; / He kissed mine eyes—could falser be? / His mirrored self he kissed—not me!"[30] Despite the rhyme, these lines could come straight from the *Greek Anthology*, that potpourri of Alexandrian verses which returned to fashion in the fin de siècle.

Although most quatrain writers never got beyond rhymed moralizing, by the 1890s poets like Eleanor B. Caldwell had begun using the form to suggest up-to-date-ness also, as in Caldwell's "Creation," published in the 1896

Fig. 9. Walking and Tennis Gowns

Chap-Book. The most self-evidently "proto-modernist" moment in this poem comes in the last line, in an image which not only lacks moral valence but approaches the sort of quasi-nonsensical playfulness we associate with early Wallace Stevens (for example, "Bantams in Pine-Woods"): "Aeons of time, infinite space, / Blackness and chaos interlace. / Sudden, a streak of light shot through—/ On a pin-head of earth, a red cock crew" (*NAWP* 495). Nor is "Creation" mere nonsense. On the contrary, Caldwell's deft allusion to scientific discourse in the poem's first line gives it a Stevens-ish substance as well. As a whimsical re-write of the Book of Genesis, "Creation," cock and all, wakes us up to the fact that we now live in a new world, cosmologically speaking as in every other respect. Brevity does not get much wittier than this.

That poems generally were getting shorter in the century's last decade can be seen just about everywhere in the period's magazines and journals. By the last decade of the century one can find significant numbers of poems by women—and men (Father Tabb and Stephen Crane, for instance)—that are only a few stanzas long, and whose diction and focus are strikingly modern. Martha T. Tyler's "Seaward" is a particularly illuminating example. Published in the *Overland Monthly* in 1893, "Seaward" dramatically fails of its own nascent poetic: strict reliance on the patterning of words and syntax to create poetic effect/meaning. By this token, however, the poem also illustrates just how little distance separated late-nineteenth-century women's poetry from what was to come:

> A line of mist, a line of shore (quoth I),
>   Tall masts that like black shadows intervene,
> A rain-bewildered sea, a barren sky,
>   And the wild sweep of restless wings between.
>
> O desolated sea and sunless sky!
>   O bitter winds and mists that intervene!
> A dream of Life, a dream of Death (quoth I),
>   And the wild sweep of restless wings between![31]

"Seaward" skewers itself with each parenthetical "quoth I," making it hard not to wish that, like H.D. and T. S. Eliot, Tyler had had the advantage of Pound's editorial pen. At the same time, however, with its disjunctive syntax, succinct and carefully chosen phrases, and sweeping refrain, her poem is something more than Victorian, something "new." Bold and timorous, modern and traditional, bound yet moving toward freedom with its "restless wings," "Seaward" mirrors what were probably Tyler's own confusions and contradictions as she entered the new era, an era for which she was and was not prepared. This same kind of conflict can also be seen in Mary McNeil Scott (Fenollosa)'s imitations haikus, for example, in "A Friend," published in *Century* in 1895: "The plum-tree bends, all dumb with snow, and pale / With mockery of the coming bloom, / But ah! with one sweet cry, the nightingale / Leaps to her bough and sings perfume."[32]

Like her second husband, the esteemed sinologist, Ernest Fenollosa, Scott was committed to introducing Far Eastern aesthetic principles to Western writers,; and she was, to my knowledge, the first U.S. poet to attempt to anglicizing Japanese poetic forms.[33] In "A Friend," she tries to capture the haiku's condensation and its delight in startling juxtapositions ("sings perfume"). But in recasting the haiku as a quatrain, Scott violated the integrity of the very principles she sought to introduce. The result is an awkward hybrid, neither fish nor fowl, traditional or modernist. For every fully successful women's poem written in the fin de siècle—such as Deland's "Noon in a New England Pasture" or Caldwell's "Creation"—one can find dozens that exhibit internal stylistic contradictions such as those in "Seaward" and "A Friend." These contradictions were, I would suggest, the birth pangs of the new. "New Women" the authors might be, but the meaning and shape of newness was still something toward which they were groping, and meanwhile they clung to bits and pieces of the past—Scott's nightingale, Tyler's "quoth I"s. It was precisely here that modernists had the advantage. They not only recognized themselves as "new" but knew what that "new" was; and, thanks to the savvy promotional efforts of writers like Pound and Lowell, they also knew how to achieve it.[34] Without a critical mass of material necessary to define the new poetry as a free-standing category—a period or movement—their fin-de-siècle precursors could only work by trial and error toward this goal.

Irony and the Unsentimental Speaker of the Fin de Siècle

If fin-de-siècle women poets never achieved a consistently modernist poetic, however, they did make one major contribution to the emergence of U.S. literary modernism for which they deserve full credit; namely, they evolved a new kind of poetic irony, what I call "affective irony"—the irony of "cool." Unlike the women's irony discussed in earlier chapters, which used sentimentality against itself in service to political goals, affective irony was a rhetorical strategy—a way, or style, of writing—designed to help writers assert control over the medium itself. That is, it addressed issues of craft as much as it did those of perspective. Its use identified the "New Woman" poet qua poet, making her *lack* of sentimentality the signature of her professionalism and the purity of her status as "maker," not feeler. Of Lizette Woodworth Reese, the fin de siècle's most skilled practitioner of affective irony, Louis Untermeyer wrote admiringly in 1930, "In a period of sugared sentiment and lace valentine lyrics, Miss Reese's crisp lines were an entire generation ahead of the times and were consequently appreciated only for their pictorial felicities."

Considering that, scarcely seven years earlier, Untermeyer had imagined Reese wearing "black lace mitts" to write, his comment is telling—not about

Reese, however. From the 1880s to the end of her lengthy career Lizette Reese wrote the same way, letting the newly emerging literary establishment catch up with—and then overtake—her, but the comment is telling about Untermeyer himself. It took modernism's most prestigious anthologist over thirty years to appreciate just how prescient Reese's "straightforward, undidactic speech" was, marking, as it did, a definitive end to "sugared sentiment and lace valentine lyrics."[35] Had Untermeyer cared to drop more of his biases, he would have discovered that Reese was not the only woman poet writing without black lace mitts. Here I want to look briefly at four: Reese herself, and three from minority communities, Louise Imogene Guiney, E. Pauline Johnson, and Henrietta Cordelia Ray, all poets for whom the practice of affective irony was, as it turned out, far more problematic than it was for Reese.

Among fin-de-siècle women poets, none used affective irony more consistently or with greater success than did Lizette Reese, who from her first publications on made the practice of emotional restraint the defining characteristic of her verse. However bitter the ironies of Dickinson's and Piatt's perceptions, both these latter poets wrote with the intense emotionalism of "romantic/sentimental" sensibility. With respect to feeling, if not necessarily verbally, they were poets of Victorian excess. Reese, on the other hand, is the epitome of cool. Like the majority of U.S. poets writing in the twentieth century, she uses the vernacular, speaking—aside from an occasional poeticism—in everyday language about everyday things. Her poems, much like those of Maxine Kumin, celebrate the daily epiphanies of a quiet and largely private life: a tuft of flowers, the coming of spring, gossip in a rural village, a mother's death. Reese neutralizes the potential "sentimentality" of these themes, as many poets still do today, by her art, in particular by her determination to pare everything unneeded away. Published in 1896, "Telling the Bees," with its very Victorian subject, a mother's death, superbly illustrates those aspects of Reese's technique that kept her work in circulation through most of the twentieth century:

> Bathsheba came out to the sun,
> Out to our wallèd cherry-trees;
> The tears adown her cheek did run,
> Bathsheba standing in the sun,
> Telling the bees.

> My mother had that moment died;
> Unknowing, sped I to the trees,
> And plucked Bathsheba's hand aside;
> Then caught the name that there she cried
> Telling the bees.

Her look I never can forget,
I held her sobbing to her knees;
The cherry-boughs above us met;
I think I see Bathsheba yet
Telling the bees.

(NAWP 304)

Like Dickinson and Piatt, Reese brings complexity as well as control to her poems through irony, but where the former poets used irony to raise difficult issues of divine and social justice, Reese's irony, like that of Frost, whom she deeply influenced, addresses the emotions. In place of the earlier poets' searing rage at an unjust God/universe, Reese assumes a voice as soft and soothing as a child's hand. The servant's tears, the child's recognition, the ancient colonial ritual meant to stave off the bees' flight,[36] are all presented without promise, judgment, expectation, or guilt. What her mother's death means to the speaker as she looks back on this childhood trauma and how she feels about the servant's reenactment of the ancient ritual now are not disclosed. With a few swift brush strokes, for example, the cherry boughs, Reese gives the reader a vivid portrait of the scene and leaves it there, refusing to tip her hand emotionally or in any other way and, equally important, refusing to impose on the reader any particular response. Reese's poetry is full of moments such as this, wherein we are simultaneously allowed to share and excluded outright, the speaker's absence of affect leaving us free to respond as much or as little as we wish or even to find our greatest satisfaction in appreciating the poem's telling, its "art," instead.[37]

Written on the brink of a century in which, according to Suzanne Clark, the chief literary order of the day was the unwarranting of emotion in art, Reese's ironizing form of understatement—her ability (no less than Hemingway's, for example), to play in the gap between stripped-down style and emotion-laden subject matter—points firmly to where U.S. high culture poetry would soon be heading. That one finds this technique so fully anticipated in a late-nineteenth-century woman poet problematizes, however, those arguments, like Clark's, that have made male discomfort with emotion the principal factor in sentimentality's twentieth-century delegitimation. No less than Frost, Reese worked to desentimentalize her verse, making it, as Kilcup puts it, "quintessentially modern and associatively masculine," despite her often nostalgic, even sentimental, subject matter.[38] Servants and children may weep in Reese's poems; the speaker does not. On the contrary, Reese's artistic sensibility and her skill as "maker"—the root meaning of poet—best register in her ability to turn tears into art. In Reese, the wheel of literary sentimentality as the primary discourse of artistic sensibility comes full circle. Stripped of all the excess language, feeling, and high-minded moralizing that made the sentimental so popular in its own day, the art of poetry now lay in the stripping itself, the energizing tension or power of a poem resided precisely in lines made "crisp" by what the poet did not say.

Hands down, Reese was affective irony's most influential female exponent in the fin de siècle, in good part because her distancing techniques meshed so perfectly with her otherwise nostalgia-ridden subject matter. One could read Reese, as, in my opinion, one can read much of Hemingway, Frost, and dozens of other early-twentieth-century male writers, and feel nostalgic without, at the same time, incurring the guilt of sentimentality. In a far more scholarly way, Louise Imogen Guiney made use of the same strategy in her backward-looking poetry. The best-known Irish American woman poet of the fin de siècle, Guiney rarely wrote on Irish themes and only occasionally published in the *Pilot*, Fanny Parnell's venue of choice. After suffering grievously from anti-Irish prejudice in the States, she joined the first cadre of expatriate U.S. artists, living in Britain. Yet if Guiney felt outrage over the way in which she and other Irish Catholics were treated, she did not put it in her verse. Rather, like Pound and H.D., Guiney dealt with her dissatisfactions by installing herself in a past that was truly past. No less than Annie Fields, Guiney was fascinated by classical antiquity. But in a way that measures the gulf between her and earlier poets, she made no attempt to Victorianize (i.e., moralize) classical themes. Rather, she recreates the past in the present through literary feats of full-blown cultural nostalgia. Her imitation "Alexandriana" (1893) are so on the mark that some readers mistook them for the real thing, much to Guiney's delight. Number 7, a blank verse elegy for the youthful athlete Cnopus, demonstrates the skill that she brought to these re-creations:

> Here lies one in the earth who scarce of the earth was moulded,
> Wise Æthalides' son, himself no lover of study,
> Cnopus, asleep, indoors: the young invincible runner.
> They from the cliff footpath that see on the grave we made him,
> Tameless, slant in the wind, the bare and beautiful iris,
> Stop short, full of delight, and shout forth: "See, it is Cnopus
> Runs, with white throat forward, over the sands to Chalcis!"
>
> (*NAWP* 320)

If the "wise Æthalides" and his son, Cnopus, "the young invincible runner," are imaginary figures, Guiney makes the Greek view of death as metamorphosis exquisitely real. With its dense rhythms full of starts and stops, and its twisted word order, "Here lies one" is an engaging poem, a moving one also, if one allows oneself to imagine its youthful subject as a white-throated iris, "slant in the wind." But, ironically, the poem's most modernist aspect, other than its linguistic control, is its global rejection of the modern world. No less than Walter Benjamin's, Guiney's is an austere turning back to an earlier time, a time when art itself was, presumably, uncompromised by mechanical reproduction and the vulgarities of commercialized taste. In such a poem, the kind of intimacy and immediacy on which literary and high sentimentality depended is no longer possible. No slave mother's cry can interrupt Guiney's poem, no call to arms, nor even grief for a dead loved one. Everything that happens happens too far away, in a world too unlike our own. We are asked to admire the author's craft instead, moved, if we are moved, by the sheer beauty of the telling and by Guiney's ability to imagine with such precision and grace something to which neither she nor we have any exposure except in books.

Like "Telling the Bees," Guiney's Alexandrian imitation is an artistic success. Indeed, its aesthetic integrity is a tribute to its maker, especially if one compares Guiney's handling of classical matter to that of a writer like Annie Fields. However, this integrity comes at the cost of the present, its jagged pains and ephemeral joys, and it comes, therefore, at the cost of the political as well. It is maker's art. When the distancing of affective irony is applied to sorrows in the present, its use, as we have already seen in Piatt's "Night-Scene at the Rock of Cashel, Ireland," becomes much more problematic. Two examples, one from E. Pauline Johnson, the other from Henrietta Cordelia Ray, will help illustrate what I mean. In these poems, we see what happened when, in effect, turn-of-the-century poets tried to mediate high-sentimental subject matter by means of rhetorical strategies designed to address formal concerns connected with the control—not the expression—of emotion.

As noted in chapter 4, E. Pauline Johnson wrote two very different kinds of Indian poems: her dramatic performance poetry, which came out of the high-sentimental tradition, and another, more contemplative and "modern" strain. In the latter, Johnson writes of her people's present, rather than their fantasized past, in ways a number of scholars have called proto-imagist because of the poems' reliance on sharply defined detail. "The Corn Husker," published in *Harper's Weekly* in 1896, is such a poem:

Hard by the Indian lodges, where the bush
　　Breaks in a clearing, through ill-fashioned fields,
She comes to labour, when the first still hush
　　Of autumn follows large and recent yields.

Age in her fingers, hunger in her face,
　　Her shoulders stooped with weight of work and years,
But rich in tawny colouring of her race,
　　She comes a-field to strip the purple ears.

And all her thoughts are with the days gone by,
　　Ere might's injustice banished from their lands
Her people, that to-day unheeded lie,
　　Like the dead husks that rustle through her hands.
　　　　　　　　　　　　　　　　(*NAWP* 330)

No less than the Johnson poems discussed in earlier chapters, "Corn Husker" is a politically charged poem; but the political burden is distributed very differently. In the performance poetry, the poem's power arises out of a rhetorically dramatic situation in which we become emotionally involved as the speaker herself is involved. In "Corn Husker," the power resides in a single, highly focused image, that of the husks themselves. Not only, as suggested in chapter 4, does Johnson use these husks to symbolize the emptying out of tribal culture, but she reinforces this meaning through submerged aural and kinetic figures: the "rustling" sound of dry and lifeless vegetation and the feel of the dried husks as they "rustle" (run like sand?) "through [the cornhusker's] hands." Yet packed as this image is, to appreciate its power, one must first unpack it. That is, we are back at Piatt's problem in "Night-Scene." Johnson has succeeded in avoiding high sentimentality's emotional and rhetorical excess, but only by leaving things out, here, most strikingly, any sense of complaint. Oblique, subtle, carefully crafted, respectful, elegiac—this poem shows us "might's injustice," but asks nothing of us beyond aesthetic appreciation in return. On the contrary, the aestheticizing of the corn husker's situation forces us to view it as the way things are, if not as they should be. We, that is, like the speaker herself, stand outside the experience she describes, observing it but otherwise unengaged, the husks an "objective correlative" for the author's despair.

The need that Reese, Johnson, and Guiney all exhibit to distance their speakers emotionally through controlled affect can also be seen in the work of Henrietta Cordelia Ray, one of a number of black women poets publishing at the end of the century. The apparent absence of political writing in Ray has caused some disappointment among scholars, and she has come in for some heavy pounding by her modern editor, Joan Sherman, in particular, who has no use for the "wax flowers, stuffed birds, and canvas sunsets in her verse museum."[39] Nevertheless, Ray's "Niobe," published in the *A.M.E. Church Review* in 1893, is an extremely powerful rendition or re-visioning of the *stabat mater* or grieving-mother theme, reworked to fit the circumstances of "Mother" Africa and the African American slave mother at once:

O Mother-Heart! when fast the arrows flew,
Like blinding lightning, smiting as they fell,
One after one, one after one, what knell
Could fitly voice thine anguish! Sorrow grew
To throes intensest, when thy sad soul knew
Thy youngest too must go. —Was it not well,
Avengers wroth, just one to spare? —Aye, tell
The ages of soul-struggle sterner? —Through
The flinty stone, O image of despair,
Sad Niobe, thy maddened grief did flow

In bitt'rest tears, when all thy wailing prayer
Was so denied. Alas! what weight of woe
Is prisoned in thy melancholy eyes!
What mother-love beneath the stoic lies!
                    (*NAWP* 289–90)

Even more than with "Corn Husker," what makes this poem so powerful is precisely what it leaves out: here, the actual reason for Niobe's punishment, her insult to the goddess Latona. In Ovid's *Metamorphoses*, as in Phillis Wheatley's youthful translation of Ovid, the focus is on the deaths of Niobe's fourteen children, the seven sons and seven daughters who pay the price for their mother's overweening pride. Read this way, Niobe's is a story of crime and punishment, an object lesson in the dangers of hubris. However, as Alicia Ostriker observes, this emphasis gets muddied in Wheatley: "the heavy degree of melodramatic woe," Ostriker writes, "suggests that ["Niobe"] may be a veiled portrait of [Wheatley's] own powerlessness—or even, more radically, a lament on behalf of the mother from whom she herself had been torn."[40]

I find Ostriker's argument cogent and further believe that it was on Wheatley's translation that Ray built. Not only does Ray focus wholly on the queen but she constructs Niobe explicitly and exclusively as grieving "mother-love." Although the speaker mentions "avengers," they are not named, nor does the speaker explain why these avengers are killing Niobe's children. Ray also withholds the children's names, given in Ovid and Wheatley. All the speaker says is that they are destroyed, "[o]ne after one, one after one," down to the youngest. By leaving so much out, Ray gives the reader no choice but to view Niobe's loss—not her "crime" or even the pain suffered by her children—as the poem's central experience. Ravaged by a grief no human flesh could bear, the queen turns to stone, her "weight of woe" henceforth forever "prisoned in [her] melancholy eyes."

Psychologically speaking, Niobe's fate—in today's parlance, "numbing out"—fits the pattern of dissociated response that great loss tends to elicit, a fact that Dickinson exploits in any number of poems but most notably in "After great pain" (F372). By suppressing all mention of Niobe's misdeeds, Ray turns the mythological queen into a powerful figure for any woman's mother-grief. Well beyond Niobe, this figure seems to gesture, therefore, toward "Mother" Africa and toward two centuries of African American slave mothers, denied the right to grieve, let alone protest, when their children were ripped from them.[41] Ironically turning the Greek tale—theme of many an illustrious bard—inside out, Ray effectively collapses the distance between the mythological Phrygian queen and the nameless slave mothers who lived out her fate, without ever having committed any of her crimes. Ray is *their* bard.

By never making her viewpoint or her politics explicit, Ray prevents our reading this heartbroken "Mother-Heart" sentimentally. At the same time, however, as Sherman's problems with Ray indicate, one must read the poem carefully indeed to catch what is going on in it. Ironic understatement here amounts to not stating at all and trusting one's readers will put in the effort to get it right. The drive for artistic control could be said at this point to overwhelm all other forms of authorial intention, particularly the political intention, turning the poem back on itself. From Oedipus on, this is, of course, how irony reveals itself. Rhetorically speaking, it is a figure of self-subversion, of endings that both confirm and undo their beginnings. Artistically, "Niobe" is Ray's greatest success.

Nonetheless, it is also an uncomfortably short step from "Niobe" to the modernist conviction that the most powerful way to express emotion is not to express any emotion at all—surely, the ultimate form of dissembling (the root meaning of "irony" itself); and as politics, should politics be wanted, not likely to work. To appreciate Ray's poem, one must read it, in other words, for the word or, as T. S. Eliot put it, for the "medium" itself.[42] Ironically, perhaps bitterly, "Niobe"'s great power derives from the way in which it turns its back on that host of antebellum texts whose overt political commitment made it possible in the first place. That is, its ironization of its relationship to the past and to past texts marks it definitively as postabolitionist, precisely because it is produced by the shift not just from sentiment to emotional control but from politics to art. Is it possible, then, that the writings of other fin-de-siècle women are "post-" also? Are all these poets writing in the aftermath, as David Porter argues so eloquently of Dickinson, if not in the aftermath of slavery, or of the final termination of precontact tribal culture, than of the domestic Angel's demise?[43]

Conclusion

Just as the eighteenth-century line of wit remained an option throughout the nineteenth century, fin-de-siècle women continued to write poems exploiting the props and themes of earlier women's verse. But the dead housewives and dead babies, the spirit-haunted domestic hearth, and the pain of their own and others' oppression that so preoccupied earlier women no longer held center stage, when touched on at all. Living in a generation parallel to our own—postsentimental if not postmodernist—fin-de-siècle women poets took their writing in playful and disinterested directions instead, a professional concern with craft taking up the slack left by failed commitments to religion, morality, domesticity, and social justice. In their poems, fin-de-siècle women poets embodied, as one *Chap-Book* reviewer put it in 1897, "the modern doctrine that woman is the unsentimental sex."[44] Their loyalty was to a poetics of affective irony whose subtlety could make any modern poet proud. Sarah Cleghorn's "Behold the Lilies" (1896) is an unusually happy example, one possibly inspired by Dickinson's "Some keep the Sabbath" (F236), but, if so, targeted very differently:

> Drowsy weather, eleven o'clock;
>   Tall white daisies blow in the sun,
> And dust blew lightly on Martha's frock;
>   (Morning Service must have begun).
>
> The anthem sounded along the street;
>   Winds breathed up from the fresh-cut hay.
> She lingered a little; the fields are sweet,
>   They toil not, neither do they pray.
>   (*NAWP* 497–98)

Even compared to a poem as playful as "Some Keep the Sabbath," Cleghorn's is a very cool poem. The new Martha is not just tossing out churchgoing and domestic labor as paths to female salvation but Dickinson's nature-is-my-road-to-God approach as well. What is left is physical pleasure—the sweet scent of fresh-cut hay—nothing else. The attitude—and this is a poem with an attitude—is as flippantly close to pagan agnosticism and as cheerfully mocking as one can get and still be recognizably "nineteenth-century." Cleghorn's freedom is the freedom of the New Woman, a woman determined to control both her life and her art, living and writing for herself alone, a woman, that is, much more like the flapper of the 1920s, than like the Victorian mother who bore her. What defines her, what makes her modern, is precisely her ability to view herself as "post-."

Cleghorn's distinctly unsentimental little ditty—irreverent, whimsical, above all, smart—seems a fitting poem with which to conclude this book's explorations of the changing fate of nineteenth-century U.S. women and their verse. All the evidence suggests that contrary to everyone's opinion, including their own, nineteenth-century bourgeois women writers were never unambivalently comfortable with sentimentality. If the 1837 *Knickerbocker* Belle used wit, not tears, to play the sex game, Margaret Fuller no less emphatically disassociates herself from tears when arguing the case for Native Americans in 1843. In 1854, Phoebe Cary unmasks literary sentimentality as a set of male delusions fatal to women, while in an 1869 *Galaxy* review, Spofford praises Lucy Larcom's poetry for its freedom from that "maudlin sentimentality that sickens the pages of so many poets."[45] In 1874, a hard-nosed Mary Booth, founding editor of *Harper's Bazar* (*sic*), echoes the supposedly "soft-minded" Lydia Sigourney of twenty years before in a scathing condemnation of the "sentimental cant" surrounding the realities of motherhood and marriage.[46] In 1880, Piatt in "His Mother's Way" targets the utter ineffectuality of tears as a means to bring about progressive social change.

Helen Gray Cone's 1890 denunciation of sentimentality in *Century Magazine*, as having "infected both continents," filling the world with "flocks of quasi swan-singers," is indistinguishable, as Kilcup observes, from the attacks on sentimental nineteenth-century poetry launched by modernist women poets years later—Amy Lowell's in 1923, for example, or Louise Bogan's in 1935.[47] In 1891, Annie Nathan Meyer saw clearly how sentimental constructions of womanhood worked to disadvantage women in the marketplace. "Sentimentalists," she wrote in *Women's Work in America* "who certainly include as many women as men, argue that every woman is the natural companion of man. . . . [making it] highly supererogatory that a woman should be taught to stand upon her own feet."[48] Cleghorn, future author, among other things, of "Comrade Jesus" ("Ah, let no local him refuse! / Comrade Jesus has paid his dues. / Whatever other be debarred, / Comrade Jesus has his red card"), seems merely bent on laughing sentimentality to death.[49] It took a late-twentieth-century feminist back-formation to restore sentimentality's positive valence, unhappily, by once more hanging it like a rhetorical albatross around women's necks.[50] But even Pound knew that nineteenth-century male writers were at least as sentimental as their womenfolk, although this did not prevent him from blaming women anyway.

When, between 1890 and 1910, "the sentimental" became nascent modernism's "Other," the pole against which literary modernity defined itself, female modernists no less than their male counterparts, participated in an auto da fé that sent hundreds, perhaps thousands, of earlier women poets into the fire. In the final irony of this critical narrative so shot through with ironies, postsentimental, postfeminist, post–fin-de-siècle women writers did away with their own past, even while enjoying the plentiful fruits of earlier women's labor: "none of you has any word for me." Right. As in H.D.'s "Sea Rose" (1916), the woman poet who emerged from the ashes was one who learned to live and bloom for herself alone, in a literary world which, now identified as high culture, was once more a male-dominated domain, run by men for their own benefit, certainly not for the benefit of fellow-traveling women:

Rose, harsh rose,
marred and with stint of petals,
meagre flower, thin,
sparse of leaf,

more precious
than a wet rose
single on a stem—
you are caught in the drift.

Stunted, with small leaf,
you are flung on the sand,

you are lifted
in the crisp sand
that drives in the wind.

Can the spice-rose
drip such acrid fragrance
hardened in a leaf?[51]

If "Sea Rose" 's speaker exhibits a good deal of tenderness toward her ocean-battered floral surrogate, that tenderness is only justified by the flower's tight-lipped courage in enduring, "flung on the sand," beaten by "crisp sand" and driven "in the wind," all without complaint. This, the poem seems to say, is the way things are. Malnourished, isolated, battered, acrid-smelling, and hard—this is the way I am, and must be, to be a poet, that incomparable "fragrance / hardened in a leaf." No (sissy?) spice-roses need apply. Women poets had come a long way from the lush, superabundant pleasure in female sexuality and female creativity—summed up in the figure of the daedal seamstress—that Spofford celebrated in "Pomegranate-Flowers." Whether this long way led to a superior destination I cannot say. Like the difference between free verse and bound forms and that between the sentimental and the ironic, the difference between Spofford's and H.D.'s poems may reflect an exchange of possibilities, nothing more.

CODA

After 1910

this way of grief
is shared, unnecessary
and political
— ADRIENNE RICH, "Translations," 1972[1]

In an 1884 editorial, "Girl Graduates," in *Harper's Bazar*, Mary L. Booth confidently predicted that women students, currently housed in the "Harvard Annex," would soon be found within the ivy-clad walls of the college itself.[2] In her typically caustic manner, Booth could not resist observing that the name of the present institutional solution to the woman problem was "as barbarous as the bestowal of the privilege [was] ungracious." Harvard's esteemed president, Charles William Eliot, undoubtedly a man of sterling quality in most respects, was a well-known foe of women's higher education; and Harvard's medical school was home base for one of its most virulent opponents, Dr. Edward Clarke, author of the notorious *Sex in Education* (1874). Nevertheless, the Annex, "barbarously" named or not, was, Booth announced, "the thin edge of the wedge which will irresistibly lead to the full admission of women to all the rights and benefits of a collegiate course."[3]

A woman not given to fruitless hoping for pie in the sky, Booth had every reason to be optimistic. By the mid-1880s, nineteenth-century women, both white and of color had racked up an astonishing number of "firsts."[4] The first women enrolled in a college (Oberlin) in 1837. By 1850, the first two medical schools for women, one in Boston, the other in Philadelphia; had opened their doors; and by 1855, so did the first women's college, Mary Sharp College, in Winchester, Tennessee. In 1853, Antoinette Brown became the first woman minister ordained by a mainstream congregation. In 1864, the first black woman, Rebecca Lee, completed a medical degree. In 1866, Lucy Hobbs became the first U.S. woman graduate from a dental school. In 1869, a U.S. law school (St. Louis Law School) admitted women for the first time. In 1872, the first African American woman (Charlotte E. Ray, sister of Henrietta Cordelia Ray), received her law degree. In 1873, the first African American woman (Susan McKinney) was formally certified as a physician. In 1877, the first U.S. woman (Helen Magill) earned her Ph.D. In 1881, Spelman College, the first black women's college, was opened. In 1886, Susan La

Flesche, a graduate of Hampton Institute, became the first Native American woman to go to medical school.

Not just for Booth but for any woman working to improve women's lot, the years between 1850 and 1890 must have been heady indeed as these barriers came down "one after one." Well before Meyer's *Woman's Work in America* (1892) and Mossell's *The Work of the Afro-American Woman* (1894), Booth celebrated women's advances in her editorials. Heretofore, she wrote in "Women and the Centennials" (1875), there were only three ways "in which a woman could earn a respectable living—as teacher, as seamstress, as servant." Now, the picture had dramatically changed.

> [Women] have the care of parishes and minister to minds diseased. . . . Women now are at the head of hospitals, carry on large practices, and are not scorned as consulting physicians by the most eminent; women edit successful newspapers; women are heard before the bar, are respected on the Change, are architects, are sculptors, are painters, are printers, are multitudinous as authors—in short, are vindicating their equal right with men to work, to live, to think, as complementary halves of the same creation.[5]

In light of these accomplishments a mere quarter-century after Seneca Falls, one can forgive Mary Booth, therefore, the wildness of her optimism where Harvard was concerned, especially since, ultimately, she was right. Pushed to the wall by feminist protest beginning in the late 1960s, Harvard University—along with Princeton, Columbia, and Yale—finally yielded, extending to women students "all the rights and benefits of [the] collegiate course" their brothers enjoyed. But in the one-hundred-year interim, Harvard's women remained, perforce, in the "Annex," re-named Radcliffe in 1894. There they were encouraged to study to their hearts' content, knowing that, whatever else their education did for them, it would make them better wives for Harvard men—or at least, so, I have it on good authority, they were told.[6]

Two of my teachers, both part-timers, as I recall—Barbara Seward in English and Susan Taubes in religion—committed suicide while I was getting my B.S. at Columbia University's School of General Studies in the tag end of the 1950s. Relatively speaking, Columbia was one of the better Ivies for women, whether as students or teachers. However, what women discovered on the long, uneven road to the late 1960s was that having an education without the freedom to use it did you little good. Indeed, as a chagrined Frederick Douglass learned, being educated could make you feel worse off than you were before. I do not know why Seward and Taubes committed suicide—but I do know that suicide was a remarkably attractive option to many educated women in the fifties. It was, if nothing else, one sure way to solve the problem that being educated and being a woman had become. To this day, I find Sylvia Plath's *Bell Jar* a compelling read.

Sometime around 1910—according to T. S. Eliot, the year when modern poetry was born—a complex concatenation of forces came together to bring the forward momentum of the nineteenth-century women's rights movement to a halt. Women got the vote in 1919, but otherwise, the years between 1910 and 1960 brought less progress than loss. For some they were a *saison en l'Enfer*, with the nadir for educated women coming in the 1950s, when professional women's numbers and prospects dipped well below those that turn-of-the-century women had enjoyed. Where poetry was concerned, the retrenchment went well beyond the erasure of eighteenth- and nineteenth-century women poets. With Brooks and Warren's *Understanding Poetry* in hand—possibly the single most influential text in U.S. literary history—male academics and reviewers, using "New Critical" standards, finished what the early modernists began.

The fruits of this labor are on view in two highly prestigious studies: Roy Harvey Pearce's *The Continuity of American Poetry* (1961, reprinted in 1987), a 434-page book that mentions fifteen women poets but discusses only three (Bradstreet, Dickinson and Moore); and David Perkins's *A History of Modern Poetry* (1976), a 602-page tome wherein, counting wives, queens, bookstore managers, mothers, and fiction writers, sixty women's names appear but, again, only three poets are discussed (H.D., Lowell, and Moore). Comments on Guiney by Perkins, John P. Marquand Professor of English and American Literature at Harvard University, help explain why he, like Pearce, could only find three women poets worth serious consideration or, indeed, any consideration at all. "Louise Imogen Guiney," Perkins declares, "was a gallant lady, who had, along with diffuseness, vagueness, and clichés, a sense of rhythm . . . and a loving heart."[7]

The "loving heart" was what got women in the end, disqualifying them as poets and scholars both, or, at least, so John Crowe Ransom opined in "The Poet as Woman," his 1937 review of Elizabeth Atkins's *Edna St. Vincent Millay and Her Times* in the *Southern Review*:

> A woman lives for love, if we will but project that term to cover all her tender fixations upon natural objects of sense. . . . Less pliant, safer, as a biological organism [than man], she remains fixed in her famous attitudes, and is indifferent to intellectuality. I mean, of course, comparatively indifferent; more so than a man. Miss Millay is rarely and barely very intellectual, and I think everybody knows it.
>
> I will try to express this by a more literary locution. The age may perhaps be defined with respect to its characteristic plunge into poetry. It is the age which has recovered the admirable John Donne; this is the way to identify its literary taste. Therefore it is hardly the age of which it may be said that Miss Millay is the voice. Donne is the poet of intellectualized persons; he always was.[8]

Were Ms. Millay truly the representative "voice of the age," these would be perilous times indeed for intellect and "literary taste." Fortunately, however, she was not, at least, she was not representative of those who mattered—the writers and readers of the *Southern Review*, for instance. At the *Review*, "intellectualized persons" like Ransom continued to defend high art and civilization—embodied in the writings of the "admirable" John Donne, seventeenth-century Anglican divine, monarchist, and so-called "metaphysical" poet—against women.

Where academe was concerned, Ransom and his cohorts were successful, possibly beyond their wildest expectations. Even those women poets fortunate enough to receive early modernism's imprimatur—H.D., Amy Lowell, Mina Loy, et al.—were subject to erasure, most disappearing as if they had never been. When Adrienne Rich attended Radcliffe in the late 1940s all, or virtually all, of her instructors were male, and all, or virtually all, of the poets she studied were also: "Frost, Dylan Thomas, Donne, Auden, Mac-Niece, Stevens, Yeats." Poetry, Rich wrote in her highly influential rethinking of her undergraduate education, "When We Dead Awaken: Writing as Revision" (1971), was supposed to be "'universal,' which meant, of course, non-female."[9] Under the banner of the "universal," as both Kate Millet's *Sexual Politics* (1970) and Judith Fetterly's *The Resisting Reader* (1977) argued, women were taught to read and write against themselves, learning to admire the virtues of authors, from Milton to Mailer, whose contempt for the opposite sex could hardly be blamed, given what "everybody" knew women's "tender fixations" and "famous attitudes" were like. Disqualified as teachers, as critics, as scholars, as readers, and as writers, by their "need to be loved"—as one psychoanalyst put it in a 1962 book on adolescence still in use today—women had reached a dead end.[10] Their very lack of a recorded history proved that they had done nothing worth recording. Fed a steady diet of male writing, those women who did manage to become literary workers did so by publicly disavowing their connections with (and taste for) other women's writing. It was a catch-22, and one hardly knows where to begin in totting up the losses. Shall I then end my story of nineteenth-century women's struggle for emancipation here in this graveyard of broken dreams?

Open Endings

In *Repression and Recovery*, Cary Nelson, a guiding spirit for this entire study, comments that "No single story can be told about modern poetry and its varied audiences that is even marginally adequate."[11] In *Is Literary History Possible?* David Perkins—of all people—extends this perspective into a critique of the project of literary history itself.[12] Any attempt to narrativize literary history—be it in terms of style, period, genre, or the role of single

(major) authors—is always already incomplete, because the generic require-
ments of narrative demand a unity that the evidence itself can never support.
Rather more, I suspect, than Perkins, who clearly is unhappy with his own
conclusion, I accept this fact. And in its spirit, I want to give my narrative
one last turn of the screw, looking, however briefly, at three writers who
carried the nineteenth-century tradition of poetry as social/political discourse into the twentieth century in ways that gave it fresh new life. That is, I
want to reverse the forward thrust of my previous chapter, looking not at
how modernism in women's writing emerged from a rejection of earlier
poetic practices—a fact by now well established—but rather at how vital
aspects of nineteenth-century poetics managed, even at the height of the
modernist period, to survive.

None of the three poets to whom I now turn—Frances Densmore (1867–
1957), Alice Ruth Moore Dunbar-Nelson (1875–1935), and Dora Read
Goodale (1866–1953)—was, strictly speaking, a professional poet, certainly
not as John Crowe Ransom would define the phrase. Densmore was an eth-
nomusicologist, who spent her life recording Native American poetry and
music, much of which would have been lost without her work. Best known
as the wife of the black poet Paul Dunbar, Alice Dunbar-Nelson was an
educator, public lecturer, club woman, fiction writer, political activist, and,
on occasion, a poet. Dora Read Goodale, the younger sister of the much
better-known Elaine Goodale Eastman, spent the final decades of her life as a
teacher and health care worker in the Appalachian highlands of Tennessee.
There, at the end of a very long, but intermittent and relatively undistinguished, literary career, she flourished as a poet.

Personal interest and the model of Alice Cunningham Fletcher led Frances
Densmore, a young musicologist from Red Wing, Minnesota, to her life-
work. Using portable cylinder equipment, Densmore spent forty years travel-
ing over rugged terrain, under primitive conditions, recording thousands of
songs given to her by individual Indian singers, from the Chippewa in Minnesota to the pueblo peoples of the American Southwest. Densmore was not
the only Euro-American to engage in this activity, which had been pioneered
by early-nineteenth-century ethnographers like John Heckewelder and Henry
Rowe Schoolcraft. She was, however, one of the few who treated Native
American song as an independent art form, with its own cultural roots, and
as one in which instrumentality was an integral and legitimate part of its
aesthetic. That is, she accepted Native song on its own terms, rather than
trying to Europeanize it to make it fit with Western (Kantian/Arnoldian)
theorizations of an autonomous aesthetic.

Along with a musical analysis of each song she recorded, Densmore provided whatever information she could on the singer's background, the song's
origins, the occasion or reason for its creation, and any rituals it might have
accompanied. Her preservation record was a monumental achievement for a

number of reasons, not least that it avoids both the nineteenth century's blatantly ethnocentric use of Native materials and the exploitive aestheticizing of the so-called "primitive" in which early modernists indulged. Because of this, Densmore's work constituted a major intervention into the imaginative representation of Native American poetries, cultures, and subjectivities in both white and Native American literary texts—an intervention whose effects are still felt today. Quite simply, she provided a literary model for the representation of Native cultures that respected the integrity of individual difference.

From this book's perspective, the most important transcriptions Densmore made are those of the medicine songs of Juana Manwell, or "Owl Woman," an elderly Papago medicine woman to whose work I have already referred several times. To my knowledge, Manwell's songs are the only extant representations of the thoughts and practices of a traditional Native American woman shaman, a tribal function generally fulfilled by men.[13] These songs are also among the relatively few examples of nineteenth-century Indian women's poetry that have come down to us largely unmediated by Western poetic conventions. They represent, therefore, a very different kind of "Indian" poetry than that of E. Pauline Johnson and Zitkala-Sa, both of whom were not only writing for white audiences but using white poetic conventions to do so. Presenting Manwell's songs in terms of their performance context, Densmore preserves Manwell's alterity and the alterity of her way of life. These transcriptions provide as a result invaluable insight into the issue of authorship in traditional shaman culture. As Manwell explains it to Densmore, all her songs were given to her in dreams, by people who had died. Because the songs come from the spirit world, they act as conduits for the transmission of spiritual power. As such, they form the basis of Manwell's healing practices; but, in a very real sense, the songs themselves are not hers, nor does she in any way seem to think of herself as their author, although she does claim that they "belong" to her.

Manwell's disavowal of authorship tallies with what Mary Austin calls the "communal" perspective in Native American cultures generally. "The development of pronominal words," Austin writes in the Introduction to *The American Rhythm*, "points to some sort of group-identity antedating the personal. Even yet there are tribes that have no word for 'I' as distinguished from 'ourselves.' Also among tribal groups we find communal song more highly developed than any form of personal expression."[14] Although an individual singer, Manwell replicates this communality by giving authorship back to those from whom the songs came. Far from being personally expressive, the songs are a quasi-historical record of the life of her tribe. "Brown Owls," for example, was given to Manwell by a man who was killed near Tucson, Arizona: "Brown owls come here in the blue evening, / They are hooting about, / They are shaking their wings and hooting." According to Manwell, the man who gave her this song was also the one to tell her that she should become a medicine woman and she always began her healing sessions with it. Another song, "Sadly I was treated," was given to her by a man named Ciko, who had been killed in a bar fight. His body was carried about in a buggy and finally laid on some railroad tracks to make it look as if he had died in a train accident (*NAWP* 359 and 360).

Coinciding with the rise of early modernism, Densmore's publications undoubtedly contributed to the exploitation of Native American song by Euro-American authors in search of the exotic. However, these transcriptions also allowed theoreticians of American poetry like Austin to expand the European base of American literature to include the actual cultural production of indigenous peoples, not just works by writers, whether white or Indian, attempting to reimagine what Native cultures were like. As a result, the bridge between the various Indian cultures and the Euro-American mainstream that nineteenth-century poets, from Sigourney to Zitkala-sa, had hoped to build was finally constructed from materials that Native Americans themselves could use and are using to this day, as even cursory, examination of recent Indian poetry will show.

Alice Dunbar-Nelson and Dora Read Goodale fit the conventional paradigm of the poet in Western society better than either Manwell or Densmore; but each of these writers, in her own way, was also committed to the principle of communality and to an instrumental view of art, engaging in it as part of an ongoing cultural or political dialogue. Like so many of the end-of-the-century poets I have discussed, Dunbar-Nelson can be viewed as a writer of the late nineteenth or of the early twentieth century. Born July 19, 1875, in New Orleans, she came of age as a writer too early to be squarely part of the Harlem Renaissance but too late (she died in 1935) to be classified as a nineteenth-century writer, especially given the influence modernism eventually exerted over her work. The liminal position of her poetics reflects something of the liminality of her own position, as a member of the first generation of black "New Women," women for whom issues of modernity—equality, professionalism, agency within the culture—could claim equal attention with those of race and civil rights.

The daughter of a former slave, Patricia Wright, a mixed-blood seamstress, and Joseph Moore, a Creole seaman, Dunbar-Nelson received an unusually solid education for a woman of her day. After getting a teacher-training degree from Straight University in New Orleans, she earned a master's degree in English Literature at Cornell and took courses in psychology and educational testing at the University of Pennsylvania and at Columbia University. The breadth of her educational experience mirrors the breadth of her accomplishments as teacher, writer, public speaker, and activist. Light-skinned and auburn-haired, Dunbar-Nelson used her ability to "pass" to take advantage of cultural opportunities that would otherwise have been denied her.

However, unlike those who built their identity on passing, Dunbar-Nelson never severed her ties to the black community either socially or in her writing, much of which appeared in black publications such as the A.M.E. *Church Review* and the *Crisis*, a highly politicized periodical which identified its audience as "the darker races" on its masthead.

From comments Dunbar-Nelson made after Paul Dunbar's death, her initial allegiance in poetry was to the genteel tradition.[15] As summarized by Ora Williams in the *Dictionary of Literary Biography*, Dunbar-Nelson believed that the poet "should be a keen observer, have a sense of humor, be close to nature and dramatize the 'delicate perception of the power of suggestion' with the right meter."[16] As Dunbar-Nelson's heated arguments with Paul Dunbar over his use of dialect suggest, she was particularly uncomfortable with black writers who exploited racialized stereotypes, accounting, perhaps, for why scholars have tended to take her commitment to the genteel at face value. Her oft-anthologized "Violets," with its turn away from contemporary life, exemplifies Dunbar-Nelson's contribution to the genteel. In this poem the speaker turns from "garish lights, and mincing little fops / And cabarets and songs, and deadening wine," toward "sweet real things," "[t]he perfect loveliness that God has made" (*NAWP* 374).

But Dunbar-Nelson wrote another kind of poetry wherein she positioned herself quite differently. If writing love poetry brought out the genteel in Dunbar-Nelson, with all of literary sentimentalism's attendant narcissism, writing political poetry resituated her in the here and now. When Dunbar-Nelson looked at white images of blacks, what she found was, as she put it, "A black savage dropped bodily into a white culture, a senseless prostitute: Negro primitivism, atavism, reversal to types, to an African . . . a hideously ugly ever-grinned [*sic*] harlot."[17] However, a great deal of room exists between these degrading stereotypes and the equally stereotyped image of the "genteel" black woman poet who only wants "sweet real things." This is the space that Dunbar-Nelson's political poetry occupies, in particular poems such as "The Proletariat Speaks" (*Crisis*, 1929) and "Harlem John Henry Views the Airmada" (*Crisis*, 1932) and "April is on the Way" (*Ebony and Topaz*, 1927), a biting poem on lynching:

April is on the way!
I sped through the town this morning. The florist shops have put yellow
    flowers in the windows,
Daffodils and tulips and primroses, pale yellow flowers
Like the tips of her fingers when she waved me that frightened farewell.
And the women in the market have stuck pussy willows in the long necked
    bottles on their stands.
(Willow trees are kind, dear God. They will not bear a body on their
    limbs.)[18]

In this poem, the lynched bodies of black men become an ironizing commentary on the genteel flower imagery of "Violets." The lines that literally spill over with their sweet burden—"yellow flowers in the windows, / Daffodils and tulips and primroses, pale yellow flowers / Like the tips of her fingers"—provide and then deny the comfort they seem at first to offer. They can distract for a moment, but then the memory of lynchings reasserts itself, and April, that most hopeful of months, becomes an anticipation of horrors also "on the way." Purporting to represent the thoughts of a black man in flight from those set to lynch him, "April is on the Way" can also be read as Dunbar-Nelson's protest against the way in which racism perverts even the most naturally positive of human responses—to beauty, to spring, to love, to the effulgent hope we associate with seasonal rebirth.

In "The Proletariat Speaks," Dunbar-Nelson again writes from the position of a speaker whose subjectivity is split between an idealizing love of beauty, on the one hand, and her knowledge of the mockery that various forms of social inequality make of this love, on the other. This poem's speaker is a young woman whose love of "beautiful things"—"Carven tables laid with lily-hued linen / And fragile china and sparkling iridescent glass"— only makes her own environment more repellent to her: "In the food-laden air of a greasy kitchen, / At an oil-clothed table: / Plate piled high with food that turns my head away / . . . / Or in a smoky cafeteria, balancing a slippery tray / To a table crowded with elbows / Which lately the bus boy wiped with a grimy rag" (*NAWP* 376). For the alienated young woman in this poem, beauty does not lead to a sense of spiritual unity or attachment to the "Whole"; the yearning for beauty only intensifies pain.

In "Harlem John Henry"—to my mind, Dunbar-Nelson's most important poem, but one too long and complex to do justice to here—she rewrites the genteel completely, giving her voice over to John Henry, the heroic male figure of black folklore. Published in 1932, "Harlem John Henry" mingles identifiably modernist concerns over mechanized warfare with remembrances of black contributions to U.S. culture and snatches of spirituals and folksongs. In the latter, Dunbar-Nelson, apparently making peace with the long-dead Paul, uses dialect to capture the black past ("Go down, Moses, way down in Egypt's land, / Tell ol' Pharaoh, let my people go!" and "Sometimes I feel like an eagle in de air, / Some-a dese mornin's bright an' fair" [*NAWP* 378 and 379]). Insofar as "Harlem John Henry" mixes modernist elements with a commitment to community and to poetry as public/political discourse, like so much of the material Cary Nelson discusses in *Repression and Recovery*, it suggests that definitions of modernism that leave political poetry out represent in themselves political readings of the past, readings that push their own high-culture agendas.

Although different in kind, the poems in Dora Read Goodale's final, volume *Mountain Dooryards* (1941; revised and enlarged for the 1946 edition) also suggest that our notions of the parameters of modernism need rethinking. Sister of Elaine Goodale Eastman, wife of Charles Eastman (Santee Sioux), a noted Indian memoirist, Dora Read Goodale was born in 1866 on Sky Farm, the Goodale family homestead in the Berkshires, Massachusetts. Like her sister, Dora was educated at home and began writing poetry at a very young age. After her first collaboration with Elaine in *Apple-Blossoms* (1879), Dora continued to publish volumes of poetry on an intermittent basis, the poems themselves well-written, but largely conventional in form and theme. Only when she took a position as a health care worker at Uplands Hospital in Pleasant Hill, Tennessee, in the 1930s did her talent, her desire to write, and her politics finally come together.

Written entirely in free verse and in the mountain dialect of the Appalachian highlands, Goodale's last poems are a moving testimony to the linguistic wealth and personal dignity of the rural poor. They are also a powerful testimony to the flexibility and genius of a woman who late in life made the transition to a twentieth-century poetic while still retaining the best of high sentimentality's commitment to those who, having suffered "might's injustice," survived, their spirits intact. Because of dialect poetry's inherent drive toward objectifying those whose voices it claims to reproduce, this kind of poetry, which was in great demand during the fin de siècle, exhibits a persistent and deeply troubling tendency to devolve into caricature, or as Goodale puts it, "burlesque." As with Paul Dunbar and Charles Chesnut, this can be true even when the writers are themselves members of the ethnic or racial community whose dialect they claim to reproduce, which was precisely what disturbed Alice Dunbar-Nelson so in her husband's work.

In Goodale's brief introductory comments to *Mountain Dooryards*, she makes clear that she was aware of this problem and sought to adjust for it, refusing, as she says, to reproduce "inflections *literatim*."[19] Her poems are not mimicry but re-creations of the language and people whose speech and ways of thought she sought to preserve. Like Densmore's notes on Manwell's songs and the brief dialect passages in Dunbar-Nelson's "Harlem John Henry," Goodale's use of dialect in *Mountain Dooryards* is a reminder of difference that at the same time avoids objectifying or stereotyping the speakers themselves. That is, it captures and respects difference even while situating it within the broader spectrum of shared humanity in which all have equal part. The result is poems that can, in their very simplicity and directness, be deeply moving. "Portraits" is one example. Its theme is one that we have encountered many times in this book—a mother's death—yet rarely done with such an exquisite balance of feeling and control, a control that does not undermine itself with irony at the same time:

—That's her likeness, yes,
But I never knowed her. My daddy, he went first,
And she died a-birthing me.

My oldest brother,
I reckon he favored her. 'Twas him as raised us
And never quit
Till he'd saw the last one married.
He was more like a daddy than a brother.
He alays had a kind look out of his eyes,
My brother had. . . .

That other likeness—that's my husband's mother.
I wasn't long married when she come to live with us
And we never had what you'd call a disagreeance—
Not really.
She holp me out a-many a time
Best way she could.
She was a good woman.
But *her*, my mother. . . . Well, it's like I said;
She died a-birthing me.

Although some readers may view this poem as sentimental, I cannot. It is written with too careful and caring a respect, reflecting even in its repetitions, and hesitations, the voice of the woman to whom it is attributed—a woman who is not in any way like Goodale herself. There is sympathy in this poem, but also acknowledgment of difference. There is communality without merging, appropriation, or sham identification. There is love without fusion or exploitation, as the speaker calls each dead family member back into life, even the mother whom she never knew, who died giving her birth.

Dora Goodale was no major poet. Strictly speaking, I am not sure she qualifies even as a minor poet. But like Densmore, Manwell, and Dunbar-Nelson, she understood poetry's power to create, even if only for the brief moment of the individual poem's existence, the illusion of an individual voice speaking across the barriers of time, space, and social/cultural difference. Centuries later the voices of these women remain with us, both those who internalized and reproduced the dominant ideology of their day and those who, "one after one," dissented from it. I have chosen to focus primarily on the latter, because, however deep their internal contradictions ran and however much they compromised their own best intentions, they are the women who worked collectively to give us birth, passing their songs on, as I pass them on here.

Notes

Notes to Introduction

1. Jerome J. McGann, *The Beauty of Inflections: Literary Investigations in Historical Method and Theory* (Oxford: Clarendon Press, 1985), p. 21.

2. T. S. Eliot, *On Poetry and Poets* (New York: Noonday Press, 1957), p. 106.

3. My definition of the complaint as a protest against injustice comes from Lauren Berlant, "The Female Complaint," *Social Text: Theory / Culture / Ideology* 9 (Fall 1988): 243. The complaint was a recognized lyric genre in the eighteenth century. For instance, see "The Lady's Complaint," *Virginia Gazette*, October 15–22, 1736, p. 3; and Stella, "The Female Complaint," *Philadelphia Minerva*, February 13, 1796, p. 3. The first is an especially clever put-down of the double standard. I should note, however, that Berlant herself does not believe that the female complaint actually rises to the elevated standard she sets for true protest literature in this essay. On the contrary, she treats the *female* complaint the same way that she treats female sentimentality, as a form of bad-faith politics that reinscribes existing gender relationships instead of pushing for rectification of their inequities. I obviously disagree—strongly—and would suggest that both male and female complaint poetry runs the gamut from utterly narcissistic passivity to passionate struggle against injustice, as chapters 1, 2, and 6 will discuss.

4. Barbara Johnson, "Apostrophe, Animation, and Abortion," in *Feminisms: An Anthology of Literary Theory and Criticism*, ed. Robyn R. Warhol and Diane Price Herndl (New Brunswick: Rutgers University Press, 1991), p. 642. In attempting to reconcile a poststructuralist definition of the lyric with the political intentions of abortion poetry, Johnson both elaborates on and to some extent critiques the more conventional approaches of Jonathan Culler and Paul de Man, both of whom, she claims, identify lyric poetry as paradigmatically and unproblematically apostrophic. For a Bakhtinian critique of the apostrophic model, see Michael Macovski, *Dialogue and Literature: Apostrophe, Auditors, and the Collapse of Romantic Discourse* (New York: Oxford University Press, 1994); and the essays collected in *Dialogue and Critical Discourse: Language, Culture, Critical Theory*, ed. Michael Macovski (New York: Oxford University Press, 1997). While Macovski focuses on the role played by multiple speakers *within the poem*, other scholars have begun to explore the role played by *multiple audiences* in lyric production. In an essay on lyric forms, Heather Dubrow advances an argument that, despite its formalist bent, offers a concept of indirect address that is central to my own theorization of the lyric as public and political discourse:

> To be sure, some poems, notably in the sonnet tradition, are indeed internalized meditations, and often their so-called plots are far more amorphous than critics more accustomed to reading narrative and drama like to acknowledge. But many Renaissance lyrics evoke a social situation, whether it be that of

the shepherd communicating with other shepherds or of the elegiac poet addressing the dead person or other mourners. And even the poems that involve internalized reflection often presume as well an audience who is not simply overhearing private thoughts but rather being indirectly addressed. . . . Thus, though this predilection has not received the attention it deserves, Renaissance lyrics frequently address not just a single audience but rather multiple and different audiences.

See Heather Dubrow, "Lyric Forms," in *The Cambridge Companion to English Literature, 1500–1600*, ed. Arthur F. Kinney (Cambridge: Cambridge University Press, 2000), p. 197.

5. McGann, *The Beauty of Inflections*, p. 21. See also Macovski, introduction to *Dialogue and Critical Discourse*, p. 6.

6. James P. Danky and Wayne A. Wiegand, *Print Culture in a Diverse America* (Urbana: University of Illinois Press, 1998), p. 1.

7. Habermas effectively sanctions this approach to poetry when responding to Martin Jay's criticism of his treatment of modernist art in *Habermas and Modernity*:

If aesthetic experience is incorporated into the context of individual life-histories, if it is utilized to illuminate a situation and to throw light on individual life-problems—if it at all communicates its impulses to a collective form of life—then art enters into a language game which is no longer that of aesthetic criticism, but belongs, rather, *to everyday communicative practice*. It then no longer affects only our evaluative language or only renews the interpretation of needs that color our perceptions; rather, it reaches into our cognitive interpretations and normative expectations and transforms the totality in which these moments are related to each other.

Jürgen Habermas, "Questions and Counterquestions," in *Habermas and Modernity*, ed. Richard J. Bernstein [Cambridge: MIT Press, 1994], p. 202; italics mine.

8. See Mary Loeffelholz, "Who Killed Lucretia Davidson? or, Poetry in the Domestic-Tutelary Complex," *Yale Journal of Criticism* 10.2 (1997): 271–93; Elizabeth Petrino, *Emily Dickinson and Her Contemporaries: Women's Verse in America, 1820–1885* (Hanover: University Press of New England, 1998); Adela Pinch, *Strange Fits of Passion: Epistemologies of Emotion, Hume to Austen* (Stanford: Stanford University Press, 1996); Yopie Prins, *The Victorian Sappho* (Princeton: Princeton University Press, 1999); and Cheryl Walker *The Nightingale's Burden: Women Poets and American Culture before 1900* (Bloomington: Indiana University Press, 1982).

9. Habermas, "Questions and Counterquestions," p. 202.

10. To illustrate just how tendentious this poetry was, and how personal at the same time, in one instance three writers exchanged two poems and one very long letter in the *South Carolina Gazette* on the rights and wrongs of interracial sex. See "The Cameleon Lover," *South Carolina Gazette*, March 4–11, 1731/2, p. 3; "Albus" and "To the Author of the *Gazette*," *South Carolina Gazette*, March 11–18, 1731/2, pp. 1–2; "Sable" and "Cameleon's Defence," *South Carolina Gazette*, March 11–18, 1731/2, p. 3.

11. Earlier Andrew Bradford ran a column under the nom de plume "Cato," a name associated with (masculine) political interests. His switch to the folksy "Mr.

Busy-Body" in 1729 may suggest his recognition that there were sales to be made in the domestic quarter.

12. See the following: "Lovia," Letter, *American Weekly Mercury*, January 14–21, 1723/24, p. 1; The Widow R——lt, "A Dream," and "A Lady" (Elizabeth Magawley?), "The Answer," *American Weekly Mercury*, May 27, 1725, p. 2; "Martha Careful" and "Caelia Shortface," Two Letters, *American Weekly Mercury*, January 28, 1728/9, p. 1; Matilda and Anon., Two Letters, *American Weekly Mercury*, May 22, 1729, p. 1; "Florio," Letter in Response, *American Weekly Mercury*, June 5, 1729, p. 1; Anon. Letter, *American Weekly Mercury*, June 26, 1729, p. 1; Anon., "The Journal of a Modern Lady in a Letter to a Person of Quality," *American Weekly Mercury*, August 6, 1730, pp. 1–2; [Andrew Bradford?], Editorial, *American Weekly Mercury*, September 10, 1730, p. 1; "Generosa" [Elizabeth Magawley], Letter to the Editor, *American Weekly Mercury*, December 29–January 5, 1730, p. 1; "Generosus" [Joseph Breintnall], Poetic Reply to Generosa, *American Weekly Mercury*, January 5–12, 1730/31, p. 1; "Ignavus" [Jacob Taylor], Poetic Reply to Generosa, *American Weekly Mercury*, January 12–19, 1730/31, p. 1; "Ignavus," Second Poetic Reply to Generosa, *American Weekly Mercury*, January 19–26, 1730/31, p. 1; "E.M.," "The Wits and Poets of Pennsylvania, a Poem. Part I," *American Weekly Mercury*, April 29–May 6, 1731, p. 1. I am accepting the attributions of David Shields here, and I am particularly indebted to him, as to Sharon Harris, for bringing the Generosa contest to my attention. See *Civil Tongues & Polite Literature in British America* (Chapel Hill: University of North Carolina Press, 1997), pp. 92–104. According to Shields, Magawley's last poem also received at least one unpublished response, a verse satire by Joseph Norris, "On E. Magawley's Pres[um]ing to Write." See Shields, *Civil Tongues*, p. 93.

13. Sharon Harris, "Elizabeth Magawley," in *American Women Writers to 1800*, ed. Sharon M. Harris (New York: Oxford University Press, 1996), p. 137. Harris reprints Magawley's first letter and her poem.

14. Penelope Aspen, Letter to the Editor, *South Carolina Gazette*, June 10, 1731, p. 3.

15. Untitled squib, *South Carolina Gazette*, April 7–14, 1733, p. 3.

16. "On the noted & celebrated Quaker Mrs. Drummond," *American Weekly Mercury*, March 9–16, 1735/6, p. 2.

17. "To the *Visitant*, from a circle of Ladies, on reading his paper, No. 3, in the *Pennsylvania Chronicle*," March 7–14, 1768, p. 2.

18. Habermas's response to feminist critiques can be found in "Further Reflections on the Public Sphere," in *Habermas and the Public Sphere*, ed. Craig Calhoun (Cambridge: MIT Press, 1992), pp. 421–61; see in particular pp. 422–30. For the feminist position, see Carole Pateman, "The Fraternal Social Contract," in *Civil Society and the State: New European Perspectives*, ed. John Keane (London: Verso, 1988), pp. 101–27; and Nancy Fraser, "Rethinking the Public Sphere: A Contribution to the Critique of Actually Existing Democracy," in *Habermas and the Public Sphere*, ed. Calhoun, pp. 109–42; and her chapter on Habermas's theory of communicative action, "What's Critical about Critical Theory? The Case of Habermas and Gender," in *Unruly Practices: Power, Discourse and Gender in Contemporary Social Theory* (Minneapolis: University of Minnesota Press, 1989), pp. 113–43. Habermas first presented his thinking on these two issues in *The Structural Transformation of the Public Sphere: An Inquiry into a Category of Bourgeois Society* (1962) and *The Theory of Communicative Action* (1981). Although I, like many others, find Habermas's definitions of such key terms

as "reason" and "public" vague and his approach excessively idealistic, this is not the place, nor am I the person, to pursue such criticism. Those interested in these issues may find essays in the following texts helpful: *Habermas and Modernity*, ed. Bernstein; *Habermas and the Public Sphere*, ed. Calhoun; and Bruce Robbins, ed., *The Phantom Public Sphere* (Minneapolis: University of Minnesota, 1993). Also see Joan Landes, *Women and the Public Sphere in the Age of the French Revolution* (Ithaca: Cornell University Press, 1988); and Mary P. Ryan, *Women in Public: Between Banners and Ballots, 1825–1880* (Baltimore: Johns Hopkins University Press, 1990).

19. This exchange is reprinted in *The Heath Anthology of American Literature*, ed. Paul Lauter et al., 3d ed., 1:905–6 (Boston: Houghton, Mifflin, 1998).

20. Habermas, "Further Reflections," in *Habermas and the Public Sphere*, ed. Calhoun, p. 429.

21. Fraser, "Rethinking the Public Sphere," in *Habermas and the Public Sphere*, ed. Calhoun, p. 139 n. 14.

22. See Mukhtar Ali Isani, "'Gambia on My Soul': Africa and the African in the Writings of Phillis Wheatley," *MELUS* 6 (Spring 1979): 67–68. According to Isani, this letter, which was Wheatley's strongest antislavery statement, was also her most often reprinted piece in her lifetime.

23. See Landes, *Women and the Public Sphere*, pp. 2–3, for a full discussion of "public"'s various meanings in relation to gender. Used for women, the word signified a prostitute, as the phrase "street woman," with its connotation of publicity, also does. The identification of agency with female modernity can be found ubiquitously in post-1848 women's poetry. See, for example, "Woman's Modern Aspirations," published anonymously in 1874: "I tell thee what we want, a clearer space. / More breathing room, some stirring work to do! / "To climb life's hill"—how well you state the case! / Those climb the hill who would enjoy the view. / If true strength lies in a calm nothingness, / Then idiots are all mighty men, I guess." "Woman's Modern Aspirations," *Woodhull & Claflin Weekly*, March 14, 1874, p. 4.

24. To cite a few examples, Sarah Piatt, whose range and complexity make her the closest thing this study has to a "central" or "major" figure, published and republished poems under different titles, signed her poems in different ways, and sometimes published them without attribution. Variant versions of her poems also appear simultaneously in different venues. Although Piatt, or more likely her husband, J. J. Piatt, was largely responsible for the chaotic state of her oeuvre, other poets might find this chaos introduced into their work by newspaper and periodical editors who felt free to lift poems at will. Thus, Richard Stoddard's "On the Town," a sympathetic poem on a prostitute (a popular thematic genre in the century), was published twice in the *Woodhull & Claflin Weekly*, first anonymously, the next time—three years later—under the name H. H. Stoddard.

25. In my original attempt to distinguish different strains of sentimentality in the nineteenth century, I missed the importance of what I am now calling "literary sentimentality" altogether. See Bennett, "'The Descent of the Angel': Interrogating Domestic Ideology in American Women's Poetry, 1858–1890," *American Literary History* 7 (Winter 1995): 592, 594, and 606 n. 2. I now see at least three forms of sentimentality: "high," as in "high-minded," the sentimentality associated with social reform, "literary," as in drawn from a particular set of Continental literary texts; and "popu-

lar," as in part of either mass or popular culture. At least in my own mind, these epithets are not evaluative. I would add, however, that the distinctions they mark are theoretical; in practice, these strains were often blended, since many writers—e.g., Sigourney, Stowe, Piatt, et al.—worked all three veins. For a trenchant critique of my nomenclature, see Karen Kilcup, *Frost and Feminine Literary Tradition* (Ann Arbor: University of Michigan Press, 1998), p. 259 n. 17.

Notes to Chapter 1

1. Mary Wollstonecraft, *A Vindication of the Rights of Woman* (Harmondsworth, England: Penguin, 1975), pp. 81–82.

2. *FPA 232.*

3. Review of *Recent Poems,* by Edmund Clarence Stedman, *Harper's New Monthly Magazine* 56 (March 1878): 628.

4. Reynolds, Introduction I to *Victorian Women Poets: An Anthology,* ed. Angela Leighton and Margaret Reynolds (Oxford: Blackwell Publishers, 1995), p. xxv.

5. Ibid., p. xxvi.

6. Gwen Davis and Beverly A. Joyce, comps., *Poetry by Women to 1900: A Bibliography of American and British Women Writers* (Toronto: University of Toronto Press, 1991), p. ix.

7. Davis and Joyce, introduction to *Poetry by Women to 1900,* p. x.

8. Ibid., p. xiv.

9. Contemporary memoirs provide a rich source of information on this score. See, for example, Julia Ward Howe, *Sketches of Representative Women of New England* (1904); Lilian Whiting, *Louise Chandler Moulton, Poet and Friend* (1910); Elizabeth Oakes-Smith, *The Autobiography of Elizabeth Oakes Smith,* ed. Mary Alice Wyman (1924); Harriet Prescott Spofford, *Our Famous Women: an Authorized Record of the Lives and Deeds of Distinguished American Women of Our Times* (1884); and *A Little Book of Friends* (1916).

10. The homogeneity of genteel poetry was a butt for jokes in the period. "Mosaic Poetry," for example, consists of thirty-two lines, pieced together from the works of twenty-two poets, from Wordsworth and Coleridge to Frances Osgood, Bayard Taylor, and Alice Cary. E.g.:

> 'Tis twelve at night by the castle clock
> —Coleridge.
> Beloved, we must part!"
> —Alice Cary.
> "Come back! come back?" he cried in grief,
> —Campbell.
> "My eyes are dim with tears,
> —Bayard Taylor.
>
> "Mosaic Poetry," *Cincinnati Israelite*
> 18 (March 15, 1872): 4

11. Unhappily, Walker, basing her attributions on Joan R. Sherman's edition of the Schomburg Library of Nineteenth-Century Black Women Writers misidentifies two

poets as black: Menken and Mary Tucker Lambert. See John Cofran, "The Identity of Adah Isaacs Menken: A Theatrical Mystery Solved," *Theatre Survey* 31 (May 1990): 47–54; and Jean Fagan Yellin and Cynthia D. Bond, introduction to *The Pen Is Ours: A Listing of Writings by and about African-American Women before 1910* (New York: Oxford University Press, 1991), p. 8.

12. The following texts have lodged significant challenges to the homogeneity hypothesis: Melba Joyce Boyd, *Discarded Legacy: Politics and Poetics in the Life of Frances E. W. Harper, 1825–1911* (Detroit: Wayne State University Press, 1990); Laura Christine Wendorff, "Race, Ethnicity, and the Voices of the 'Poetess,' in the Lives and Works of Four Late-Nineteenth-Century American Women Poets: Frances E. W. Harper, Emma Lazarus, Louise Guiney, and Ella Wheeler Wilcox" (Ph.D. dissertation, University of Michigan, 1992); Joanne Dobson, "Sex, Wit, and Sentiment: Frances Osgood and the Poetry of Love," *American Literature* 65 (December 1993): 631–50; Elizabeth Fox-Genovese, *Within the Plantation Household: Black and White Women of the Old South* (Chapel Hill: University of North Carolina Press, 1988), pp. 281–89 and passim (on Louisa McCord); Cheryl Walker, "Rose Terry Cooke, 1827–1892," *Legacy: A Journal of American Women Writers* 9 (Fall 1992): 143–50; "In Bluebeard's Closet: Women Who Write with the Wolves," *LIT* 7 (1996): 13–25; and "Nineteenth-Century American Women Poets Revisited," in *Nineteenth-Century American Women Writers: A Critical Reader*, ed. Karen Kilcup (Oxford: Blackwell Publishers, 1998), pp. 231–44; and Gary Williams, *Hungry Heart: The Literary Emergence of Julia Ward Howe* (Amherst: University of Massachusetts Press, 1999).

13. Herman Melville, *Pierre; or, The Ambiguities* (Evanston: Northwestern University Press, 1971), p. 245.

14. Johann Wolfgang von Goethe, *The Sorrows of Young Werther, Elective Affinities*, trans. Victor Lange and Judith Ryan (New York: Suhrkamp, n.d.), p. 14.

15. Erich Auerbach, *Mimesis: The Representation of Reality in Western Literature*, trans. Willard Trask (New York: Doubleday, 1957), p. 352.

16. Ann Douglas, *The Feminization of American Culture* (New York: Doubleday, 1977), p. 256.

17. David E. Wellbery, "Afterword," in Goethe, *Werther*, p. 283.

18. The absurdity of this scene was not lost on nineteenth-century wits. Both the *Southern Literary Messenger* and the *Springfield Republican* reprint Thackeray's satirical "Sorrows of Werther" in 1853. Sarah Piatt may be responding to Thackeray as well as Goethe in her 1872 "The Sorrows of Charlotte," suggesting that the mawkishness of Goethe's novel was so well known that parodies of it could still entertain readers one hundred years later.

19. Yopie Prins, *The Victorian Sappho* (Princeton: Princeton University Press, 1999), pp. 19–20.

20. Goethe, *Werther*, p. 15.

21. For example: "I sit in my grief: I wait for morning in my tears! Rear the tomb, ye friends of the dead. Close it not till Colma comes. My life flies away like a dream. Why should I stay behind?" and so on. After five pages of this kind of thing, Charlotte and Werther let loose a "torrent of tears" (*Werther*, pp. 77 and 80).

22. Judith Fetterly, *The Resisting Reader: A Feminist Approach to American Fiction* (Bloomington: Indiana University Press, 1977), p. xx.

23. Wollstonecraft, *A Vindication of the Rights of Woman*, p. 156 n. 8.

24. *The Poems of Charlotte Smith*, ed. Stuart Curran (New York: Oxford University Press, 1993), p. 27.

25. For a discussion of Robinson's revision of Ovid's revision of Sappho's fictive life, see Jerome McGann, *The Poetics of Sensibility: A Revolution in Literary Style* (Oxford: Clarendon Press, 1996), pp. 94–116; and Prins, *Victorian Sappho*, pp. 180–84.

26. See Prins, *The Victorian Sappho*, pp. 65–67.

27. See Adela Pinch, *Strange Fits of Passion: Epistemologies of Emotion, Hume to Austen* (Stanford: Stanford University Press, 1996), pp. 1–16, 51–71, and 164–92. I am indebted to Pinch for drawing my attention to Charlotte Smith. Also see Julie Ellison, *Cato's Tears and the Making of Anglo-American Emotion* (Chicago: University of Chicago Press, 1999), pp. 1–22.

28. Beginning with Santayana's essay on the genteel tradition (reprinted in *The Genteel Tradition: Nine Essays*, ed. Douglas L. Wilson [Cambridge: Harvard University Press, 1967]), the putative "feminization," that is, sentimentalization, of American literature, has been a recurrent and sometimes hysterical concern of much twentieth-century U.S. literary scholarship. See, for example, Van Wyck Brooks, *New England Indian Summer, 1865–1915* (New York: E. P. Dutton, 1940), pp. 134, 491–543; Fred Lewis Pattee, *The Feminine Fifties* (New York: Appleton-Century, 1940); David Perkins, *A History of Modern Poetry from the 1890s to the High Modernist Mode* (Cambridge: Belknap Press of Harvard University Press, 1976), pp. 51–59 and passim; Douglas, *The Feminization of American Culture*; and, perhaps most bizarre, Lauren Berlant, "Poor Eliza," *American Literature* 70 (September 1998): 635–66, which seems determined to place *Uncle Tom's Cabin* at the heart of all that is meretricious and corrupt in contemporary American political culture.

For more complicated and nuanced presentations of the origins of sentimentality and the relationships between male and female sentimental texts, see Auerbach, *Mimesis*; Mary Chapman and Glenn Hendler, eds., *Sentimental Men: Masculinity and the Politics of Affect in American Culture* (Berkeley: University of California Press, 1999); Ellison, *Cato's Tears*; Glenn Hendler, *Public Sentiments: Structures of Feeling in Nineteenth-Century American Literature* (Chapel Hill: University of North Carolina Press, 2001); Fred Kaplan, *Sacred Tears: Sentimentality in Victorian Literature* (Princeton: Princeton University Press, 1987); Karen Kilcup: *Robert Frost and Feminine Literary Tradition* (Ann Arbor: University of Michigan Press, 1999); Carlin T. Kindilien, *American Poetry in the Eighteen Nineties* (Providence: Brown University Press, 1956); Laurence Lerner, *Angels and Absences: Child Deaths in the Nineteenth Century* (Nashville: Vanderbilt University Press, 1997); David Marshall, *The Surprising Effects of Sympathy: Marivaux, Diderot, Rousseau, and Mary Shelley* (Chicago: University of Chicago Press, 1988); Jerome McGann, *The Poetics of Sensibility: A Revolution in Literary Style* (Oxford: Clarendon Press, 1996); Anne K. Mellor, *Mary Shelley: Her Life, Her Fiction, Her Monsters* (New York: Routledge, 1988); and Pinch, *Strange Fits*.

29. *PB* 33.

30. I have not been able to locate a reliable set of numbers for books published between 1800 and 1825. The American Antiquarian Society lists twenty-four among its holdings; Oscar Wegelin's bibliography, *Early American Poetry*, lists twenty-six (overlapping eight with the AAS) but only goes to 1820.

31. "Written by a Young Lady to Her Seducer," *Ladies' Monitor* 1 (May 1, 1802): 296.

32. "Dr. Caustick," "The Fop: A Song," *Weekly Inspector* 1 (September 6, 1806): 16. Even more disturbing than "The Fop's" sexism is its racism: "He please the ladies! very good; / Why then I wouldn't if I could, / So notable my spunk is; / I'd let them sooner seek gallants / From Afric's coast, or that of France. / Brisk Sans Callottes—or monkies."

33. Anna Maria, "The Bachelor's Soliloquy; or, A New Puzzle in Praise of Women," *Ladies' Literary Cabinet* 6 (July 6, 1822): 72. A pro-bachelor version of Anna Maria's poem also exists, raising the possibility that hers is a retort poem: using the same structure but written from the opposite point of view. Since the only versions of the "male" alternative I have found, however, were published well after "The Bachelor's Soliloquy," it is also possible that men chose to "retort" to her. See "Matrimony," *Cherokee Phoenix* 4 (July 14, 1832): 4. Also see "Editor's Drawer," *Harper's New Monthly Magazine* 11 (August 1855): 423–24.

34. "Clementina," Reply to "Tray," *Boston Gazette* 14 (June 27, 1803): 2. Kicked off on June 6, 1803, this debate began with "The Dog and the Elbow: A Metrical Tale," by "Trim." Then, on June 16, came "The Surly Dog: or a Short Metrical Address to 'Tray' in answer to his Tale." Other poems, possibly by different hands but addressing the same issue, followed on June 20, June 27, July 4, July 11, and July 14, at which point everyone had had enough and the debate was suspended without a winner declared.

35. "Verses to my First Born," *Ladies' Literary Cabinet* 4 (July 21, 1821): 88. The poem was reprinted from the *New Monthly Magazine*.

36. Osgood, "Ah! Woman Still" (*AWP* 133).

37. See Mary Kelley, *Private Woman, Public Stage: Literary Domesticity in Nineteenth-Century America* (New York: Oxford University Press, 1984), pp. vii–xiii.

38. Richard Brodhead, "Sparing the Rod, Discipline and Fiction in Antebellum America," *Representations* 21 (Winter 1988): 67–77.

39. For "belle," see *The Letters of Emily Dickinson*, ed. Thomas H. Johnson and Theodora Ward (Cambridge: Belknap Press of Harvard University Press, 1958), 1:13. For "Wayward Nun," see *The Poems of Emily Dickinson*, ed. R. W. Franklin (Cambridge: Belknap Press of Harvard University Press, 1998), 2:707. Henceforth, all references to Dickinson's letters and poems will appear parenthetically in my text with their assigned Johnson or Franklin number only, preceded by the letters *L* or *F*.

40. See Paula Bennett, *My Life a Loaded Gun: Female Creativity and Feminist Poetics* (Boston: Beacon Press, 1986), pp. 15–37. I still view Dickinson's rebellion against usefulness as a key element in her self-positioning as artist.

41. Sarah Bryan (Piatt), "Lines," *Louisville Daily Journal* 27 (July 1, 1857): 2.

42. Osgood's indifference to politics is striking in "Lines," her poetic response to married women's property rights legislation. In this exceedingly clever poem, Osgood argues that the "real" wealth men steal from women is that in "woman's heart, / As fancies, tastes, affections;— / . . . / Do we not daily sacrifice, / To our lords—and Creation's / Some darling wish—some petted whim, / Ah, me! in vain oblations!" In *The Heath Anthology of American Literature*, ed. Paul Lauter et al., 3d ed. (Boston: Houghton Mifflin, 1998), 1:2715. Like Dickinson, who also saw "duty" as soul-killing, Osgood is more concerned with protecting the imaginative life and the life of the spirit than in trying to rescue humanity from its hopeless ditch, but the attitude is socially regressive and amounts to a politics of the right.

43. Edgar Allan Poe, Review of *Poems,* by Frances S. Osgood, *Broadway Journal* 2 (1845): 353.

44. As quoted in Caroline May, *The American Female Poets* (Philadelphia: Lindsay and Blakiston, 1859), p. 382.

45. Eliza Richards, "Poetic Attractions: Gender, Celebrity, and Authority in Poe's Circle" (Ph.D. dissertation, University of Michigan, 1997), p. 88. Let me add that Richards also exhibits substantial concern with poetry as a form of public dialogue and a keen awareness of the importance of cross-gender exchange, placing her work significantly outside the more standard scholarship in the field.

46. Joanne Dobson, "Sex, Wit, and Sentiment: Frances Osgood and the Poetry of Love," *American Literature* 65 (1993): 632.

47. Nancy F. Cott, "Passionlessness: An Interpretation of Victorian Sexual Ideology, 1790–1850," *Signs: Journal of Women in Culture and Society* 4 (1978): 219–36.

48. Dobson, "Sex, Wit, and Sentiment," p. 646.

49. Dobson made this discovery at the American Antiquarian Society at a time when I had the good fortune to be working there also. She deserves full credit both for the discovery, which she has kindly permitted me to share here, and for opening this entire side of Osgood up for exploration in the first place. Our difference, insofar as there is one, lies more in emphasis than interpretation.

50. Other women poets of the period also brought their affairs forward on the public stage, in Adah Menken's case, literally. See Renée Sentilles, "Performing Menken: Adah Isaacs Menken's American Odyssey" (Ph.D. dissertation, College of William and Mary, 1997), pp. 128–67; and my comments on Sarah Piatt's juvenile productions above. A woman given to in-your-face politics on a heroic scale, Menken defended herself against charges of bigamy with poems published in the New York City press. In August 1860, she even rented Hope Chapel for a night to defend her honor before a surprised audience that had come to hear a dramatic reading. The audience was not pleased.

51. Richards, "Poetic Attractions," pp. 85–143.

52. Mary P. Ryan, *Women in Public: Between Banners and Ballots, 1825–1880* (Baltimore: Johns Hopkins University Press, 1990), pp. 58–94.

Notes to Chapter 2

1. Frances D. Gage, Letter, *Una: A Paper Devoted to the Elevation of Women,* May 1854, p. 265.

2. Rita Felski, *Beyond Feminist Aesthetics: Feminist Literature and Social Change* (Cambridge: Harvard University Press, 1989), p. 71.

3. "Another Woman's Rights Convention," *Cherokee Advocate* 4 (September 18, 1848): 4.

4. Angelina Grimké to Jane Smith, in *The Public Years of Sarah and Angelina Grimké: Selected Writings 1835–1839,* ed. Larry Ceplair (New York: Columbia University Press, 1989), p. 272.

5. Margaret Fuller, *Woman in the Nineteenth Century* (New York: W. W. Norton, 1971), p. 35.

6. Nineteenth-century feminists did not use the labels "equality" and "difference," but the distinction was in the air. See, for example, Samuel Miller's 1803 warning: "when women carry the idea of their *equality* with the other sex so far as to insist

that there should be no *difference* in their education and pursuits, they mistake both their character and their happiness." As quoted by Rosemarie Zagarri in "The Rights of Man and Woman in Post-Revolutionary America, *William and Mary Quarterly* 55 (April 1998): 218 (italics mine). Feminist historians have yet to settle on one consistent set of terms to define differences within nineteenth-century feminism. See, for example, "utopian-radical" versus "conservative-sentimental," in Jill Ker Conway, "Utopian Dream or Dystopian Nightmare? Nineteenth-Century Feminist Ideas about Equality," *Proceedings of the American Antiquarian Society* 96 (part 2, 1986): 285–94; and "ultraists" versus conservatives in Lori D. Ginzberg, *Women and the Work of Benevolence: Morality, Politics, and Class in the Nineteenth-Century United States* (New Haven: Yale University Press, 1990), pp. 81–92. Also see Joan C. Scott, "Deconstructing Equality-Versus-Difference, or the Uses of Poststructuralist Theory for Feminists," *Feminist Studies* 14 (Spring 1988): 33–50, for a cogent critique of difference-equality labels as used today. I employ them anyway, because I believe they are still relevant to nineteenth-century feminism, where the split between essentialist and constructionist perspectives runs extremely deep.

7. Julia Ward Howe, *Julia Ward Howe and the Woman Suffrage Movement* (Boston: Dana Estes and Co., 1913), p. 372.

8. *Cherokee Phoenix* 3 (March 12, 1831): 3. There is a distinct edge to Sigourney's phrasing in this passage as she draws an implied analogy between the oppression of the Cherokee and the oppression of women; and this might help to explain why the good ladies of Connecticut who had commissioned the memorial ultimately decided not to send it, declaring it "too bold & too political." Sigourney ended by giving the manuscript to an autograph hunter a few years later, declaring with some bitterness that it was a "useless thing." Tricia Lootens discusses this incident in "Hemans and Her American Heirs: Nineteenth-Century Women's Poetry and National Identity," in *Women's Poetry, Late Romantic to Late Victorian: Gender and Genre, 1830–1900*, ed. Isobel Armstrong and Virginia Blain (London: University of London, 1999), p. 250. I am indebted to Lootens for calling my attention to this particular bit of the memorial's sad history; but I would disagree with her conclusion that the memorial's rejection marked the effective end of Sigourney's political involvement.

9. Zagarri, "The Rights of Man and Woman," p. 216. I am deeply indebted to Zagarri for much of my thinking in this chapter.

10. The citations in this and the preceding paragraph come from Zagarri, "The Rights of Man and Woman," pp. 209, 220, 220, 224, and 225, respectively.

11. Cf. the famous epitaph of "John Jack, a native of Africa," written in much the same spirit: "Though born in a land of SLAVES / He was born FREE; / Though he lived in a land of LIBERTY, / HE lived a SLAVE . . ." *Philadelphia Minerva* 2 (September 17, 1796): 2.

12. "Rights of Woman," *New York Weekly Museum*, April 25, 1795, n.p.

13. Ada, "The Panic," *Kentucky Reporter* 22 (March 4, 1829): 4.

14. See Debra Gold Hansen, *Strained Sisterhood: Gender and Class in the Boston Female Anti-Slavery Society* (Amherst: University of Massachusetts Press, 1993), pp. 101–6 and passim. To date, this is the most thorough and carefully documented study of the fractures within the feminist-abolitionist movement that I have encountered and makes very sobering reading.

15. See Sarah Grimké, Letter III, in *Public Years*, ed. Ceplair, pp. 212–16.

16. Nancy A. Walker, *A Very Serious Thing: Women's Humor and American Culture* (Minneapolis: University of Minnesota Press), pp. 78–79.

17. As quoted in S. Grimké, Letter III, p. 216.

18. S. Grimké, Letter III, p. 216.

19. Although copyright was on the books, the reprinting of poetry was largely carried out on an honor system requiring only that editors name their source for "selected" poems. This, taken together with the free exchange between newspapers, meant that poems could circulate widely in very short order. (Personal communication from Melissa Homestead.) Squibs also circulated freely. For example, the following peroration came from a Fourth of July speech given by a Miss Green in Augusta, Maine, in 1834, which found its way into the *Kentucky Observer and Reporter* two months later:

> If I shall have been so happy as to gain the approbation of those for whose sake
> I have so far departed from the strict limit which ancient prejudices have long
> prescribed to our sex, I shall be amply repaid for all the sneers of witlings and
> fools. (Cheers.) . . . and I say unto you, lords of creation, as you call yourselves,
> if you doubt my sincerity—I proclaim it here, in the face of all Augusta . . .
> and you may believe me or not, as you please—that there is not one among
> you, Tom, Dick, or Harry, that I would give a brass thimble to call "husband"
> to-morrow. (*Kentucky Observer and Reporter* 3 [September 3, 1834]: 3)

Whether or not this lively young lady went on to bigger and better things in the woman's rights movement does not matter. For the moment, she was doing the woman's movement's political work, and word of her action spread to others.

20. "The Rights of Wives," *Irish Nationalist* 1 (May 3, 1873): 2.

21. On the whole, equality feminism, unlike difference feminism, was strikingly free from religious cant, and I hesitate therefore to introduce God into the picture at this point. However, I do not think it possible to understand equality feminism's theorization of civil free agency without first taking into account its roots in religious thought. It is no accident that so many of the women's rights movement's initial leaders and most powerful advocates were Hicksite Quakers. For women like the Grimké sisters, insofar as the principle of coverture stripped women of personal agency, it made it impossible for them to act according to the dictates of their conscience, thus risking the damnation of the very persons it claimed to protect. This concern lies at the core of Angelina Grimké's "Appeal to the Christian Women of the South" (1836) and Sarah's *Letters on the Equality of the Sexes* (1838), two of the most important documents in the history of U.S. women's political engagement. Quite simply, in the absence of free choice, women could neither act responsibly nor be held accountable for their actions. For an unusually helpful discussion of the differences among Quakers and the progressive role played by Hicksite Quakers see Kathryn Kish Sklar, "'Women Who Speak for an Entire Nation': American and British Women at the World Anti-Slavery Convention, London, 1840," in *The Abolitionist Sisterhood: Women's Political Culture in Antebellum America*, ed. Jean Fagan Yellin and John C. Van Horne (Ithaca: Cornell University Press, 1994), pp. 301–33.

22. It is, of course, precisely the public sphere's legitimation of debate that allows it, as Habermas says (contra Foucault) both to encourage "the individuating effects of

socialization" and to accommodate itself to them, making individual agency possible at the same time. See Jürgen Habermas, *The Philosophical Discourses of Modernity: Twelve Lectures*, trans. Frederick G. Lawrence (Cambridge: MIT Press, 1993), p. 286.

23. Zagarri makes this point respecting the nontraditional sources that she uses to track the rights debate: "[l]adies' magazines, literary periodicals, and prescriptive literature for women." See "Rights of Man and Woman," pp. 203–4. Like myself, Zagarri believes that these sources served finally as a "Habermasian public sphere . . . that incorporated women into the discussion of political ideas." See "The Rights of Man and Woman," p. 207.

24. As quoted in Hansen, *Strained Sisterhood*, p. 57.

25. See Ann Douglas, *The Feminization of American Culture* (New York: Doubleday, 1977) and the essays on Stowe and Warner in Jane Tompkins, *Sensational Designs: the Cultural Work of American Fiction, 1790–1860* (New York: Oxford University Press, 1986). The core issue in this debate centers on whether high-sentimental sympathy politics (as I call it) is a politics of bad faith, with the preponderance of scholars holding that it is. See, for example, the essays in Shirley Samuels, ed., *The Culture of Sentiment: Race, Gender, and Sentimentality in Nineteenth-Century America* (New York: Oxford University Press, 1992). In *Feminism without Women: Culture and Criticism in a "Post-Feminist" Age* (New York: Routledge, 1991), 23–28, Tania Modeleski rightly points out the disturbing number of gynophobic stereotypes embedded in Douglas's critical narrative. However, many of the most notable defenders of sentimentality have relied on sexist stereotypes also, praising women, on the one hand, as caretakers and nurturers, and damning men, on the other, for their emotional indifference and selfishness. In this writer's opinion, the Douglas-Tompkins debate will continue as long as scholars persist in viewing sentimentality as a *female* discourse rather than a *feminized* one. That is, as a rhetorical mode, sentimentality is identified with the "feminine" not because women originated it (they didn't) but because, as we saw in chapter 1, it exhibits traits that have been *traditionally identified as "feminine," whichever sex exhibits them*: softness, a focus on domestic life, fragile interiority, concern with social and affective bonds, and so on. Douglas's title signals this possibility; but her obsessive focus on, and intense discomfort with, women writers undermines the distinction. What troubles me most about this debate, beside the fact that it is driven by stereotypes, is that it has also choked off virtually all other areas of discussion.

26. Hannah Mather Crocker, *Observations on the Real Rights of Women, with their Appropriate Duties, agreeable to Scripture, Reason and Common Sense* (Boston: printed for the author, 1818), pp. 15 and 20.

27. In the *Massachusetts Spy* (66 [February 1, 1837]: 3), Earle or her brother provided a note identifying Wollstonecraft as the specific target of this stanza: "Alluding to the works of M. Wolstonecraft [*sic*], the latter written while she was yet an Infidel—the former, after she embraced the Christian religion."

28. Shirley J. Yee notes that no black woman is known to have attended the Seneca Falls convention. See *Black Women Abolitionists: A Study in Activism, 1828–1860* (Knoxville: University of Tennessee Press, 1992), pp. 91–95. Since many black women, including the Forten sisters and the Douglasses, were active in the feminist-abolitionist movement, their absence from Seneca Falls speaks volumes.

29. See Margaret McFadden, "Boston Teenagers Debate the Woman Question, 1837–1838," *Signs: Journal of Women in Culture and Society* 15 (Summer 1990): 844–45.

30. McFadden, "Boston Teenagers," pp. 833–34, 836–38. This exchange is a study in brief of the kinds of dynamic interaction this book documents. The debate was set off by a woman's rights lecture the two girls attended in 1837. Cheney and her sister then wrote a poem, published in the *Transcript*, a local Boston newspaper, in response to the lecture. Dall and Cheney then proceeded to debate the issue privately in letters, which then led to Dall's essay in the *Casket*. Can one trace these two young women's willingness in later life to pursue professional careers to a lecture they heard one day in 1837 and to the position-clarifying debate it then precipitated between them? I believe so.

31. William Lloyd Garrison, Editorial, *Liberator* 2 (July 14, 1832):110.

32. See Todd Gernes, "Poetic Justice: Sarah Forten, Eliza Earle, and the Paradox of Intellectual Property," *New England Quarterly* 71 (June 1998): 229–30 and 257–62. I want to thank Janet Gray, Jean Fagan Yellin, Julie Winch, and Todd Gernes for their generous assistance in clarifying this matter for me.

33. One can find many examples of this sort of eulogy in abolitionist venues. In 1837 alone, for example, the *National Enquirer* published "Lines Written on Reading 'Right and Wrong in Boston'" (1 [March 11]: 104); "The Female Abolitionists," by "S. J."; and "To a Female Abolitionist," by "H." (3 [October 5]: 16); and "Female Efforts," by "Julia" (3 [October 12]: 20). Jean FaganYellin reviews similar material in *Women & Sisters: The Antislavery Feminists in American Culture* (New Haven: Yale University Press, 1989), pp. 66–69.

34. According to Benjamin Lundy, Chandler was the "first American female author" to have made a career out of antislavery protest. Like Earle, however, she walked a fine line between duty and desire, claiming that her poetry was not political but philanthropic. Lundy's description of Chandler's intentions makes the link between nineteenth-century high sentimentality and its eighteenth-century precursor, moral sentiment, inarguable: "The philosophic and sentimental piety manifested in [her works]; the liberal principles of charity and benevolence which they inculcate; and the lessons of justice, humanity, and active philanthropy, that are taught by them, cannot fail to recommend the book" Lundy, preface to *The Poetical Works of Elizabeth Margaret Chandler with a Memoir of her Life and Character*, by Benjamin Lundy (Philadelphia: Lemuel Howell, 1836), p. 3. This is also one of the few unequivocally positive uses of the term "sentimental" that I have found in the century. Lydia Maria Child's very self-contradictory views on the political character of her antislavery work have been canvassed thoroughly by her biographer, Carolyn L. Karcher, in *The First Woman in the Republic: A Cultural Biography of Lydia Maria Child* (Durham: Duke University Press, 1994). While Chandler and Child preceded Grimké, the latter was the first to offer a full-blown theorization of the morality justifying women's participation in the abolitionist movement.

35. In two letters, one addressed to Weld and Whittier jointly, the other to Jane Smith, Angelina makes her strategy explicit, noting that she uses the words "responsibilities" or "duty" (not "rights") when speaking on the platform. See Angelina Grimké to Theodore Dwight Weld and John Greenleaf Whittier, August 20, 1837; and

Angelina Grimké to Jane Smith, August 26, 1837, both in *Public Years*, ed. Ceplair, pp. 285 and 286.

36. Karen Sánchez-Eppler, *Touching Liberty: Abolition, Feminism, and the Politics of the Body* (Berkeley: University of California Press, 1993), p. 16.

37. Sánchez-Eppler, *Touching Liberty*, p. 19. As I see it, Sánchez-Eppler is conflating positions that need to be kept separate. As Grimké pointed out to Weld and Whittier in response to their opposition to her woman's rights activity, it would have been not only logically inconsistent for her to fight against one form of enslavement while swallowing another but impossible, since she would thereby deny the grounds for her own agency as speaker on *any* subject. "*We must Establish this right*, for if we do not, it will be impossible for *us* to *go on with the work of emancipation*" (Letter to Weld and Whittier, p. 282).

38. Charlotte Forten Grimké, "The Angel's Visit," reprinted in William Wells Brown, *The Black Man: His Antecedents, His Genius, and His Achievements* (Boston: James Redpath, 1863), pp. 196–99.

39. Charlotte Forten Grimké, "The Two Voices," *National Anti-Slavery Standard* 19 (January 15, 1859): 4.

40. "Ada" [Sarah Louisa Forten], "The Slave Girl's Address to her Mother," *Liberator*, January 29, 1831, 18.

41. Sánchez-Eppler, *Touching Liberty*, p. 20.

42. See *King Lear*, 4.1.67–70, 4.6.147, and 4.6.217. Edgar's description of himself to his blinded father seems especially pertinent: "A most poor man, made tame to fortune's blows, / Who, by the art of known and feeling sorrows, / Am pregnant to good pity."

43. Adam Smith, *The Theory of Moral Sentiments; or, An Essay towards an Analysis of the Principles by which Men naturally judge concerning the Conduct and Character, first of their Neighbors, and afterwards of themselves*, 9th ed. (London: Cadell and Davies, 1801), 1:3. See David Marshall, *The Surprising Effects of Sympathy: Marivaux, Diderot, Rousseau, and Mary Shelley* (Chicago: University of Chicago Press, 1988), pp. 3–5; and Howard, "What is Sentimentality?" p. 7, both of whom discuss this passage.

44. Angelina Grimké, *Letters to Catherine* [sic] *E. Beecher, in reply to An Essay on Slavery and Abolitionism, addressed to A. E. Grimké*: Letter VII: Prejudice," July 23, 1837, in *Public Years*, ed. Ceplair, p. 171.

45. James Scott, "A Reply to Ada," *Liberator* 4 (February 22, 1834): 32; and "Reply to Ada," by "Augusta," *Liberator* 4 (March 1, 1834): 36 ("For shame is ours that we begin so late. / Though 'skins may differ,' thou dost justly claim / A sister's privilege in a sister's name").

46. In a passionate letter to Angelina Grimké, Forten responds to Grimké's request that she describe the " 'effect of prejudice' " by portraying a pervasive racism that in small ways and large subjected even free, upper-middle-class blacks like herself to degradation. Sarah L. Forten to Angelina Grimké, April 15, 1837, in *Letters of Theodore Dwight Weld, Angelina Grimké Weld and Sarah Grimké, 1822–1844*, ed. Gilbert H. Barnes and Dwight L. Dumond (New York: D. Appleton-Century, 1934), 1:379–82.

47. As quoted in Jane Thompson Follis, "Frances Wright: Feminism and Literature in AnteBellum America" (Ph.D. dissertation, University of Wisconsin, Madison, 1982),

31–33. Also see Phillip Lapsansky, "Graphic Discord: Abolitionist and Antiabolitionist Images," in Yellin and Van Horne, *The Abolitionist Sisterhood*, pp. 201–30.

48. "Ella" [Sarah Mapps Douglass], "The Mother and Her Captive Boy," *National Enquirer* 1 (October 8, 1836): 20.

49. See Nina Baym, "Reinventing Lydia Sigourney," *Feminism and American Literary History* (New Brunswick: Rutgers University Press, 1992), pp. 151–66.

50. L. H. Sigourney, "The Lost Lily," in *The Western Home and Other Poems* (Philadelphia: Parry and McMillan, 1854), p. 349.

51. Ibid., p. 348.

Notes to Chapter 3

1. As quoted in Diane Lichtenstein, *Writing Their Nations: The Tradition of Nineteenth-Century American Jewish Women Writers* (Bloomington: Indiana University Press, 1992), p. 112.

2. K. Anthony Appiah, "Race, Culture, Identity: Misunderstood Connections," in K. Anthony Appiah and Amy Gutman, *Color Conscious: the Political Morality of Race* (Princeton: Princeton University Press, 1996), p. 76.

3. J. Hector St. John de Crèvecoeur, *Letters from an American Farmer and Sketches of Eighteenth-Century America* (New York: Penguin, 1986), p. 68.

4. Margaret Fuller, "American Literature: Its Position in the Present Time, and Prospects for the Future," in *Margaret Fuller, American Romantic: A Selection from Her Writings and Correspondence*, ed. Perry Miller (Garden City: Doubleday Anchor, 1963), p. 231.

5. Walt Whitman, preface to *Leaves of Grass* (1855), in *Leaves of Grass and Selected Prose*, ed. Lawrence Buell (New York: Modern Library, 1981), pp. 450–51.

6. According to the *Oxford English Dictionary*, the use of "race" to denote a "tribe, nation, or people, regarded as of common stock" was current by 1600. The primary definition of "nation" was fully elaborated by 1800: "A distinct race or people, characterized by common descent, language, or history, usu. organized as a separate political state and occupying a definite territory." The conflation of race and nationality prevailed through most of the twentieth century. See, for example, the sample question and answer taken from a 1933 United States Application for Citizenship form: "What race do you belong to? A white citizen of France is of French race and French nationality." As quoted in Jacques Barzun, *Race: A Study in Superstition*, rev. ed. (New York: Harper Torchbooks, 1965), p. 7. Also see Nicholas Hudson, "From 'Nation' to 'Race': The Origin of Racial Classification in Eighteenth-Century Thought," *Eighteenth-Century Studies* 29.3 (1996): 247–64.

7. See Benedict Anderson, *Imagined Communities: Reflections on the Origin and Spread of Nationalism* (London: Verso, 1983), pp. 1–7.

8. K. Anthony Appiah, "Race, Culture, Identity: Misunderstood Connections," in Appiah and Gutman, *Color Conscious*, p. 76.

9. My argument here is strictly political. What Gayatri Spivak calls "strategic essentialism" was enormously effective for late-twentieth-century "liberation" movements. See "Subaltern Studies: Deconstructing Historiography," in *The Spivak Reader*, ed. Donna Landry and Gerald Maclean (New York: Routledge, 1996), pp. 203 and passim.

10. The idea of "counter-public spheres" was first elaborated by scholars writing from a feminist or Marxist revisionist perspective, who tended to treat them as sites for (implicitly progressive) oppositional minority thinking. As will become evident later in this chapter, although I accept the idea of counter-public spheres, I do not view them as necessarily progressive. See the essays by Baker, Eley, Fraser, and Garnham in *Habermas and the Public Sphere*, ed. Craig Calhoun (Cambridge: MIT Press, 1996). Also see Georgina Taylor, *H. D. and the Public Sphere of Modernist Women Writers 1913–1946* (Oxford: Clarendon Press, 2001), pp. 1–21, for an interesting application of the concept of the counter-public sphere to modernist women writers' affiliations. I am deeply indebted to Taylor—at the time a struggling graduate student—for first making me realize how relevant Habermas was to women's poetry, and I am delighted to return the favor by calling attention to her excellent study here. For a sobering view of a reactionary ethnic "counter-public sphere," see Rudolph Vecoli's "The Italian Immigrant Press and the Construction of Social Reality, 1850–1920," in *Print Culture in a Diverse America*, ed. James P. Danky and Wayne A. Wiegand (Urbana: University of Illinois Press, 1998), pp. 17–33.

11. Hutchins Hapgood, *The Spirit of the Ghetto*, ed. Moses Rischin (Cambridge: Belknap Press of Harvard University Press, 1967), p. 79.

12. "The New Face of America: How Immigrants Are Shaping the World's First Multicultural Society," *Time*, Fall 1993 (special issue), cover.

13. See Crèvecoeur, Letter XII, in *Letters from an American Farmer*.

14. See Elizabeth Young, *Disarming the Nation: Women's Writing and the American Civil War* (Chicago: University of Chicago Press, 1999), pp. 11–14, for a lively and suggestive discussion of the multiple meanings of "civil," meanings that, among other things, reinforced the identification of *civil* (citizen) status with the putative *civility* of bourgeois values.

15. Louise Michele Newman, *White Women's Rights: The Racial Origins of Feminism in the United States* (New York: Oxford University Press, 1999), pp. 6–11.

16. "Freedom's Gift to Women," *Southern Workman* 2 (November 1873): 3.

17. Barbara McCaskill, "'To Labor . . . and Fight on the Side of God': Spirit, Class, and Nineteenth-Century African American Women's Literature," in *Nineteenth-Century American Women Writers: A Critical Reader*, ed. Karen Kilcup (Oxford: Blackwell Publishers, 1998), p. 168.

18. Noel Ignatiev, *How the Irish Became White* (New York: Routledge, 1995), p. 2.

19. See Matthew Frye Jacobson, *Whiteness of a Different Color: European Immigrants and the Alchemy of Race* (Cambridge: Harvard University Press, 1998), pp. 72–75 and passim.

20. Richard Brodhead, *Cultures of Letters: Scenes of Reading and Writing in Nineteenth-Century America* (Chicago: University of Chicago Press, 1993), pp. 1–12.

21. Aldon Nielsen, *Reading Race in American Poetry: An Area of Act* (Urbana: University of Illinois Press, 2000), p. 16.

22. Miscellaneous News Items, *Springfield Daily Republican*, August 16, 1860, p. 2.

23. For example, in an 1860 editorial, "What Shall be Done with the Darkies?" Bowles urged the voluntary exodus of all American blacks from the United States. "If they had any pluck—if the best of them had a particle of the spirit of the white man," American blacks would, he says, build their own "independent state. . . . There is Mr Fred Douglas [*sic*]—a genius—a man of power—but he apparently never

dreams of anything better for his race than freedom and mixture with white society. We hear of no large plans for benefiting them—we see no striking out for a future that indicates capacity for self-government." (*Springfield Daily Republican,* July 14, 1860, p. 4). It is possible that those Dickinson scholars who find Bowles admirable have only read the *Republican* in its weekly format. The daily version of the newspaper decidedly took the low road; and as sole publisher, Bowles must be held accountable for both newspapers' views, as he must also be held accountable for the generally retrograde position the newspaper took on women's issues. To gauge Bowles's degree of responsibility, one could note that during the same years that the *Springfield Republican* in Amherst, Massachusetts, was most fully engaged in dishing out racial hatred with one hand and trying to keep women in their place with the other (1859–61), the *Louisville Journal* in Louisville, Kentucky, under the guidance of George Prentice, opposed the South's separatist fantasies and supported the aspirations of women writers, if anything, almost too enthusiastically.

24. Anna Brackett, "Indian and Negro," *Harper's New Monthly Magazine* 61 (September 1880): 627 and 628.

25. "The Heathen Chinee," *New Varieties,* March 27, 1871, p. 12. Harte's poem appeared after "The Heathen Chinee" came out and is only minimally less nasty.

26. Lizzie W. Champney, "That Small Piecee Boy from China," *Harper's Young People* 2 (December 21, 1880): 157.

27. See the essays in *Satire or Evasion? Black Perspectives on* Huckleberry Finn, ed. James S. Leonard (Durham: Duke University Press, 1992).

28. Well before Bowles and Dickinson became personal friends, the poet voices her admiration for the peculiar tone of the *Republican* squibs in an 1853 letter to Dr. and Mrs. J. G. Holland (L133). Although Dickinson's attitude toward individual Irish undoubtedly softened as she grew close to the Irish servants who worked for her family, her sense of class difference remained very much intact and as exclusionary as ever. Only one Dickinson poem ever asserts social equality, "Color - Caste - Denomination" (F836). However, this poem deploys the medieval trope of death-the-leveler, thus locating equality in the afterlife while doing nothing to disrupt the status quo here. See Betsy Erkkila, "Emily Dickinson and Class," *American Literary History* 4 (Spring 1992): 1–27.

29. Dickinson's image of the tropical, sensuous black man is, of course, a stereotype that she could have picked up just about anywhere in her culture; however, her image also resonates with some particularity in the *Daily Republican's* pages. Cf. "The Ebony Idol," *Springfield Daily Republican,* August 15, 1860, p. 2: "The inexorable law of civilization, work or starve, is one that Sambo, from the very tropical sensuousness of his being, is exceedingly slow to learn." Like most nineteenth-century exponents of orientalism, Dickinson also plays positively with the trope associating color with sensuality, most notably in "Civilization - spurns - the Leopard!" (F276).

30. See Peter Gay, *The Cultivation of Hatred,* vol. 3 of *The Bourgeois Experience Victoria to Freud* (New York: W. W. Norton, 1993), 68–95.

31. Louisa Anna, "Zuleika," *Cincinnati Israelite* 14 (April 17, 1868): 1.

32. Mary P. Ryan, *Women in Public: Between Banners and Ballots, 1825–1880* (Baltimore: Johns Hopkins University Press, 1990), p. 35.

33. See Rebekah Hyneman, "Woman's Rights," in *She Wields a Pen: American Women Poets of the Nineteenth Century,* ed. Janet Gray (Iowa City: University of Iowa

Press, 1997), p. 58: "It is her right, to bind with warmest ties, / The lordly spirit of aspiring man, / Making his home an earthly paradise, / Rich in all joys allotted to life's span," and so forth. Rosa Levy, of Augusta, Georgia, tried to move beyond this position in "Woman's Destiny," published in the *Cincinnati Israelite* in 1873. Her poem bemoans how women were forced to squelch their aspirations, their "brother / To benefit, and beautify." The poem elicited a swift rebuttal from an angry male reader: "For happiness was woman placed on earth; / But if she crosses designated limits / She finds a wilderness of pain and dearth." This nasty bit of chauvinism then moved a second woman, Courtney from Mobile, Alabama, to defend Levy: "And would the selfish cynic strive to teach / That there are hights [*sic*] her genius may not reach? / 'Tis a base libel; she may side by side / Walk with her brother man in all his pride." See *Cincinnati Israelite* 21 (August 8, 1873): 1; *Cincinnati Israelite* 21 (August 22, 1873): 1; and "To R.A.L.," *Cincinnati Israelite* 21 (September 26, 1873): 1. Among other things, this printed exchange provides more evidence for the survival of eighteenth-century newspaper debate practices right through the 1800s. Since Levy's feminism is relatively conservative, however—for example, she makes no mention of the vote—it also suggests that the bar for allowable protest was very low even in the reform Jewish community that the *Israelite* served.

34. "Una" [Mary McMullen Ford], "St. Agnes," *Irish World* 6 (May 6, 1876): 5. See also Mary A. McMullen [Ford], *Snatches of Song* (St. Louis, Mo.: Patrick Fox, 1874), p. 26.

35. "Una" [Mary McMullen Ford], "Unite," *Irish World* (May 6, 1876): 5.

36. For lengthier treatments of this problem in the Jewish and Irish communities, see the discussions in Diane Lichtenstein, *Writing Their Nations: The Tradition of Nineteenth-Century American Jewish Women Writers* (Bloomington: Indiana University Press, 1992), pp. 60–94; and in Hasia R. Diner, *Erin's Daughters in America: Irish Immigrant Women in the Nineteenth Century* (Baltimore: Johns Hopkins University Press, 1983), pp. xiii–xiv, 139–53. Ryan's *Women in Public* also provides an excellent analysis of the play between progressive and repressive elements within those nineteenth-century urban counter-public spheres that developed around differences of class, region, and ethnicity. Her treatment of the variety of ways working-class Irish women found to interact with men in the public sphere is especially enlightening.

37. Mrs. N. F. Mossell, *The Work of Afro-American Woman*, with an introduction by Joanne Braxton (New York: Oxford University Press, 1988), pp. 81–82, 83–84.

38. Qua-Tsy, "Female Influence," *The Wreath of Cherokee Rose Buds* 2 (August 1, 1855): 5.

39. Zallie Rulo, "The Indian Woman," *Southern Workman* 14 (June 1885): 62. In fairness to Rulo, she also puts up a spirited defense of her people's culture at various points in her essay, only cleaving the party line where gender roles are concerned.

40. As quoted in Josephine E. Richards, "The Training of the Indian Girl as the Uplifter of the Home," *Southern Workman* 29 (September 1900): 507. Richards opens her paper, which she gave before the Indian Department of the National Education Association, with Sitting Bull's plea. Unfortunately, her solution to this problem is to teach young Indian women the inestimable values of "order," "cleanliness," and happy homemaking, suggesting that she understood nothing the man said.

41. Veronica Strong-Boag and Carole Gerson record in *Paddling Her Own Canoe: The Time and Texts of E. Pauline Johnson (Tekahionwake)* (Toronto: University of

Toronto Press, 2000), pp. 150–51, that "A Cry of an Indian Wife" also received poetic replies when it was first published in Canada's prestigious literary magazine *This Week*. According to Strong-Boag and Gerson, the poem itself represents Johnson's direct response to news reports on the Northwest Rebellion. Similarly, the biographers suggest that "The Corn Husker," which I treat in chapter 8, also represents Johnson's response to a white perspective on Indian affairs, here poetry by Duncan-Campbell Scott. I mention these possibilities because they establish that in Canada, as in the United States, a culture developed around newspaper and periodical poetry that converted it into an open site for political protest by women and peoples of color, who were otherwise excluded from both the political and the editorial process. Although technically Johnson, as a Canadian, has no place in this book, her writings were widely published in the United States as well as in Canada—appearing in the *Independent, Harper's Weekly,* and the *Mother's Magazine,* among other places—and these publications qualify her therefore as a participant in the debates I sketch out.

42. Compare, for example, Victor Hugo's "Souvenir of the Night of the Fourth of December, 1851," trans. Maria Weston Chapmen (*NAWP* 427–28).

43. Zitkala-Sa, "A Sioux Woman's Love for Her Grandchild," *American Indian Magazine* 5 (October–December 1917): 231. I wish to thank Karen Kilcup for calling this poem to my attention.

Notes to Chapter 4

1. Margaretta Odell, "Memoir," in *Phillis Wheatley and Her Writings*, ed. William H. Robinson (Boston: Hall, 1982), pp. 11–12.

2. Carla Peterson, *Doers of the Word: African-American Women Speakers and Writers in the North (1830–1880)* (New York: Oxford University Press, 1995), p. 3.

3. Katherine Clay Bassard, *Spiritual Interrogations* (Princeton: Princeton University Press, 1999), p. 128.

4. Bassard, *Spiritual Interrogations*, p. 9.

5. As quoted in Barbara McCaskill, "'To Labor . . . and Fight on the Side of God': Spirit, Class, and Nineteenth-Century African American Women's Literature," in *Nineteenth-Century American Women Writers: A Critical Reader*, ed. Karen Kilcup (Oxford: Blackwell Publishers, 1998), p. 174.

6. *A Brighter Coming Day: A Frances Ellen Watkins Harper Reader*, ed. Frances Smith Foster (New York: Feminist Press, 1990), p. 130. Subsequent references to Harper's writings in this volume will appear parenthetically in the text.

7. As quoted in Foster, introduction to *A Brighter Coming Day*, p. 4.

8. Peterson, *Doers*, p. 210. Also see Maryemma Graham, introduction to *Complete Poems of Frances E. W. Harper*, ed. Maryemma Graham (New York: Oxford University Press, 1988), p. xliii. For a detailed analysis of "Moses" itself, see Melba Joyce Boyd, *Discarded Legacy: Politics and Poetics in the Life of Frances E. W. Harper, 1825–1911* (Detroit: Wayne State University Press, 1994), pp. 88–109.

9. Peterson, *Doers*, p. 210. See also Boyd, *Discarded Legacy*, pp. 156–66; and Graham, introduction to *Complete Poems*, p. xliii.

10. McCaskill, "'To Labor,'" p. 176.

11. See Foster, introduction to *A Brighter Coming Day*, p. 21. Also see Boyd, *Discarded Legacy*, p. 224.

12. As quoted in Boyd, *Discarded Legacy*, p. 224.

13. See Louise Michele Newman, *White Women's Rights: The Racial Origins of Feminism in the United States* (New York: Oxford University Press, 1999), pp. 56–85. Also see the material under "The 'Expediency' Argument I: Racism and Xenophobia Enlisted in the Cause of Woman Suffrage," in *Up from the Pedestal: Selected Writings in the History of American Feminism*, ed. Aileen S. Kraditor (New York: Quadrangle, 1975), pp. 253–65. Boyd provides a well-balanced account of suffrage politics in the reconstruction era (*Discarded Legacy*, pp. 126–29).

14. [John Boyle O'Reilly], "Parnell," *Pilot* 45 (July 29, 1882): 1. My description of Parnell's two funerals is drawn entirely from the *Pilot*. See "Miss Fanny Parnell's Obsequies," *Pilot* 45 (October 28, 1882): 1 and 5. O'Reilly was not exaggerating. According to Parnell's biographer, Jane McL. Côté, Fanny's poems "were invariably reprinted in newspapers . . . in Ireland, England, North America and Australasia, bringing to her a celebrity almost equal to that of her brother Charles." *Fanny and Anna Parnell: Ireland's Patriot Sisters* (New York: St. Martin's Press, 1991), p. 220.

15. Parnell's remains are still lodged in the Tudor family vault in Mount Auburn, and the Parnell society of Ireland has recently installed a memorial to her on the site.

16. Hasia Diner, *Erin's Daughters in America: Irish Immigrant Women in the Nineteenth Century* (Baltimore: Johns Hopkins University Press, 1983), p. 27. For Parnell's political activities on behalf of the Ladies' Land Leagues, see Côté, *Fanny and Anna Parnell*, pp. 130–47.

17. As quoted in Côté, *Fanny and Anna Parnell*, p. 131.

18. Diner, *Erin's Daughters*, p. 128.

19. O'Reilly, "Parnell," p. 1.

20. As quoted in Côté, *Fanny and Anna Parnell*, p. 61. Generally, modern critical assessments of Parnell's poetry are mixed. Côté cites Parnell's "[e]xtravagant language, verging at times on the ludicrous" (p. 130). Eagleton lets his aesthetics take over from his politics, calling Parnell a "penner of politically forceful if artistically feeble verses." *Heathcliff and the Great Hunger: Studies in Irish Culture* (New York: Verso, 1995), p. 291. O'Reilly's comment that Fanny sacrificed "polish to force" are closer to the mark (as quoted in Côté, *Fanny and Anna Parnell*, p. 131). My view is, her poems work.

21. Côté, *Fanny and Anna Parnell*, p. 132. According to Côté, Fanny held more sentimentally inclined women poets, like Felicia Hemans, in contempt (p. 61).

22. Fanny Parnell, "She is Not Dead," *Pilot* 43 (September 4, 1880): 2.

23. Fanny Parnell, "Michael Davitt," *Pilot* 43 (December 18, 1880): 1.

24. Fanny Parnell, "What Shall We Weep For?" *Pilot* 43 (July 3, 1880): 1.

25. Fanny Parnell, "To the Land Leaguers," *Pilot* 43 (July 24, 1880): 1.

26. Fanny Parnell, "To My Fellow-Women," *Pilot* 43 (November 27, 1880): 1.

27. Fanny Parnell, "To the Irish Farmers—Hold the Harvest!" *Pilot* 43 (August 21, 1880): 2.

28. Côté, *Fanny and Anna Parnell*, p. 61.

29. Parnell, "Ireland, Mother!" *Pilot* 43 (November 6, 1880): 1.

30. "Fanny Parnell," in *The Poetry and Song of Ireland*, ed. John Boyle O'Reilly, 2d ed. (New York: Gay Brothers and Co., 1887), p. 103.

31. For a contrary view see her sister Josephine's memoir in *Century* magazine, which opens "One hesitates to lift the veil and throw the light upon a life so hidden and a personality so withdrawn as that of Emma Lazarus." See "Emma Lazarus," *Century* 36 (October 1888): 875. Bette Roth Young comments that this perspective on

the poet "has remained remarkably unchanged . . . since it was written." See *Emma Lazarus in Her World: Life and Letters* (Philadelphia: Jewish Publication Society, 1995), p. 13.

32. According to Ellen Emerson, Ralph Waldo's daughter, the entire family was filled with excitement at meeting "a real unconverted Jew (who had no objections to calling herself one. . . .)." Quoted in Francine Klagsbrun, foreword to Young, *Emma Lazarus*, p. x.

33. Young, *Emma Lazarus*, p. 5.

34. Ibid., p. 43.

35. Emma Lazarus, "Fog," *Lippincott's* 20 (August 1877): 207, and "Among the Thousand Islands," *Century* 22 (December 1881): 289.

36. Emma Lazarus, "Scenes in the Woods (Suggested by Robert Schumann)," *Lippincott's* 16 (August 1875): 178.

37. Emma Lazarus, "Epistle to the Hebrews," *American Hebrew*, November 3, 1882–February 23, 1883, reprinted in *Emma Lazarus: Selections from Her Poetry and Prose*, ed. Morris U. Schappes, 3d ed., rev. and enl. (New York: Emma Lazarus Federation of Jewish Women's Clubs, 1967), p. 79.

38. George Eliot, *Impressions of Theophrastus Such*, ed. Nancy Henry (Iowa City: University of Iowa Press, 1994), p. 47. According to Henry's notes "Hep! Hep! Hep!" refers to "an anti-Semitic cry which may have originated during the Crusades as an abbreviation of '*Hierosolyma est perdita*' (Jerusalem is lost), or perhaps as a cry used for driving herds of animals" (pp. 183–84 n. 1). I want to thank my colleague, K. K. Collins, for sharing information on Eliot with me.

39. Ibid., p. 155. In all fairness to Eliot, Theophrastus goes on to argue passionately that Jews as a group have suffered far less moral degradation than one would expect given the conditions under which they were forced to live (pp. 155–59).

40. Emma Lazarus, "Epistle to the Hebrews," in Schappes, *Emma Lazarus*, pp. 79 and 80.

41. Emma Lazarus, *The Poems of Emma Lazarus* (Boston: Houghton, Mifflin and Co., 1889), 2:114. All subsequent citations to this edition will appear directly in the text.

42. Diane Lichtenstein, *Writing Their Nations: The Traditions of Nineteenth-Century American Jewish Women Writers* (Bloomington: Indiana University Press, 1992), p. 252.

43. Emma Lazarus, "The Last National Revolt of the Jews," in *Emma Lazarus*, ed. Schappes, p. 101.

44. Lazarus, "Last National Revolt," p. 100.

45. Johnson not only employed slave labor on his Louisiana plantation but was the owner of a dairy cited in a *New York Times* article as directly responsible for the deaths of thousands of city children. Although Moses Lazarus was not involved directly in either concern, he did not break off his relationship with Johnson either. Indeed, the two men remained partners until 1885. See Young, *Emma Lazarus*, pp. 48–49.

46. Ibid., p. 51.

47. On this point, I would add that my own attitude toward Lazarus, one Jew to another, undoubtedly suffers from the same dynamic. I would have much preferred an Emma Lazarus who nobly inveighed against slavery with all the passion that she

inveighed against anti-Semitism. Unfortunately, she did not, nor do I think Lazarus's attacks on anti-Semitism are a displacement of her feeling about slavery, as Young argues. Is this because I am facing facts? Or is it because she embarrasses me? It is probably both, but I find my attitude troubling nonetheless.

48. E. Pauline Johnson, "My Mother," in *The Moccasin Maker*, ed. A. LaVonne Brown Ruoff (Tucson: University of Arizona Press, 1987), p. 69.

49. Ruoff, introduction to *The Moccasin Maker*, p. 6. The preceding quotation in this paragraph can be found on the same page.

50. Veronica Strong-Boag and Carole Gerson, *Paddling Her Own Canoe: The Time and Texts of E. Pauline Johnson (Tekahionwake)* (Toronto: University of Toronto Press, 2000), pp. 102–3.

51. Strong-Boag and Gerson, *Paddling*, p. 110.

52. In striking contrast to Parnell's funeral, Johnson's funeral in 1913 was not a community affair. According to Theodore Watts-Dunton, a "large crowd of silent Red Men . . . lined Georgia Street [in Vancouver] and . . . stood motionless as statues . . . until the funeral cortège had passed on the way to the cemetery." The Squamish presence indicates local tribes were respectful of Johnson's efforts on their behalf, but they had no control over what whites did with her. See Dunton's introduction to *Flint and Feather: The Complete Poems of E. Pauline Johnson*, 13th ed. (Toronto: Musson Book Co., 1930), p. xvi. In *Paddling*, Strong-Boag and Gerson comment that "To the end, Johnson's life was mediated and appropriated by White admirers and friends" (67).

53. See "The Silent News Carriers: How the Indian Carries and Sends Tidings," published in the London *Express* in 1906, and "The Iroquois of the Grand River," published in *Harper's Weekly* in 1894, both available on the Writings/Journalism section of the E. Pauline Johnson website: *http://www.humanities.mcmaster.ca/-pjohnson*.

54. For Eastman, see *NAWP* 546–50. For Manwell, see *NAWP* 357–62 and the coda to this book.

55. "Ojistoh," in *Flint and Feather*, p. 3. Subsequent citations from this collection of Johnson's poetry will appear directly in the text. Most of Johnson's poems also appeared in periodicals.

56. For a discussion of this same problem in Johnson's fiction, see Ruoff's, Introduction to *Moccasin Maker*, pp. 31–34.

57. In her article "The Iroquois of Grand River," Johnson acknowledges how much was being lost even as she wrote, giving the essay a strongly elegiac note.

58. Ruoff, introduction to *Moccasin Maker*, p. 6.

59. Although this may be unfair to Johnson, one could compare her account of Indian culture with that of Mary Jemison (1743–1833). A white woman taken in captivity by the Seneca when still quite young, Jemison lived as an Indian her entire life, even after the breakup of her tribe following the American Revolution—the same event that sent Johnson's Mohawk ancestors north to Canada. In relaying her story to James Seaver late in life, Jemison focused entirely on her experience as a Senecan woman, leaving "men's affairs" to men to discuss. It is possible, therefore, that Johnson's paternal grandmother's lack of English may have been decisive in shaping her granddaughter's vision of pre-reservation Indian society. The only stories Pauline heard were those told by men.

60. Johnson, "My Mother," in *Moccasin Maker*, p. 71.

61. Ibid., p. 78. See also p. 235 n.64. In their biography of Johnson, Strong-Boag and Carole Gerson provide a more balanced account of this conflict than does Johnson, stressing that economic (class?) interests also separated the two parties. That is, the "traditionalists," who so resented George Johnson's interference, also came from the poorest of the six nations—the Seneca, the Onondaga, and the Cayuga—and they were angry at being dominated by the more wealthy and powerful, as well as more acculturated, Mohawk. See *Paddling*, pp. 35–39.

62. Strong-Boag and Gerson, *Paddling*, pp. 38–39.

63. Eagleton, *Heathcliff*, p. 144.

Notes to Chapter 5

1. Ralph Waldo Emerson, "The Poet," in *The Complete Works of Ralph Waldo Emerson: Essays*, 2d ser. (Boston: Houghton, Mifflin, 1903), 3:18–19.

2. "Mrs. Sigourney on Woman's Rights," in *Una: A Paper Devoted to the Elevation of Women*, June 1854, p. 282.

3. Mary Clemmer Ames, "A Memorial of Alice and Phoebe Cary," in *The Poetical Works of Alice and Phoebe Cary with a Memorial of Their Lives*, ed. Mary Clemmer [Ames] (Boston: Houghton, Mifflin, 1876), p. 61.

4. Raymond Williams, "Base and Superstructure in Marxist Cultural Theory," in *Contemporary Literary Criticism: Literary and Cultural Studies*, ed. Robert Con Davis and Ronald Schleifer, 3d ed. (New York: Longmans, 1994), p. 458.

5. Terry Eagleton, *Heathcliff and the Great Hunger* (London: Verso, 1995), p. 27.

6. Williams, "Base and Superstructure," pp. 445–46.

7. Ibid., pp. 458–59.

8. Eagleton, *Heathcliff*, p. 28.

9. Williams, "Base and Superstructure," p. 458.

10. Mary Louise Kete, *Sentimental Collaborations: Mourning and Middle-Class Identity in Nineteenth-Century America* (Durham: Duke University Press, 1999), p. 6. Dobson makes a similar argument in "Reclaiming Sentimental Literature," *American Literature* 69 (June 1997): 263–88.

11. See Kete, *Sentimental Collaborations*, pp. xiv–xix.

12. Emerson, "The Poet," 3:18–19.

13. A Mary F. Lowe submitted Sigourney's essay to *Una*. Lowe gives no source, but the essay seems complete. See Sigourney, "Woman's Rights," p. 282.

14. Cary never again included parodies in a book, but she continued to write satirically on gender issues. See, for example, "Dorothy's Dower" and "Was He Henpecked?" (*NAWP* 105–6, 106–9). The best analysis of Cary's parodies is Jonathan Hall, "Alice Cary [and] Phoebe Cary," in *Encyclopedia of American Poetry: The Nineteenth Century*, ed. Eric L. Haralson (Chicago: Fitzroy Dearborn, 1998).

15. Cynthia Griffin Wolff, *Emily Dickinson* (New York: Alfred A. Knopf, 1986), p. 68 and passim.

16. See Kete, *Sentimental Collaborations*, pp. 19–58. For women's role when death occurs, see also, Ann Douglas, *The Feminization of American Culture* (New York: Doubleday, 1977), pp. 200–207; and Karen Halttunen, *Confidence Men, Painted Women: A Study of Middle-Class Culture in America, 1830–1870* (New Haven: Yale University Press, 1982), pp. 125–26, 132–33.

17. Mary Forest, "Rosa Vertner Johnson," in *Women of the South Distinguished in*

Literature, ed. Mary Forest (Mrs. Julia Deane Forest) (New York: Derby and Jackson, 1861), p. 246.

18. Johnson, "Angel Watchers," in *Women of the South,* ed. Forest, p. 257.

19. Forest, "Rosa Vertner Johnson," pp. 247–48.

20. Grace Aguilar, "Angels," *Occident* 1 (1843): 599.

21. Clara Longdon, "Sister Josie," *Woodhull & Claflin Weekly* 9 (August 28, 1875): 2. For scholarly discussions of nineteenth-century women and spiritualism, see, among others, Ann Braude, *Radical Spirits: Spiritualism and Women's Rights in Nineteenth-Century America* (Boston: Beacon, 1989); Barbara Goldsmith, *Other Powers: The Age of Suffrage, Spiritualism, and the Scandalous Victoria Woodhull* (New York: HarperCollins, 1998); and Jean McMahon, *Gifts of Power: The Writings of Rebecca Jackson, Black Visionary, Shaker Eldress* (Amherst: University of Massachusetts Press, 1981). The following anecdote may help readers understand more fully the power that dreams of the dead once had and, apparently, still do have for many people. In a small town near my home in Vermont, the mother of a child who had been severely injured in an automobile accident dreamt that her daughter came to her, telling her that she had died and was now an angel in heaven. Shortly thereafter the hospital called to tell the mother that Katie had in fact died, according to the mother's account, at the same time that she had had the dream. To a skeptic such as myself, the most obvious explanation is that the mother's unconscious recognized the inevitable and engaged in self-comforting; but Katie's small mountain community took the dream at face value, finding great comfort in it. If this can happen today, in the nineteenth-century, when virtually every family was touched by child death one way or another, such dreams were undoubtedly rampant, as not just these poems but the many illustrations of child-haunted mothers suggest (see fig. 5).

22. Sigmund Freud, "The Uncanny," in *Papers on Metapsychology; Papers on Applied Psychoanalysis,* vol. 4 of *Collected Papers,* trans. under the supervision of Joan Riviere (London: Hogarth Press, 1953), pp. 368–407. Freud views experiences related "to death and dead bodies, to the return of the dead, and to spirits and ghosts" as "the most striking of all, of something uncanny" (395). Interestingly, Freud opens his famous discussion by observing that there was very little scholarship on the presence of the uncanny in literature at the time he wrote because aestheticians preferred "in general . . . to concern themselves with what is beautiful, attractive and sublime . . . rather than with the opposite feelings of unpleasantness and repulsion."

23. See Cheryl Walker, "Teaching Dickinson as a Gen(i)us: Emily among Women," *Emily Dickinson Journal* 2 (February 1993): 172–80.

24. See Clara Barton, *The Women Who Went to the Field,* privately published pamphlet (Washington, D.C., 1892). Also see Frances Dana Gage, *Poems* (Philadelphia: J. B. Lippincott and Co., 1867). Unhappily, as is so often the case with these writers, Gage's failures match her strengths. She is best known today for her slanted "reconstruction" of Sojourner Truth's famous 1851 "Ain't I a woman?" speech. See Peterson, *Doers of the Word,* for a discussion of the racist undertones of Gage's text (pp. 51–55).

25. See, for example, Sandra M. Gilbert and Susan Gubar, *The Madwoman in the Attic: The Woman Writer and the Nineteenth-Century Literary Imagination* (New Haven: Yale University Press, 1979), p. 33, and passim; Eve Kosofsky Sedgwick, *The Coherence of Gothic Conventions* (New York: Methuen, 1987), pp. 97–139; and Da-

neen Wardrop, *Emily Dickinson's Gothic: Goblin with a Gauge* (Iowa City: University of Iowa Press, 1996). For more socially oriented treatments, see Gillian Brown, *Domestic Individualism: Imagining Self in Nineteenth-Century America* (Berkeley: University of California Press, 1990); Teresa A. Goddu, *Gothic America: Narrative, History, and Nation* (New York: Columbia University Press, 1997); David Anthony, "Class, Culture, and the Trouble with White Skin in Hawthorne's *The House of the Seven Gables*," *Yale Journal of Criticism* 12.2 (Fall 1999): 249–68; and David Reynolds, *Beneath the American Renaissance* (New York: Alfred A. Knopf, 1988).

26. Gage, "The Maniac Wife," in *Poems*, p. 167.

27. Gage, "The Faded One," in *Poems*, p. 166.

28. Phoebe Carey [*sic*], *Poems and Parodies* (Boston: Ticknor, Reed, and Fields, 1854), p. 10. All subsequent references to this volume will appear parenthetically in the text.

29. Dickinson was not necessarily speaking figuratively. According to the San Francisco–based *Irish Nationalist*, which got its information from the Chicago *Tribune*, the use of opium among women was skyrocketing by the 1870s; in 1840, 24,000 pounds of opium were consumed; in 1870, 154,842; and in 1872, over 250,000, half of which was apparently being used by women. *Irish Nationalist*, August 22, 1874, p. 7.

30. Osgood, "Ah! Woman Still" (*AWP* 133). I have discussed mid- and late-nineteenth-century women poets' general revolt against domestic ideology and against marriage in particular in "'The Descent of the Angel': Interrogating Domestic Ideology in American Women's Poetry 1858–1890," *American Literary History* 7 (1995): 591–610. To save space here, I refer the reader to the poems cited in that article.

31. Elizabeth Akers Allen, "Her Sphere," *Scribner's Monthly* 4 (June 1872): 218.

32. For a serious, complex, and highly nuanced analysis of the many pitfalls of reading irony, especially in a political context, see Linda Hutcheon, *Irony's Edge: The Theory and Politics of Irony* (London and New York: Routledge, 1994), pp. 9–36 and 116–24. I would agree with Hutcheon completely that irony, taken in itself, is "trans-ideological," that is, as a rhetorical mode it, like all other rhetorical modes, can be and is used by people arguing from every point on the political spectrum. My desire in this study, therefore, is not to claim that irony is a sign of political progressiveness in nineteenth-century women's writing or that, since these writers use irony, they must of necessity be progressive. Rather, it is show how the many ironies of their situations not only appear in and shape their verse but are often, as this chapter has demonstrated, manipulated by them for political ends. That is, this book deals with many of the theoretical issues around irony that Hutcheon discusses in her study but makes no attempt to theorize irony itself. I am, however, indebted to Hutcheon for the title of chapter 6 and in general for her brilliant coverage of a subject I would not dare touch.

33. Review of *Poems and Parodies*, by Phoebe Carey (*sic*), *Southern Literary Messenger*, February 1854, p. 126.

34. As quoted in Jonathan Hall, "Alice Cary," p. 68.

35. L[ydia] H[untley] Sigourney, *Letters of Life* (New York: D. Appleton and Co., 1866), p. 376. Sigourney's comment, which has too often been read unironically, comes after she lists the various kinds of requests that people sent her for poems. For example, "A father requests elegiac lines on a young child, supplying, as the only

suggestion for the tuneful Muse, the fact that he was unfortunately 'drowned in a barrel of swine's food'" (373). While this boy's death may have elicited sentimental grief in the father, clearly sentimentality's putative high priestess was not moved.

36. David Leverenz, *Manhood and the American Renaissance* (Ithaca: Cornell University Press, 1989), pp. 62–63. Given Whitney's own Brahmin status, it is quite possible that Emerson was one of her targets in *Mother Goose*. The fact that the book was wildly popular also suggests it was "in-reading."

Notes to Chapter 6

1. Jerome McGann, *Social Values and Poetic Acts: The Historical Judgment of Literary Work* (Cambridge: Harvard University Press, 1988), p. 5.

2. Gay L. Gullickson, "*La Pétroleuse*: Representing Revolution," *Feminist Studies* 17 (Summer 1991): 241–65. According to Gullickson, the *pétroleuse* "was almost entirely a figment of the government's and the conservative press's imagination" (242).

3. "The End of the Commune," *Harper's Weekly* 15 (July 8, 1871): 628.

4. My point here is not that Piatt is a modernist but that in using irony as the structuring principle of her verse, she shifted the balance in her writing away from having readers get the message of her poems to having them exercise interpretive skills locating it. I view this as a modernist move. See Jerome J. McGann's discussion of the tension between textually oriented, de Manian, deconstructive readings and his own Habermasian concern with literature as a form of social activity in *Social Values*. McGann situates de Manian deconstruction as the endgame in a process that began with the turn against positivism in both historiography and morality at the end of the nineteenth century (see pp. 1–10).

5. Andreas Huyssen, *After the Great Divide: Modernism, Mass Culture, PostModernism* (Bloomington: Indiana University Press, 1986), pp. 3–62.

6. See Lawrence W. Levine, *Highbrow/Lowbrow: The Emergence of Cultural Hierarchy in America* (Cambridge: Harvard University Press, 1988), p. 96.

7. Piatt uses the romance of Anthony and Cleopatra to allegorize the South's illusions in "The Lily of the Nile" (1869) and "Her Rescue" (1872). Both poems suggest that she viewed the Confederacy as, at best, a heroic but suicidal gesture made for a prize that was poisonous in itself. Also see "Sour Grapes" (*PB* 45). To my knowledge, there is no parallel for Piatt's war poetry anywhere in U.S. nineteenth-century verse.

8. John James Piatt, "Firelight Abroad," in *Western Windows and Other Poems*, 3d ed. (Boston: James R. Osgood,1878), pp. 96 and 97.

9. John James Piatt, "Charity at Home," in *Western Windows*, pp. 90–91.

10. John James Piatt, "Firelight Abroad," p. 82. I have discussed the Piatts' marriage at much greater length in the introduction to *The Palace-Burner*, pp. xxiv–xxviii. My opinion of John James Piatt is obviously low, but he could have been worse. However many mistakes he made, he does seem to have loved Sarah (or, at any rate, been highly dependent on her), and he was, despite occasional fits of jealousy, devoted to promoting her career.

11. Piatt has many other poems parodying, or simply attacking outright, nineteenth-century gender ideology, including "The Sorrows of Charlotte," discussed in chapter 5, and "A Woman's Counsel," explicitly addressed to "My fine Narcissus of to-day" (*PB* 67). Some of these poems, in particular "A Pique at Parting," have a very modern feel to them. For example, the lines "One woman can hardly care, I think, to

remember another one's eyes, / And—the bats are beginning to flit. . . . We hate one another? It may be true. / [W]hat else do you teach us to do? / Yea, verily, to love you" (*PB* 91), eerily echo both Sylvia Plath's "Lesbos" and Adrienne Rich's "Snapshots of a Daughter-in-Law."

12. See Bennett, "'The Descent of the Angel': Interrogating Domestic Ideology in American Women's Poetry, 1858–1890," *American Literary History* 7 (Winter 1995): 601–3.

13. John James Piatt, "The Birthdays," in *The Nests at Washington and Other Poems*, by John James Piatt and Sarah Morgan Bryan Piatt (New York: Walter Low, 1864), p. 94.

14. In a poem of this title, Piatt draws mocking parallels between Columbus, Confederate soldiers, and Christians, all of whom, like lovers, "keep the faith" (see *PB* 69–70).

15. But according to Laurence Lerner, Oscar Wilde had the final say on Little Nell: "One must have a heart of stone to read the death of Little Nell without laughing." Quoted in *Angels and Absences: Child Deaths in the Nineteenth Century* (Nashville: Vanderbilt University Press, 1997), p. 180. Lerner provides an excellent discussion of the entire role played by Little Nell in nineteenth-century sentimental culture (174–212).

16. Piatt treats these themes in "Her Blindness in Grief," "The Little Boy I Dreamed About," and "No Help." The last line of "Her Blindness"—"God has his will. I have not mine"—is probably the single most powerful statement of apostasy Piatt made. The poem appeared in the *Independent* three months after her newborn's death in 1873 (see *PB* 51). Piatt's emphasis on the trouble children cause has at least partial biographical roots. According to Katherine Tynan's memoir of the Piatt family, her four surviving sons were a tumultuous crew, whom the family's Irish hosts were wont to compare to wild Indians. See Katherine Tynan, *Memories* (London: Eveleigh, Nash and Grayson, 1924), p. 190.

17. Review of *Dramatic Persons and Moods*, *Scribner's Monthly* 19 (February 1880): 635. I have discussed Piatt's reception and her poetics at length in the introduction to the selected edition (*PB* xviii–xl).

18. Virginia Woolf, "Professions for Women," in *The Death of the Moth and Other Essays* (London: Hogarth Press, 1942), pp. 150–53.

19. In a letter to E. C. Stedman describing Victor's death in a freak Fourth of July accident, J. J. mentions in passing that Sarah incorporated his "quaint expressions" in a number of her poems. John James Piatt to Edmund Clarence Stedman, August 2, 1874, Edmund Clarence Stedman Papers, Rare Book and Manuscript Library, Columbia University.

20. See, for example, Sigourney's "The Sick Child" (*AWP* 17). In this poem, a mother tending the sickbed of her child struggles to attain a correct state of mind: "That start, that cry, that struggle! / My God—I am but clay, / Have pity on a bruised reed, / Give thy compassion sway; / Send forth thy strength to gird me, / Impart a power divine, / To wring out sorrow's dregs, and say / 'Oh! Not my will but thine.'" Obviously, this struggle could go the wrong way, and in Piatt's case, it did. Rampant in its self-destructive emotionalism, Piatt's refusal of acceptance radically differentiates her child elegies from those of her peers, and she was criticized roundly for them. In a letter to Bayard Taylor, J. J. rightly attributes the criticism to Northeastern

evangelical bias. See Bennett, introduction to *Palace-Burner,* pp. xlvi–xlvii and p. lviii n. 31.

21. The text she uses (or abuses) is Psalm 91:5–6: "Thou shalt not be afraid for the terror by night, nor for the arrow that flieth by day, nor the pestilence that stalks in the darkness, nor the destruction that wastes at noonday."

22. Joanne Dobson, "Reclaiming Sentimental Literature," *American Literature* 69 (June 1997): 263–88.

23. Margaret Fuller, *Summer on the Lakes in 1843* (Urbana: University of Illinois Press, 1991), p. 143.

24. This poem also appears in *Summer on the Lakes,* pp. 143, 144–48.

25. Pamela J. Kincheloe, "Through the Claude Glass: Nineteenth-Century American Writers and Monumental Discourse" (Ph.D. dissertation, Southern Illinois University, Carbondale, 1997), pp. 110–16.

Notes to Chapter 7

1. As quoted in Nancy F. Cott, "Passionlessness: An Interpretation of Victorian Sexual Ideology, 1790–1850," *Signs: Journal of Women in Culture and Society* 4 (1978): 236. Stanton was reading Whitman's "There Is a Woman Waiting for Me."

2. Jacques Lacan, "God and the *Jouissance* of The Woman," in *Feminine Sexuality: Jacques Lacan and the École Freudienne,* ed. Juliet Mitchell and Jacqueline Rose, trans. Jacqueline Rose (New York: W. W. Norton, 1982), p. 146.

3. Margaret Fuller, "A Dialogue," in *The Transcendentalists: An Anthology,* ed. Perry Miller (Cambridge: Harvard University Press, 1950), p. 402.

4. Gay believes this oft-cited work is probably a collection of sexual fantasies. See Peter Gay, *Education of the Senses,* vol. 1 of *The Bourgeois Experience Victoria to Freud* (New York: Oxford University Press, 1984), p. 468.

5. See Gay, *Education of the Senses,* pp. 461–62.

6. See Rachel P. Maines, *The Technology of Orgasm: "Hysteria," the Vibrator, and Women's Sexual Satisfaction* (Baltimore: Johns Hopkins University Press, 1999).

7. Cott, "Passionlessness," p. 221.

8. William Acton, selection from *Functions and Disorders of the Reproductive Organs,* in *Victorian Women: A Documentary Account of Women's Lives in Nineteenth-Century England, France, and the United States,* ed. Erna Olafson Hellerstein, Leslie Parker Hume, and Karen M. Offen (Stanford: Stanford University Press, 1981), p. 177.

9. Clarke, in particular, drew down feminist wrath upon himself for his attacks on higher education for women. See the essays in Julia Ward Howe, ed., *Sex and Education: Dr. E. H. Clarke's "Sex in Education"* (Boston: Roberts Brothers, 1874).

10. As quoted in Cott, "Passionlessness," p. 236.

11. As quoted in Charles N. Degler, *At Odds: Women and the Family in America from the Revolution to the Present* (New York: Oxford University Press, 1980), p. 267.

12. As quoted in Degler, *At Odds,* p. 268.

13. See Cott, "Passionlessness," p. 236.

14. Both Prins and Watts document multiple allusions to Sappho by British and U. S. women poets. See Yopie Prins, *The Victorian Sappho* (Princeton: Princeton University Press, 1999), pp. 174–245 and passim; and Emily Stipes Watts, *The Poetry of American Women from 1632 to 1943* (Austin: University of Texas Press, 1977), pp. 75–81 and passim.

15. As quoted in Joan DeJean, *Fictions of Sappho, 1546–1937* (Chicago: University of Chicago Press, 1989), p. 256.

16. Harriet Prescott Spofford, "The Amber Gods," in *The Amber Gods and Other Stories*, ed. Alfred Bendixen (New Brunswick: Rutgers University Press, 1989), p. 38. All subsequent references will appear parenthetically in the text.

17. According to the *OED*, "climax" only began signifying orgasm in the first decade of the twentieth century, but this sense of the word was in circulation well before. For example, one of Mabel Todd's journal entries in 1879 speaks of her love-making as a "thrilling sort of breathlessness—but at last it came—the same beautiful climax of feeling I knew so well." As quoted in Peter Gay, *Education of the Senses*, p. 84.

18. "The Amber Gods" is obviously about a great deal more than sex; it deals with a range of gender issues linking male power to female oppression, from the role of the artist's model to the exploitation of slave women's sexuality as well as their labor. I am at a loss to explain why this story has received so little attention from scholars, given how much, comparatively speaking, they have paid to another Spofford story, "Circumstance." If, as I suspect, it is because Dickinson mentions only the latter, this would be sad testimony indeed to the way in which the privileging of major writers distorts our perception of what is important in their presumably "lesser" peers. Spofford warrants and deserves study in her own right, not just for her ties to E. D.

19. See Kelly Dennis, "Playing with Herself: Feminine Sexuality and Aesthetic Indifference," in *Solitary Pleasures: The Historical, Literary, and Artistic Discourses of Autoeroticism*, ed. Paula Bennett and Vernon A. Rosario II (New York: Routledge, 1995), p. 49. My deep debt to this excellent essay permeates my discussion of Spofford's story.

20. Maines, *Technology of Orgasm*, pp. 5–7. Maines argues that Victorian men's androcentric concern with their own pleasure was probably the principal reason for bourgeois women's sexual frustration, a frustration she amply demonstrates. I would agree but believe that coverture would have exacerbated the situation greatly. Not only did many women find intercourse with their husbands unpleasurable because of their husbands' ignorance with respect to how women's bodies worked, but they also, under coverture, had no right to refuse. Under such circumstances women's privileging of masturbation should not be surprising.

21. The role played by turn-of-the-century sexologists and psychoanalysts in re-pathologizing female sexuality and indeed all forms of sexuality exclusive of bourgeois male heterosexual desire has been extensively explored elsewhere. Among the works to which I am personally most indebted are Degler, *At Odds*, pp. 144–77, 249–97; Gay, *Education of the Senses*; S. Haller, Jr., and Robin M. Haller, *The Physician and Sexuality in Victorian America* (Carbondale: Southern Illinois University Press, 1974); Vernon Rosario, *The Erotic Imagination: French Histories of Perversity* (New York: Oxford University Press, 1997); the essays in Bennett and Rosario, *Solitary Pleasures*; and, of course, Michel Foucault, *The History of Sexuality, vol. 1, An Introduction*, trans. Robert Hurley (New York: Vintage Books, 1978). As I read Lacan, and admittedly I am no fan, he flatly denies women's status as sexual agents in their own right. Woman (his singular, not mine) is "excluded by the nature of things, which is the nature of words." They have, to be sure, a "*jouissance*" proper to them, but it is "supplementary" to phallic *jouissance*. "Woman," he writes, is a "'her' which does not exist and which signifies nothing." Moreover, she herself knows "nothing" of it (i.e.,

her *jouissance*) "except that she experiences it" ("God and the *Jouissance* of The Woman," in *Feminine Sexuality*, pp. 144, 145.)

22. Going well back before Milton, the image of woman making love to herself in front of a mirror (see Eve's creation in book 4 of *Paradise Lost*) can be found ubiquitously in male art and literature. For a relatively tame nineteenth-century version see Paul H. Hayne's "Before the Mirror": "Where in her chamber by the Southern sea, / Her taper's light shone soft and silvery." "[R]obed for restful sleep . . . / . . . / Her dew-bright eyes, and faintly flushing face / Viewed in the glass their delicate beauty beam, / Strange as a shadowy dream within a dream. / . . . / Her lips—twin rosebud petals blown apart— / Quivered, half breathless; then subdued but warm, / Around her perfect face, her pliant form," and so on (*Galaxy* 24 [December 1877]: 755). See also Bram Dijkstra, *Idols of Perversity: Fantasies of Feminine Evil in Fin-de-Siècle Culture* (New York: Oxford University Press), 1986, pp. 64–82 and 129–59.

23. Freud outlines his theory of "mature" vaginal sexuality versus immature clitoral sexuality in "Some Psychological Consequences of the Anatomical Distinction between the Sexes." See Paula Bennett, "Critical Clitoridectomy: Female Sexual Imagery and Feminist Psychoanalytic Theory," *Signs: A Journal of Women in Culture and Society* 18 (Winter 1993): 235–59. In this essay, I also discuss Dickinson's "Crisis is sweet" (F1365), which is remarkably similar to "My Heart."

24. "My Heart," *Frank Leslie's* 7 (June 1879): 670.

25. Collette [Loomis,] "Only a Shadow," *Springfield Republican* 16 (September 24, 1859): 2.

26. Sara J. Lippincott [Grace Greenwood], "Siri, The Swimmer," in *Poems* (Boston: Ticknor, Reed, and Fields, 1851), pp. 66–68.

27. Eleanor Mary Ladd, "The Waiting Rain," *Overland Monthly* 21 (January 1893): 77–78.

28. In Gloria C. Erlich, *The Sexual Education of Edith Wharton* (Berkeley: University of California, 1992), pp. 175–76.

29. See Ariel and Chana Bloch, *The Song of Songs*, trans. with introduction and commentary by Ariel and Chana Bloch (New York: Random House, 1995), for a reliable discussion of the text's history from a secular perspective.

30. Maria Gowen Brooks, *Zóphiël; or, The Bride of Seven*, ed. Zadel Gustafson (Boston: Lee and Shepard, 1879) canto I: 19, 58, pp. 9 and 24.

31. As an ex-Renaissance scholar, I am in full accord with Lawrence Lipking's observation, quoted by Prins (*The Victorian Sappho*, p. 41), that "A history of lyric poetry could be written by following the ways that later poets have adapted [the Longinian fragment] to their own purposes."

32. Longinus, *On the Sublime*, trans. Thomas R. R. Stebbing (London: Oxford, 1867), pp. 36 and 37.

33. Mary E. Hewitt, "Imitation of Sappho," in *The Songs of Our Land and Other Poems* (William D. Ticknor and Co.), 1846), pp. 43–44.

34. In her book on lesbian poetry, Judy Grahn places Dickinson squarely in the Sapphic tradition. See *The Highest Apple: Sappho and the Lesbian Poetic Tradition* (San Francisco: Spinsters, Ink, 1985), p. 98. In particular, Grahn points to Sappho's lines "The Sweet apple reddens on a high branch / high upon highest, missed by the applepickers: / no, they didn't miss, so much as couldn't touch." Fragment 48, in *Sappho's Lyre: Archaic Lyric and Women Poets of Ancient Greece*, trans. Diane Rayor (Los Angeles: University of California Press, 1991), p. 74.

35. Longinus, *On the Sublime*, p. 37.

36. Helen (Burrell) D'Apery (Olive Harper), "Cleopatra," in *Cleopatra* (n.p., n.d.), p. 5. All subsequent references to D'Apery's and Story's poems will appear parenthetically in the text.

37. It is worth noting that in Canticles these lines are spoken by the man to the woman, just as the woman uses imagery that "feminizes" the man: "O my dove, that art in the clefts of the rock . . . let me hear thy voice; for sweet is thy voice, and thy countenance is comely. / . . . / My beloved is mine, and I am his: he feedeth among the lilies" (2: 14 and 16). That is, where Canticles consistently provides balance and harmony, equalizing the two lovers, the D'Apery and Story poems, despite their attribution of transgressive desire to Cleopatra, reengage polarized gender roles. D'Apery published another poem on Cleopatra, "My Antony's Away," in the *Daily Eastern Argus* (Portland, Maine) in 1880, so "Cleopatra" was probably written in the early 1880s (see *NAWP* 462).

38. Fragment 57, in *Sappho's Lyre*, trans. Rayor, p. 78.

39. Annie Fields, "Antinous," *Under the Olive* (Boston; Houghton, Mifflin and Co., 1881), p. 99. All subsequent references to this poem will appear parenthetically in the text.

40. See Ruth A. Roman, *Annie Adams Fields: The Spirit of Charles Street* (Bloomington: Indiana University Press, 1990), pp. 1–13, 42–55, and passim. I am also indebted to provocative discussions with Susan Harris, Marjorie Pryse, and Judith Fetterly on Fields and the Fields-Jewett relationship.

41. It is perhaps worth noting that by virtue of Fields's authorship, her treatment of Antinous involves all three of the primary forms of sexual relationships: male-male, female-female, and male-female, with the same problems arising, as it were, in each. What this suggests is that there is nothing necessarily liberating in same-sex relations or, to put it another way, that heterosexuality per se is not repressive. Obviously, this is not an opinion shared by queer theorists.

42. Suzanne Clarke, *Sentimental Modernism: Women Writers and the Revolution of the Word* (Bloomington: Indiana University Press, 1991), p. 1.

43. As quoted in Carolyn Burke, *Becoming Modern: the Life of Mina Loy* (Berkeley: University of California Press, 1997), p. 6.

Notes to Chapter 8

1. Marianne Moore to Bryher (Winfred Ellerman), January 16, 1823, in *The Gender of Modernism*, ed. Bonnie Kime Scott (Bloomington: Indiana University Press, 1990), p. 337.

2. Mary Lawson, "Realism," *Penny Magazine* 3 (Midsummer 1897): 30.

3. C.E.L., "A Biography," *Penny Magazine* 3 (October 1897): 32.

4. See Frederick Winthrop Faxon, *Ephemeral Bibelots: A Bibliography of the Modern Chap-Books and Their Imitators* (Boston: Boston Book Co., 1903). The average lifetime for these magazines was two or three years, if that. By 1900, the craze for them was pretty much spent.

5. See Ezra Pound, *Make It New* (New Haven: Yale University Press, 1935).

6. Peter N. Stearns, in *American Cool: Constructing a Twentieth-Century Emotional Style* (New York: New York University Press, 1994), comments that "It is the very un-Victorian suspicion of intense emotional experience, far more than a simple renunciation of Victorian repression, that forms the essence of the transition in American

emotional culture" at the beginning of the twentieth century (p. 11; see also pp. 16–57, 139–82). I would place the turn somewhat earlier, but basically what I describe here is the initial phase of this social transformation.

7. Rita Felski, *The Gender of Modernity* (Cambridge: Harvard University Press, 1995), p. 146. I am much indebted to Felski throughout this chapter, especially to her theorization of female modernity with respect to "the multiplicity and diversity of women's relations to historical processes" (7).

8. Walter Blackburn Harte, "The Stir in Literature," *Fly Leaf* 1 (December 1895): 3–4.

9. Mina Loy, "Aphorisms of Futurism," in *Gender of Modernism*, ed. Scott, p. 245.

10. Scholarly works treating the gynophobic component in modernism are legion. Among those that have influenced me the most are Suzanne Clark, *Sentimental Modernism: Women Writers and the Revolution of the Word* (Bloomington: Indiana University Press, 1991); Marianne DeKoven, *Rich and Strange: Gender, History, Modernism* (Princeton: Princeton University Press, 1991); Bram Dijkstra, *Idols of Perversity: Fantasies of Feminine Evil in Fin-de-Siècle Culture* (New York: Oxford University Press, 1986); Sandra Gilbert and Susan Gubar, *The War of Words*, vol. 1 of *No Man's Land: The Place of the Woman Writer in the Twentieth Century* (New Haven: Yale University Press, 1988); Andreas Huyssen, *After the Great Divide: Modernism, Mass Culture, Post-Modernism* ((Bloomington: Indiana University Press, 1986); Eunice Lipton, *Looking into Degas: Uneasy Images of Woman and Modern Life* (Berkeley: University of California Press, 1986); and Griselda Pollock, *Vision and Difference: Femininity, Feminism and the Histories of Art* (New York: Routledge, 1988).

11. See H. L. Davis, "Enter the Woman," review of *Ballads of the Singing Bowl*, by Marjorie Allen Seiffert, *Poetry* 30 (September 1927): 339. Interestingly, Davis found British, Italian, and German anthologies of the period similarly emasculated, but he blames the problem on "the Americanization of Western civilization," which made it "impossible for a man to follow the calling of a poet." Thus, it would appear that nineteenth-century U.S. women were responsible for having "feminized" not only their own country but the entire West. No mean trick, one must admit.

12. As quoted in Gilbert and Gubar, *War of Words*, p. 154.

13. Amy Lowell, "Sisters," in *The Complete Poetical Works of Amy Lowell* (Boston: Houghton Mifflin, 1955), p. 461.

14. Felski, *Gender of Modernity*, p. 9. See also pp. 14, 145–73.

15. Sarah Norcliffe Cleghorn, "Ballade of Queens and Great Ladies," *Philistine: A Periodical of Protest* 9 (June 1899): 1–2.

16. William D. Forest, "Woman," *Chips from Literary Workshops* 2 (December 1895): n.p.; and Marjorie R. Johnson, "Man," *Chips from Literary Workshops* 3 (February 1896): n.p.

17. Clara Cahill Park, "The Manners Tart," *Philistine: A Periodical of Protest* 1 (September 1895): 116 and 117.

18. Carolyn Burke, *Becoming Modern: The Life of Mina Loy* (Berkeley: University of California Press, 1998), p. v.

19. According to my own, admittedly rough, tally, postbellum male poets' periodical publication rates on average exceeded that of women by 2 to 1 until the 1890s, when women poets began to outpublish men.

20. Karen Kilcup, *Robert Frost and Feminine Literary Tradition* (Ann Arbor: University of Michigan Press, 1998), p. 44.

21. Robert Frost, *The Poetry of Robert Frost* (New York: Holt, Rinehart and Winston, 1969), p. 6.

22. Ezra Pound, "A Virginal," in *Personae* (New York: New Directions, n.d.), p. 71.

23. See Ezra Pound, *Literary Essays of Ezra Pound*, ed. T. S. Eliot (New York: New Directions, 1968), p. 11. For Frost's letter, see Kilcup, *Frost*, p. 153.

24. Wallace Stevens, "Sunday Morning," in *The Collected Poems of Wallace Stevens* (New York: Alfred A. Knopf, 1961), p. 70.

25. Stevens, "Sunday Morning," p. 67.

26. Ralph Waldo Emerson, "The Rhodora," in *Poems* (Boston: Houghton Mifflin Co., 1904), pp. 37–38.

27. That is, I view Deland's poem as fulfilling the very standards for craftsmanship and objectivity mandated by New Critics years later: "Impersonality, craftsmanship, objectivity, hardness and clarity of a kind, a union of emotion with verbal object, a norm of inclusiveness and reconciliation and hence a close interdependence of drama, irony, ambiguity, and metaphor, or the near equivalence of these four." William K. Wimsatt and Cleanth Brooks, *Literary Criticism*, as quoted in Kevin Dettmar, introduction to *Rereading the New: A Backward Glance at Modernism*, ed. Kevin Dettmar (Ann Arbor: University of Michigan Press, 1992), p. 6.

28. Cynthia Griffin Wolff, *Emily Dickinson* (New York: Alfred A. Knopf, 1986), pp. 9–10 and 524.

29. See, for example, "A New Education for Girls," *Harper's Bazar* 21 (June 23, 1888): 410.

30. S. S. Cohen, "False Kisses," *Current Literature* 2 (March 1889): 230.

31. Martha T. Tyler, "Seaward," *Overland Monthly* 21 (January 1893): 4.

32. Mary McNeil Scott, "A Friend," *Century* 50 (August 1896): 619.

33. Unhappily, Scott has come down in literary history only as the woman who persuaded Pound to poeticize her husband's transcriptions of two Japanese Noh plays. See Van Wyck Brooks, *Fenollosa and His Circle with Other Essays in Biography* (New York: E. P. Dutton, 1962), p. 67. She had, in fact, an independent interest in the Orient, having lived there for a number of years before meeting Fenollosa. Her divorce from her first husband and marriage to Fenollosa, at that time the curator of Asian art at the Museum of Fine Arts in Boston, created a scandal that cost Fenollosa his job. Her life, in other words, was very much a public one of the sort increasing numbers of bourgeois women were enjoying.

34. See Timothy Materer, "Make it Sell! Ezra Pound Advertises Modernism," in *Marketing Modernisms: Self-Promotion, Canonization, Rereading*, ed. Kevin Dettmar and Stephen Watt (Ann Arbor: University of Michigan Press, 1996), pp. 17–36.

35. Untermeyer, "Lizette Woodworth Reese," in *Modern American Poetry: A Critical Anthology* (New York: Harcourt, Brace, and Co., 1931), p. 116; and "Lizette Woodworth Reese," in *American Poetry since 1900* (New York: Henry Holt and Co., 1923), p. 300.

36. Whittier describes "telling the bees" as a colonial custom meant to prevent the bees from swarming after a death in the family. See *The Complete Poetical Works of John Greenleaf Whittier* (Boston: Houghton, Mifflin, 1892), p. 529 n. 66.

37. I wish to thank Victoria Wilson-Schwartz, my copy editor at Princeton University Press, for challenging my initial presentation of this poem and thus helping me clarify my thinking here. To her, the success of Reese's poem lay in its restraint, and

she found the poem *more* deeply moving than the work of writers like Dickinson and Piatt as a result. As she explained it, it was the delicacy of Reese's style that freed her to respond emotionally to the poem's otherwise tear-jerking subject matter. From my viewpoint, this is just what renders the poem ironic: it plays on the sizeable gap between what it describes (a child's response to her mother's death) and the way the poem's speaker (tearlessly) describes it. Put another way, the poem is ironic precisely because its language—its style or manner of expression—understates an experience we expect to see overstated. Thus Vicky writes: "What gets me about this poem is that it forswears words in favor of a picture, almost like a haiku, and is trying for something like what the Zen tradition calls 'direct mind transmission.' I think it's no accident that the last lines are 'I think I *see* Bathsheba yet / Telling the bees.' The whole idea of the poem is to create this unforgettable picture—and, as we all know, one picture, etc. etc. That is why the poem is so laconic; it doesn't need a voice track, so to speak." At the same time, in allowing craft to trump content in this way, Vicky was reading as a twentieth-century modern, whether she realized it or not. That is, finally, it was the particular quality of the craft (its restraint in the face of otherwise highly emotional content) not the content per se that moved her.

38. Kilcup, *Frost*, p. 202. Reese's strategy was very successful. Even David Perkins, who has very little good to say about any woman poet other than Marianne Moore, praises Reese, calling her "a foe to sloppiness and sentimentality" and finding intimations of imagism in her precise handling of metaphor. See *A History of Modern Poetry from the 1890s to the High Modernist Mode* (Cambridge: Belknap Press of Harvard University Press, 1976), pp. 110 and 109.

39. Joan Sherman, introduction to *Poems*, by Henrietta Cordelia Ray, vol. 3 of *Collected Black Women's Poetry* (New York: Oxford University Press, 1988), p. xxx.

40. Alicia Suskin Ostriker, *Stealing the Language: The Emergence of Women's Poetry in America* (Boston: Beacon Press, 1986), p. 22.

41. Poems on African slave mothers torn from their children were, of course, a staple in abolitionist poetry. However, the greatest influence on Ray may have been Maria Lowell's description of Africa, personified in the Sphinx, lamenting her children's fates: "Her great lips closed upon her moan; / Silently sate she on her throne, / Rigid and black, as carved in stone." See "Africa" (*AWP* 193).

42. As quoted by Paul Lauter in an unpublished comment on my edition of Sarah Piatt. A propos of the reading of political poetry, Lauter writes, "It seems to me that what sixty or seventy years of formalist criticism has done is to disable us, and most of our students, [from reading for something other than the word] by discounting the virtues of anything but what Eliot so powerfully points to, the 'medium' in which the poet works." Quoted with permission of the author.

43. David Porter, *Dickinson: The Modern Idiom* (Cambridge: Harvard University Press, 1981), p. 9.

44. See "The West in Women's Hands," *Chap-Book* 7 (September 15, 1897): 323.

45. Harriet P. Spofford, "Literature and Art," *Galaxy* 7 (February 1869): 300. I want to thank Karen Kilcup for calling my attention to this review.

46. [Mary Louise Booth], "The Commonplace Mother, " *Harper's Bazar* 7 (June 6, 1874): 362.

47. Kilcup, *Frost*, p. 19.

48. Annie Nathan Meyer, ed., *Women's Work in America* (New York: Henry Holt, 1891), pp. iv and v.

49. Sarah N. Cleghorn, *Threescore: The Autobiography of Sarah N. Cleghorn*, with an introduction by Robert Frost (New York: Harrison Smith and Robert Haas, 1936), p. 160.

50. I am not denying the power of sentimental discourse, especially high sentimentality, which has a long and dignified history, only sentimentality's gendering. Like Piatt and Grimké, I believe that high sentimentality is only meaningful when its humanistic concerns are accompanied by an active commitment to equal rights and social justice, both of which are (or should be) gender blind. When this commitment is lacking, sentimental sympathy becomes precisely the kind of bad-faith politics against which scholars like Douglas and Berlant inveigh, whether it is practiced by men or women and no matter how seemingly powerful in some respects. *Uncle Tom's Cabin* is to my mind the quintessential example of this particular paradox.

51. H.D., "Sea Rose," in *Collected Poems, 1912–1944*, ed. Louis L. Martz (New York: New Directions, 1983), p. 5.

Notes to Coda

1. Adrienne Rich, "Translations," in *Diving into the Wreck: Poems 1971–1972* (New York: W. W. Norton, and Co., 1973), p. 41.

2. Booth was not alone in her conviction. Theodore Tilton confidently predicted that "President Eliot will live to see the women capture Harvard." *Golden Age*, June 14, 1873, p. 4.

3. [Mary L. Booth], "Girl Graduates," *Harper's Bazar*, April 5th, 1884, p. 218.

4. I have taken the following statistics from a variety of sources, each of which seems to have its own system for dating. Whatever the exact date, the point here is that almost all these "firsts" had to be revisited again in the 1960s and 1970s, as women found themselves once more having to challenge barriers that nineteenth-century women thought they had knocked down for good.

5. [Mary L. Booth], "Women and the Centennials," *Harper's Bazar*, August 28, 1875, p. 554.

6. Personal communication from Constance Trowbridge, Radcliffe, 1958.

7. David Perkins, *A History of Modern Poetry: From the 1890s to the High Modernist Mode* (Cambridge: Belknap Press of Harvard University Press, 1976), p. 107.

8. John Crowe Ransom. "The Poet as Woman" (1937), rept. in *The World's Body* (Baton Rouge: Louisiana State University Press, 1968), p. 78.

9. Adrienne Rich, "When We Dead Awaken: Writing as Re-Vision" (1971), in *On Lies, Secrets, and Silence: Selected Prose 1966–1978* (New York: W. W. Norton, 1979), pp. 39 and 44.

10. Peter Blos, *On Adolescence: A Psychoanalytic Interpretation* (New York: Free Press of Glencoe, 1962), p. 167.

11. Cary Nelson, *Repression and Recovery: Modern American Poetry and the Politics of Cultural Memory* (Madison: University of Wisconsin Press, 1989), p. 7.

12. David Perkins, *Is Literary History Possible?* (Baltimore: Johns Hopkins University Press, 1992), pp. 1–27.

13. I want to thank Dawn Janke for calling this to my attention in a seminar paper

on the Shaman figure in nineteenth- and twentieth-century Native American literature by women.

14. Mary Austin, *The American Rhythm* (New York: Harcourt, Brace, 1923), p. 20.

15. See Alice Dunbar-Nelson, "Paul Laurence Dunbar: Poet Laureate of the Negro Race," A.M.E. *Church Review*, October 1914, pp. 5–19.

16. Ora Williams, "Alice Moore Dunbar Nelson," *Dictionary of Literary Biography* 50: 229.

17. As quoted in Williams, "Dunbar Nelson," p. 229.

18. Alice Dunbar-Nelson, *The Works of Alice Dunbar-Nelson*, ed. Gloria T. Hull (New York: Oxford University Press, 1988), 2:90.

19. Dora Read Goodale, "By Way of Introduction," in *Mountain Dooryards* (Berea, Ky.: Council of the Southern Mountains, 1958), p. 5.

Index

abolitionists, 103; black female, 55–58, 228n28; feminist, 45, 50–58, 83–87, 88, 89, 121, 229n34. *See also* Grimké sisters: Angelina

Acton, Lord William, 34, 161, 166, 170

Ada, "The Panic," 45–46, 47

Adams, Hannah, 8

Adams, John, 8–9; Abigail (JA's wife), 8

Advertiser (Springfield, Missouri), 118

aesthetics and communicative practices, 4–6, 218n7, 242n4; Freud on, 240n22; in genteel tradition, 19–27, 29, 35, 69, 132; in high culture (modernist) tradition, 3–4, 87–89, 186–200, 209. *See also* complaint; poetry: fin de siècle women's; Walker, Cheryl: nightingale tradition

agency, 4, 41, 47–49, 54, 79, 114, 220n23, 227n21, 227n22; as collective, xii, 52, 134; and modernity, 10, 116, 211; in relation to sexuality, 32, 34, 245n21; situational, 53–54. *See also* Grimké sisters: Angelina

Aguilar, Grace, "Angels," 118

Alcott, Louisa May, 120

Aldrich, Thomas Bailey, "A Death-Bed," 130, 131–32

Allen, Elizabeth Akers, "Her Sphere," 128–29, 131, 133, 138

A.M.E. Church Review, 198, 212

American Hebrew, 97, 99

American Indian Magazine, 84

American Weekly Mercury, 6, 7

Ames, Mary Clemmer, 113

Amherst, Massachusetts, 32, 35

Anderson, Benedict, 63

"Angel in the House, The," xi, 3, 28, 29, 79, 166, 182, 185, 186, 200; as channel to the dead, 118–20, 127; as figure for lack, 24–25, 47; as ideological ideal, 28–29, 32, 35, 126–29, 138; as sexual ideal, 163, 166, 167, 179, 180; as site for resistance, 115–16, 130–32; as universal female victim, 120, 121–29. *See also* Piatt, Sarah Morgan Bryan

Anna, Louisa, 64; "Zuleika," 77–78, 79, 81

Anna Maria [Wells?], "The Bachelor's Soliloquy," 30, 224n33

Anthony, Susan B., 90

Antinous, 180

apostrophe, 1, 4, 21–22, 26, 123, 177, 217n4

Appiah, K. Anthony, 62

Arnold, Matthew, 3, 156

Aspen, Penelope, 7

Atkins, Elizabeth, 207–8

Atlantic Monthly, 97, 139, 163, 165, 168, 179, 183

Auerbach, Erich, 23, 24

"Augusta," "Reply to Ada," 57

Austin, Mary, 210, 211

"bare elbows" debate. *See* newspapers: "debates" in ("bare elbows")

Barnes, Djuna, 152

Barton, Clara, "The Women Who Went to the Field," 121

Bassard, Katherine, 87

Baym, Nina, 58

Beecher, Catherine, 50, 51, 56

belle / coquette poems, 28, 32; Southern, 3, 143. *See also* Osgood, Frances Sargent

"Belle's Philosophy, The," 32–34, 48, 201

Bellini, Vincenzo: *Norma*, 142, 143; "Here me, Norma," 143

Benjamin, Walter, 196

Bercovitch, Sacvan, 85

Berlant, Lauren, 134, 217n3, 223n28, 251n50

Bethune, George, *The British Female Poets*, 18

Blackwell, Elizabeth, 162

Bleecker, Ann Elizabeth, 8

Bogan, Louise, 202

Boone, Aunt "Annie" (Sarah Piatt's aunt), 144

Booth, Mary Louise, 201. Works: "Girl Graduates," 205; "Women and the Centennials," 206

Boston, Massachusetts, 28, 70, 93

Boston Gazette, 31

Boston Weekly Magazine, 44